5995
AF782863

SUNDAY.

Legal Aspects

OF THE

First Day of the Week.

BY

JAMES T. RINGGOLD,

OF THE BALTIMORE BAR.

"Put up again thy sword into his place: for all they that take the sword shall perish with the sword."—*The Master on the Union of the Church and State.*

THE LAWBOOK EXCHANGE, LTD.

Clark, New Jersey

2003

ISBN 1-58477-332-4

Second printing 2005

Printed in the United States of America on acid-free paper

THE LAWBOOK EXCHANGE, LTD.
33 Terminal Avenue
Clark, New Jersey 07066-1321

Please see our website for a selection of our other publications and fine facsimile reprints of classic works of legal history:
www.lawbookexchange.com

Library of Congress Cataloging-in-Publication Data

Ringgold, James Trapier, 1851-1898.
Sunday: legal aspects of the first day of the week / by James T. Ringgold.
p. cm.
Originally published: Jersey City, N.J. : F.D. Linn & Co., 1891.
Includes bibliographical references and index.
ISBN 1-58477-332-4 (alk. paper)
1. Sunday legislation—United States. I. Title.

KF2009 .R5 2003
343.73 ‘088—dc21

2002042758

SUNDAY.

Legal Aspects

OF THE

First Day of the Week.

BY

JAMES T. RINGGOLD,

OF THE BALTIMORE BAR.

"Put up again thy sword into his place: for all they that take the sword shall perish with the sword."—*The Master on the Union of the Church and State.*

JERSEY CITY, N. J.:
FREDERICK D. LINN & CO., LAW PUBLISHERS.
1891.

Entered according to Act of Congress, in the year 1891, by
FREDERICK D. LINN & CO.,
In the office of the Librarian of Congress, at Washington.

THE ELECTRIC PRINTING CO.,
TRENTON, N. J.

THIS BOOK IS INSCRIBED,

IN

TESTIMONY OF THE AUTHOR'S KINDLIEST REGARD AND ESTEEM,

TO

HON. CHARLES G. KERR,

STATE'S ATTORNEY FOR BALTIMORE CITY.

"*Cujus et vita et oratio consecuta mihi videtur difficilimam illam societatem* GRAVITATIS CUM HUMANITATE."

—*Cic De Leg. III.*, 1.

PREFACE.

A law book ought to be a working tool. The practitioner should be safe in trusting that he will find in it fairly stated the result of the authorities upon the subject with which it deals.

But no good reason is perceived why a law book should not be something more than this—why suggestions as to what the law ought to be should not accompany the statement of what the law is. The lawyer does not earn his living by merely citing cases; he has to cultivate the faculty of criticism and comparison in his practice. A critical and comparative way of dealing with a legal topic may, therefore, save him labor even when he does not accept the writer's conclusions.

But lawyers have a higher function in society than that of making a living. They are, to a greater extent than any other class, makers of law—in the legislatures by enactment, on the bench by construction, at the trial table by persuasion. They are, therefore, above all others, the class to whom those should appeal who would have the law made or unmade along certain lines.

In this little book the endeavor has been to include every point of technical interest, and at the same time to treat the subject in a manner worthy of its vast political and economical importance. On the success of the undertaking in either direction, others must decide.

J. T. R.

CONTENTS.

CHAPTER I.

CONSTITUTIONALITY OF SUNDAY LAWS IN THE UNITED STATES.

CHAPTER II.

CONSTITUTIONALITY OF SUNDAY LAWS IN THE UNITED STATES—CONTINUED.

CHAPTER III.

CONSTITUTIONALITY OF SUNDAY LAWS IN THE UNITED STATES—CONTINUED.

CHAPTER IV.

CHAPTER V.

NATURE OF THE ILLEGALITY OF A SUNDAY CONTRACT.

CHAPTER VI.

CHAPTER VII.

SUNDAY AS A DIES NON JURIDICUS.

CHAPTER VIII.

SUNDAY IN THE COMPUTATION OF TIME.

CHAPTER IX.

SUNDAY LIQUOR-SELLING.

CHAPTER X.

THE PROHIBITION OF SUNDAY LABOR.

I. The Forbidden Acts.

II. The Exceptions of "Necessity" and "Charity."

CASES CITED.

C.

D.

H.

I.

J.

K.

L.

M.

S.

T.

SUNDAY.

Legal Aspects of the First Day of the Week.

CHAPTER I.

CONSTITUTIONALITY OF SUNDAY LAWS IN THE UNITED STATES.

In General.

Special regulations for the conduct of citizens on the first day of the week are usually among the first enactments of an American commonwealth. The manner in which such legislation has been treated by the courts forms a most curious and interesting chapter in our constitutional history. What follows is an attempt to digest the decisions on this subject, and to analyze their reasoning, in order to ascertain how far the conclusions reached are defensible in themselves, and how far they must depend for acceptance on mere weight of authority. For this purpose the points which may be regarded as settled have been arranged in a series of propositions, corollaries, &c., showing their connection and inter-dependence. The following general statement, made in Louisiana in 1879, fitly introduces the subject:

"The constitution of the United States forbids the congress from making any law respecting an establishment of religion, or prohibiting the free exercise thereof. But this is an inhibition to congress only, leaving to the state governments the whole power over the subject of religion. There are considerable differences in the various state constitutions on this subject, but the general provision of the most perfect equality before the law of all shades of religious belief is common to all of them."[1]

PROPOSITION I.

Inhibitions of Work, Business, Amusements and Liquor-selling are Constitutional.

I. THE PROPOSITION DENIED.—The constitutionality of inhibitions of labor, business, &c., on Sunday has been denied in a few instances. The Supreme Bench of Indiana thus dealt with the question in 1860:

"Can the Sunday law be maintained as a mere police regulation, without reference to an institution of religion? Could the legislature enact a law that no man should labor on New Year's day? The legislature enacts a law that no man shall compel his children, apprentices or employes to labor more than ten hours a day, and it may be well. Such a law may be a reasonable regulation of labor, to protect the weak from the oppression of the strong, but has the legislature ever attempted to enact a law that the father or employer should not himself labor more than ten hours a day, if he preferred to do so?[2] So, perhaps, the legislature, on the same principle, might enact a law that no man should compel those under him to labor more than six days in a week; that he should allow one-seventh of the days for rest; but could it enact that no individual should labor for himself but six-sevenths of the days? We express no fixed opinion on this point, as the case does not require it. Does it not

[1] *Bott's Case*, 31 La. Ann. 663.

[2] The only legislation limiting the power of adult employers to contract with adult employes for so many hours' work per day as may be agreeable to both, except the Sunday laws, is the outcome of "labor agitation"—that is to say, agitation for the promotion of idleness, which is the precise object and result of Sunday laws. An example may be found in the Maryland statute, 1886, ch. I., p. 63, wherein horse railway companies are forbidden to "require, *permit* or *suffer*" their employes to work more than twelve hours in each twenty-four.

involve the patriarchal theory of government?"[1] And the court refers to *Newman's Case*, in California, cited *post*. The question was involved in a case at *nisi prius*, in South Carolina, in 1846. A Jew was arrested for selling goods in violation of an ordinance of the city of Charleston. The recorder who decided the case below declared that, according to his own religious faith, Sunday was peculiarly devoted and set apart to Christian worship, and was a day on which the ordinary secular employments of men, or, in the language of the church, "all servile works" should be suspended. But he asked, "By what authority, consistent with the entire freedom of religious faith and worship, guaranteed to all alike, of whatever religious sect or community, whether Jew or Christian, can the civil power ordain that on the day kept by Christians as a holiday or day of worship peculiar to them, the Jew shall be made to keep in the same way, or to some extent at least, the Christian holiday; although, according to his religious faith, he is required to keep another and a different day as sacred to religion? * * * The constitution professes to give to all mankind an entire and perfect equality of freedom in religious faith and worship, without discrimination or preference. Is it no discrimination or preference to select, by the civil law of the state, the day considered sacred in a religious sense by the Christian, and to compel the Jew to unite, externally at least, in its observance? To protect from possible disturbance those who worship on that day by requiring all others to abstain from every species of labor or employment, while the Jewish Sabbath is protected by no similar regulation? * * * It may well be asked whether, if the Jews should happen to have a majority, they could require by law on the part of the rest of the community the same observance of the Jewish Sabbath which is now required of them in regard to the Christian Sunday. * * * In truth, this provision appears to furnish ample security, and perhaps the only one, against undue encroachments on religious liberty by the legislative power, amidst all fluctuations, and to place, at all times and forever, freedom of conscience beyond the reach of any dominant or preponderating opinions, which numbers may at any time give to a particular religious sect, or to any prevailing

[1] *Thomasson's Case*, 15 Ind. 449.

creed of the day." He then points out that the ordinance was copied almost literally from a section of a statute enacted in 1712, when the people were required, under penalty, to attend their parish church and remain there devoutly during divine service, and forbidden to travel, except to and from church, or on an errand of charity; which statute, he thinks, is obsolete, and is repealed by the provision guarding against discrimination between religions. And he holds that this old act was not revived, in any of its features, by the city ordinance. He then considers the argument that the law is a mere police regulation. He says that all laws and ordinances connected with the observance of Sunday are not necessarily inoperative, for, "while it may be held that no law of the state or of any subordinate corporation can require the conscientious Israelite to keep the Christian Sunday by abstaining from an occupation, honest and in itself innocent and wholesome to society, or even that it does not pertain to the civil power of the state to compel the religious observance of any particular day by abstaining from labor, or in any other way, there may be enactments founded on the observance *in fact* by a large majority of its citizens of any particular day as a holy day." And he instances the law against retailing liquor, the act exempting slaves from labor (necessary occasions of the family excepted), the act forbidding the issue or service of legal process, and the act punishing those who disturb a religious corporation, which is not confined to the Lord's day. He adds that he does not deem it pertinent to refer in this connection to the English statutes or decisions, because "where, as in that country, church and state are united, and not only particular religious faith, but a particular form of religious worship prescribed by law, it is in vain to look for illustrations of the freedom of religious faith and worship which it was the glory of our ancestors to attain * * * and it is the design of the constitution to secure and perpetuate." He considers that it is equally unnecessary to trace the history of the day in the decrees of councils, &c.[1] But by far the most important case holding the negative of this question, is that decided in California in 1858. The statute under consideration was entitled "An act for the better observance of the Sabbath," and the body of

[1] *Benjamin's Case*, 2 Strob. 508. This decision was reversed on appeal. See *post*.

the act alluded to the first day of the week as "The Christian Sabbath." Terry, C. J., and Bennett, J., delivered opinions setting forth the views of the majority of the court. The former proceeded to show that it was a "discrimination" between religions, saying, in reference to decisions to the contrary in other states, that, "While we entertain a profound respect for the courts of our sister states, we do not feel called upon to yield our convictions of right to a blind adherence to precedent. * * * It is not so much the decision as the reason upon which the decision is based which makes it authority and requires it to be respected;" and that it gave a "preference" to one form of belief over another, and was, therefore, repugnant to the constitution of the state. And, considering the argument that the act was a mere police regulation, the Chief Justice said that the legislature could not enforce compulsory abstinence from lawful and ordinary occupation for a given period without apparent civil necessity. Of the position that the Sunday law was a necessity, for the benefit of the citizen's health and the restoration of his powers, he said: "This argument is founded on the assumption that mankind are in the habit of working too much, and thereby entailing evil on society, and that without compulsion they will not seek the necessary repose which their exhausted natures demand. This is to us a new theory, and is contradicted by the history of the past and the observation of the present. We have heard, in all ages, of declamations and reproaches against the vice of idleness, but we have yet to learn that there has ever been any general complaint of any intemperate, vicious, unhealthy or morbid industry. On the contrary, we know that mankind seek cessation from toil from the natural influences of self-preservation in the same manner and as certainly as they seek slumber, relief from pain, or food to appease their hunger. Again, the amount of rest which would be required by one-half of society may be widely disproportionate to that required by the other. It is a matter of which each individual must be permitted to judge for himself. As well might the legislature fix the days and hours for work and enforce their observance by an unbending rule which shall be visited alike upon the weak and strong." And he likened the Sunday law to the sumptuary laws of the ancients, and added: "The truth is, however much it may be disguised, that this one day of rest is purely a religious idea.

Derived from the sabbatical institutions of the ancient Hebrews, it has been adopted into the creeds of the succeeding religious sects, and, whether it be the Friday of the Mahometan, the Saturday of the Israelite, or the Sunday of the Christian, it is alike fixed in the affections of its followers beyond the power of eradication, and in most of the states of our confederacy the aid of the law to enforce its observance has been given under the pretence of a civil, municipal or police regulation." Of the argument that the question was one of police, and exclusively for the legislature, he said: "One of the objects for which the judicial department is established, is the protection of the constitutional rights of the citizen. The question presented is not merely one of expediency, or abuse of power; it is a question of usurpation of power." And he also held that the act was "in conflict with the first section of article I. of the constitution, because, without necessity, it infringes upon the liberty of the citizen by restraining his right to acquire property."[1] Judge Burnett observed that the constitution protected unbelievers as well as believers; and held that the act was unconstitutional, because it established a compulsory religious observance, and not because it made a discrimination between different systems of religion. He said that the fact that the Christian voluntarily kept the first day did not authorize the legislature to make that observance compulsory; that the principle was the same, whether the many or the few were concerned; that, in considering whether the act could be sustained on the ground that it was a mere municipal regulation, the reasons which operated on the minds of members in voting on the measure were wholly immaterial, and he concurred with the Chief Justice in the opinion that the act interfered with the "inalienable right of acquiring, possessing and protecting property," guaranteed by the California Bill of Rights. Finally, Judge Burnett observed, "The question is quite distinguishable from the case where a legislature passes an act for the protection of a slave against the inhumanity of a master, in not allowing sufficient rest. Had the act been confined to infants, or persons bound by law to obey others, the question presented would have been very different. If the legislature could prescribe the days of rest for free agents, it would seem that the same power could prescribe the hours to work, rest

[1] See Table B.

and eat." On the other hand, Judge Field, in his dissenting opinion, held that the law treated of business matters, not religious duties; that the legislature had the right to pass laws for the preservation of health and the promotion of good morals, and so to require periodical cessation from labor, if of opinion that it would tend to both; and he said: "It is no answer to say that mankind will seek cessation from labor by the natural influences of self-preservation. The position assumes that all men are independent and at liberty to work whenever they choose; whether this be true or not in theory, it is false in fact; it is contradicted by every day's experience. The relations of superior and subordinate, master and servant, principal and clerk, always have and always will exist [*sic*], and labor is in a great degree dependent upon capital; the law steps in to restrain the power of capital. Its object is not to protect those who could rest at pleasure, but to afford rest to those who needed it, and could not, from the condition of society, otherwise obtain it. Authority for the enactment we find in the great object of all government, which is protection. Labor is a necessity imposed by the condition of our race, and to protect labor is the highest object of our laws." And, considering the argument that the regulation must be a religious one, because of the title and phraseology of the act, he said that the terms "Christian Sabbath," or "Sunday," were used simply to designate the day, and afforded no evidence that the intention was to enforce a religious institution. And he added, that the fact that the law operates with inconvenience to some is no argument against its constitutionality; such inconvenience is an incident to all general laws. And he instanced the provision against certain judicial and official business, and the rule that notes, when the last day of grace falls on Sunday, shall be presented to the maker on Saturday to hold the endorser, and asked, "Would the complaint of an Israelite that this was a discrimination in an important class of contracts in favor of the Christian, be listened to for a moment? * * * The simple fact is, that the legislation is not based upon any idea of enforcing a religious observance, but of establishing, as a civil regulation, a day of rest from judicial and other official labor; and the constitution itself contains a recognition of Sunday as a day of rest, in the clause which provides that a bill presented to the governor shall become a law in like manner as if he had signed it, if not returned by him within ten days, Sundays excepted," &c. And he continued: "The fact that the civil regulation finds support in the religious opinions of a vast majority is no argument against it * * * the establishment by law of Sunday as a day of rest from labor is none the less a beneficial and humane regulation because it accords with the divine precept that upon that day 'thou shalt do no manner of work; thou and thy son and thy daughter, thy man servant and thy maid servant, thy cattle and the stranger that is within thy gates.'"[1] He then proceeded to observe that the title of an act could not control its intent; that the law would be equally obligatory if entitled "An act to promote the general health;" and that the court had nothing to do with the legislature's motives in passing the act. He then cited various cases in which Sunday laws had been sustained, which he said "ought to conclude the case before us." And, referring to the clause of the state constitution which placed among "inalienable rights" that of "acquiring, possessing and protecting property," &c., he said: "The mode and manner of the acquisition, possession and protection are matters upon which laws are passed at every session of the legislature. The legislature possesses the power to legislate for the good order and peace, welfare and happiness of society. The means by which these ends are to be effected are left to its discretion. It is no argument against the existence of the power to establish a day of rest that it may be exerted to a prohibition of labor for six days in the week. The only limitation upon the exercise of the taxing-power is, that the taxation must be equal and uniform * * * frequent elections furnish the only protection against the abuse of an acknowledged legislative power." And he added: "If it be admitted that the legislature has the right to restrain each one's freedom of conduct only so far as necessary to secure protection to all others, the character and necessity of this protection must be left to its determination."[2]

[1] It is not necessarily true that the distinguished jurist's law is as much at fault as his Scripture. Several portions of his opinion show greater accuracy than might be expected of a man capable of asserting that the Fourth Commandment had any reference to Sunday.

[2] *Newman's Case*, 9 Cal. 502.

II. THE PROPOSITION SUSTAINED.—But the overwhelming weight of authority is against the view of these cases. The California case just cited was expressly overruled. And the court said: "Unless restrained by the organic law, the legislature has power to pass laws regulating the relations, contracts, intercourse and business of the general society, and of the particular members in respect to each other."[1] So, it was said in New York in the same year: "If precedents were necessary to establish the right to legislate upon the subject, they could be cited from the statutes and ordinances of every government, really or nominally Christian, and from the earliest period." The court admitted that acts to compel attendance at church, &c., would be unconstitutional in New York, but said there were times when Sunday was "greatly profaned in England, and practices tolerated which would meet, at this time, with little public favor either there or here." But this fact, it said, "does not detract from the force of the long series of acts of the British parliament, representing in legislation the sentiment of the British nation, as precedents, and as a testimony in favor of a legislative regulation of the Sabbath."[2] And it was considered in Pennsylvania, in 1848, that the question was a settled one in that state, and that the Sunday law "is essentially but a civil regulation, made for the government of man as a member of society, and obedience to it may properly be enforced by penal sanction."[3] And in 1859, in the same state, the court observed: "We do not feel called upon to give any opinion as to the policy, the propriety or the justice of the law itself; that stands settled by authority, so far as authority can settle it, and that authority is not to be overlooked by individual sentiments, or by private opinion, whatever that may be."[4] So, in Ohio, in 1849, it was said: "There is no reason to doubt that the legislature had power given them by the constitution to pass a law prohibiting all persons who do not conscientiously observe another day as the Sabbath from engaging in sports or labor on that day. Whether the power ought to be exercised would depend on their sense of the public good; and, in our representative government, it is very certain that they would reflect, in

[1] *Andrews' Case*, 18 Cal. 678.

[2] *Lindenmuller's Case*, 33 Barb. 548.

[3] *Specht's Case*, 8 Pa. 312.

[4] *Minock's Case*, 3 Phila. 347.

that particular, as in others, the public and general sentiment."[1] And, in Tennessee, in 1883, "The question as to the power of the state to compel, by penal enactments, the observance of the Sabbath day, so far as cessation from secular pursuits is concerned, and to punish its open violation, has not been seriously questioned, and is too well settled to admit of question, or require discussion."[2] And in 1854, in Missouri, the court said: "We are of opinion that there is nothing inconsistent with the constitution, as it was understood at the time of its adoption, with a law compelling the observance of Sunday as a day of rest; the constitution itself recognizes that day as a day of rest, and, from the circumstances under which it was done, we are warranted in the opinion that a power to compel a cessation from labor on that day was not designed to be withheld from the General Assembly."[3]

Equally decided is the opinion in New York that Sunday amusements may be forbidden. The court said, in 1861: "The act, in substance, declares a Sunday theatre to be a nuisance and deals with it as such. It was conceded upon the argument that the legislature could entirely suppress theatres, and prohibit theatrical exhibitions. This, I think, yields the whole argument, for, as the whole includes all its parts, and the greater includes the less, the power of total suppression includes the power of regulation and partial suppression."[4] So, considering another case of a Sunday theatre, in 1877, the court said of a certain act: "The title is general—'to preserve the public peace and order on the first day of the week, commonly called Sunday.' Though the words 'public peace and order' are general, they indicate every particular which goes to make up those things. That a cessation from dramatic representations or the like on Sunday is a particular thereof needs no discussion since the case of *Lindenmuller* v. *The People*, which has never been questioned in a court of higher or equal authority. * * *

[1] *Sellers* v. *Dugan*, 18 Ohio 489.

[2] *Linck's Case*, 12 Lea 499.

[3] *Amb's Case*, 20 Mo. 214. The Supreme Court of the United States, in 1827, decided that a state could not require an importer to take out a license. *Brown's Case*, 12 Wheat. 419.

Query. Could it forbid him to exhibit his merchandise for sale on Sunday? The court in Maryland, in 1848, thought this point would probably never arise, but held that its power to impose such a restriction on the retailer whom it had licensed could not be doubted. *Bode's Case*, 7 Gill 326.

[4] *Lindenmuller's Case* cited.

It is contended that, though the general subject of the act is to preserve the public peace and good order, yet as this is sought to be effected by the particular method of prohibiting dramatic representations and the like, the title of the act should have contained some phrase or phrases declaring that particular subject. We do not think that this was requisite. The legislature had the right to assume that the law was reasonably well settled, and sufficiently declared by competent judicial and legislative authority that such representations on the first day of the week were a breach of the public peace and good order. The legislature was therefore right in conceiving that the title which expressed the purpose of legislating to preserve that peace and good order gave notice that such representations might be affected by it. It is not to be forgotten that the title does not point to legislation on the subject of the public peace and good order in general, that is, on any and every day, but only on the first day of the week. So that the title is fitted to call particular attention to whatever is likely to disturb that peace and order on that day." Church, J., dissenting on other grounds, agreed with the opinion of the majority, that the provision for closing theatres is within the general scope of the subject-matter indicated in the title, as one of the means of preserving the peace on Sunday.[1]

As to liquor-selling, it was said in Indiana, in 1860: "It is competent for the legislature to prohibit, as a police regulation, under penalties, the sale of liquor by retail on Sunday, as well as upon election and other public days, on which increased danger of drunkenness and rioting and public disturbance exists; the law is not an unwarrantable interference with individual right."[2] And in Michigan, in 1870, it was held that such a prohibition was within the title of an act "to prohibit the sale of liquor to minors," &c., the legislature assuming that to keep saloons open on Sunday was to tempt youths, &c., into intoxication. And it was said: "If there is any possible ground for holding that belief, it certainly is no function of a court to determine that the legislature were mistaken. We are not prepared to say that it is such a palpable error as to show they cannot be regarded as acting within their province in accepting it."[3] It was said in California, in 1881, that "regarding the

[1] *Neuendorff* v. *Duryea*, 69 N. Y. 557.
[2] *Thomasson's Case*, 15 Ind. 449.
[3] *Kurtz's Case*, 33 Mich. 279.

matter from a purely secular standpoint, the law is a proper and salutary one."[1] And a North Carolina judge, in 1860, said: "I entertain no doubt the legislature of the state has the power, under the constitution, to prohibit work on Sunday, as a matter pertaining to the civil well-being of the community."[2]

The proposition that Sunday laws are constitutional in the United States being established by a decided weight of authority, certain corollaries follow, which have also received express judicial sanction.

COROLLARY I. *Inhibitions of Work do not Violate the Constitution of the United States.*—The objection to Sunday laws on this score was urged in New York in 1883, where an injunction was sought against police interference with an express company's business. It was said: "So far as the Sunday laws attempt to restrict the transportation of merchandise, by an express company, consigned beyond the state on one side, to be delivered beyond the state on the other side, they are unconstitutional and void, under the constitution of the United States. A different rule prevails, however, where the state is the initial and terminal point. There the regulation above quoted has no application * * * therefore, as to domestic matters, that is, goods to be received and delivered in this city, the injunction is denied; as to goods in transit, the injunction against the defendant is continued."[3]

In 1884 an indictment against a railroad company for carrying freight was sustained in West Virginia. The court held that the Sunday law of that state did not conflict with the constitution of the United States, "for the simple reason that it in no manner undertakes to regulate commerce between the states;" observed that the fact that this point was not taken in a certain previous case argued by the same counsel for the company indicated that it was "far-fetched," and added, that though "unquestionably the statute would have the effect of diminishing the transportation of freight, it is well settled that everything which affects commerce is not, simply for that reason, a regulation of it, within the meaning of the constitution of the United States," and that the law came within

[1] *Bruke's Case,* 59 Cal. 619.

[2] Manly, J., in *Melvin* v. *Ensley,* 7 Jones 356.

[3] *Dinsmore* v. *Police,* 12 Abb. (N. Y.) N. Cas. 436.

the definition of an "internal police law, which any state has a right to pass, though it does affect interstate commerce." The court referred to a case, wherein a law of Missouri, prohibiting the driving of "Texas cattle," &c., into the state between March 1st and November 1st, was held unconstitutional, and said it was passed to make a discrimination which the constitution intended to prevent, but the Sunday law was passed "for the sole purpose of promoting the mental, moral and physical well-being of our people." It further maintained that the statute did not operate to discriminate against non-residents; that the difficulty in determining whether an act was a regulation of interstate commerce arose because of the difficulty in determining the object of the legislature; that an incidental effect could not convert a law of internal police into a law regulating commerce, and "if the trade of all the states be carried on with equality and freedom, all that was intended by this provision of the constitution is accomplished."[1] It was held in Pennsylvania that the objection to the jurisdiction of a justice on the ground that the boats ran into tide-water under registry or license from the United States government was not tenable, and that "however independent of any other than federal law and jurisdiction they might be when navigating the tide-waters of the United States, when navigating an interior stream, and especially an artificial one, erected and governed by a state, they are amenable to local laws." And the court added: "No federal legislation can give any one authority to travel on any of the public works of Pennsylvania, erected by herself within her own borders, without being subject to such rules and regulations as the state may lay down."[2]

COROLLARY II. *Inhibitions of Work do not Interfere with Rights of Property.*—A second objection to Sunday laws has been found in their alleged interference with rights of property. Thus, where a prohibition of work was under consideration, it was said, in California, in 1861, that the fact that the citizen is guaranteed the right of acquiring property does not deprive the legislature of the power of prescribing the mode of acquisition, or of regulating the conduct and relations of the members of society in respect to property rights,

[1] *State* v. *Railroad*, 24 W. Va. 783.

[2] *Minock's Case*, 3 Phila. 347.

and that the power to regulate did not involve the power to destroy, and that "the legislature has the power to repress what is hurtful to the general good, and must generally be the exclusive judge of what is or is not hurtful." And the court then speaks of acts in reference to mines, &c., and says that the duty of government comprehends the moral as well as the physical welfare of the state, and that the physical and moral necessity of the law, its advantage as a protection against the results of competition, &c., are considerations for the law-giver.[1]

A similar point was raised in reference to the prohibition of amusements in New York, and was thus disposed of in 1861: "The law does not touch private property, or impair its value. The restraint upon the use of property is incidental to the exercise of a power vested in the legislature to legislate for the whole state. Public safety requires that powder magazines should not be kept in a populous neighborhood; public health requires that certain trades and manufactures should not be carried on in crowded localities; public interest requires that certain callings should be exercised by a limited number of persons, and at a limited number of places, and legislative promotion of these objects necessarily qualifies the absolute ownership of property to the extent that it prohibits the use of it in the manner and for the purpose deemed inconsistent with the public good; but that deprives no man of his property, or impairs its legal value. The fact that the plaintiff in error leased the property with a view to its occupancy for the purposes of a Sunday theatre does not vary the question. He might have bought it for the same purpose, but that would by no means lessen the power of the legislature, or give him an indefeasible right to use it for the purpose intended, or to establish or perpetuate a public nuisance * * * The contract with the performers, if one exists, for their services on the Sabbath, stands upon the same footing." And the court says the statute "rests upon the same foundation as a multitude of other laws, such as those against gambling, lotteries, keeping disorderly houses, polygamy, horse-racing, profane cursing and swearing, disturbance of religious meetings, selling of intoxicating liquors on election days within a given

[1] *Andrews' Case*, 18 Cal. 678.

distance of the polls, &c. All these and many others do, to some extent, restrain the citizen, and deprive him of some of his natural rights; but the legislature have the right to prohibit acts injurious to the public and subversive of the government, or which tend to the destruction of the morals of the people, and disturb the peace and good order of society. It is exclusively for the legislature to determine what acts should be prohibited, as dangerous to the community. The laws of every civilized state embrace a long list of offences which are such merely as *mala prohibita*, as distinguished from those which are *mala in se*. If the argument in behalf of the plaintiff in error is sound, I see no way of saving the class of *mala prohibita*."[1] And, in a later case in the same state, where, also, a party had been indicted for giving theatrical exhibitions, the court reviewed the charter of the Province of New York, &c., and sustained the prohibition of public amusements on the same ground as that of work, in the following words: "I cannot see a substantial distinction between the interdiction of the employment of cattle in ordinary agricultural labor, or the selling of merchandise in a person's ordinary business, and the prohibition of the use of premises for certain specified purposes on the Sunday. The restriction in each instance rests upon the principle of the preservation of good order and the public morality and peace. In each the full enjoyment of property is restrained. In the old statutes, no distinction is found between cases of property possessed at the passing of the statute and that subsequently acquired; nor is there a trace of it in the authorities. Rights may exist of which the owner cannot be deprived, but still their exercise and enjoyment may be restrained and regulated by law, so far as the public interest may render proper. The rights must be exercised in such a manner as not to affect prejudicially the tranquility or morality of the local public."[2]

COROLLARY III. *Sunday Laws do not Infringe Religious Liberty, nor do they Give any Preference to One Religion over Another.*—Repeated attacks have been made on Sunday laws as in their nature religious ordinances, and therefore inconsistent with American theories of government. We have seen that, in a few

[1] *Lindenmuller's Case*, 33 Barb. 548. [2] *Hayne's Case*, 20 How. Prac. 76.

cases, this objection has been regarded as fatal. But the majority hold otherwise. In Georgia, in 1859, the court declined, as unnecessary to the decision of the case before them, to decide the question whether the law gave a preference to those religious societies which believed that the Lord's day was the first day of the week over those which believed that it was the seventh day.[1] So, it was laid down, in 1861, that the California statute "does not discriminate in favor of any sect, system or school in the matter of their religion."[2] And this was affirmed in 1882.[3] On this subject, the following remarks were made in New York in 1861: "It would be strange that a people, Christian in doctrine and worship, many of whom or whose forefathers had sought these shores for the privilege of worshiping God in simplicity and purity of faith, and who regarded religion as the basis of their civil liberty and the foundation of their rights, should, in their zeal to secure to all the freedom of conscience which they valued so highly, solemnly repudiate and put beyond the pale of the law the religion which was dear to them as life, and dethrone the God who they openly and avowedly professed to believe had been their protector and guide, as a people. Unless they were hypocrites, which will hardly be charged, they would not have dared, even if their consciences would have suffered them to do so. Religious tolerance is entirely consistent with a recognized religion. * * * Different denominations of Christians are recognized, but this does not detract from the force of the recognition of God as the only proper object of religious worship, and the Christian religion as the religion of the people, which it was not intended to destroy, but to maintain." And, as to leaving the conscience free, we are told: "Wisdom is justified of her children in the experiment, which could hardly be said if blasphemy, Sabbath-breaking, incest, polygamy and the like were protected by the constitution. The framers of it did not suppose they had abolished the Sabbath as a day of rest for all, and of Christian worship for those who were disposed to engage in it, or had deprived themselves of the power to protect their God from blasphemy and revilings, or their religious worship from unseemly interruptions * * * if there were any doubt about the mean-

[1] *Sanders* v. *Johnson*, 29 Ga. 526.
[2] *Andrews' Case*, 18 Cal. 678.
[3] *Koser's Case*, 60 Cal. 177.

ing of the constitution securing freedom in religion, the contemporaneous and continued acts of the legislature under it would be very good evidence of the intent and understanding of its framers, and of the people who adopted it as their fundamental law. As early as 1788, traveling, work, labor, and exposing goods to sale on that day were prohibited. In 1789 the sale of spirituous liquors was prohibited, and from that time statutes have been in force to prevent Sabbath desecration, and prohibiting acts upon that day which would be lawful on other days of the week. Early in the history of the state government, the objections taken to the act under consideration were taken before the council of revision to an act to regulate Sabbath observance, because the provisions, as was claimed, militated against the constitution, by giving a preference to one class of Christians and oppressing others; because it, in some manner, prescribed the mode of keeping the Sabbath, and because it was inexpedient to impose obligations on the consciences of men in matters of opinion. The council overruled the objections, and held them not well taken." And, considering the constitutionality of a prohibition of amusements, the court added: "It is urged that it is the right of the citizen to regard the Sabbath day as a day of recreation and amusement, rather than as a day of rest and religious worship, and that he has a right to act upon that belief and engage in innocent amusements and recreations. This position it is not necessary to gainsay. But who is to judge and decide what amusements and pastimes are innocent—as having no direct baneful influence upon the community, as not in any way disturbing the peace and quiet of the public, as not unnecessarily interfering with the equally sacred rights of conscience of others? * * * It is a matter within the legislative discretion and power, and their will must stand as the reason of the law. We could not, if we would, review their discretion and sit in judgment upon the expediency of their acts. * * * The constitution makes provision for this case, by providing that the liberty of conscience secured by it 'shall not be so construed as to excuse acts of licentiousness or justify practices inconsistent with the peace and safety of the state.' The legislature have declared that Sunday theatres are of this character, and come within the description of acts and practices which are not protected by the constitution, and they are the sole judges. * * *"[1] And later (1877), the reasoning of this case was referred to and approved as follows: "Here, again, it is enough to refer to the decision and opinion in *Lindenmuller* v. *The People,* which, having never been appealed from, or in other manner questioned, will be held as declaring the law of this state. It is there held, with great force of argument, that the Christian Sunday may be protected from desecration by such laws as the legislature, in its wisdom, may deem necessary, and that it is the sole judge of the acts proper to be prohibited with a view to the public peace. The subject is exhausted in the *Lindenmuller Case,* and the true ground of judgment there occupied, and all the arguments upon this branch of the case, in the present state of civil society, in this country, are there advanced and elaborated."[2] In Pennsylvania, in 1859, after reviewing the early legislation of the state in regard to Sunday, the court said: "These various acts are illustrative of the views and feelings of the founders of the colony of Pennsylvania and of its ancient inhabitants, men who sustained Christianity upon the one hand and civil and religious liberty upon the other, so that the acts themselves are but the embodiment of the usages and customs of the people, and are therefore all illustrative of the common law of the state. In further illustration of these views, it will appear that by the constitution of the state, which is beyond all question the great embodiment of the customs, usages and will of the people, Sunday is excepted from the calculation fixing the number of the days allowed to the executive for the consideration of legislative bills, thus imparting to it an extraordinary position in the calendar of days, and which, [*sic*] coupled with the natural and indefeasible right to worship Almighty God according to the dictates of conscience, guaranteed by the same constitution, goes far to settle the question now under consideration. The judges who have either written or spoken upon this subject have invariably given to the 'Lord's day' the position now contended for."[3] Liberty of conscience and compulsory idleness on Sunday were thus reconciled in that state in 1861: "The constitution of this state secures freedom of conscience and equality of right. No man living under the protection of our institutions can be

[1] *Lindenmuller's Case,* 33 Barb. 548.

[2] *Neuendorff* v. *Duryea,* 69 N. Y. 557.

[3] *Jeandelle's Case,* 3 Phil. 509.

coerced to profess any form of religious belief, or to practice any mode of worship in preference to another. In this respect, the Christian, the Jew, the Mohammedan and the Pagan are alike entitled to protection. Nay, the infidel, who madly rejects all belief in a divine essence, may safely do so in reference to civil punishment, as long as he refrains from the wanton and malicious proclamation of his opinions with intent to outrage the moral and religious convictions of a community, the vast majority of whom are Christians. But beyond this, conscience, doctrines and practices can claim no immunity from the operation of general laws, made for the government and to promote the welfare of the whole people. The right of conscience, as understood in our organic law, is simply the right to worship the Supreme Being according to the dictates of the heart; to adopt any creed or hold any opinion whatever, or to support any religion, and to do or forbear to do any act for conscience sake, the doing or forbearing of which is not prejudicial to the public weal."[1] We are also indebted for the following exposition of the subject to the Pennsylvania judiciary: "People always know their moral and physical wants much better than the reasons or the remedy for them. They must have institutions according to their wants, whether they can give philosophical reasons for them or not. As long as they are unable to distinguish clearly between religion, morality and law, it is of their very nature that their political institutions must be more or less theocratical or religious; no number of rational principles, set in array in bills of rights, can prevent this. The natural order of events cannot be arrested by such barriers. We are not forgetting that the public acts of our Pennsylvania ancestors abound with declarations in favor of liberty of conscience, and that some regard these declarations as inconsistent with the Sunday laws. But a little reflection shows that they indicate the moral ideal to which all government ought to approach, as nearly as possible, rather than a positive principle of legislation. And, in applying such declarations, we must bear in mind that they proceeded from an earnestly Christian people and must receive a practical interpretation. They never thought of tolerating Paganism, or the principle of ecclesiastical

[1] *Specht's Case*, 8 Pa. 312.

supremacy in civil affairs, on the ground of liberty of conscience. They could not admit this as a civil justification of human sacrifices, or parricide, or infanticide, or thuggism, or of such modes of worship as the disgusting and corrupting rites of the Dionysia, the Aphrodisia, the Eleusinia and other festivals of Greece and Rome. They did not mean that the pure, moral customs which Christianity has introduced should be without legal protection, because some Pagan or other religionist or anti-religionist should advocate, as matter of conscience, concubinage, polygamy, incest, free love and free divorce, or any of them. They did not mean that phallic processions, and satyric dances, and obscene songs, and indecent statues and paintings, of ancient or of modern Paganism, might be introduced, under the profession of religion, or pleasure, or conscience, to seduce the young and the ignorant into a Corinthian degradation; to offend the moral sentiment of a refined Christian people; to compel Christian modesty to associate with the nudity and impurity of Polynesian or of Spartan women. No Christian people could possibly allow such things. No written law, founded on such bold and impotent rationalism, could present the slightest obstacle to the sentiment and action of a people in opposition to such things. Every Christian man is sure that it is his religion that has suppressed the Pagan customs just alluded to, and that to it is due the large advance in justice, benevolence, truth and purity that belongs to modern civilization; that it has purified and elevated the family relations; that it has so elevated the moral standards of society that the indecencies and cruelties and cheats of Paganism are now condemned by custom and by law as crimes. And he is very sure that the Sabbath and its institutions were the prominent means of this progress, and are essential to its maintenance and continuance. How, then, is it possible for a Christian people to avoid protecting such a day and its institutions? If there are men who oppose them as superstitions, let them at least respect them, as essential constituents of the people's life which cannot possibly be laid aside at will."[1]

It follows from Corollary III. that inhibitions of work and amusements on the first day of the week may be enforced against those

[1] *Nesbit's Case*, 34 Pa. 398.

who deny its "sacred" character, and who "observe" another day. Doubt upon this point has been intimated in Massachusetts, where it was said, in 1861: "Though a Jew's conscientious belief might protect him from a prosecution for violating the law prohibiting acts of secular labor, it is no excuse for his violation of the law respecting the sale of intoxicating liquors."[1] But later (1877), it was said in the same state: "That one who conscientiously observes the seventh day of the week may also be compelled to abstain from business of the kind expressly forbidden on the first day, is not occasioned by any subordination of his religion, but because, as a member of the community, he must submit to the rules which are made by lawful authority to regulate and govern the business of that community."[2] And in Pennsylvania, in 1848, it was held that the statute did not meddle with the right of men to worship according to their consciences, nor enter on any discussion of the rival claims of the first and seventh days, nor infringe upon the Sabbath of any sect; that it gave no preference to any religious establishment or mode of worship; that the selection of the day of rest was a question of expediency, and if the Jew and Seventh Day Christian suffered the inconvenience of two successive days of withdrawal from worldly affairs, it was an incidental worldly disadvantage, conferring no superior religious position on others; that the law intended no preference, and the inconvenience was the result of the generality of the provision.[3] It was ingeniously argued in Pennsylvania, in 1817, that the Jew might deem it a religious duty to work on Sunday, under the command "Six days shalt thou labor," coupled with the prohibition of work on Saturday. On this point the court said: "The defendant's counsel has not contended that the prohibition of work immediately opposes the received doctrine of the Jews, as disclosed in the five books of Moses; but has asserted that there may be persons of that religious persuasion who may suppose that the command in the decalogue, 'Six days shalt thou labor, and do all that thou hast to do,' imperiously binds them to work six days in each week, and firmly believing Saturday to be the day set apart for rest, they can only cease to work on that day, consistently with their ideas of religious duty. It has also been urged that there may be others

[1] *Hyneman's Case*, 101 Mass. 30.

[2] *Has' Case*, 122 Mass. 40.

[3] *Specht's Case*, 8 Barr 312.

who may make it a point of conscience to show, by plain, open, unequivocal acts, that the Christian institution of Sunday is abhorrent to their minds. To this we answer that we have never heard of the Fourth Commandment having received this construction by any persons who profess to believe either in the Old or New Testament. And that the Jewish Talmud, containing the traditions of that people, asserts no such doctrine. The true meaning of the command is uniformly supposed to be that we should abstain from our usual labor the one seventh part of our time, and devote the same to the worship of the Deity, and the exercise of our religious duties. Upon this subject the sense of the adherents to the Mosaic dispensation is strongly evinced by the religious holidays which they keep."[1] In 1848 this point was again raised in Pennsylvania, in the case of a "Seventh Day" Baptist. The court said: "The one remaining ground on which the plaintiff in error attacks the validity of the statute is found in the assumption that in conscience he is as fully bound to attend to his secular affairs upon the first six days of the week as to cease from labor on the seventh. Were this so, the law which compels him to inaction on one of the six days of the week might well be regarded as an invasion of his conscientious convictions. But for this supposed article of his faith his counsel refers us to no other warrant than that command of the decalogue which teaches, 'Remember the Sabbath day to keep it holy; six days shalt thou labor and do all thy work, but the seventh is the Sabbath of the Lord thy God; in it thou shalt not do any work.'" But, without other evidence than the mere suggestion of counsel, we can not believe that the religious sect to which the plaintiff belongs have so construed this enactment as to make it imperative on its members literally to labor on every day of the week other than the seventh. Such is not rationally its meaning, nor is it that assigned to the word by the ancient people to whom it was originally delivered by the Deity. From the beginning even until now it is regarded by them as intended to set apart a day of religious rest, but not as commanding six days of labor. Within six days the Israelite was directed to do all his work, in order that he might devote the seventh uninterruptedly to the service of God. But it was never imagined that he was under an imperative obligation to

[1] *Wolf's Case*, 3 S. & R. 48.

fill up each day of the other six with some worldly employment. In *The Commonwealth* v. *Wolf* the court rightly repudiates such a notion, and in this it has been followed by other tribunals. Indeed, the meaning of the command is so obvious as scarcely to leave room for construction; and, accordingly, so far as we are informed, the practice of all who profess to believe in the Old and New Testaments has been in consonance with the original interpretation. The case in Cincinnati (150 Ohio 225) was determined on the proviso, that nothing in the statute should be construed to extend to those who conscientiously observed the seventh day of the week as the Sabbath. Did our statute offer a similar provision, this controversy would probably never have arisen.[1] And, in Alabama, in 1867, it was held that the rule "which," said the court, "the Jew prescribes for himself," *i. e.*, to work on all the six days except his own Sabbath—which the party claimed to believe a command of God—could not be regarded as otherwise than as an industrial regulation, which is not required by a sentiment in fact religious, although so conscientiously regarded by him.[2]

In some states, as was indicated in *Specht's Case*, *ante*, there are exceptions made in favor of those who observe another day than the first of the week. Only one case—and that was decided under the civil law—has been found which denies the constitutionality of this exception. In Louisiana it was said of a city ordinance forbidding trade: "If it stopped there, perhaps it might do very well. But it goes on and provides further, that it shall not apply to any person or persons who close up their places of business and keep them closed during the whole day. It is admitted in the record that a large proportion of persons engaged in mercantile pursuits in the city of Shreveport are Jews, many of whom observe the Jewish Sabbath. Before the constitution, Jews and Gentiles are equal; by the law they must be treated alike, and the ordinance of a city council which gives to one sect a privilege which it denies to another violates both the constitution and the law, and is, therefore, null and void."[3] On the other hand, it was laid down in New York, in 1861, that "There is no ground of

[1] *Specht's Case*, 8 Pa. 312.

[2] *Frolickstein* v. *Mayor of Mobile*, 40 Ala. 725.

[3] *Shreveport* v. *Levy*, 26 La. Ann. 671.

complaint in the respect paid to the religious feelings of those who conscientiously observe the seventh, rather than the first day of the week, as a day of rest, by the legislation upon that subject, exempting them from certain public duties and from the service of process on their Sabbath, and excepting them from the operation of certain other statutes regulating the observance of the first day of the week."[1] And in Indiana, in 1881, it was held that a proviso that "nothing herein contained shall be construed to affect such as conscientiously observe the seventh day of the week as the Sabbath," did not conflict with a constitutional provision that "the General Assembly shall not grant to any citizen, or to any class of citizens, privileges or immunities which, upon the same terms, shall not belong equally to all citizens," as the terms on which the immunity might be enjoyed were denied to none, and it was left to the consciences of the citizens whether they would refrain from work on the first day or the seventh.[2]

PROPOSITION II.

Sunday Laws May be Passed by Municipal Corporations.

That the legislature of a state may authorize them to do so "has not been seriously questioned, and is too well settled to admit of question or require discussion."[3] Moreover, it appears that these corporations may possess this authority without its being conferred upon them in express terms. So it was held in Georgia, in 1871, that a city council had power to pass an ordinance prohibiting a dealer from keeping his store open.[4] And in Ohio, in 1859, the authority of a municipality in the premises was sustained, as included in the "power to provide for the preservation of the health, morals, &c., of their inhabitants."[5] In Tennessee the question arose as to what charter provision conferred this authority on the city of Nashville. The court said it was not included in the power "to make regulations to secure the general health and prevent and remove nuisances," but was embraced in the power "to tax and regulate" dealers of various sorts, and was also conferred by that clause in the

[1] *Lindenmuller's Case,* 33 Barb. 548.
[2] *John's Case,* 78 Ind. 332.
[3] *Linck's Case,* 12 Lea 499.
[4] *Karwisch's Case,* 44 Ga. 204.
[5] *Canton* v. *Nist,* 9 Ohio St. 439.

act of incorporation which authorized the passage of ordinances necessary for the health, convenience and safety of the citizens, "and to carry out the meaning of this act and accomplish the object of this incorporation." And the court added: "As the object of the city's incorporation was the proper regulation, good order and well-being of the community, and as a people whose traditions, laws and religion have accustomed them to an observance of the Christian Sabbath by a cessation from secular employments, and to consecrate it as a day of rest and devotion, [*sic*] it is not straining a construction to hold it would be a serious inconvenience, to say the least, if trading houses and places of business are to be permitted kept open for the sale of wares or merchandise and the transaction of secular business upon that day." And as to the argument that the fact that special authority in regard to other matters was given excluded the idea of power to pass ordinances on the subject of Sabbath-breaking under a general clause, the court said: "The rule, as we understand it, is, that if the power to pass ordinances upon any subject is specifically given, the power so granted cannot be enlarged or changed by the general clause, but if the subject is omitted altogether in the specific powers, authority to pass ordinances upon such omitted subject may be conferred under the general clause."[1]

It is an unsettled point whether the fact that there is a state law regulating Sunday conduct is a bar to municipal action in the same direction. It was held in New York, in 1852, that a city might pass an ordinance prohibiting liquor-selling, though already prohibited by state statute, and the court said: "The act to incorporate the city expressly authorizes the corporation to impose penalties for various acts rendered penal under the laws of the state * * * there is good reason why city corporations should be authorized to impose penalties in addition to those inflicted by the laws of the state. Particular acts may be far more injurious, while the temptation to commit them may be much greater in a crowded city than in the state generally. They consequently require more severe measures for prevention. State laws are for the general good, and cannot always answer the peculiar wants of particular localities * * * local legislation may be delegated to municipal corporations. Their acts under the power are valid when there is no con-

[1] *Linck Case*, 12 Tenn. 499.

flict and the superadded penalties are not inconsistent with those previously imposed."[1] On the other hand, it was held in Georgia, in 1882, that the prohibition of labor by a city ordinance was void because a similar prohibition was already made by a statute, and "it has been decided by this court that a municipal corporation cannot legislate upon subjects already made offences and punishable by the laws of the state."[2] But it is, at any rate, settled that a city ordinance on the subject cannot invalidate a statutory exception. Thus it was held, in 1852, that as the New York statute authorizes the sale of liquors by licensed inn-keepers to lodgers and travelers, a city ordinance forbidding liquor-selling is void as to such a sale.[3] So, in Ohio, where the statute excepts those who observe the seventh day, &c., from its obligations, it was held, in 1859, that the exceptions expressed the state's policy equally with the prohibition, and that a municipal ordinance, in ignoring the statutory exceptions and assuming to punish acts which the statute, by clear inference, authorizes, was inconsistent with the state's law and policy, and to that extent void.[4] If the municipal corporation cannot of itself, or under the doctrine of implied powers, interfere with the local operation of a statute, can the legislature expressly authorize it to do so? The Michigan Supreme Court, in 1876, spoke of the "somewhat extraordinary" proviso in the Sunday laws of that state, that saloons, &c., shall close, unless otherwise determined by the council, &c., of the city, &c., and said: "This seems to be based on the idea that a municipality can be allowed to suspend the penal laws of the state."[5] It was provided in the Virginia statute forbidding liquor-selling, that it should not apply to any city having police regulations on the subject and an ordinance inflicting a penalty equal to that of the statute. It was held, in 1878, that an ordinance to fulfill this description must *plainly* come within the meaning of the proviso. And the court said: "If the proviso had plainly declared that the law should not apply to any city having police regulations and an ordinance to the same effect with the body of the law, both as to the definition

[1] *Wood* v. *Brooklyn*, 14 Barb. 425.

[2] *Rothschild's Case*, 59 Ga. 503. As to the power of municipal corporations to pass ordinances on subjects already regulated by statute, see *Dillon Mun. Corp.* (*ed.* 1881), § 317, *notes*.

[3] *Wood* v. *Brooklyn*, 14 Barb. 425.

[4] *Nist's Case*, 9 Ohio St. 439.

[5] *Kurtz's Case*, 33 Mich. 279.

of the crime.and the nature and measure of the penalty, there would have been, perhaps, nothing unreasonable in the law, and certainly no room for doubt as to the legislative meaning. * * * If the proviso had plainly declared that the law should not apply to any city having police regulations and an ordinance *not* to the same effect with the body of the law, either as to the definition of the offence or as to the nature and measure of the penalty, such an effect would have been very unequal and unreasonable, even if such a law would have been valid—a question which need not be here decided." A Richmond ordinance required the bar where liquors were sold to be closed, &c. The statute declared that no intoxicating drink should be sold in any bar, &c. The fine was the same, but the statute contained a provision for the forfeiture of the license, which was not in the ordinance. The court said there were several material differences between the offences prohibited; and that a person might violate the ordinance by keeping a bar open, though he did not sell a single drink, but could not violate the statute without selling; that the two laws were enacted *diverso intuitu*, and without any reference to each other; and though the city council might have intended to supersede the statute by an amendment of the ordinance which they passed seventeen days after the enactment of the statute, they could not do this except in the mode prescribed—defining the same offence, and prescribing the same punishment; that it was not enough to make the fine the same, and prescribe the forfeiture of license "at the court's discretion." And the court added: "Without deciding whether the penalties are the same, it is enough to say that they are not substantially the same * * * and we have further to say that the statute embraces a period not embraced in the ordinance, that is, from twelve o'clock Sunday night till sunrise Monday morning * * * this would create a palpable difference in the law governing different localities, which could not have been contemplated by the legislature * * * there is another reason for saying that neither the offences nor the penalties are substantially the same—a person may be convicted under the statute for every act of selling on the same day, whereas he can be convicted under the ordinance of only one offence of not closing 'on Sunday during the whole day.'"[1]

[1] *Thon's Case*, 31 Grattan 887.

The preceding cases have dealt with the constitutionality of general Sunday laws, that is, of laws which prescribe special rules of conduct on the first day of the week, but prescribe them for all citizens alike. But there are certain Sunday laws which are concerned with particular classes only. The objection has been made to these that they are "special legislation." Blackstone says: "Special acts are rather exceptions than rules, being those which only operate upon particular persons and private concerns."[1] Dwarris says: "Public acts relate to the public at large, and private acts concern the particular interest or benefit of certain individuals or particular classes of men."[2] Judge Cooley says: "The authority that legislates for a state at large must determine whether particular rules shall extend to the whole state and all its citizens, or, on the other hand, to a subdivision of the state or a single class of its citizens only. The circumstances of a particular locality, or the prevailing public sentiment in that section of the state may require, or make acceptable, different police regulations from those demanded in another, or call for different taxation, and a different application of the public money. The legislature may, therefore, prescribe, or authorize, different laws of police, allow the right of eminent domain to be exercised in different cases, and through different agencies, and prescribe peculiar restrictions upon taxation in each distinct municipality, provided the state constitution does not forbid. These discriminations are made constantly; and the fact that the laws are of local or special operation only is not supposed to render them obnoxious in principle * * * If the laws be otherwise unobjectionable, all that can be required in these cases is, that they be general to the class or locality to which they apply, and they are then public in character, and of their propriety and policy the legislature must judge."[3] In Idaho, in 1870, a provision against keeping open saloons in one county was held to be a general law, uniform in its operation upon the same classes of people throughout that county, and not "vindictive" any further than necessary to vindicate good order; and in response to the suggestion that the law was against public policy, it was observed: "It is not for this court to determine whether the law is politic or not; it

[1] *Sharswood's Bl.*, bk. I., 85.
[2] *Pot. Dwar. Stat.* 53.
[3] *Cooley Const. Lim.* 390 (marg.)

may be against public policy for the people to rest one day in seven, but the court cannot be asked to so determine for the purpose of destroying any law."[1] An act prohibiting baking on Sunday was pronounced void, as special legislation, in California in 1880. Judge Myrick said: "The baking of bread is in itself lawful and necessary; * * * even if there were authority to restrain the labor on some one day, it must be under a general law." And McKintay, J., concurring, observed: "The act does not declare the business of baking, as ordinarily conducted, to be a nuisance, nor does it contain any intimation that the business of baking may tend to interrupt divine worship by any class of sectaries, or can otherwise interfere with the rights or privileges of any class of citizens. The baking of bread is not only lawful and necessary, but we will take notice that there is nothing so peculiar in the occupation as that those engaged in it require—as a sanitary measure, or for the protection of their morals—a period of rest not required by those engaged in many other employments; the general law must include within its sanction all who come within its purpose and scope. It must be as broad as its object. If it is to be made a crime not to refrain from labor, it must be made equally a crime as to all who do not so refrain. Or the prohibitory law must be made applicable to all of a class, the members of which, for reasons apparent upon mention of the class, may, at least, require, for the benefit of their health or morals, a period of rest not beneficial to any other class or individual." And he added that "Though a law might be general which did not include clergymen, or others whose pursuits might involve works of necessity, yet there could be no rule which would permit the prohibition of a particular kind of labor in itself innocent and beneficial to the public, and that there was no reason, and could be none, why bakers should be forced to rest periodically which was not applicable to many other artisans and workmen."[2] In the following year, in the same state, the court, after remarking that a constitutional prohibition of special laws applied to subsequent, but not to previous, legislation, referred to the provision that "laws of a general nature shall have a uniform operation," and said of a Sunday law: "It is true a section of the act excepts from the operation of the law

[1] *Griffin Case,* 1 Idaho (N. S.) 476.

[2] *Westerfield's Case,* 55 Cal. 350.

certain kinds of business; but this it was perfectly competent for the legislature to do, without violating the constitutional provision respecting uniformity."[1] The law in question required the closing of places of business, &c., and made an exception of "hotels, barber-shops," &c. It was again attacked as "special" in 1882, and again upheld, upon the ground that in making the exceptions, the legislature "merely declared that, in its judgment, there was something in the callings specified which rendered it improper to include them; that the exclusion was not arbitrary and the discrimination was reasonable, and that to declare the sections invalid would be to strike at the power of the legislature to determine what acts of those not *malum in se* shall be punished, and what shall not be punished." And, referring to the law against baking, which had been held "special," the court repeated its opinion that it was clearly so, and added: "It may be further said that the discrimination made by such act was not on any reasonable grounds, but appeared to be entirely arbitrary."[2] And Judge Myrick, who had delivered an opinion against the law forbidding baking, now observed: "Whatever may be individual opinion from a religious standpoint, I cannot say, as a matter of law, that a man will not be more benefited by bathing, or by being shaved, or by having meals or a drive on Sunday, than he will by visiting a store, saloon or banking-house. Such distinctions are for the consideration of the legislature."[3] It will be observed that the two cases last cited differ in this regard: the first deals with a positive prohibition of the practice of a particular trade on Sunday, the second, with an exception of certain lines of business from a positive prohibition which applies to all others. But the principle is the same; the decisions are irreconcilable, except on the ground that while the legislature may discriminate in its Sunday laws between one pursuit or another, the discrimination must be reasonable, and of its reasonableness the courts are to judge.

We may also remark here that these special Sunday laws are not generally considered by legislatures with reference to their reasonableness or unreasonableness, but are passed under the urgent pressure, either of employes who wish to secure seven days' pay for

[1] *Burke's Case*, 59 Cal. 6.
[2] *Id.* 192.
[3] *Koser's Case*, 60 Cal. 177.

six days' work (*e. g.*, a late Maryland law forbidding the delivery of ice on Sunday, to the great detriment of poor housekeepers, unprovided with means of storing their ice from Saturday to Monday), or of principals who wish to close their places of business for holiday purposes, and are prevented by the competition of a less luxurious class from so doing, except under the penalty of a loss of custom (*e. g.*, the law for closing barber-shops in the same state).

Finally, we may notice an objection to a certain Sunday law which was based on its title. It is provided by the New York constitution that "no local bill shall be passed which shall embrace more than one subject, and that shall be embraced in its title." A bill entitled "An act to preserve the public peace and order on the first day of the week," whose provisions, by their terms, applied to the city of New York alone, was held, in 1877, not to be invalid under this constitutional requirement. And the court said: "It will be seen that the title is broad enough in its language to apply to the whole state. This, however, is not enough to determine that it is improper. The constitutional purpose was not to insure that there should be no legislation discriminating for or against any locality. It was to insure that such legislation should not be had without such locality being apprised of the intention so to legislate, with opportunity to urge or oppose. If the title of the bill be so general as to indicate to every portion of the state that possibly it may be brought within the scope of the law, that purpose is effected; so that, though the act deals with New York city alone, and the title indicates the whole state, the dealers in New York city were apprised that there was a law proposed which might affect them." But Church, J., dissented, in an able opinion, and said of the above mode of reasoning: "This argument, if sound, would annihilate the constitutional provision in its practical application." And he continued: "The title is deceptive and calculated to mislead. It does not indicate the real purpose of the bill. On the contrary, it expresses an entirely different purpose." And he pointed out that the citizens of New York city might object to special police regulations for their city, and not to the same rules if established for the whole state.[1]

[1] *Neuendorff* v. *Duryea*, 69 N. Y. 557.

CHAPTER II.

CONSTITUTIONALITY OF SUNDAY LAWS IN THE UNITED STATES—CONTINUED.

Cases Sustaining Them as Religious Regulations.

The preceding chapter was confined to a statement of the established propositions in reference to the constitutionality of Sunday laws, and of the principal objections to them which have been overruled. We come now to consider the positive grounds upon which these laws have been sustained.

According to their reasoning, the favorable decisions naturally divide themselves into two classes—those which consider Sunday laws as legislative sanctions of a religious tenet, and those which regard them simply as civil regulations. And the first class may be separated again into two subdivisions—the first comprising those cases which hold that, as religion is concerned with conduct in its relation to the individual man, these laws for the enforcement of religion must be construed with reference to him alone, and have nothing to do with the effect of his behavior on others; and the second maintaining that their object is not to exact a religious observance from the individual, but to prevent his interference with the religious practices of other people.

This classification, however, refers only to the reasoning of the cases, and not to the cases themselves. The same case sometimes takes in one paragraph the view of what is here called the first subdivision, and in another that of the second, and occasionally religious and sanitary or social considerations are indissolubly blended. But the above analysis is believed to cover the entire ground occupied by decisions upholding laws for the enforcement of Sunday idleness.

The following propositions may be demonstrated by the cases which hold that Sunday laws are religious regulations, and may be sustained as such.

PROPOSITION I.

Sunday is a Holy Day.

That is to say, it is a period of time to which a peculiar sanctity attaches, such as attaches in the estimation of believers to certain places, as churches and the like.

An English judge said, in 1824: "It seems to me that the object of the statute was to prevent persons keeping open shop and *disregarding the decency of the Lord's day* by the public show of their ordinary trades and occupations."[1]

And Judge Kent, in 1811, said of Sunday idleness, that, in New York, "the statute has, for over a century, recognized the *sanctity* of the obligation, and punished its violators;"[2] and, in 1834, another judge spoke of "the public order and *solemnity* of the day;"[3] while still later (1859) we are assured that the New York statute "explicitly recognizes the first day of the week as '*holy* time;' and, thus, it has brought us back to the full, enlarged and absolute rule of interdiction which we find prevailed in the earliest laws of Christian states, and which the construction of the statute of Charles II. has tended somewhat to narrow and impair."[4] And it was asked, in 1882: "Is it not obvious that, by reason of keeping a store open for business, a temptation is presented to those who have no regard for Sunday, as *holy* time, to violate the law?"[5] So, a Pennsylvania judge holds that "the day is clothed with peculiar *sanctity;*"[6] and it was observed concerning two Kentucky statutes, that "one applied exclusively to Sunday, as *sacred*, and the other to holidays, as secular;"[7] and, in Iowa, Sunday is "*sacred*, set apart for rest by the voice of wisdom, experience and necessity;"[8] and, in North Carolina, while alluding to Sunday laws, it was observed, that "all

[1] Littledale, J., in *Bloxsome* v. *Williams*, 5 D. & R. 82.

[2] *Ruggle's Case*, 8 Johns. 290.

[3] *Boynton* v. *Page*, 12 Wend. (N. Y.) 57.

[4] *Campbell* v. *International Soc.*, 4 Bos. (N. Y.) 298.

[5] *Anonymous*, 12 Abb. N. C. (N. Y.) 455.

[6] *Jeandelle's Case*, 3 Phil. 509.

[7] *Moore* v. *Hagan*, 2 Duv. 437 (1866).

[8] *Davis* v. *Fish*, 1 Green 406 (1848).

religions and moral codes permit works of necessity and charity on their *sacred* days;"[1] and, finally, it has been said in Georgia, that "all courts should abstain from the transaction of ordinary business on this *holy* day;"[2] for, "in every form, by all the different authorities of this state—by its organic laws, its civil and criminal code, and by every judicial decision upon the question—the Sabbath day is regarded as the Lord's day, and it is protected from violation by so many guards, that the courts should not be allowed to invade its *sanctity*, and, in so doing, make a record to be read by all men in all time;"[3] and in Georgia, as in England, Sunday is a *holy* day. The code denominates it the Lord's day, and as the Lord's day all courts and magistrates are to consider it."[4]

Having established the proposition, as a matter of law, that Sunday is "holy," the inquiring mind is next inclined to examine the manner in which it became so, and to ascertain by what authority its peculiar sanctity was conferred upon it. There are cases which hold that its sanctification was accomplished by statute. Thus, one reason given for "separating" the day as a "holy" one in Massachusetts is the fact that "the *legislative power* has exacted the observance of it as such."[5] And Judge Kent assures us that, in New York, "the *statute* for preventing immorality *consecrates* the first day of the week as holy time;"[6] and Judge Robertson, of Kentucky, speaks of the law in his state as "the statute *consecrating* the Sabbath;"[7] and so, in Georgia, courts and magistrates are to regard Sunday as the Lord's day "*as matter of mere law*, irrespective of religious obligation and duty."[8]

Now, it cannot be denied that this assertion of authority in an American legislature to "sanctify" or "consecrate" a particular time attributes ecclesiastical functions to such a body which are not commonly ascribed to it in the theory of our jurisprudence. And if a portion of the week may be made "holy," "as a mere matter of law," of course a portion of territory may be so made by the same power; so that the "consecration" of a church or cathedral

[1] *Ricketts' Case*, 74 N. C. 184 (1876).

[2] *Gholston* v. *Gholston*, 31 Ga. 625 (1860).

[3] *Bass* v. *Irvin*, 49 Ga. 436.

[4] *Weldon's Case*, 62 Ga. 449.

[5] *Pearce* v. *Atwood*, 13 Mass. 324.

[6] *People* v. *Ruggles*, 8 Johns. 290 (1811).

[7] *Moore* v. *Hagan*, 2 Duv. 437.

[8] *Weldon's Case*, 62 Ga. 449 (1879).

comes directly within the purview of legislative enactment. But no association of believers would acknowledge the jurisdiction of an American legislature in such matters as these. Sacred times and sacred places with us are determined by the religious organization to which one is attached; and "consecration," or "setting apart" of days or buildings, is the work of those whom each citizen chooses to recognize as his spiritual guides. If the "sanctity" of Sunday, then, is to be maintained, it should seem that it must be on some other ground than that of legislative decree.

The following citations establish judicially that it is divine authority, and not any statute of New York, Kentucky or Georgia, which has sanctified Sunday. Thus, we find that, contrary to Judge Kent's view, Judge Allen, of New York, holds that the statute merely recognizes an attribute of holiness already bestowed by a higher law. He says: "It does not detract from the moral or legal sanction of the law of the state that it conforms to the *law of God*, as that law is recognized by the great majority of the people;"[1] and it is held in Pennsylvania that "Sabbath-breaking is a violation of a *divine* as well as a human law;"[2] and in a later case it is observed: "The learned counsel for the plaintiff has entered largely into the question of the origin and sanction of the Christian Sabbath. It may not be essential, but it is far from being irrelevant, to the decision of the present case, to sustain the *divine* authority of its institution," and the day is declared to be "set apart by *divine* command and human legislation as a day of rest;" and the court adds: "We have no right to give up this institution. It has come down to us with the most *solemn sanctions, both of God* and man, and, if we do not appreciate it as we ought, we are at the least bound to preserve it."[3] It was an Arkansas judge who assured certain Sunday card-players that the day "is set apart by *divine* appointment, as well as by the law of the land, for other and better engagements."[4] In Iowa, it is said that Sunday has been "established by laws, both human and *divine*, for public worship and private devotion—a time-honored and *heaven-appointed* institution;"[5] and, in Maryland, we are told that "the Sabbath is emphatically the day of rest, and the

[1] *Lindenmuller's Case*, 33 Barb. 548 (1861).

[2] *Eyre's Case*, 1 S. & R. 347 (1815).

[3] *Johnston's Case*, 22 Pa. 102 (1853).

[4] *Stockden's Case*, 18 Ark. 186 (1856).

[5] *Davis* v. *Fish*, 1 Green 406 (1848).

day of rest here is the Lord's day or Christian Sunday. Ours is a Christian community, and the day set apart as a day of rest is the day *consecrated by the resurrection of our Saviour*, and embraces the twenty-four hours next ensuing the midnight of Saturday."[1] The Georgia view is as follows: "The law fixes the day recognized as the Sabbath day all over Christendom, and that day, *by divine injunction*, is to be kept holy—'on it thou shalt do no work.' The Christian Sabbath is a civil institution *older than our government*, and respected as a day of rest by our constitution, and the regulation of its observance as a civil institution has always been considered to be, and is, within the power of the legislature as much as any regulations and laws having for their object the preservation of good morals, and the peace and good order of society;"[2] and is thus further elucidated in a later case: "Independently of the moral obligation, resting upon all men, to obey the law of the Lord, and to observe by abstaining from all secular business on the day set apart for His worship throughout Christendom, the rest of one day in seven from all physical and mental labor is a great conservative, refreshing, invigorating means, *designed by Almighty wisdom for the preservation of health* and the recreation of our mental and bodily faculties. But neither the law of God nor the law of man forbids us to do good on the Sabbath day. The Saviour rebuked the Pharisees who questioned His divinity, because He healed the impotent man on the Sabbath, and bade him take up his bed and walk; and He, who spake as never man spake, said that the Sabbath was made for man, not man for the Sabbath, and that it was lawful to do good on the Sabbath day; and His own pure and perfect life illustrated His teaching by deeds of constant kindness and beneficence on the Sabbath day. When the statute of Georgia, therefore, excepts works of benevolence and charity from the operation of this penal statute, it but *re-enacts the law of the Almighty* as announced by the Saviour and beautified by His example."[3]

[1] *Kilgour* v. *Mills*, 6 G. & J. 268 (1834).

[2] *Karwisch's Case*, 44 Ga. 204 (1871).

[3] *Salter* v. *Smith*, 55 Ga. 244 (1875).

PROPOSITION II.

The Holiness of Sunday is to be Recognized by Remaining Idle on that Day; and Not to so Remain is to be Immoral.

However the quality of sanctity came to be bestowed on Sunday, two points are settled by the class of cases now under consideration—first, that this quality can only be respected by remaining idle; and, secondly, that not to remain idle is something over and above a mere infraction of a statutory rule of public conduct, and is properly to be taken cognizance of by our civil courts as an "immorality" or "sin." Thus, Judge Kent said, in New York, "the statute considers the violation of the first day of the week as *immoral;*"[1] and, in the same state, the court spoke of "the mere making of a bargain, however much it may violate the *moral* law;"[2] and the Pennsylvania courts allude to "our Sunday laws, and our other laws against *vice and immorality*,"[3] and remark, in connection with the Sunday law, that "the prevention of *vice and immorality*, and the suppression of dissipation, [*sic*] are state objects,"[4] and say that these laws "have heretofore been regarded as efficient protectors of *public morals* and of social happiness."[5] In Georgia, the court sustained the law, holding that the power to make it was collected from the general powers delegated to maintain good order, &c.; which evidently confines the reasoning to a question of police. But it proceeded to add: "The power is a very high prerogative, and is supported by the principle involved in the preservation of the *morals and duties* of the citizens upon the Lord's day."[6] In Alabama, it is said that the object of the Sunday law is "to prevent *vice and immorality*,"[7] and that contracts made on Sunday are "void for *immorality;*"[8] and, in Ohio, where a deed was executed on Sunday, the court announced that "both parties partook of the *sin* of violating the Sabbath."[9]

[1] *People* v. *Ruggles*, 8 Johns. 290 (1811).

[2] *Miller* v. *Roessler*, 4 E. D. S. 234 (1855).

[3] *Nesbit's Case*, 34 Pa. 398 (1859).

[4] *Omit's Case*, 9 Harris (Pa.) 426.

[5] *Tieman's Case*, 1 Phil. 460 (1853).

[6] *Karwisch's Case*, 44 Ga. 204 (1871).

[7] *Hooper* v. *Edwards*, 18 Ala. 280.

[8] *Rainey* v. *Cuffs*, 22 Ala. 288 (1853).

[9] *Swisher* v. *Williams*, Wright (Ohio) 754 (1834).

To appreciate the true significance of these citations, it must be borne in mind that the "immorality," "vice" and "sin" consists not in the acts done, but in the doing of them on Sunday. That is to say, the language, if it means anything, means that Sunday labor, &c., should be regarded by our secular courts just as an ecclesiastical tribunal would regard boisterous behavior in a church, unauthorized intrusions upon a sanctuary, &c., as "violations" of a holy time, akin to desecrations of a holy place. Strange as this spiritual view of a civil jurisdiction may seem, in our age and country, there is ample and high authority for it. Thus, Blackstone gives as "*the ninth offence against God and religion,*" "*Profanation* of the Lord's day, vulgarly (but improperly) called 'Sabbath-breaking;'"[1] and our friend, Judge Kent, insists that the New York Sunday statute is "only a continuation in substance of the law of the colony, which declared that the *profanation* of the Lord's day was the great scandal of the Christian faith;"[2] and it was said later, in the same state, "a public arrest may be a greater *desecration* of the Sabbath than the act for which it is made, and for many violations of a corporation ordinance it certainly would;"[3] and we are told that, since 1789, "statutes have been in force to prevent Sabbath *desecration,* and prohibiting acts on that day which would be lawful on other days of the week;"[4] so that the doctrine may be considered as settled, that by legislative act "Sunday may be protected from *desecration.*"[5] In Pennsylvania, also, we read of "the *violation* of the Sabbath,"[6] and of "Sabbath *desecration,*"[7] and how, from a judicial standpoint, "it would be a small boon to the people of Pennsylvania to declare their indefeasible right to worship God according to the dictates of their consciences amid the din and confusion of secular employments and the *desecrations* on every hand of what they conscientiously believe to be *holy* time."[8] So, in Arkansas, where a party was indicted for liquor-selling, the court said: "The gravamen of the charge is a *desecration* of the Sabbath, an offence against public

[1] *Blackstone IV.*, 63 (marg.)

[2] *People* v. *Ruggles,* 8 Johns. 290 (1811).

[3] *Wood* v. *Brooklyn,* 14 Barb. 425 (1852).

[4] *Lindenmuller's Case,* 33 Barb. 548 (1861).

[5] *Neuendorff* v. *Duryea,* 69 N. Y. 557 (1877).

[6] *Eyre's Case,* 1 S. & R. 347 (1815).

[7] *Nesbit's Case,* 34 Pa. 86 (1859).

[8] *Johnston's Case,* 22 Pa. 102 (1853).

morals and not against an individual;"[1] and later, in the same state, it was said, "the object of the statute was to prohibit the *desecration* of the Sabbath by engaging in the vicious employment of playing cards on that day; * * * no matter what the purpose of the game may be, it is a *desecration* of the day, and vicious to public morals in its tendencies."[2] And again: "One great object of the American statutes, though differing in their expressions, is to prevent the *desecration* of the Sabbath by the doing of ordinary work, or secular business."[3] The object of the Kentucky provisions for idleness, &c., on Sunday, is "to aid in securing it against *desecration*,"[4] &c. And, in Alabama, "the obvious design of the legislature was to prevent the spread of vice and immorality by the *desecration* of the first day of the week to common secular purposes, unless justified by the necessity of the case."[5] And, in Minnesota, "the law is not enforced for the benefit of either of the parties, but to prevent a *desecration* of the day."[6]

PROPOSITION III.

Sunday Idleness is Enforced as a Religious Duty in the Individual.

As work on Sunday is a "desecration," and only that which is sacred can be desecrated, and as the ascription of this quality of sacredness, whether to a time or a place, is altogether a matter of religious belief, it follows that, if the sacredness of Sunday is, as we are told by some judges, created by the legislature, then, as already observed, the legislature has exercised ecclesiastical functions in the passage of Sunday laws; but it is no less true that, if these laws are simply a recognition of a sanctity already bestowed on the day by some other authority, the legislature has, in their passage, applied the civil authority to the enforcement of a religious dogma, and to that extent identified the State with the Church. The English authorities are clear and decided on this point. Let us begin with Coke. He says, referring to the Sunday laws: "It is truly said,

1 *Parnell's Case*, 16 Ark. 506.
2 *Stockden's Case*, 18 Ark. 186.
3 *Tucker* v. *West*, 29 Ark. 386 (1871).
4 *Moore* v. *Hagan*, 2 Duv. 437.
5 *Colten* v. *Huey*, 4 Ala. 56 (1842).
6 *Brackett* v. *Edgerton*, 14 Minn. 174 (1869).

'*reges, qui serviunt Christo, faciunt leges pro Christo.*'"[1] And, again, "'*Sabbath dies non dies juridicus,*' for that ought to be *consecrated to divine service.*"[2] So, Blackstone, more at length: "Profanation of the Lord's day is a ninth offence against God and religion punished by the municipal law of England. For, beside the notorious indecency and scandal of permitting any secular business to be transacted on that day, in a country professing Christianity, and the corruption of morals which usually follows its profanation, the keeping one day in the seven *holy*, as a time of relaxation and refreshment, as well as for *public worship*, is of admirable service to a state, considered merely as a civil institution. It humanizes, by the help of conversation and society, the manners of the lower classes, which would, otherwise, degenerate into a sordid ferocity and savage selfishness of spirit; it enables the industrious workman to pursue his occupation in the ensuing week, with health and cheerfulness; it imprints on the minds of the people that *sense of their duty to God*, so necessary to make them good citizens; but which, yet, would be worn out and defaced by an unremitting continuance of labor, without any stated time of *recalling them to the worship of their Maker*."[3] And, in a comparatively recent case, it was said of the English Sunday law. "The spirit of the act is to advance the interests of *religion*, to turn a man's thoughts from his worldly concerns, and to direct them to the duties of piety and religion. Labor may be private and not meet the public eye, and so not offend against public decency, but it is equally labor, and equally interferes with a man's religious duties. The statute, in express terms, provides that every person shall apply himself to the *observation of the Lord's day publicly and privately*, so that private, as well as public, conduct, was expressly within its contemplation."[4] And there is no lack of American authorities which recognize the logical consistency of the English view, and adopt the same reasoning. Thus, attention was called to the fact that the Rhode Island statute is a "transcript" of 29 Car. II.;[5] and, in another case, we are told that it is "almost an exact transcript," and that it is "different from the Sunday laws of other states, except that of New Hampshire, which more

[1] 2 Inst. 264.

[2] *Coke on Littleton*, L. II., 135*a* (g).

[3] *Com. IV.*, 6 (marg.)

[4] *Fenneller* v. *Ridler*, 5 B. & C. 406 (1829).

[5] *Allen* v. *Gardiner*, 7 R. I. 22 (1861).

nearly resembles it."[1] So, the New Hampshire court observed, "traveling, as the case finds the plaintiff did, would be no violation of law, however we might be disposed to regard it, in a moral, or *religious* point of view."[2] And again: "The policy of the English act, and of our Provincial act of 1700, is disclosed in the commencement of those acts, providing that all and every person and persons whatsoever shall on that day apply themselves to the *duties of piety, and religion*, publicly and privately. The object of the English statute was to promote the due observance of the Lord's day, by putting a stop to unnecessary worldly labor and business, at least among the persons and classes enumerated, and others like them, whether such labor and business was open and public, or in private; and this, not only for the sake of public decency and order, but to withdraw a man's own thoughts from secular concerns, and turn them to the *duties of religion*. In respect to the Provincial act of 1700, and the law of 1799, we can entertain no doubt that their purpose and object were substantially the same, although the act of 1799 had a larger scope, and was more general in its application, reaching all persons and all secular occupations alike; and we think it too clear to admit of question that, with the view of enforcing the observance of *religious duties* on the Sabbath, unnecessary secular business and labor were forbidden equally, whether public or private." And of a later statute, prohibiting "disturbance" of others, the court said: "We perceive no intention to diminish the restraints upon those unnecessary worldly acts which interfere with the public observance of the Lord's day; and, therefore, such acts, when done openly or publicly, in the presence of others, are prohibited, because they are calculated to turn the attention of those who are present from their appropriate *religious* duties, to matters of mere worldly concern. * * * The policy of the act is still to encourage the due observance of the Sabbath, as a day of rest from worldly labors and traffic, *and of devotion to religious duties;* to give every citizen an opportunity to discharge the *religious* duties incumbent upon him on that day."[3] In Massachusetts, we are told, "all arguments, drawn from the Jewish law respecting the Sabbath, are out of place, except so far as any provisions of that law may

[1] *Sayles* v. *Wellman,* 10 R. I. 465 (1873).

[2] *Corey* v. *Bath,* 35 N. H. 530 (1857).

[3] *George v. George,* 47 N. H. 27 (1866).

have been recognized and promulgated by our Saviour, or *by the legislative authority* of our own commonwealth. We are far from questioning the *religious* obligation which all Christians are under to separate to *religious uses* the first day of the week, since the legislative power has exacted the observance of it *as such.*"[1] And, again, in the same state, it was said: "Our Puritan ancestors intended that the day should be not merely a day of rest from labor, but also a day *devoted to public and private worship, and to religious meditation and repose,* undisturbed by secular cares or amusements. They saw fit to enforce the observance of the day by penal legislation, and *the statute regulations which they devised for that purpose have continued in force, without any substantial modification, to the present time.*"[2] And in New York, the judges have said: "The same principles of policy, as well as of *religion* and morality, would interdict the issuing, as well as the service, of process,"[3] and "we think ourselves bound by the statute, and the moral and *religious* sense of the community."[4] And of the serving of process, it was further observed, "with respect to many persons, this might, and probably would, violate their *religious* feelings and principles." So, it was declared that "The statute is in harmony with the *religion* of the country and the *religious* sentiment of the public;"[5] and, "if the act is not prohibited, it is lawful, however improper it may be, as a violation of decorum and *religious* duty;"[6] and a doubt is expressed "whether, in a *religious* point of view, the distinction between selling and exposing for sale be a sound one."[7] And, in the following extract, though we find "duties to the state" mentioned towards the close, it is evident that it is to the religion of the state, and not to any of its civil institutions, that the deference required by the statute is to be accorded by the unwilling citizen. The court said, in the case of a Sunday theatre, "Liberty of conscience in matters of faith and practice, in fact, of the Christian *religion, entitled to, and enjoying the protection of the law as the religion* of the people of the state, and as furnishing the best sanctions of moral and social obligations. The public peace

[1] *Pearce* v. *Atwood*, 13 Mass. 324.

[2] *Davis* v. *Somerville*, 128 Mass. 594 (1880).

[3] *Van Vechten* v. *Paddock*, 12 Johns. 177 (1815).

[4] *Field* v. *Park*, 20 Johns. 140 (1822).

[5] *Smith* v. *Wilcox*, 24 N. Y. 353 (1862).

[6] *Sayles* v. *Smith*, 12 Wend. 57 (1834).

[7] *Smith* v. *Wilcox*, 19 Barb. 581 (1853).

and public welfare are greatly dependent upon the protection of the *religion* of the country, and the preventing or punishing of offences against it, and acts, wantonly committed, subversive of it. * * * The claim of the defence, carried to its necessary sequence, is that the Bible and *religion*, with all its ordinances, including the Sabbath [*sic*], are as effectually abolished as they were in France during the revolution, and so effectually abolished that duties may not be enforced as duties to the state, because they have been heretofore associated with acts of *religious* worship or connected with *religious* duties."[1] So, it was said in Pennsylvania: "Laws cannot be administered in any civilized government, unless the people are taught to revere the sanctity of an oath, and look to a future state of rewards and punishments for the deeds of this life. It is of the utmost moment, therefore, that they should be reminded of their *religious* duties at stated periods."[2] And again: "The policy of these acts, I think, ought not to be questioned. I presume it will be admitted by an intelligent mind that *religion* is of the utmost importance to every community. The history of the past furnishes abundant evidence of the truth of this proposition. It is the basis of civilization. Without it, we should be in a state of moral darkness and degradation such as usually attend the most barbarous and savage states. It is to the influence of it that we stand indebted for all that social order and happiness which prevails among us. It is by the force of *religion*, more than by that of our municipal regulations, or our boasted sense of honor, that we are kept within the line of moral rectitude, and constrained to administer to the welfare and comfort of each other. In short, we owe to it all that we enjoy either of civil or *religious* liberty. Blessings which cannot be too highly appreciated, but ought not, as the defendants are said to have done upon this occasion, to be used as a cloak to cover a design to disturb the public peace and to promote a sinister end. Here, then, give me leave to say that the institution of the Sabbath is, in my humble opinion, not only admirably adapted to promote and establish *religion* among us, but to secure and preserve our physical as well as moral health and strength."[3] And later: "For the ease of creation," said the old act of 1705, "as well as that

[1] *Lindenmuller's Case*, 33 Barb. 548 (1861).

[2] *Wolf's Case*, 3 S. & R. 48 (1817).

[3] *Dupuy's Case*, Bright. 44.

people may enjoy *religious* privileges, the first day of the week shall be observed. They [the early settlers] justly regarded it as essential to *religious* freedom, as well as to physical health and strength. It is an institution deeply seated in the *religious* affections of the community, and one of the foundations of public morals and of our political fabric."[1] And, in the same year, the court quoted the language of Coke and Blackstone, just cited, and said: "It is apparent from these authorities, as well as from the whole history of the statute Sabbath, and particularly from the preamble to our old act, that rest and the *public worship of Almighty God* were the primary objects of the institution, both as a divine and civil appointment."[2] And again it was said: "It was necessary that prohibitory statutes should be passed to regulate and restrain such proceedings as were considered inconsistent with the *observance* of Sunday as a day of rest," and it was added that the idle Sunday seemed to be universally recognized as "an institution deeply seated in the *religious* affections of the community, and one of the foundations of public morals and of our political fabric;" and, the court continued, the design of the law is to secure not only a day of rest, but, as it is termed in the act of 1705, a day on which "*the people may devote themselves to religious and pious exercise;* * * * a period of *religious observance* and of rest from wordly business."[3] And we are told that the idle Sunday is "a *religious* institution held in high reverence by great numbers, a civil institution which the state has always cherished,"[4] and that "people are forbidden to carry on worldly business, in order that they may devote the *day to rest, and the worship of God;*"[5] and "a special purpose of the day is, that people may enjoy *religious worship and instruction* * * * *conducting and attending religious worship* are among the very purposes, for which the law protects the day;"[6] and we are further assured that "Law can never become entirely infidel; for it is, essentially, founded on the moral customs of men, and the generating principle of these is most frequently *religion*,"[7] and "so far as the legislation of the state is concerned, as well as that of the Colony and

[1] *Omit's Case*, 21 Pa. 426 (1853).
[2] *Johnston's Case*, 22 Pa. 102 (1853)
[3] *Teaman's Case*, 1 Phil. 460.
[4] *Barr's Case*, 34 Pa. 86 (1859).
[5] *Nesbit's Case*, 34 Pa. 398 (1859).
[6] *Ibid.*
[7] *Ibid.*

Province of Pennsylvania, the Lord's day is recognized not only as a day of rest, but as a day of *religious* rest and quiet;"[1] and later still, as illustrating the spirit of the existing law, the court cited the act of 1682, which was avowedly passed "to the end that license, *irreligion* and atheism may not creep in under a pretence of conscience, and that the people may better dispose themselves to *read the scripture of truth at home, or frequent such meetings of religious worship abroad* as may best suit their respective persuasions."[2] And, in the concurring opinion delivered by Judge Read in the same case, he says he is "deeply impressed with the necessity of a proper observance of Sunday as a day of *worship and prayer* and of rest from labor;"[3] and so late as 1870, the Pennsylvania Sunday law has been spoken of as "legislation intended to prevent the commission of acts at variance with the observance of the day, as *a day of rest, and of religious worship.*"[4] Likewise in Kentucky "the Christian Sabbath is wisely recognized by law as *a day of rest to be devoted to religious contemplation and observance* free from secular disturbance,"[5] and it is not a holiday, within the meaning of the statute prohibiting the service of process on holidays, "for in both a popular and a legal sense, a holiday is a day dedicated by usage not to *rest and religious devotion*, but to amusement and festivity, marked by a general liberty and hilarity of all classes of the people. As early as the reign of Edward VI., England established holidays by law, but in the statutory enumeration of such free days Sunday was not included. Before the adoption of our code, legal process on Sunday was unlawful, but as lawful on a holiday as on any other secular day. We cannot perceive how or why Sunday shall be treated as a holiday, or a holiday shall be considered as synonymous with Sunday."[6] And, in Tennessee, it was said: "It is correct, as advanced by the defendant's counsel, that no worldly labor or business ought to be carried on on the Sabbath day. It is, at the least, unseemly, subversive of good morals, and, as it appears to me, not in union with the principles of *our holy religion.*"[7] And again, "The object of the legislature in the law

[1] *Jeandelle's Case*, 3 Phil. 509 (1859).

[2] *Sparhawk* v. *Union R. W.*, 54 Pa. 401 (1861).

[3] *Ibid.*

[4] *Granger* v. *Grubb*, 7 Phil. 350 (1870).

[5] *Moore* v. *Hagan*, 2 Duv. (Ken.) 437 (1866).

[6] *Ibid.*

[7] *Amis* v. *Kyle*, 2 Yerg. 31 (1820).

against liquor-selling was to prevent the *desecration* of the day which by our law is dedicated to the *duties of religion* by the sale of an article the use of which is calculated to produce the most shameless disregard of *those duties.*[1] And we find the Sunday laws of Delaware cited as "legal proofs of what has been, and now is, the *religion* preferred by the people of Delaware;"[2] and the court added: "Independent of these, and other evidence existing on the statute book of the state, we are bound to notice, as judges acting under the authority of the people at all times, what is that religion which they have voluntarily preferred. We know not only from the oaths that are administered by our authority to witnesses and jurors, but from that evidence to which every man may resort without these walls, that the *religion* of the people of Delaware is Christian."[3] It is also the opinion of the North Carolina court that Sunday is "A day set apart expressly for recreation, *and for the worship of Almighty God,*"[4] and that Sunday work "offends us not so much because it disturbs us in practicing for ourselves the religious duties, or enjoying the salutary repose, or recreation of that day, as that it is, in itself, a *breach of God's law,* and a violation of the party's *own religious duty;*"[5] and the court quotes the passage cited above from Blackstone, and proceeds as follows: "We perfectly concur in the eloquent passage in the commentaries on the propriety and political necessity of keeping one day of the week for the purposes of *public worship,* relaxation and refreshment. The institution, wherever it has existed, has proved to be a great good, promoting private virtue and happiness among all classes, and the public morals and prosperity. It is, therefore, fit that every commonwealth, and especially one in which Christianity is generally professed, *should set apart by law* a day for *these purposes,* and enforce its due observance by such sanctions as may seem adequate." So, in South Carolina, "all temporal business transacted is void, as the day is *set apart* by our *holy religion* for the *worship of the Almighty,* and the necessary preparations for that purpose;"[6] and in Mississippi the Sunday law is spoken of as "a statute wisely intended to promote public morals, and to induce *the observance of*

[1] *Eskridge's Case,* 1 Swan 413 (1852).
[2] *Chandler's Case,* 2 Harr. 553 (1837).
[3] *Ibid.*
[4] *Melvin* v. *Easley,* 7 Jones 356 (1860).
[5] *Williams' Case,* 4 Ired. 400 (1844).
[6] *Shaw* v. *McCombs,* 2 Bay 232 (1799).

the duties of religion in society;"[1] and in Alabama its object is declared to be "to promote morality, and *advance the interests of religion*."[2]

PROPOSITION IV.

There is a Divine Command that Men Shall be Idle on Sunday; and this Command is an Element of Christianity.

It is evident that the reasoning of the preceding cases establishes for the Sunday statutes a position absolutely unique in American jurisprudence. Their sanction is drawn not from the will of the people, but from a "revelation" of the will of Deity. Whether the legislature, in passing them, is itself a sanctifying agent, or whether it is merelv "recognizing" a sanctity already possessed, it is acting as the channel or declarer of divine will, like Moses of old, and not as the representative of the people. For such laws, the phrase "Be it enacted" is a meaningless formula, and "Thus saith the Lord" is their proper mode of introduction. It is no wonder, then, that, in the view of the judges who have adopted this construction of the Sunday laws. "the consent of the governed" disappears altogether as a basis of government, and the right by which kings and emperors claim to reign is postulated as their true foundation. Thus, in England, Park, J., said: "I should be sorry to be supposed to recede from the cases decided on this point and the principle established to enforce the observance of the Lord's day, which tends so eminently to the advantage of society, since no laws can be of any avail *except so far as they are founded on religion*;"[3] and, in Pennsylvania, we are told, "Rest one day in seven was enjoined by the precept and example of the Author of our existence, and *government, founding itself on divine appointment*, has made it a civil institution;"[4] for "worldly employment on the Lord's day *is in violation of the divine command*."[5] But there is a Pennsylvania

[1] *Kountz* v. *Price*, 40 Miss. 341 (1866).

[2] *O'Donnell* v. *Sweeney*, 5 Ala. 467 (1843).

[3] *Williams* v. *Paul*, 6 Bing. 653 (1830).

[4] *Omit's Case*, 21 Pa. 426 (1853).

[5] *Foreman* v. *Ahl*, 53 Pa. 325 (1866). In a previous case in this state we find the court broadly hinting that an infraction of this "divine" law might affect one's property rights, independent

decision which expressly repudiates jurisdiction of the civil courts in matters of divine law, saying of a defendant, "guiltless before the civil law, by the *divine* law, as such, we have no authority to judge him."[1] And the cases generally do not deem it necessary to claim, in express words, a "divine" foundation for civil government, in order to justify the statutory requirements of Sunday idleness. The reasoning of most of the decisions which regard such laws as designed to enforce a religious tenet seems to be about as follows: (1) The "observance" of Sunday consists in being idle; (2) this observance is a part of Christianity; (3) Christianity is a part of the common law; (4) the common law is a part of our law; (5) constitutional limitations of the legislative authority in matters of religion and constitutional guaranties of religious liberty are to be construed with reference to these fundamental principles; (6) so construing them, they do not restrain the legislature from making idleness on Sunday compulsory.

The first of this series of propositions is generally taken for granted, and will be recurred to hereafter. The second is judicially established. An English judge said of Sunday: "It was extremely wise to put a mark on that day; *by observing it Christianity may be kept alive;*"[2] and we are told, in New York, that, "as a civil institution, the selection of a day is at the option of the legislature; but, for a *Christian* people, it is highly fit and proper that the day observed should be that which is regarded as the *Christian Sabbath;*"[3] and, in Vermont, "whatever might be the feelings of any member of the court in regard to the propriety of observing other days also as religious fasts or festivals, there could be but one opinion in regard to the *strict observance* of the Lord's day among *consistent Christians;*"[4] and, in Pennsylvania, "*Christians* of all denominations look upon the *institution of the Sabbath* as of divine origin;"[5] and, alluding to the discharge of their duties by public officials, the

of any statute on the subject. In 1841 it was said that zeal for Sabbath observance "cannot avail a defendant, who has the possession of property, without paying for it, *unless he proves that the plaintiff has violated some law, human or divine*" [*sic!*] *Hadly* v. *Snevily*, 1 W. & S. 477.

[1] *Nesbit's Case*, 34 Pa. 398.

[2] Kenyon, C. J., in *Younger's Case*, 5 T. R. 449 (1793).

[3] *Lindenmuller's Case*, 33 Barb. 548 (1861).

[4] *Adams* v. *Gay*, 19 Vt. 358 (1847).

[5] *Jeandelle's Case*, 2 Grant 506 (1859).

court said: "These form their *worldly business*, which the policy of our law, *founded on principles of Christianity*, interdicts them from performing. If the public functionaries are to open their offices for the transaction of their ordinary employments, I scarcely need to observe that the vestige of a Sabbath would not long remain amongst us;" and the Illinois court considers it "clear, that to permit officers to intrude upon families on Sundays, for service of civil process, would be a violation of the spirit and policy of this law, and unbecoming a *Christian* community;"[1] and, in Arkansas, "Sunday, or the Sabbath, is properly and emphatically called *the* Lord's day, and *is one amongst the first and most sacred institutions of the Christian religion;*"[2] while a North Carolina judge says: "It is well known that the *Christian Sabbath*, sometimes called the 'Lord's day,' but more commonly 'Sunday,' is a *Christian institution*, and I cannot perceive any good reason why our legislature may not direct it to be observed by any person, and in any manner which their wisdom may suggest, for the happiness of the people and the welfare of the state, saving and reserving always to every person the right to worship God according to the dictates of his own conscience."[3]

PROPOSITION V.

This Divine Command is a Part of American Constitutional Law.

Almost all the states have, by the language of their constitutions, adopted the common law of England, though frequently they add, "so far as applicable," or some equivalent phrase. The constitutions also provide, in language more or less explicit, against any "preference" being given by the state to one form of religion over any other. Under the established rules of construction, both these provisions must stand, if it be reasonably possible for them to do so; and this can only be accomplished by taking their joint significance to be that the common law is adopted with the exception of

[1] *Scammon's Case*, 40 Ill. 146 (1866).

[2] *Shover's Case*, 10 Ark. 259 (1850).

[3] *Melvin* v. *Easley*, 7 Jones 356.

that portion of it, if any, which implies a preference of one form of religion to another. But it is settled judicially that Christianity is "preferred" by the common law to such an extent that it is actually a component part of it; that the common law, again, preference and all, is a part of the fundamental law of American commonwealths; and that thus the idle Sunday is an "institution" which is beyond legislative control, which legislatures may indeed "recognize," but which derives its sanction primarily from a system of religious belief which has been adopted into the constitutions of the several states.

This position of the idle Sunday in American law is established by the following citations:

"*Christianity*, in its enlarged sense, as a religion revealed and taught in the Bible, *is not unknown to our law.* The statute for preventing immorality consecrates the first day of the week as holy time, and considers the violation of it as immoral. This was only the continuation, in substance, of a law of the colony, which declared that the profanation of the Lord's day was the great scandal of the Christian faith."[1] "The *Christian Sabbath is one of the civil institutions of the state*, to which the business and duties of life are, *by the common law*, made to adapt and conform themselves. The same cannot be said of the Jewish Sabbath, or the day observed by the followers of any other religion. The respect paid to such days, other than that voluntarily paid by those observing them as days of worship, is in obedience to positive law."[2] "With us, *the Sabbath, as a civil institution, is older than the government. The framers of the first constitution found it in existence*; they *recognized* it in their acts, and they did not abolish it, or alter it, or lessen its sanctions, or the obligations of the people to observe it."[3] "In this state, *the Sabbath exists, as a day of rest, by the common law, and without the necessity of legislative action* to establish it, and all that the legislature attempts to do in the Sabbath laws is *to regulate its observance*."[4] "It is no violation of the rights of conscience that the day should be respected by the law-making power. The *exist-*

[1] *People* v. *Ruggles*, 8 Johns. 290 (1811).

[2] *Lindenmuller's Case*, 33 Barb. 548 (1861).

[3] *Id.* 568.

[4] *Id.* 569.

ence of the Sabbath day, *as a civil institution,* being conceded, as it must be, the right of the legislature to control and regulate it and its observance is a necessary sequence."[1] In Pennsylvania: "*The common law adopted it* (the idle Sunday) *along with Christianity,* of which it is one of the bulwarks;"[2] "the declaration that *Christianity is part of the law of the land* is a summary description of an existing and very obvious condition of our institutions. We are a *Christian people,* in so far as we have entered into the spirit of *Christian institutions,* and become imbued with the *sentiments and principles of Christianity,* and we cannot be imbued with them, and yet prevent them from entering into, and influencing, more or less, all our social institutions, customs and relations, as well as all our individual modes of thinking and acting. It is involved in our social nature that even those who object to Christianity cannot possibly get clear of its influence, or reject those sentiments, customs and principles, which it has spread among the people, so that, like the air we breathe, they have become the common stock of the whole country, and essential elements of its life. It is perfectly natural, therefore, that *a Christian people should have laws to protect their day of rest from desecration.* Regarding it as a day, *necessarily and divinely set apart for rest from worldly employments, and for the enjoyment of spiritual privileges,* it is simply absurd to suppose that they would leave it without any legislative protection from the disorderly and immoral. The sentiment that sustains it must find expression through those who are elected to represent the will of their constituents. So far as relates to the criminality of the act, which we are now to consider, the mind of the state is expressed in the law which forbids all worldly employment on the Lord's day, under a penalty of four dollars."[3] "The right to *repose and quiet* upon the Lord's day rests upon the *same basis* with the law *which declares Christianity to be part of the common law,* and would have existed, though the statutes prohibiting work upon the Lord's day had never been enacted. * * * If Christianity is a part of the common law of the state, and the observance of Sunday is a distinctive feature of Christianity; if the ancient colonial, provincial and state legislature, and the constitution itself, are all based on

[1] *Id.* 570.

[2] *Johnston's Case,* 22 Pa. 102 (1853).

[3] *Mohney* v. *Cook,* 26 Pa. 342 (1853).

Christianity, as part of the common law, and distinctly recognize Sunday, then it follows that the day itself is clothed with peculiar sanctity, and is intended by law to be a day of extraordinary quiet and repose."[1] "It has been decided over and over again that *Christianity is a part of the common law of the land.* Upon this ground, statutes against profanity and blasphemy have been sustained, and upon this also rests, in part, the decisions in support of *laws intended to maintain and defend the Christian Sabbath.* To enact a by-law, or to make a rule which falls in with the religious custom of the people; which acknowledges the propriety, if not the duty, of a recognition of the Sabbath; which secures to the employes of the company an opportunity for rest and worship on that day, cannot be held to be other than in entire accord with the common law, which our fathers brought with them to this country. This common law, which includes a recognition of Christianity, as well as the Christian Sabbath, was the foundation upon which they built, and which yet remains the law of the land, except in so far as the statute law has abrogated or changed it."[2] In Arkansas: "*This system of religion* (the Christian) *is recognized as constituting a part and parcel of the common law, and, as such, all of the institutions growing out of it, or in any way connected with it,* in case they shall not be found to interfere with the rights of conscience, are entitled to the most profound respect, and *can rightfully claim the protection of the law-making power of the state.*"[3] In Michigan: "*The Christian religion has largely affected the great body of our laws, and to it we must trace the laws which punish what the Christian regards as the desecration of the first day of the week* * * * the general sense of a *Christian people has demanded, and secured, the law,* and their method of observing the day must be some evidence of the sense in which the law is enacted."[4] In North Carolina: "It cannot be denied *that ours is a Christian country, and that the constitution of North Carolina recognizes the Christian religion as a part of our system of government.*"[5] In Georgia: "The *Christian Sabbath* is a *civil institution, older than our government.*"[6] In California: "It may be conceded that the *acts prohibited are*

[1] *Jeandelle's Case*, 3 Phil. 509 (1859).
[2] *Granger* v. *Grubb*, 7 Phil. 350 (1870).
[3] *Shover's Case*, 10 Ark. 259 (1850)
[4] *Allen* v. *Duffie*, 43 Mich. 1.
[5] *Melvin* v. *Easley*, 7 Jones 356 (1860).
[6] *Karwisch's Case*, 44 Ga. 204 (1871).

only prohibited because they are such as would be offensive to public morals according to the standard of Christianity, but if the prohibition does not interfere with any man's liberty of conscience, it is no valid objection to the law because it prohibits acts to be done which are deemed immoral according to the standard of one religion or another. *Doubtless the law was passed under the influence of Christianity.* The legislature, in the course and character of legislation, can recognize no other standard of moral ideas. As the prevailing religious opinion of the people, public morals are largely dependent upon it."[1]

We may here observe, that, as Christianity, in one phase or another, is the religion professed by an overwhelming majority of our people, and compulsory idleness on Sunday is a vital and essential element of Christianity, it follows that permitting people who desire to work on that day to yield to their inclinations would be fraught with the most tremendous consequences. In fact, if the Sunday laws were repealed, it appears that the United States would be in danger of becoming reduced to the condition of the Sandwich Islands when the first missionaries reached them. It is well known that the natives were found to be absolutely destitute of religious belief, having a short time before arrived at a conviction of the fallacy of their ancient creed, and destroyed all their idols. That a similar extinction of Christianity would be threatened by a repeal of the statute which imposes a small fine for Sunday labor is strongly implied in the following extracts. And it will be perceived that the social wreck involved is scarcely less complete and horrifying than that of the country's religious faith. In Pennsylvania, it is said: "*Sunday is a part of Christianity. Upon its peaceful observance Christianity in a great measure depends for its support.* Destroy this day, and a revolution of the most astounding character is produced. Whatever conclusion may be arrived at upon the evidence, we cannot assert as law a principle which must lead to the most disastrous results, which *must shake Christianity itself.*"[2] And a picture no less impressive is thus drawn in Missouri: "*Convert Sunday into a worldly day by law, and what becomes of Christianity?* How can we reconcile the idea to our understand-

[1] *Koser's Case*, 60 Cal. 177 (1882).

[2] *Jeandelle's Case*, 3 Phil. 509 (1859).

ing that a people professing Christianity would make a fundamental law by which they would convert Sunday into a worldly day? It would have been an act of deadly hostility to the religion they professed, exposing it to the danger of being reduced to the condition in which it was before the Roman world was governed by Christian princes. Though it might not be persecuted by the arm of the civil power, it would be driven by the annoyances and interruptions of the world to corners and by-places, in which to find a retreat for its undisturbed exercise. How startling would the announcement be to the people of Missouri that, by their organic law, they had abolished Sunday as a day of rest, and put it out of the power of their legislators ever to restore it as such; with what sorrow would the toil-worn laborer receive the intelligence that there was no longer by law a day of rest from his labor. The poor beasts of burden would soon find, by experience, that our laws were no longer tempered by the softening influences of Christianity, and all the social advantages which great and good men have attributed to the observance of Sunday as a day of rest would be taken away."[1]

Thus far our consideration has been altogether directed to the prohibitions of labor contained in Sunday laws. This method of dealing with the subject has been followed because all the reasons for sustaining such statutes are at their strongest and best when applied to the question of work. If the reasons prove insufficient or untenable when so applied, of course they are not worth a moment's consideration as vindication of a prohibition of amusements or games as such. But we have now arrived at a point where Sunday legislation must be viewed as a whole, and the arguments in its favor must be weighed with reference not merely to its restrictions on work, but also to its no less universal restrictions on play. To sustain such legislation, as we have it in America, on religious grounds, it is necessary to demonstrate not merely that the idle, but also that the cheerless Sunday is an "institution" of Christianity.

It is clear that the "sacredness" of a day, and the obligation to observe it, may be conceded, and still, in the absence of authoritative definition, the exact nature of the observance required may

[1] *Amb's Case*, 20 Mo. 214 (1854).

remain in doubt. One man might say: "I recognize the day as holy; I will honor it by taking that recreation which I find best calculated to refresh and reinvigorate me for my worldly labors;" another might reason thus: "I have a family dependent on me for support; I feel no need of idleness; I will make this sacred day a marked and distinguished one in my life by doubling my labor and my earnings, and thus rendering a double service to those whom I cherish, and to work for whom is my highest act of love and worship;" a third might fast as an observance; a fourth indulge in a feast, and so on. Now, the Sunday laws prohibit both amusements and work. Viewing them, therefore, as civil adoptions of a religious dogma, the assumption underlying them is, that play is obnoxious to religion and idleness required by it. The legislature, in passing such laws, takes it for granted that a particular religion—which the courts say is Christianity—has not merely required the observance of Sunday, but has rigidly defined the nature thereof. Is this a fact? Doubts on this point were thus insinuated in Vermont: "Although the holy observance of the Sabbath, like charity, is a positive duty, yet, like charity, it is undefined; and different denominations of Christians, even as well as individuals, vary much in the degree of strictness with which it ought to be observed; and, though an admitted duty, yet the manner of its observance is perhaps described with less certainty than almost any other Gospel requirement. How ungracious, then, for a court to mark the law upon this duty for all denominations to be governed by, and with judges usually belonging to different religious societies. It would be like a synod composed of the dignitaries of several sects. Unanimity could scarcely be expected."[1] And, again, in the same state, noticing the argument that making a contract on Sunday "shocked the moral sense," the court said: "I have no doubt that such is the fact in regard to a portion of the most serious-minded, earnest and strenuously religious of our citizens. And no one can doubt that the feelings of so considerable and influential a portion of the citizens of the state are entitled to the highest consideration. But, in making inquiry into the state of the moral feeling of the whole community, we must not forget that upon religious matters

[1] Mattock's dissenting opinion in *Lyon* v. *Strong*, 6 Vt. 219 (1834).

it is almost infinitesimally divided; and before we could determine that any given cause shocked the moral feeling of the community, we must be able to find but one pervading feeling upon that subject—so much so, that a contrary feeling in the individual would denominate him either insane or diseased in his moral perceptions. Now, nothing is more absurd to my mind than to argue the existence of any such universal moral sentiment in regard to the observance of Sunday. It is in no just sense a moral sentiment at all which impels us to the observance of Sunday for religious purposes more than any other day. It is but education and habit in the main, certainly. Moral feeling might dictate the devotion of a portion of our time to religious rites and solemnities, but could never indicate any particular time above all others. But this will best be seen by the actual state of opinions among us upon this subject. Some of our citizens are Atheists, perhaps; a considerable number Deists, or Rationalists; and among Christians there is almost an infinite diversity of opinion in regard to this subject. The Irish Catholic who may have become a denizen of the republic regards St. Patrick's day, perhaps, as the most sacred in the calendar. The French Catholic is willing to labor every day in the year almost, except on St. Peter's day. If well informed and conscientious, he will hardly forget Good Friday, or Christmas, or Ash Wednesday. The same is true in regard to these latter days with the consistent members of the Church of England, or of the Lutheran Church, or of the Greek Church, if any such there be among us. Now, all these regard Sunday, but not as more sacred than some other days. It is but in commemoration of the miracle of the Lord's day, the Resurrection. But Easter day, which is the annual festival of the Lord's day, is truly the great day of the feast—the Sunday of Sundays, the crowning festival of the year; and this, with Good Friday, Ash Wednesday, Christmas, and some few other prominent fasts and festivals, is most religiously observed in all ancient churches, and in all the Lutheran Churches—which embrace Holland, Sweden and Denmark, Prussia and Germany, so far as they are Protestant—and all its branches. And so are all the Sundays in the year, but with far less solemnity than the greater fasts and festivals above named. In addition to this, it must be remembered that we have among us some Jews, perhaps, and some Seventh-day Baptists, who do not regard Sunday at all, and many of the Friends, who regard all days alike. This may be all very unwise, or very unreasonable, in the estimation of some, but it is none the less true, and we must take things as they are."[1] So, referring to a previous decision (*Johnston* v. *Commonwealth*, 22 Pa. 109), a Pennsylvania judge said: "The cardinal error is in treating Sunday as set apart by divine command;" and from the whole decision two judges, two-fifths of the court, dissented, in opinions of very great weight and force.[2] So, in West Virginia: "It is argued that the statute requires this observance of the Sabbath day, as a religious duty, imposed upon us by God, and that, as corporations can owe no religious duty, the statute cannot be construed to extend to them. In this argument, it is assumed as universally admitted that God has imposed on all mankind the duty of keeping the first day of the week as holy. This assumption is far from being conceded. It is, of course, not admitted by those of our citizens who are disbelievers in the Christian religion. * * * Nor is it true that it is admitted by all believers in Christianity."[3] And, in North Carolina, we are told: "The extent of the obligation of the Sabbath under the Gospel is a point on which the professors and teachers of Christianity have been far from agreeing."[4] If we substitute for "the rational observance of the Sabbath" the words "abstention from labor and amusement on Sunday," in the following extract, we shall find it frankly asserted that the mode of spending the day enjoined by our statutes is not a requirement of Christianity at all, but simply a dogma of one particular school, or communion, or sect of Christians. And, moreover, that the "change" which it involved in the existing and universal practice of Christendom was not made in England until the reign of a king who ascended his throne fifteen hundred years after the founder of Christianity was crucified. It was said in New Hampshire: "The toleration of amusements, and the existence of fairs in England, to a greater or less degree, upon the Sabbath, are readily accounted for by their known accordance with the practice of Roman Catholic countries, among which was England, until the reformation in the reign of Henry VIII. With the spread of the

[1] *Adams* v. *Gay*, 19 Vt. 358 (1847).

[2] Read's concurring opinion in *Sparhawk's Case*, 54 Pa. 401.

[3] *B. & O.'s Case*, 15 W. Va. 362 (1879).

[4] *Williams' Case*, 4 Ired. 400 (1844).

reformed religion, and the consequent improvement in civilization, the views and manners of the people changed on the subject of the rational observance of the Sabbath, and in all Protestant communities laws were enacted to secure it, varying in their provisions with the peculiarities of the people."[1] Finally, we must quote the pointed words in which a Missouri judge disposes of the underlying principle of the cases which have just been considered. The reader is aware that a certain New England university has, till very recently, made what were called "compulsory prayers" a feature of its course. Compulsory idleness on Sunday this remarkable judge appears to consider on a par with such performances, when regarded as an act of religion. He says the object of the law is to compel a cessation of labor, but disposes of the notion that enforced idleness can commend the idler to the good-will of his Creator in the following decided manner: "Such an idea can only be based on the supposition of an entire ignorance in the legislature of the nature of the worship which God exacts from His creatures. A compliance with the law, *induced by a fear of its penalties*, could never be regarded as an act acceptable to the Deity. No act of worship, unless dictated by a heartfelt love, can be pleasing to the Almighty. God listens alone to the voice of the heart."[2]

We pass now to the consideration of the second subdivision of the first class of cases. Here the courts are still busy with the religious aspect of the question. They still affirm that religion is the justification and source of laws prescribing Sunday idleness. But they depart altogether from the theory that it is the soul of the unwilling idler which the state is intent upon conserving, and hold that the object in view is to restrict him from disturbing the proceedings of other people for securing the safety of their souls. That is to say, A is required to be idle not because he thus propitiates the Deity in his own behalf, but because B's devotions would be interfered with if A were to pursue his ordinary avocations on Sunday. A New York case maintains that Sunday restrictions on labor, and the use of property, "rest upon the principle of the preservation of *good order* and the *public morality and peace;*"[3] and the court adds: "Rights must be exercised in such a manner as not to affect preju-

[1] *Allen* v. *Deming*, 14 N. H. 133 (1843).

[2] *Amb's Case*, 20 Mo. 214 (1854).

[3] *Hoym's Case*, 20 How. Pr. 76 (1860).

dicially the *tranquility and morality of the local public.*"[1] So, we read: "The Christian Sunday may be protected from *desecration* by such laws as the legislature, in its wisdom, may deem necessary; and it is the sole judge of the acts proper to be prohibited, *with a view to the public peace.*"[2] These decisions, coupling "morality" with "peace" and "tranquility," and seeming to imply that it is the breach of the peace involved in Sunday work which constitutes the "desecration" that Sunday laws are designed to prevent, constitute, so to speak, connecting links between those cases which hold that such laws are justified by reason of the ill-effect of the sin on the sinner's own soul, and those which maintain that their only concern is with the "consequential damage" done to the souls of others by interference with the religious devotions of the latter. In Massachusetts, it is said that the law was "enacted for the *sole* object of insuring *reverence and respect* for one day of the week, in order that *religious exercises should be performed without interruption* from common and secular employments."[3] And this view of the subject was elucidated in Vermont as follows: "The constitution of this state (and herein it is a transcript from the first constitution of government established in this state), while it carefully protects and guards religious freedom, and asserts that the conscience of no one can be controlled, declares 'that every sect or denomination of Christians ought to observe the Sabbath, or Lord's day, and keep up some sort of religious worship which to them shall seem most agreeable to the revealed will of God.' To carry into effect the spirit of this constitution, to enable each religious sect to keep up religious worship on the Sabbath, and to enable all to enjoy the benefits to be derived from a day of religious retirement, the legislature, among other first laws, made provision for the prohibition of secular labor on that day. Aware of the benefits to be derived from stated periods of rest from manual labor, and the importance of having the same day observed by all, and recognizing that every denomination of Christians among them regarded the Sabbath as a day set apart for moral and religious duties, they determined that every one should be protected in the enjoyment of his religious privileges and in the performance of his religious duties, and have

[1] *Id.* 85.

[2] *Neuendorff* v. *Duryea*, 69 N. Y. 557.

[3] *Pearce* v. *Atwood*, 13 Mass. 324 (1816).

made provision that those who are thus disposed may, on that day, perform those great and necessary duties which they believe are required of them, without disturbance from the secular labor of others; and further, that all, whether high or low, prisoner or free, master or servant, shall be permitted to rest, and that none shall compel them to labor on that day; and, lest, through avarice or cupidity, any one should be disposed so to do, they have enacted that the day shall be observed as a day of rest from secular labor and employment, except such as necessity and acts of charity shall require."[1] And again: "In this state full immunity for all religions and no religion is equally given by the fundamental law of the state. No man can be abridged of his perfect liberty in that respect. And while this does not forbid the legislature from passing general laws against blasphemy, the desecration of the Lord's day and the disturbance of public worship, it does, impliedly, at least, forbid the adoption of any law which is not necessary for the quiet enjoyment of religious feeling and religious worship. So that all law, which it is competent for the legislature to adopt, must have reference solely to preventing the disturbance of our citizens in their religious feelings or devotions. Beyond this the constitution of the state absolutely prohibits any law."[2] So, speaking of an early statute of New Hampshire, it was said: "It has both an individual and a general purpose. While it protects the solemnities of religion from interruption, and secures the public in their peaceful performance, it reminds the individual that he has religious duties to fulfill, and religious duties alone. It tends to secure to him time and opportunity for their fulfillment by prohibiting him from performing other things, and induces him to turn his attention, for one day in the week, to religious reflection, by refusing him permission to distract his mind by occupying himself with his worldly affairs. It cannot legislate him into a religious man, but it keeps him from business and forbids business to come to him, and aims at doing what may reasonably be attained, without infringing his freedom of conscience. It is not considered expedient, by the revised statutes, to attempt to attain one object which the act of 1799 had in view, that is, the good effect upon the individual, by prohibiting

[1] *Lyon* v. *Strong*, 6 Vt. 219 (1834).

[2] *Adams* v. *Gay*, 19 Vt. 358 (1847).

him from exercising his secular calling. By the act of 1799, he could not do this under any circumstances. By the revised statutes, he may do it, with a qualification, a condition, and that is, that it be not 'to the disturbance of others.' This provision aims only at protecting the public in their devotions and religious reflections; others, the law says, shall not be disturbed. It leaves each individual to employ himself as he may choose, subject only to this limitation. It does not aim at guarding him from himself. It does not seek to interest him in religion by forbidding him to interest himself in things not religious. It leaves him to his own conscience, and does not attempt to furnish any other guarantee for the religious and devotional employment of his time than such as may be afforded by his own views of his religious obligations. This, then, is an important change in the law. It shows that there is a radical difference in the theories on which the two statutes proceed."[1] It has been said of the New York Sunday statute that "its design is not to enforce the conscience, or compel comformity to any religious rites and ceremonies, but simply to secure to the day that outward respect and observance which is due to it, as the acknowledged Sabbath of the great mass of the people, to protect the religion of the community from contempt and unseemly hindrances, and to its professors the liberty of quiet and undisturbed worship on the day set apart for that purpose." And a sale of newspapers was held to be within the mischiefs which the act was designed to remedy, because "it disturbs the public peace and quiet; interferes with the proper religious observance of the day; is opposed to good morals, and tends to draw men away from the duties of piety and religion."[2] And, again, it was said, in the same state: "It is the right of the citizen to be protected from offences against decency, and against acts which corrupt the morals and debase the moral sense of the community. Regarding the Sabbath as a civil institution well established, it is the right of the citizen that it should be kept and observed in a way not inconsistent with its purpose, and the necessity out of which it grew, as a day of rest rather than a day of riot or disorder, which would be effectually to overthrow it, and render it a curse rather than a blessing."[3] And again: "Our fathers, who

[1] *Varney* v. *French*, 19 N. H. 233.

[2] *Smith* v. *Wilcox*, 24 N. Y. 353 (1862).

[3] *Lindenmuller's Case*, 33 Barb. 548 (1861). It was, of course, under the

planted in our fundamental law the assertion of those immortal truths, that all men have a natural and indefeasible right to worship Almighty God according to the dictates of their own consciences, that no man can be compelled to attend, erect or support any place of public worship, and that no human authority can control or interfere with the rights of conscience, enacted also the statutes for the suppression of worldly employments on Sunday. So far from conflicting with these invaluable rights of conscience, they regarded such statutes as indispensable to secure them. It would be a small boon to the people of Pennsylvania to declare their indefeasible right to worship God according to the dictates of their consciences amid the din and confusion of secular employments, and the desecrations on every hand of what they conscientiously believe to be holy time. The statutes were not designed to compel men to go to church, or to worship God in any manner inconsistent with personal preferences, but to compel a cessation of those employments which are calculated to interfere with the rights of those who choose to assemble for public worship. The day was set apart for a purpose, and the penal enactments guard it, but they leave every man free to use it for that purpose or not. If he wish to use it for the purpose designed, the law protects him from the annoyance of others—if he do not, it restrains him from annoying those who do so use it. Thus, the law, without oppressing anybody, becomes auxiliary to the rights of conscience. And there are other rights, intimately associated with the rights of conscience, which are worth preserving. The right to rear a family with a becoming regard to the institutions of Christianity, and without compelling them to witness hourly infractions of one of its fundamental laws—the right to enjoy the peace and good order of society, and the increased

influence of this view of the spirit and objects of Sunday legislation that the Pennsylvania law-makers passed an act which recited that to grant men the right to worship God was nugatory, without securing the peaceable and quiet enjoyment thereof, and authorized religious societies in Philadelphia to fasten chains across the streets during divine service, to "hinder and obstruct coaches, wagons," &c. In 1816 the act was extended to embrace other districts around Philadelphia, and in 1831 both acts were repealed. The iron sockets, in which were fixed the posts to which the chains were attached, were still to be seen opposite some of the old churches in 1867. See Read's concurring opinion in *Sparhawk's Case*, 54 Pa. 401.

securities to life and property, which result from the decent observance of Sunday—the right of the poor to rest from labor, without a diminution of wages or loss of employment—the right of beasts of burden to repose one-seventh of their time from their unrequited toil—these are real and substantial interests which the legislature sought to secure by these enactments; and when has legislation aimed at higher objects?"[1] And again, "By our Sunday laws, and our other laws against vice and immorality, we do not mean to enforce religion; we admit that to be impossible. But we do mean to protect our customs, no matter that they may have originated in our religion, for they are essential parts of our social life. Instinctively we defend and protect them. It is mere social self-defence, and not a matter of choice. In doing so, we must be as generous towards those who differ from us as we know how to be, or as circumstances will allow us to be. No more than this can reasonably be expected of us."[2] And yet again: "By the common law of the commonwealth, every citizen is entitled to enjoy the first day of the week in undisturbed quiet and repose, that he may exercise his natural and indefeasible right to worship Almighty God according to the dictates of his own conscience, and whatever actual noise or disorder hinders seriously, or destroys altogether, this inalienable right, is, and always has been, a breach of the peace."[3] In West Virginia, after dwelling on the importance of providing a day of uniform compulsory idleness, or "rest," as it is called, the court proceeds: "This, I conceive, is the main object of our law; but it is not its only object. While I am thus resting on the Sabbath, in obedience to law, it is right and reasonable that my rest should not be disturbed by others. Such a disturbance by others of my rest is, in its nature, a nuisance, which the law ought to punish, and Sabbath-breaking has been frequently classed with nuisances, and punished as such. That these are the objects of our statute are, [*sic*] to my mind, clearly shown by the wording;" and, after alluding to the exception by which those who consent to remain idle on some other day in the week are graciously allowed to pursue their ordinary avocations on Sunday, the court continues: "But, if you do not rest on the Sunday, you must take care not to disturb those

[1] *Johnston's Case*, 22 Pa. 102 (1853).

[2] *Nesbit's Case*, 34 Pa. 368 (1859).

[3] *Jeandelle's Case*, 3 Phil. 509 (1859).

who do, and not to compel others to work, who should rest on that day. The obvious purposes of the law are not to enforce the performance of a religious or moral duty, for it expressly provides that this supposed religious duty may be neglected by any one, who will rest the required seventh part of his time. It may be said, however, that the section prohibiting hunting or shooting on Sunday; shows that the true and real spirit of the law is to enforce the keeping of the Sabbath holy as a religious duty. But it must be obvious that this section does not prohibit hunting or shooting on Sunday, it only prohibits it from being done in a way which shall be to the annoyance of the public. That is, your hunting and shooting must not be done so as to make it a public nuisance. And this is in full accord with the general purpose, as I have explained it. No inference can be drawn from the act prohibiting a person to 'employ his minor children, apprentices or servants in labor.' That purpose was to enforce on parents the social duty of training religiously their children, as has been suggested in argument. The spirit of this clause is simply to forbid masters from compelling their servants to labor more than six-sevenths of their time; and minor children are named simply because minor children are the servants of their parents. Nor can any inference be drawn that the whole scope of this law has not been correctly stated because it is placed in the chapter headed 'Offences against morality and decency.' There are other sections in this chapter punishing offences or acts which cannot be regarded as *malum in se*, or as contrary to religion or abstract morality, as the marriage of a white person with a negro. If these be correct views of the true meaning and purpose of this act, it is obvious that there is no reason why its observance should not be enforced against corporations, and why they should not be fined, according to the provisions of this act, for employing their servants in labor. The punishment inflicted is not because they, in employing their servants in labor on Sunday, are violating the Fourth Commandment, or committing any immoral act, but they are requiring their servants to labor more than six-sevenths of their time; and this is regarded by the state as prejudicial to their well-being. The corporation is, therefore, punished not for the violation of any social, or moral obligation, but simply because it is violating a positive law, forbidding it to employ its servants in labor on

Sunday, or because it is annoying others, who are thus resting in obedience to law."[1] It is said in Illinois: "The unquestionable object of this law is to secure to every individual in the community the right to pass the Sunday either in religious exercises or in the quiet and seclusion of his home, without liability to annoyance from the ordinary secular pursuits of life, except so far as they may be dictated by necessity, or charity. The wisdom of this provision no one doubts. Although we have departed from the austere observances of the New England colonists, we have not drifted so far in the opposite direction as to recognize no distinction between Sunday's and the other days of the week. The experience of the world has taught the necessity of setting apart one-seventh of our time for religious worship and meditation, and for complete repose from the harassing and absorbing pursuits of gain, ambition and pleasure. Even those who are not guided by the teachings of Christianity acknowledge the necessity of a rational observance of the Sabbath, as conducive, in the highest degree, to the temporal interests of society. While legislation prescribing the precise mode of its observance would be justly regarded as an unwarrantable interference with individual liberty, on the other hand, all agree that no person should be permitted to follow his ordinary secular occupations, if, by so doing, he disturbs that portion of the community which desires to devote the day to religious worship and meditation."[2] In Missouri, it was asked: "How could those who conscientiously believe that Sunday is hallowed time, to be devoted to the worship of God, enjoy themselves in its observance amidst all the turmoil and bustle of worldly pursuits, amidst scenes by which the day was desecrated, which they conscientiously believed to be holy?"[3] And keeping open a grocery was held, in Arkansas, to be unlawful, as "shocking the community's sense of propriety and common decency, and bringing into utter contempt the sacred and venerable institution of the Sabbath."[4] But one case has been found which throws any shadow of doubt on the identification of Sunday labor with nuisance, as defined by law. It is said, in Tennessee, that "it would be a strange and far-fetched construction to

[1] *B. & O.'s Case*, 15 W. Va. 362 (1879).
[2] *Seamon* v. *Chicago*, 41 Ill. 146.
[3] *Amb's Case*, 20 Mo. 214 (1854).
[4] *Shover's Case*, 10 Ark. 259 (1850).

hold that violations of the Sabbath, *per se*, would constitute a nuisance."[1]

It remains to cite a few expressions of opinion to the effect that if Sunday idleness is sought to be enforced as a religious duty by law, the statutes requiring it are unconstitutional. The following is the language of a judge who avows himself a strong believer in Puritanism: "In *Smith* v. *Sparrow*, Park, J., says the common law is founded on our holy religion, and no law can be good which is not. And other judges often express the same sentiment. Hence the national church, their tithes and their requiring officers to partake of the sacrament. Whether religion is a safer basis to found a government and the laws upon than liberty and the voice of the people, it is not for us to decide. But it is well known that our government and laws are not founded upon religion, as we have no test, or standard of belief, by law established, and because our government, they believe, is not founded upon the word of God, a portion of the Scotch emigrants in this state, although they submit to, yet refuse to qualify, or vote, or participate in the government, and have made several unsuccessful attempts before different councils to have the constitution amended in this particular."[2] So in Indiana: "It has been held by this court that the law for compelling observance of the Sabbath was valid; but the writer of this opinion, speaking on this point for himself alone, wishes to say that farther reflection has led him to doubt the power of the legislature, under our present constitution, to enact such a statute. When our existing government was created, its creators determined that there were some matters in which the majority should not control the minority; that there were some things over which the legislature should not have authority; that in some things the people should not be within the power of the legislature. Such is our organization of government—our constitution. One of the subjects withdrawn by that constitution, in the bill of rights, from legislative interference, is that of religion; and the writer has no hesitation in saying, highly as he individually values the Sabbath, that, if the Sunday law is upon the statute book for the protection, or enforcement of the observance, of that day, as an institution of the Chris-

[1] *Linck's Case*, 12 Tenn. 499 (1883).

[2] Mattock's dissenting opinion in *Lyon* v. *Strong*, 6 Vt. 219 (1834).

tian religion, it cannot be upheld, no more than could a law forbidding labor on Saturday, the Jewish Sabbath, or on any and all other days of the week, which may be, in fulfillment of a requirement of a creed, set apart for religious observance by any portion of our citizens, whether Christian, Jewish, Mahomedan or Pagan. It is not, of course, meant here to trench upon the laws to protect the meetings of those desiring to worship from disturbance on all days."[1] And Judge Manly, of North Carolina, said: "In North Carolina, it would be clearly contrary to the fundamental law to attempt an enforcement of that part of our statute which enjoins upon all persons a careful application of themselves on the Lord's day to the duties of religion and piety. To enforce such an injunction, it must first be settled by the state what specific duties are embraced in our obligations to God, and all men be then called upon to conform to the state ritual. This is forbidden by our bill of rights, and would be violative of religious freedom, without which society could not be held together by the ties which at present bind it."[2] And, in Alabama, it is declared that the compelling of a citizen by law to abstain from work on Sunday "cannot be justified upon the grounds that such abstinence is enjoined by the Christian religion."[3] And, if an ordinance forbidding the sale of liquor on Sunday had for its object the enforcement of the observance of the Christian Sabbath, it would be open to assault in Louisiana; but such an ordinance was held to be manifestly a police regulation, like a similar prohibition in regard to election day.[4]

A few general observations may be subjoined, before dismissing finally this branch of our subject. There is, of course, no requirement on a people that it shall be consistent in the expression of its will; and, as a matter of fact, statutes do frequently conflict, without formal repeal of one by the other. But no inconsistency can be allowed by the courts between a statute and a constitution; and where repugnancy plainly appears, the statute must give way. Again, an absolutely free people is unrestrained in the establishment of its fundamental law; and American states, in framing their constitutions, are only restrained by the constitution and statutes

[1] *Thomasson's Case,* 15 Ind. 449.

[2] *Melvin* v. *Easley,* 7 Jones 356 (1860).

[3] *Frolickstein* v. *Mayor of Mobile,* 40 Ala. 725 (1867).

[4] *Bott's Case,* 31 La. Ann. 663 (1879).

of the United States. Accordingly, as there is nothing in the latter prohibiting distinctions between religions by a state, it would be legitimate to incorporate in a bill of rights a provision that no church should be favored except the Christian, or none tolerated except that and the Jewish. In fact, however, no such exceptions are made, as appears by the Table B. The phraseology of the various guaranties of religious liberty there collected is diverse; but the spirit of them all is, as has been said, against a "preference" to any form of religion. Some of the early decisions on the Sunday laws show a disposition on the part of the courts to understand the adjective "Christian" before the word "religion" in such provisions. But this is unreasonable, as well as historically wrong. It is unreasonable, because it deprives the provision of its meaning altogether, leaving the majority at liberty to "prefer" and establish at any time as a state institution a church with any creed which it may suit the fancy of the majority to declare to be "Christian;" they have simply to pronounce other creeds un-Christian, and the latter's claim to equality before the state is destroyed. And it is historically wrong, because even the earliest provisions of this character were understood to place the religion of the Hebrew on a complete level with that of the Christian, so far as the government of the commonwealth was concerned. The question, then, presents itself, assuming that the idle Sunday is an "institution" of Christianity, does a statute which for that reason requires men to be idle on Sunday give a preference to one particular religion? How can it be maintained that it does not, unless a similar institution of every other religion be honored with like recognition? As to the individual aspect of the case, if the law is to assist Christianity by making idleness compulsory on its sacred day, thereby presumably commending it to those who reject it, and strengthening its hold upon its devotees, is there not a "preference" given to a religion, unless the Hebrew and all other faiths have a like recognition extended to their sacred days? And as to the social aspect, assuming that it is an advantage to have other people kept extraordinarily quiet while we pray, and to have an especial "peace" established by law on the day we select for public worship, and that we have the right to prevent our neighbor from earning his living at a certain time because the practice of his avocation interferes with our religious exercises, must it not be called a "preference" to do all this for the Christian's benefit, and not to do it for the benefit of the followers of Moses, or Mahomet, or Confucius or Buddha?

Notwithstanding that there would seem to be but one possible reply to these queries, it may be worth while to briefly examine the historical basis for the assumption that the idle Sunday is an "institution" of Christianity. Whatever the origin of the custom of dividing days into weeks, there is, admittedly, only one record of a divine sanction being given to that particular method of reckoning time, and that is in the Bible. In the common English translation of the Old Testament, we are told that the creation was completed in six days, and that its author "rested" on the seventh day; and "blessed and sanctified" it for that reason. And, by the revelation addressed to the Hebrews, through the prophet Moses, four Sabbaths, or periods of rest, were prescribed to that people. One was every fiftieth year, which they were commanded to "hallow,"[1] and during which they were forbidden to sow, or reap, or gather grapes,[2] for it was to be "holy" to them.[3] Another was every seventh year, during which they were forbidden to "sow the field or prune the vineyard."[4] A third was the tenth day of every seventh month, which was a day of "atonement," and on which the Hebrews were commanded to "afflict their souls," and abstain from work—it being proclaimed that the soul which was not afflicted should be "cut off from among his people," and the soul that worked "destroyed."[5] (This Sabbath, by the way, was to be kept from the even of the ninth day to the even of the tenth.) And the fourth was the seventh day of the week, on which no work was to be done. In one place the death penalty is fixed as the punishment of those who "defile" this day, or do any work thereon;[6] and we have a single instance of its infliction, the criminal act being the "gathering of sticks."[7] For the establishment of this last "Sabbath," we find two reasons given, as we also find two slightly different versions of the commandment for its observance. According to the

1 *Leviticus xxv.*, 8–10.

2 *Id.* 11.

3 *Id.* 12.

4 *Id.* 2–7. Compare *Lev. xxvi.*, 33–35, and *II. Chron. xxxvi.*, 20, 21.

5 *Leviticus xxiii.*, 27–32.

6 *Exodus xxxi.*, 14, 15; *xxxv.*, 2.

7 *Numbers xv.*, 32 *et seq.*

translation by King James' ministers, in Exodus it is said the Jews must not work because the Creator made the world in six days, and "rested" on the seventh, "wherefore" He "blessed, and hallowed" it;[1] but in Deuteronomy, the "rest" seems to be enjoined merely as a commemoration of the deliverance of the Jews from the Egyptians.[2] In the texts just cited, and others, referring to the same subject, we have the only "Divine" recognition of the "seventh day." If we were without the benefit of judicial illumination of this question, we might grope our way darkly to several conclusions, such as the following: (1) We can attach no human meaning or significance to the statement that the Deity "rested;" but true reverence may well dismiss the matter with acquiescence in the negative comment of St. Augustine: "It cannot be that God was spent in doing the work of His creation, and needed rest, like a man."[3] (2) The fact that a day has been "blessed" or "sanctified" is no argument that men are under an obligation to be idle on that day; in fact, idleness would not have served to distinguish the day from any other for the lower animals, at the time of the Creator's "rest," since man had not yet appeared to interfere with the unbroken Sabbath of their lives; and the first of our species could have made no distinction in this regard between one day and another, since his "labor" did not begin till he was cursed with it as a punishment, when, it will be observed, no provision was made for "Sabbaths" of any kind, but he was sentenced to work "*all* the days of his life." (3) If, therefore, the "sanctification" of the seventh day implies that idleness is a duty thereon, we must seek elsewhere for a revelation of that fact. (4) As the only "observance" prescribed for the seventh day consists in abstention from work, no amount or kind of recreation, allowable on any other day, could constitute a "violation" of the seventh—and, in thus determining, we should feel fortified by such texts as that which speaks of

[1] *Exodus xx.*, 8–11.

[2] *Deuteronomy v.*, 12–15. Dean Milman, in his "*History of the Jews*," thus combines the two statements: "The double sanction, on which the observance of the day rested, reminded every faithful Israelite of his God, under His two-fold character of Creator and Deliverer. All creation should rest, because on that day the Creator rested; Israel more particularly, because on that day they rested from their bondage in Egypt." *Harper's ed., I.*, 97.

[3] *Homilies on St. John xvii.*, 269 (Oxford, 1848).

"mirth, new moons, Sabbaths and solemn feasts;"[1] that which says that, when the Levites told the people that the day was "holy," they proceeded to "eat, drink and make great mirth," "because they understood the words;"[2] by the custom in the time of the founder of Christianity, even among that strictest of Jewish sects, the Pharisees, of entertaining guests on the Sabbath,[3] and by the high authority of Milman, who says that in later times among the Jews "rich and poor, young and old, master and slave, met before the gates of the city, and indulged in innocent mirth, or in the pleasures of friendly intercourse."[4] (5) The Sabbath or "rest" of the seventh day is no more an "obligation" than that of the fiftieth year, or the seventh year, or the tenth day of the seventh month; whoever is bound by one of these prescribed rules of life is bound by all. (6) All four of these regulations were for Jews alone, and expressly intended to mark out and distinguish them from other people—and, in arriving at this conclusion respecting the institution of the seventh day, we should feel assisted by the phraseology of the commands, *e. g.* the introductory adjuration, "Hear, O, Israel,"[5] the total lack of evidence that any other people practiced such observance,[6] the construction put upon the language by the Jews themselves, who actually punished "proselytes of the gates" for keeping the Sabbath,[7] by the texts which say "it shall be a sign between me and you,"[8] and "it is a sign between me and the children of Israel forever,"[9] and "the adversaries saw her, and did mock at her Sabbaths."[10] (7) Whatever the difficulty in ascertaining that day of our week which corresponds with the day of "rest" from the work of creation,[11] there is no doubt that the Jews accepted the

[1] *Hosea ii.*, 11.

[2] *Nehemiah viii.*, 11-12.

[3] *Luke xiv.*, 1 *et seq.*

[4] *1 History of Jews* (*Harper's ed.*) 97. See, also, *Philo Judaeus, De Vita Mosis; Josephus*, Cont., App. I., 1. An accurate statement of the practice of the modern Jews to abstain only from "productive" work on Saturday, and a scholarly vindication of the position that they thus literally fulfill the Hebrew words of the Fourth Commandment, may be found in an article in the "*Jewish Chronicle*," of London, issue of February 3d, 1865.

[5] *Deuteronomy v.*, 1. As to "strangers within thy gates," &c., see *Grotius* (*Hugo*), App. I., 34, 46 (London, 1679).

[6] See "*Sunday*," *Hessey*, 139, 142, 415 (London, 1860).

[7] *2 Barrington Theol. Wks.* 265–358.

[8] *Exodus xxxi.*, 13.

[9] *Id.* 17. See *Ezekiel xx.*, 12, 9, 20.

[10] *Jeremiah Lam.* 1, 7.

[11] On the "Patriarchal Sabbath," see

instructions of Moses as applying to the day which we call Saturday, and, in the absence of proof that they misunderstood him, or that he acquiesced in such a misconstruction of his message, we are safe in drawing the inference that the day was Saturday, and that the Fourth Commandment has no relation, either for Jews or any one else, to any other day of the week. (8) The Hebrew founder of the Christian religion appears to have rendered obedience to all the ordinances of his people. Submission to constituted authority was one of the principles of his philosophy of life; and without a careful observance of the ceremonial law, he could never have gotten a hearing among the formalists to whom his preaching was addressed. For these two reasons he antagonized no portion of the Mosaic code; and his utterances on Sabbatarianism were confined to a gentle pleading that in this, as in all other things, there should be observed what Mr. Matthew Arnold has well styled a "sweet reasonableness" and sensible moderation. But it was written that Christianity should not be limited to the Hebrew race. And when the Apostles came to lay down rules of conduct for their Gentile converts, one of the first difficulties with which they were confronted was the disposition—inherent in the nature of all men—to substitute outward ceremony for internal purity. To take the instance with which we have to deal, it is much easier to be idle one day in the week than to be honest, good-natured, kind and liberal all the time; just as it is much easier to go to church occasionally than to tell the truth under all circumstances. And the early Gentile Christians, like the rest of us, were prone to find a way to balance their accounts on the eternal books by privately indulging in pleasant or profitable sins and publicly displaying an extraordinary zeal for matters of ritual. They had not merely the Hebrew example for observing days; any one who has read Ovid's "*Fasti*" will remember how the Roman calendar was burdened with dates sacred to this God or that—times when it was "lucky" to do one thing and dangerous to attempt something else. But there was nothing in which the Apostles more thoroughly imbibed and earnestly enforced the spirit of the Master's teaching than in this thing of cleansing the inside of the platter; and the burden of their speech is incessant

Mede Wks., Dis. XV., 55–57; *Heylin's* "*History of the Sabbath,*" Pt. I., ch. 3, §§ 2, 3; "*Holmes' Essay on Sabbath*" (London, 1673).

that there is nothing meritorious in the form, and that the motive is the all essential. And while they were contending against other superstitions, the innate immorality of this superstition of days did not escape their anxious attention. They plainly discerned its dangerous tendency to be two-fold: first, in the false idea that the time of an act could have anything whatever to do with its moral nature, other things being the same; and, secondly, in the inevitable result of its acceptance to foster the notion that it was possible, by being extraordinarily good for a certain number of hours, to purchase immunity for naughtiness the balance of the time. The moral system of Christianity would be fatally incomplete if its sacred books did not contain emphatic condemnation of this, one of the most common and apparently ineradicable weaknesses of the human heart. It is immaterial to the point that so many modern Christians have wandered, as did their predecessors of the Apostolic time, away from the path in this, as in many other things. It is pointed out clearly enough for all in the fundamental Charter of Christian Liberty, from which it is necessary to make no more than the following extracts:

"Let no man therefore judge you in meat, or in drink, or in respect of an holy day, or of the new moon, or of the Sabbath days; which are a shadow of things to come; but the body is of Christ."[1]

"One man esteemeth one day above another; another esteemeth every day alike. Let every man be fully persuaded in his own mind. He that regardeth the day, regardeth it unto the Lord; and he that regardeth not the day, to the Lord he doth not regard it."[2]

"Howbeit then when ye knew not God, ye did service unto them which by nature are no Gods. But now, after that ye have known God, or rather are known of God, how turn ye again to the weak and beggarly elements whereunto ye desire again to be in bondage? Ye observe days, and months, and times, and years. I am afraid of you, lest I have bestowed upon you labor in vain."[3]

(8) We might dismiss the consideration of the religious aspects of the Sunday-law question with the remark that these laws, viewed with reference to their origin, constitute one of the most curious and surprising chapters in the history of ideas. The conception originated

[1] *Col. ii.*, 16–17.
[2] *Rom. xiv.*, 5, 6.
[3] *Gal. iv.*, 8–11.

with a sect which denounced the observance of Christmas, of Easter, of the Ascension Day, of Good Friday, and of every other Christian anniversary, as base and degrading "Popish" superstition; which repudiated and considered an easy death all too light a penalty for the slightest deference to what it styled "tradition." Yet these people seem to have concentrated, as it were, upon the first day of the week all the solemn awe and respect which Christians generally distributed among other occasions; and for doing this they had no warrant but the flimsiest of traditional authority, and in order to do it they were obliged to defy the very letter, no less than the whole spirit, of what they professed to regard as the "Written Word," and the only rule of faith and action.

But from all such erroneous views upon this subject, whether resulting from the text of Scripture, the evidence of history, or the force of reason, we are happily saved by judicial exposition. A Pennsylvania judge informs us that idleness is prescribed by *"the positive law, promulgated at Sinai;"*[1] and by an Arkansas case the transaction of business on Sunday by a Christian is brought within the prohibitions of the decalogue, as follows: "A female witness, who was present when the note was executed, stated that the parties were all members of the church, and that she knew that they were doing wrong at the time. She perhaps knew nothing of the statute, *but was, no doubt, familiar with the Ten Commandments;*"[2] and Judge Flandrean, in Minnesota, said: "The act can have no other object than *the enforcement of the fourth of God's Commandments,* which are a recognized and excellent standard of both public and private morals. A violation of the act, therefore, is *contra bonos mores,* and cannot be sustained by the courts."[3] So, it was said by Judge Lumpkin, of Georgia: "All agree that to the well-being of society, stated intervals of rest are absolutely necessary. We should not tempt mankind, therefore, to yield obedience to municipal arrangements which overlook and disregard *the moral law* of the great Jehovah who, *from the smoking top of Mount Sinai, proclaimed to all the world* [*sic*] "Remember the Sabbath day, to keep it holy; in it thou shalt not do any work."[4] And Judge Lochrane, of the

[1] *Lindenmuller's Case,* 33 Barb. 548 (1861).

[2] *Tucker* v. *West,* 29 Ark. 386.

[3] *Brimball* v. *Van Campen,* 8 Minn. 13.

[4] *Neal* v. *Crew,* 12 Ga. 93 (1852).

same state, so late as 1871, said he felt sustained in presuming the law of Kansas to be the same as that of his own state in this regard, because the contrary view would suppose the people of Kansas to have *annulled* the *decalogue*, and to have permitted by law the *disregard of Christian obligation*, and not only forgotten, but violated the injunction, "*Remember the Sabbath day, to keep it holy;* on it thou shalt do no manner of work."[1]

By which high authorities we have established the propositions that Sunday, and not Saturday, is the day referred to in the Fourth Commandment, and that the Jews have erred in their interpretation of its words during all the ages; that its injunctions are not for that race alone, as they have fondly imagined, but for all time and all men; and that what is, on its face, a mere requirement of a ceremonial or ritual observance is really a "moral" duty, such, for example, as veracity or honest dealing. These points are still more clearly elucidated in the extract which follows. "In *Campbell* v. *The International, &c.*, I have expressed my own views upon this subject. I repeat them in language far better than my own: The dedication of one day in seven to religious rest, and the worship of Almighty God, is of divine authority, and perpetual obligation, as a characteristic of revealed religion during all its successive periods; having been enjoined upon men at the creation, recognized and confirmed in the most solemn manner in the Ten Commandments, vindicated by our Divine Lord from unauthorized additions and impositions of the Jewish teachers, and transferred, upon the abrogation of the ceremonies of the Mosaic law, to the first day of the week, in commemoration of the resurrection of Christ, and, on that account, called the Lord's day. Rev. D. Wilson, Bishop of Calcutta: It is enough to say that this conclusion has not been lightly formed; nor without attention to the arguments of the eminent men who have doubted or contested it."[2] The language here quoted, and given judicial sanction, is taken from a work entitled "*The Divine Authority, &c., of the Lord's Day*" (London, 1830; Boston, 1831), which must be consulted for the authorities on which the Bishop relies. It will be observed that several distinct propositions are embraced within this brief extract. The writer speaks of "religious

[1] *Hill* v. *Wilker*, 41 Ga. 449.

[2] *Hogan's Case*, 20 How. (N.Y.) Pr. 76 (1860).

rest," a phrase found nowhere in the Bible; of Sabbath "worship," as enjoined upon men at the creation, the fact being, as already noted, that at the time of the Creator's "rest" there were no men on whom such an injunction could operate, and of course the Bible contains no record of such an injunction having been then delivered; of the primeval dedication of one day in seven to rest and worship having been "recognized and confirmed" in the Ten Commandments, whereas, so far from indicating that the "Sabbath" was existent or universal when the Commandments were promulgated, the language and context seem to indicate that it was a new thing, and, as previously remarked, that one of the great objects of its institution was to distinguish the Jews from the people around them;[1] of a "transferrence" of the obligation of "rest and worship" to the first day of the week by authority unmentioned,[2] "in commemoration of the resurrection of Christ, and on that account called the Lord's Day"—by what authority so designated we are left uninformed.[3]

It is proper to observe that the adoption of these theological positions of the Bishop of Calcutta into the law has not met with universal assent. A Pennsylvania judge has said: "I am deeply

[1] See, on this point, *White's "Treatise of the Sabbath Day"* 40–46; *Milton's "Christian Doctrine,"* Bk. II., ch. 7. "The most ancient fathers affirm that none of the patriarchs before Moses observed the Sabbath day," says Bishop White, and cites his proof. See, also, *Hughes' "Letter,"* in *"The Pamphleteer,"* vol. 27, p. 214; *Heylin's "History of the Sabbath,"* Pt. I., ch. 1. As to whether the Jews were required by Moses to assemble for worship, or perform any special devotions on Saturday, see *Josephus*, art. I., i., 1; III., v., 5; xvi., 2, 4; second book *Ag. Apion,* § 18; Bishop White's *"Treatise of the Sabbath Day"* (London, 1635), and the text cited on page 143; *British Quarterly Review*, January, 1885, 109. That "except at the Tabernacle or the Temple, no religious ceremony distinguished the Sabbath according to the law of Moses," is proven by Dr. Reichle in *"The Lord's Day Not the Sabbath"* (Dublin, 1859). Nowhere in the five Books of Moses is there found any precept in reference to prayer.

[2] Because unmentionable, see *Heylin*, Pt. II., ch. 1. That no "days" were to be "separated" according to the apostolic view is sufficiently apparent from the texts previously cited. That it was the practice of the Apostles to preach on Saturdays, appears from *Acts xiii.*, 14, 42, 44; *xvi.*, 13; *xvii.*, 2; *xviii.*, 4. See, also, on this question, *Paley's "Philosophy,"* ch. VII.; *Milton's "Christian Doctrine,"* Book II., ch. 7; *"Sunday Questions,"* in *"Christian Reformer,"* for April and May, 1856.

[3] "The Lord's Day" and "the Day of the Lord" are phrases occurring in the Bible. But in no instance is there the slightest foundation for the assump-

impressed with the necessity of a proper observance of Sunday, as a day of worship and prayer and of rest from labor, but, living under the new dispensation, and not under the old, I feel no inclination to turn the Lord's day into a Jewish Sabbath;"[1] and a judge in North Carolina spoke of Sunday as "a day set apart by the *Author of our religion*, for His peculiar service,"[2] wherein the allusion is, apparently, to some declaration of the founder of Christianity, though "chapter and verse" are strangely omitted. Parker, C. J., of Massachusetts, observes: "It is true that from the Fourth Commandment in the decalogue it may be inferred that one day in seven was, according to the divine will, to be set apart as a day of rest from labor, but none will contend that the day therein sanctified is the day which Christians are bound to keep as holy time, or that any of the rigid laws of Moses, relative to the observance of that day, are now in force. It is enough to observe that, by the universal consent of Christians, another holy day has been substituted, and that works of necessity and charity are not profanations of the Christian Sabbath; so that a poor man in these days would not be stoned to death for gathering sticks on the Sabbath, although that was the punishment inflicted in the time of Moses, and although some among our ancestors so far regarded the laws of Moses as of perpetual obligation as to propose for their code the punishment of death for the crime of disregarding or carelessly observing the Sabbath. All arguments drawn from the Jewish law respecting the Sabbath are, therefore, out of place; *except so far as any provision of that law may have been recognized and promulgated by our Saviour*, or by the legislative authority of our own commonwealth. We are not aware that there is upon record any express precept of our Saviour, or of his Apostles, enjoining the observance of one day as more holy than others; and yet we are far from questioning the religious obligation which all Christians are under to separate to religious uses the first day of the week, since that is the time which, from the days of the apostles, was set apart for that purpose, and since the legislative power, or the uniform usage of every Christian state, has exacted the observance of it as such."[3]

tion that they refer to Sunday. See *Milton's "Christian Doctrine,"* Book II., ch. 7.

[1] *Sparhawk's Case*, 54 Pa. 401.

[2] *Williams' Case*, 4 Ired. 400 (1844).

[3] *Pearce* v. *Atwood*, 13 Mass. 324.

With which extract concludes our discussion of the religious aspect of the Sunday laws. If this deserves consideration at all, it surely ought to be treated with reasonable exhaustiveness. The chapter has been a failure if it has not been demonstrated that, viewed under this aspect, such laws are anti-American, immoral and un-Christian.

CHAPTER III.

CONSTITUTIONALITY OF SUNDAY LAWS IN THE UNITED STATES—CONTINUED.

CASES SUSTAINING THEM AS CIVIL REGULATIONS.

We now leave the religious aspect of the question altogether, and take up the physical and social sanction which has been claimed for the Sunday laws. And, first, we cite the decisions which, without elaborating the temporal or worldly reasons for such laws, distinctly affirm that on those reasons alone can they be sustained. The Massachusetts court says of the Sunday law, that it "is essentially a civil regulation, providing for a fixed period of rest in the business, the ordinary avocations, and the amusements of the community. If there is to be such a cessation from labor and amusement, some one day must be selected for the purpose; and even if the day thus selected is chosen because a great majority of the people celebrate it as a day of peculiar sanctity, the legislative authority to provide for its observance is derived from its general authority to regulate the business of the community, and provide for its moral and physical welfare. The act imposes upon no one any religious ceremony, or attendance upon any form of worship, and any one who deems another day more suitable for rest or worship, may devote that day to the religious observance which he deems appropriate;"[1] and the moral aspect of Sunday business has been thus repudiated in New York: "In so far as the transaction of business is in itself immoral, the permitted sales and purchases are just as immoral as those which are prohibited. Business transactions, therefore, which are void, are void not because they are immoral *per se*, but because they are prohibited by law;"[2] and so with its religious aspect: "The constitutionality of the law does not depend on the question whether or not Christianity is a part of

[1] *Has' Case*, 122 Mass. 40 (1877).

[2] *Sayles* v. *Smith*, 12 Wend. 57 (1834).

the common law of this state. As a civil and political institution, the establishment and regulation of a Sabbath is within the just powers of the civil government;"[1] and in Pennsylvania "the law relating to the observance of Sunday defines a duty of the citizen to the state and to the state only."[2] And Judge Thurman, of Ohio, in a case often referred to, thus elucidates the subject: "The statute upon which the defendant relies, prohibiting common labor on the Sabbath, could not stand for a moment as the law of this state, if its sole foundation was the Christian duty of keeping that day holy, and its sole motive to enforce the observance of that duty. For no power over things spiritual has ever been delegated to the government, while any preference of one religion over another, as the statute would give upon the above hypothesis, is directly prohibited by the constitution. Acts evil in their nature, or dangerous to the public welfare, may be forbidden and punished, though sanctioned by one religion and prohibited by another; but this creates no preference whatever, for they would be equally forbidden and punished if all religions permitted them. Thus, no plea of his religion could shield a murderer, ravisher or bigamist; for the community would be at the mercy of superstition, if such crimes as these could be committed with impunity, because sanctioned by some religious delusion. We are, then, to regard the statute as a mere municipal or police regulation, whose validity is neither strengthened nor weakened by the fact that the day of rest it enjoins is the Sabbath day. It was within the constitutional competency of the General Assembly to require this cessation of labor and to name the day of rest. It did so, and, in accordance with the feelings of a majority of the people, the Christian Sabbath was very properly selected. But regarded merely as an exertion of legislative authority, the act would have had neither more nor less validity than had any other day been adopted. The legislative power in Ohio has never extended to the enforcement of religious duties, merely because they are religious; and politically and legally, considered, the power to prescribe a day of rest is simply a municipal power, and the injunction a civil regulation, and nothing more. 'But to

[1] *Lindenmuller's Case,* 33 Barb. 548 (1861).

[2] *Mohney* v. *Cook,* 26 Pa. 342 (1853). See, also, *Dale* v. *Knapp,* 98 Pa. 389 (1881).

allow men to make bargains on the Sabbath is to let them desecrate that holy day, and it should not be granted that the legislature would suffer that.' This is the language of the modern English cases, and perhaps it is consistently used in a country where Christianity is a part of the law, and in which there is an established church and an omnipotent parliament. But the General Assembly of Ohio is not, as we have shown, a guardian of the sanctity of any day. If it may protect the first day of the week from desecration, because it is the Christian Sabbath, it may, in like manner, protect the sixth day because it is the holy day of the Mahomedan, and the seventh day because it is the Sabbath of the Jew and the Seventh-day Baptist. Nay, more, it may protect the various festivals, which, by some of the churches, are considered scarcely less sacred than the Sabbath day. But, were the power conceded to the legislature, it has not attempted to exercise it. It would, in the opinion of most Christians, be a far greater desecration of Sunday to go to an infidel lecture on that day than to buy a tract of land, and yet the former is certainly not unlawful. The statute leaves a man to study atheism or the Bible, as he may see fit, although, in the judgment of most men, the former occupation is as vicious as the latter is laudable. There are various religious duties the performance of which on Sunday is considered peculiarly appropriate; various occupations or amusements, harmless in themselves, but deemed by most Christians irreligious, if indulged in on the Sabbath; yet the law neither enforces the one nor forbids the other. In a word, we repeat that, legally considered, Sunday is merely a day of rest. To the Christian it is far more. With him it has a sanctity not derived from human laws, but stamped upon it by the Almighty. His observance of it is not the mere performance of a civil duty, but an obedience to a precept of the Most High. In this faith he is protected; the faith itself is protected; but the law does not enforce it."[1] And again he says: "We must always keep in mind that it is no part of the object of the act to enforce the observance of a religious duty. The act does not, to any extent, rest upon the ground that it is immoral or irreligious to labor on the Sabbath, any more than upon any other day. It

[1] *Bloom* v. *Richards*, 2 Ohio St. 387 (1853).

simply prescribes a day of rest, from motives of public policy, and as a civil regulation; and, as the prohibition itself is founded on principles of policy, upon the same principle certain exceptions are made, among which are 'works of necessity and charity.' Unless we keep constantly in mind that the act rests upon public policy alone, we will be in great danger of giving it a wrong construction; and, instead of reading it in the light of the constitution, which prohibits all religious tests and preferences, find ourselves led away from its meaning by the influence of our own peculiar theological tenets."[1] So we are told in Missouri: "In this country the legislative power, since the formation of our Federal Government, has never extended to the enforcement of religious duties merely because they are religious. The rules of human conduct prescribed by the Christian religion find no vindication in the civil authority, except in so far as they have become visibly incorporated in our constitutions and laws. To these constitutions and laws, then, and not to any mere sentiment of piety, however commendable, must we look for the means and measures whereby the courts are required to preserve good order and the well-being of society. It may be sinful to make loans and promissory notes on Sunday. But if we do not find the acts clearly forbidden by the laws which we are authorized to enforce, we must leave the sin to be dealt with by a higher power."[2] And in Kentucky: "The statute is only a civil regulation, enacted from motives of public policy, and to discuss it in a religious point of view would be to attribute to the legislature the exercise of a power it does not possess; that is, the power to enforce the performance of religious duties."[3] And in California: "The policy of the law is fully committed to the secular phase of the subject only," and the requirement of compulsory idleness on Sunday is considered as "an exercise of police power;" and the court adds, that to say the state may not set apart Sunday, because to do so discriminates in favor of Christians, "seems to interpose the authority of churches against the power of the state," for, in guaranteeing religious freedom, she "did not relinquish to religious

[1] *McGatrick* v. *Wason*, 4 Ohio St. 566 (1855).

[2] *Moore* v. *Climer*, 12 Mo. App. 11 (1882).

[3] *Louisville and Nashville R. R.'s Case*, 80 Ky. 291 (1882).

bodies, nor divest herself of, the power to establish a day of rest as a municipal institution;" that the day is set apart not as a holy day, but as a holiday; that the acts under consideration were not prohibited as offences against any religion, and, conceding that they were prohibited because offensive to public morals, according to the standard of Christianity, was no valid objection, for, as that is the prevailing religious opinion of the people, public morals are largely dependent on it.[1] And in North Carolina, it was said of Sunday work: "We do not perceive how it can become an offence at common law, even when the labor is both openly and publicly performed, as in a town, for example, except upon a process of reasoning of this kind: That the Christian religion is a part of the common law; that it forbids work on Sunday, not only as a sin in itself, but as a disturbance to others and an injury to the state, and, therefore, that the law prohibits such profanation and punishes it. But we cannot believe that such a principle was established at the common law. In the first place, the extent of the obligation of the Sabbath [*sic*] under the Gospel is a point on which the professors and teachers of Christianity have been far from agreeing. It would not, then, be likely that the temporal judges would, without the enactment of parliament, assume to punish the violation of Sunday as being a breach of Christian or religious duty. We should rather expect them to leave that to the censure of the spiritual judge, who was charged peculiarly with the office of enjoining on all subjects the duties of religion and obedience to the canons of the church. Although it may be true that Christianity is a part of the common law, it is not so in the sense that an act contrary to the precepts of our Saviour, or Christian morals, is necessarily indictable. Those which were merely against God and religion were left to the correction of conscience, or the religious authorities of the church. Such, necessarily, must be the character of acts which are criminal only in respect to the day on which they are done, being a day set apart by the Author of our religion for His peculiar service. There is reason to doubt, as before said, whether work on Sunday was held to be contrary to the Christian dispensation, as early held in the English church. But, if it was, it became an offence against

[1] *Koser's Case*, 60 Cal. 177.

the state by being contrary to the religion which the state had established. In this state, however, although recognized as an existing, and as the prevalent, religion, it is not, and cannot be, established by law in any form, nor as consisting of any particular doctrines, or imposing any special duties of worship, or of worship at particular places or periods. Therefore, however clearly the profanation of Sunday might be against the Christian religion, it is not, and could not here be made, merely as a breach of religious duty, an offence; and much less can it be held an offence at common law;"[1] and accordingly a levy was held void, not because it was void at common law, or upon the idea that the day ought, upon religious or moral doctrines, to be kept holy, but because a statute made the service of process on that day unlawful. And the court said: "What religion or morality permit, or forbid, to be done, is not within our province to inquire. In different Christian countries, and in different ages in the same country, very differing opinions have prevailed upon this question. In this state, in general, every act may lawfully be done which may lawfully be done on any other day, unless there be some act of the legislature forbidding it to be done on that day."[2] And the doctrine is thus stated in Alabama: "The legislation on the subject of abstaining from worldly employments on the first day of the week is referred to the police power. It has a sanction in the teaching of experience that the general welfare and the good of society require a suspension of labor and business for one day in seven, and that that day should be one of uniform observance. The exercise of the power to enforce this theory of the public good would not infringe the constitution, whether the designated day should be the Christian or the Jewish Sabbath."[3]

The historical fact is, of course, just as well known to the pundits of the bench as to other scholars, that the Sunday laws were intended by those who passed them as the assertion of a religious dogma, and designed to force an external compliance with a portion of their ritual upon those who did not believe in the dogma or approve the ceremonial; that the men who concocted such laws were religious enthusiasts, and not physiologists; that they felt and pro-

[1] *Williams' Case*, 4 Ired. 400 (1844).
[2] *Ricketts' Case*, 74 N. C. 187 (1876).
[3] *Frolickstein's Case*, 40 Ala. 725 (1867).

fessed a supreme contempt for the physical body and its welfare, and that they would have destroyed for heresy in the early days, and laughed to scorn in the more recent times, any person who suggested that they were making idleness on Sunday compulsory because it would lengthen life and benefit the tissues and organs of men, or because it was a social advantage to have everybody loafing on the same day. But this historical consideration has been pronounced irrelevant, and even where the phraseology of the act plainly shows its spirit and purpose to be as is here stated, this is held immaterial, and the right is asserted in the courts to sustain Sunday laws on grounds admittedly not present to the minds of the legislators, and for reasons which, as we have said, every student of history knows that they would have repudiated if presented to them. That the acknowledged and specified purposes of a statute may be disregarded in deciding upon its constitutionality was thus distinctly laid down in Pennsylvania: "Though it may have been a motive with the law-makers to prohibit the profanation of a day regarded by them as sacred—and certainly there are expressions used in the statute that justify this conclusion—it is not perceived how this fact can vitally affect the question at issue. In a Christian community, where a very large majority of the people celebrate the first day of the week as their chosen period of rest from labor, it is not surprising that that day of the week should have received the legislative sanction, and, as it is also devoted to religious observance, we are prepared to estimate the reason why the statute should speak of it as the Lord's day and denominate the infraction of its legalized rest a profanation. Yet this does not change the character of the enactment. To say that one of the objects of the legislature was to assert the sanctity of the particular day selected is to say nothing in proof of the unconstitutionality of the act, unless, in this, the religious conscience of others has been offended and their rights invaded. The phraseology used may indicate a conviction of the holy character of the day, but as this simple expression of an abstract opinion carries with it no obligation, beyond the influence attendant upon the expression itself, it cannot be said that the primary object of the act was authoritatively to assert the supremacy of Sunday as of divine appointment. Had such been the intent, its framers would have commanded the performance of religious rites, or, at least, some express recognition of the day as the true Sabbath. Such a requisition, we agree, would be a palpable interference with the rights of conscience. Its operation is secular, just as much as the business on which it bears is secular, and it is purely a civil regulation. The title of the act is 'for the observance of the Sabbath.' But even if the title could be looked to as furnishing decisive evidence of its purpose, we see nothing in these words which indicate [*sic*] that the phrase was designed to imply a requirement of a religious character, or that the act was, in any respect, designed to subserve a religious purpose. The act itself, in the body of it, explains in what manner the day was to be observed, and shows that the object was only to require duties purely civic or secular; but, even if it were otherwise, it would be difficult to maintain, as the Supreme Court of Pennsylvania observed in the case in 8 Barr, from the circumstance that the act shows one of the motives of its framers was to enforce a religious respect to the Sabbath, that this invalidated it on the ground of its unconstitutionality—the body and substantive provisions of the law showing a purpose and prescribing duties or forbidding acts merely secular in their character."[1]

So, in Louisiana, it has been said: "If the object were to compel the observance of Sunday as a religious institution because it is the Christian Sabbath, to be kept holy under the ordinances of the Christian religion, we should not hesitate in declaring it to be violative of the constitution. It would violate equally the religious liberty of the Christian, the Jew and the infidel. The law in question makes no reference to Sunday as a religious holy day, and indeed the exceptions expressly made to the general prohibition conclusively show that the statute is not designed to enforce the Christian idea of the Sabbath, or to apply the rules of any religious sect to its observance. The statute is to be judged precisely as if it had selected for the day of rest any day of the week other than Sunday, and its validity is not to be questioned because, in the exercise of a wise discretion, it has chosen that day which the majority of the inhabitants of the state, under the sanction of their religious faith, already voluntarily observe as a day of rest."[2] And in Texas the court adopted the view of the assistant attorney-general, who said,

[1] *Specht's Case*, 8 Pa. 312 (1848).

[2] *Walker's Case*, 39 La. Ann. 132 (1887).

among other things: "I do not base the validity of the Sunday law under discussion on the ground of morality or religion, but simply on the broad ground of a police regulation, free from any question of religion and entirely independent of religious ideas as such, except as those laws may not interfere with such religious questions. With an ingenuity worthy of a better cause counsel for the complainant has sought to give this case a religious phase, thereby avoiding the real issue. Does the article of the Penal Code propose to dictate or control the religion of any citizen of the state? It does not. It prohibits selling on Sunday, as therein set forth; it refers not to religion; it does not prohibit or control religion. What religion or religious creed or dogma is inculcated in that statute? Or what religion is prohibited? Does it demand any religious act or service of or from any religionist or non-religionist? Does it require any professed Christian of any faith, order or denomination to do any religious act? Does it require any non-Christian or non-religionist to do any act of worship or to support any minister, build any church or other place of worship, or to contribute thereto, or to subscribe to any creed? Does it oblige any Christian, Jew, Mahomedan, Greek, Infidel, Atheist, Spiritualist, Agnostic, 'Scythian, bond or free,' to observe any religious form, rite or ceremony, or demand of him that he shall bow the knee to any Deity? If so, what or where or when? Does it enjoin upon anybody that he or she or they shall do anything religious at any time or place? Does it ask that any citizen shall believe in the God of the Bible or its teachings, or the doctrines of the Bible, the Koran, or of Confucius, or the Talmud, or the Old or New Testament? Certainly not. * * * If the legislature has the power to pass a law setting apart a day of rest, and to call the citizens off from the pursuits and avocations of life for their own protection and require the law to be observed, does it not follow as the night the day that the same body can select and set apart the day by virtue of their police powers?"[1]

[1] *Sundstrom's Case*, 25 Tex. App. 133 (1888). The following extract thus succinctly exhibits the "common law" as at once the exponent of revelation of the hygienic regulations of society---the dual functions of Moses, but not the American idea of government: "*The Creator* instituted the Sabbath as a day of rest, as *experience* has shown the necessity of its observance by mankind

Having settled, by the preceding cases, the principle that Sunday laws are mere civil regulations, we have next to examine the grounds on which their constitutionality is justified when regarded exclusively from this standpoint. By observing the dates of the decisions previously cited, it will be seen that some of the most radical religious views of the subject have been taken in recent years. Yet the weight of later authority is decidedly in favor of the secular reasoning. And if religious liberty is to be more clearly understood as time passes on, and we are to discard the word and idea of "toleration" in jurisprudence altogether, as Judge Thurman says Ohio has done, it would seem that, in order to sustain Sunday laws, it will be necessary to find reasons altogether mundane for their justification. This necessity has been manfully grappled with by the judges who have recognized its existence, and discarded the religious aspect of the subject. Facts have been assumed, of which no evidence exists; phraseology and history have been ignored, and logic strained without hesitation, wherever the good end seemed to require such methods. And, in more than one instance, there is a manifest consciousness of the fallacies maintained which suggests that the reasoner is suffering an intellectual martyrdom as sublime in its way as any physical sacrifice of the olden time. To appreciate this, the opinions now to be cited must be read in full, and "between the lines." Only the nature of the reasoning, and not the desperate attempts at self-deception as to its sufficiency, can be understood from the mere "extracts" to which we are confined. And first, we may notice, as it stands, practically, alone in its theory, the attempt of an Arkansas judge to sustain the validity of Sunday laws by likening them to the statutes which name certain days as "holidays" in various states. It was said in Arkansas: "The power of the legislature to select a day as a holiday is everywhere conceded. This state, from the beginning, has appropriated Sunday *as such.*" And after mentioning the closing of the public offices, &c., the court adds: "The principle which upholds these regulations underlies the right of the state to prescribe a penalty for the violation of the Sunday law."[1] Under the Arkansas theory, the state says to its citi-

generally as a means of preserving full mental and physical vigor." *State* v. *King*, 37 N. W. Rep. 310 (1888).

[1] *Scale's Case*, 47 Ark. 476 (1886).

zens: "You must be merry on Sunday, under a penalty of ——— dollars for each and every offence." So Mr. Squeers, marking a depressed look on the face of his pupil, Master Mobbs, "moistened the palm" of the hand in which he held his stout rattan and observed: "Cheerfulness and contentment must be kept up. Mobbs, come here!"

Now, the power of the state to close institutions which she controls and operates and to allow her own employes to remain idle on any day she chooses, if they desire to do so, is not in dispute; nor is her authority to extend the time for carrying out contracts, as by making protest, &c., illegal on certain days, in the least involved. The question is not, may she allow her employes to refrain from her own work, but may she compel them and all others to refrain from working either at her business or at business of their own?—not, may she enact that notes shall not be presented at a bank on Sunday, but may she fine the bank officials for looking into its affairs on that day? In a word, may the legislature, besides allowing and encouraging idleness in its citizens, actually *force* it upon them? The learned judge in the opinion just cited shows by his own quotations the difference between Sunday "holidays" and all others, in that the first are compulsory, the latter optional. A distinction has been attempted in Nebraska between holiday laws and Sunday laws, as follows: "The Creator instituted the Sabbath as a day of rest, and experience has shown the necessity of its observance by mankind generally as a means of preserving full mental and physical vigor; hence at common law, courts are prohibited from transacting business on Sunday. No such reasons exist however in favor of holidays. They are established usually to commemorate some event, show respect to some person or persons, or to express gratitude for favors received. In many cases they are liable to interfere with private rights; and while the legislature has undoubted authority within certain bounds to declare certain days legal holidays and prevent the courts from transacting business on such days, yet the courts could not extend such days by implication."[1] It is doubtful whether the "no such reason" here mentioned refers to the "Creator's institution" or the "experimentally demonstrated"

[1] *State* v. *King*, 37 N. W. Rep. 310 (1888).

necessity for Sunday idleness. If the latter, the reasoning cannot, apparently, afford a tangible distinction between the justification for compulsory idleness on Sunday and that for permissible idleness in certain classes on other days (the extent of true "holiday laws"), except on the grounds that human nature is so curiously constituted that its highest development can only be attained where men are compelled to be idle one day in the week, while to even allow them to be idle oftener would be injurious to the race.[1]

But there is little disposition among the authorities generally to compare Sunday laws with those establishing holidays—probably because the compulsory feature of the former has been generally felt to be a fatal objection to such an analogy. We pass, therefore, to the consideration of those cases which sustain them on secular grounds, but rightly deal with them as absolutely unique in American jurisprudence, having no kinship in their spirit or effect with any other law of our country, and of necessity to stand or fall by their own desert alone. Here, as in the other cases, two things are regarded, namely, the individual and the body politic; and Sunday laws are held to be constitutional because Sunday idleness is beneficial to the idler, and because his idleness is an advantage to the community—the latter being considered not as an aggregate of individuals, necessarily advantaged by whatever is useful to its component parts, but as a separate entity, receiving a distinct benefit to itself as a whole. According to these authorities, "the evident object of the statute was to prevent the day from being employed in servile work, which *is exhausting to the body*, or in *merely idle pastime*, subversive of that order, thrift and economy which is necessary to the *preservation of society*."[2] And "the laboring part of the community must feel the institution of a day of rest as *peculiarly adapted to invigorate* their bodies for fresh exertions of activity. *A wise policy* would naturally lead to the formation of laws calculated to subserve *these salutary purposes*."[3] "It is *a law of our nature*

[1] See the citation *post*, frankly asserting the proposition that the "precise" amount of idleness necessary is that prescribed in the Decalogue. Of course this applies to all men, and debars any one from distributing his twenty-four hours of idleness through the week, to suit his convenience or inclination, requiring him, so to speak, to take it all "at one dose."

[2] *Landers* v. *R. R. Co.*, 13 Abb. Pr. (N. S.) 338 (1872).

[3] *Waf's Case*, 3 S. & R. (Pa.) 48 (1817).

that *one day in seven must be observed as a day of relaxation and refreshment* if not for public worship. * * * *We are so constituted, physically, that the precise portion of time indicated by the decalogue must be observed as a day of rest and relaxation, and nature, in the punishment inflicted for a violation of our physical laws, adds her sanction to the positive law* promulgated at Sinai."[1] Idleness on one day in each week, then, is not merely advisable, but an absolute requirement of nature, like the principle of gravity. The legislature is authorized to add penalties of its own to those already established by nature for the violation of her laws; and as it may require each citizen to neglect his business one-seventh of his time, because nature will punish him if he fails to do so, it may require every citizen to be idle on the same one-seventh of the time, because business will be facilitated and the convenience of society subserved by having the necessary idleness of everybody indulged in on the same day, instead of having the lawyers idle one day, the doctors another, the carpenters on a third, the bricklayers on a fourth, and so on. The following citations lead us easily and naturally from the individual to the social considerations involved in this view of the Sunday laws. Thus, we are told in the case just cited, that "experience has shown that the observance of one day in seven as a day of rest is of admirable service to a state, *considered merely as a civil institution.*" "*The stability of government, the welfare of the subject, and the interests of society* have made it necessary that the day of rest observed by the people of a nation should be *uniform*, and that its observance should be, to some extent, compulsory;"[2] and by other authority it is stated: "All agree that *to the well-being of society periods of rest are absolutely necessary.* To be productive of the required advantage these periods *must recur at stated intervals*, so that the *mass* of which the community is composed may enjoy a respite from labor *at the same time.* They may be established by common consent, or, as is conceded, the legislative power of the state may interfere to enforce the time of their stated return and enforce obedience to the direction;"[3] and the Sunday law "has its sanction in the *teaching of experience that the general welfare and good of society require a suspension of labor and*

[1] *Lindenmuller's Case*, 33 Barb. 548 (1861).

[2] *Id.* 568.

[3] *Specht's Case*, 8 Pa. 312 (1848).

business for one day in seven, and that it should be a day of *uniform* observance;"[1] and the courts are "well convinced there is nothing more essential to the *physical, social and religious elevation of a people* than the institution of a *weekly day of rest*—a day set apart especially for recreation and for the worship of Almighty God;"[2] and this view of the subject is well summarized as follows: "In construing our statute, it would be our duty to give it a meaning consistent with our constitution, if its meaning were doubtful, and such meaning could reasonably be attached to its language. Its meaning is not, however, doubtful. It was obviously not intended by our statute to enforce the observance of the Sabbath as a religious duty. The legislature obviously regarded it as promotive of the mental, moral, and physical well-being of men that they should rest from their labors at stated intervals, and in this all experience shows they were right. If, then, rest is to be enjoined as a matter of public policy at stated intervals, it is obvious that public convenience would be much promoted by the community generally resting on the same day; for, otherwise, each individual would be much annoyed and hindered in finding that those with whom he had business to transact were resting on the day on which he was working. The legislature, in holding these views, in selecting the particular day of rest, doubtless selected Sunday because it was deemed a proper day of rest by a majority of our people, who thought it a religious duty to rest on that day, and, in selecting this day, for these reasons, the legislature acted wisely. The law requires that the day be observed as a day of rest, not because it is a religious duty, but because such observance promotes the physical, mental and moral well-being of the community; and Sunday is selected as this day of rest, because, if any other day had been named, it would have imposed unnecessarily onerous obligations on the community, inasmuch as many of them would have rested on Sunday as a religious duty, and the requirement of another day to be observed as a day of rest would have resulted in two days being observed instead of one, and thus time would have been uselessly wasted." The court then quotes the exception in the state statute of

[1] *Frolickstein* v. *Mayor of Mobile,* 40 Ala. 725 (1867).

[2] Manly, J.'s, dissenting opinion in *Melvin* v. *Easley,* 7 Jones (N. C.) 356 (1860).

any person who conscientiously believes that the seventh day of the week ought to be observed as a Sabbath, and does not compel an apprentice, or servant, not of his belief, to do secular work, and does not disturb others, and adds: "This, in effect, says rest on Sunday is not required of any one on the ground that it is a religious duty, but because the well-being of men require [*sic*] that they should rest the one-seventh part of their time, and public convenience requires that this rest should be taken on the day when a majority of the community would, even without a law on the subject, rest, as they regard it as a religious duty to do so, and it would be prejudicial to the public, and tend to idleness, if two-sevenths of the time was devoted to rest. If, then, any portion of the community should regard it as their religious duty to rest on some other day than Sunday, and do so rest, they are not required to rest on Sunday, as one-seventh of time is all that the public good requires to be devoted to rest."[1]

It will be perceived that most of the reasoning which relies on the consideration of the individual's physical welfare is confined to a demonstration of the expediency of a day's idleness at certain intervals, and implies that once a week is about the proper frequency for the general loafing time. But *Lindenmuller's Case*[2] assures us that the "*precise* portion of time indicated by the decalogue" *must* be spent in idleness or nature will punish us. We have here a reference to an extraordinary and awe-inspiring chapter in nature's code. And it is deeply to be regretted that the learned judge to whom we are indebted for the citation has not favored us with the tables of vital statistics or extracts from the writings on hygiene which he examined before arriving at so remarkable a conclusion. This is the more unfortunate because there are facts that seem to bear directly against his position, as well as that of the "expediency men," and to show that nature not only neglects to punish breaches of her law in this regard, but that she bestows no reward on those who observe it, in the way of especial health or longevity. And, though these are mere negative propositions, and the burden of their demonstration ought not, in law or logic, to be on those maintaining them, a few considerations in their support are here submitted.

[1] *B. & O.'s Case*, 15 W. Va. 362 (1879). [2] *Ante*, —.

Without entering upon the question of the origin and universality of the division of days into weeks,[1] we may observe that even if a "seventh day" was known from the creation, and "observed" by any people, there is no evidence in the Bible, or anywhere else, that idleness was considered a part or the whole of such observance by any one, prior to the date of Moses' command to the Israelites upon this subject. And, yet, the record which has come down to us of the great ages attained by the patriarchs, to whom no such injunction was delivered, seems to prove that tenacity of life does not bear a fixed relation to weekly idleness. And some further light on this point is perhaps to be derived from the case of the Greeks, to whom the week was unknown,[2] and who yet attained a very respectable degree of physical development, their statues remaining models for all time; and from the case of the Romans, who borrowed the week from Egypt in the second century,[3] but were powerful and sturdy of frame for many generations before, unless all accounts belie them, and the greatest glories of whose career of conquest were achieved before they began to use the weekly division of days; whereas, the famous edict of Constantine, making idleness compulsory for certain persons "on the venerable day of the sun,"[4] was passed A. D. 321, when the Roman Empire was perhaps at its zenith, but still a process of decay in men and manners had begun, which neither the Christian religion nor the very partial Sunday idleness which was thereby first established was able to arrest.[5] Coming down to the present time, we find the very existence of a "seventh day," and consequently, of course, any necessity for its observance by remaining idle, unknown to the American aborigines,[6]

[1] See *Hessey's "Bumpton Lectures,"* 139, 142, 415; *Potter's "Arch. Græca,"* Bk. II., 126; *Adams' "Roman Ant."* (ed. 1819) 303.

[2] *Potter's "Arch. Græca,"* Bk. II., ch. 26.

[3] *Adams' "Roman Ant."* (1819) 303 *et seq.*

[4] See Table B.

[5] "The military spirit evaporated. The natives of Europe were brave and robust. Spain, Gaul, Britain and Illyricum supplied the legions with excellent soldiers, and constituted the real strength of the monarchy." *1 Gibbon's Decline and Fall of Roman Empire* (*Milman's ed.*), ch. 2, p. 70 (Lippincott, 1866).

[6] *1 Humboldt's Researches* 283–6; *2 Id.* 110, 123; *1 Prescott's Conquest of Mexico* 111 (Harper's, 1843).

the Chinese,[1] Japanese,[2] and Polynesians.[3] But the observation of travelers has failed to note any physical weakness or brevity of existence among any of these races, evidencing the wrath of nature at their ignorant infraction of one of her "fundamental laws." The average height of the Chinese and Japanese is probably less than that of Englishmen; but their capacity for steady labor is certainly as great as the capacity of white men, if it does not exceed the latter. Perhaps many among the Indian and Polynesian tribes are the equals in physical development of the most highly civilized of the Caucasian race; but as the males, at least, of those fortunate branches of the human family do little work beyond hunting and fishing on any days, and substantially enjoy the blessings of a perpetual Sabbath, even if statistics in relation to their endurance of work or longevity were obtainable, they would be valueless for purposes of comparison with our own. If it be said that the exactions of civilization and the hard conditions which it imports into the struggle for existence make a weekly recurrence of an idle day essential, or even desirable, the answer might be that the Chinaman survives and develops under a fiercer competition than ours. But it is not necessary to go to China for *data*. We have among us many thousands of persons—literary men, students, lawyers, &c.—who make little or no difference between Sunday and the rest of the week in the matter of labor; many hundreds of overtaxed clergymen, whose only method of distinguishing the day is to work considerably harder than on others, and the vast army of the medical profession, the very nature of whose occupation forbids their resting at any certain interval. Yet there is absolutely not a single fact to show that the vigor of any one of these is impaired or the number of their years on earth abridged by their failure to yield obedience to the "law of our nature," which requires idleness on Sunday. And the farmer, who, as a rule, conscientiously neglects his business as much as possible every Sunday, is among the shortest lived of men, and, as a soldier, compares unfavorably in ability to stand prolonged duty and resist the attacks of disease with recruits from other classes; whereas, the physicians,

[1] *2 Davis' Chinese*, ch. 18, p. 290 (London, 1836).

[2] *Thundberg's "Voyage au Japan"* 317.

[3] *"Sabbath," "Westminster Review,"* October, 1850.

"who know no Sabbath," are notorious for their longevity, endurance, and resistance to contagion. Doubtless every member of the classes above enumerated as disregarding Sunday idleness needs and, if he is wise and careful, takes both rest and recreation; rest, and plenty of it, he should take in the night hours; recreation, whenever nature seems to an unbiased judgment to demand it, and in "quantities to suit." The only point at issue is the physical necessity or advisability of idleness for everybody during twenty-four hours in each week.

The social considerations in favor of Sunday idleness remain now to be reviewed. In dealing with these we find the courts sometimes merely dwelling on the expediency of Sunday idleness and at other times proclaiming its absolute necessity, just as we have seen that they do when they are concerned with the relation of Sunday idleness to the do individual idler. Thus, we are told that "public convenience would be much promoted by the community generally resting on the same day; for, otherwise, each individual would be much annoyed and hindered in finding that those with whom he had business to transact were resting on the day on which he was working;"[1] and that this uniformity is enjoined by the "teaching of experience;"[2] and we then pass to cases which assure us that "there is nothing *more essential* to the physical, social and religious elevation of a people than the institution of a *weekly day of rest;*"[3] and that "the stability of government and the interests of society have made it necessary that the day of rest observed by the people of a nation should be uniform, and that its observance should be, to some extent, compulsory;"[4] and we are thus prepared to receive the opinion of that West Virginia judge, who is convinced (like the one in New York, whose opinion has just been quoted,) that there is a magic potency in idleness on one day in seven, so that to idle less—say for one day in ten—would be an injury, and to idle more a superfluity; but, as in *Lindenmuller's Case*, no authorities are given for this assumption, in its relation to the individual, so, here, we find none referred to for its vindication in the social aspect; no instance is recalled of a

[1] *B. & O.'s Case*, 15 W. Va. 362 (1879).

[2] *Frolickstein* v. *Mayor of Mobile*, 40 Ala. 725 (1867).

[3] Manly, J., in *Melvin* v. *Easley*, 7 Jones (N. C.) 356 (1860).

[4] *Lindenmuller's Case*, 33 Barb. 548 (1861).

people who kept two "holy days" in the week, and "observed" them by "resting," and, consequently, fell behind some neighboring race, who, under like conditions of heredity and environment, flourished and finally subjugated the first, because they only "rested" on one day in seven. But the difference between such a rest and one of more frequent recurrence is none the less sharply defined because the *data* on which it rests are omitted. The court says: "Sunday is selected as the day of rest, because, if any other day had been named, it would have imposed unnecessarily onerous obligations on the community, inasmuch as many of them would have rested on Sunday as a religious duty, and the requirement of another day to be observed as a day of rest would have resulted in two days being observed instead of one, and thus time would have been uselessly wasted. * * * It would be prejudicial to the public, and tend to idleness, if two-sevenths of the time was devoted to rest. * * * One-seventh of time is all that the public good requires to be devoted to rest."[1] It will be observed that, in the North Carolina citation above, the words "a day set apart especially for recreation and for the worship of Almighty God," are omitted after the words "a weekly day of rest," though the former are added in the fuller citation previously given. They were retained in the first citation because the purpose was, then, merely to set out the argument as it was used, and omitted in the second quotation as irrelevant to its effectiveness, since it has never been claimed that any legislature in the United States can compel a man to indulge against his will in "recreation," even if it were possible for him to accomplish that feat; and the power of the state to set apart a day for "worship" is expressly repudiated by the authorities heretofore digested. Passing to the New York case, we may observe, as to a weekly day of idleness being essential to the "stability" of government, that the fact that it is not so is shown if a single instance is produced of a government's being maintained without it, which is, of course, easily enough done. And as to the *argumentum ab inconvenienti*, or the "annoyance" to which one man might be subjected, by finding another resting while he was working, it may be said that, if one day were prescribed for lawyers to rest, another for doctors, another for merchants, &c.,

[1] *B. & O.'s Case*, 15 W. Va. 362 (1879).

every one would easily recall the days fixed and act accordingly; so that the case is not made out in theory; while, as a matter of fact, our "orthodox". Hebrew citizens do rest on Saturday while our Christians are at work, and, in some states, they are allowed to work on Sunday while Christians are resting; and the inconvenience of this state of things has never been seriously urged as sufficiently great to warrant legislative interference, however much the propriety of the exemption last mentioned may have been impugned on other grounds.

But there is another side to this question of the social advantage of an idle Sunday which has never received fair consideration in England or America, and yet is forced upon our notice every Sunday, in field, and village, town and city. The fact is patent to all; it is only "viewed unequally," as a distinguished scientist once said. We shall start with a premise: The community being made up of individual units, whatever has an ill-effect on a large number of these units is *prima facie* an injury to the community, and the burden of showing an overbalancing benefit to the mass is on him who asserts it. The only definite worldly benefit of Sunday laws to the masses of society for which we have a judicial voucher, is that "annoyance" would be caused to some if all are not compelled to be idle at once. This argument is, of course, disposed of if it can be shown that something far worse than "annoyance," that demoralization, debauchery, and degradation are entailed on thousands by the enforced idleness of Sunday. Thus far in the present chapter, as in the greater portion of the preceding one, every advantage has been carefully conceded to the advocates of Sunday laws by treating those statutes as if they interfered with the liberty of labor alone. But a stage of the argument has again been reached when the necessity of defending them in their entirety, if they are to be defended at all, must be insisted upon. Those who uphold them as aids to religion must prove that spiritual betterment is likely to result from a general abstention once a week, under legal compulsion, from play as well as from work; and no less must those who are sticklers for them, on mere social grounds, demonstrate that the community is advantaged by having its members compelled against their wills to refrain once a week from all attempts to amuse themselves, as well as from all attempts to earn a living. The *cheerless and idle* Sunday is before the tribunal of reason; and, on this subject, we cannot do better than quote the following extract from a writer of singular clearness in thought and felicity in expression. It is not necessary for the present purpose that the reader should accept his reasoning absolutely; enough is accomplished if it serves to show that the social expediency of the idle Sunday is not the self-evident thing which the decisions assume it to be, that, at least, as much may be said against it as for it: "How small a part of the great bulk of the people have either inclination or ability to employ the weekly returns of Sabbatical idleness in religious exercises or meditations! Look around among those higher orders of men, whose situations and circumstances afford them the greatest share of leisure time; and though they, for the most part, have had the great advantage of a liberal education, how few of them employ their leisure to any valuable purpose; and how many abuse it, to their own and others' detriment! Who, then, can think it possible that the uninformed minds of the illiterate and ignorant can wisely and virtuously spend one-seventh part of their lives in idleness, or, rather, that great numbers of them should not misspend it, as we find they do, to the corruption of their own morals and the insecurity and annoyance of society in general? That admirable, perfect model of prayer to the Deity, taught us by our Lord himself, contains but four petitions that personally respect ourselves, and one of them is that we may not be led into temptation—a petition which evidently enjoins upon us, as an essential duty of our religion, the doing our utmost to preserve both ourselves and our fellow-creatures from falling into so perilous a situation. Whereas, the calling off the laboring orders of men from their usual honest occupations, and obliging them to pass every seventh day in an idleness which many of them cannot but misspend, is forcing them into a weekly state of the most dangerous temptation, the consequence of which must be, *what we experimentally find it, especially in all populous places, a most fatal depravity of their morals.* And I have no doubt it was for this very reason that the religion of the Gospel enjoins upon its professors no Sabbatical cessation from business, nor festival seasons of any kind."[1]

[1] "*Arguments For and Against Sabbatical Observance of Sunday,*" &c., 23, 24 (Ipswich, 1792).

The writer adduces, as a recognition of the ill-effects of compulsory idleness, the establishment of Sunday-schools by charitable people, in order to provide places " where the children of the laboring people, instead of lounging away the day in childish pastimes, or misspending it in doing mischief, may employ it in the acquisition of some useful knowledge."[1]

It has been maintained that some of the evils, here so graphically portrayed, may be avoided by allowing public amusements, while prohibiting labor. This view is set forth as follows by a writer in the *New Monthly Magazine*, vol. 38, p. 210: "The religious tracts and similar publications dwell on no point so strongly as the danger of Sabbath-breaking. No wonder—a poor fellow must either go to church, or to sleep, to be safe. If he is not impressed with the importance of church-going, if he finds the parson drowsy or incomprehensible, the congregation smart and proud, and, on the whole, decides upon staying away, what is he to do? Everything is dull—shut up—no sport allowed—restraint upon every movement —solemnity upon every face. Eaten up with *ennui*, he creeps into some corner, with a few fellows similarly situated, and resorts to gambling for amusement; or he collects his companions in some out-of-the-way beer shop; or, perhaps, he and they loiter, by dozens, at the town end, lounging on walls and posts, corrupting each other with loose conversation and insulting the passengers by indecent remarks; and all this because the ordinary channels of amusement are blocked up, in the vain hope of driving him and such as him, without trouble, into the arms of Mother Church. Vain hope! The poor criminal, when reduced, in prison, to reflect upon the circumstances that have contributed to his fall, always has Sabbath-breaking put into his mouth, and he confesses the justice of the charge. No doubt—*forbidden to work, forbidden to play*, uninduced to go to church—he was driven to clandestine amusement and riotous companionship in secret. No one in France ever talks of Sabbath-breaking as a cause of crime; no, for though the day is a day of worship it is also a day of pleasure; there is mass in the morning, but there is a dance at night, and thus youth and nature find a safety-valve. Injudicious duties always lead to contraband trade." But, so far as the legal aspect of the matter is concerned,

[1] *Id.* 11, 26.

all this is irrelevant. The attempt is made to sustain the constitutionality of Sunday laws on the ground of urgent social necessity, or, at least, their overwhelming advantage. To admit that they produce evil results, when applied both to labor and amusements, and to insist on retaining the former while abandoning the latter inhibition, is to shift, somewhat, the debatable ground, but it does not strengthen the argument in favor of the laws. For, then, the position of their supporters amounts to this: "We will force idleness on the citizen; but, as he is prone to injure himself when idle, we will give him every opportunity to spend his idle hours in innocent diversion; we will tempt him to vice, but we will give him a chance to avoid it." This is the method of the scientist who administers a deadly draught to a brute in order to test the value of another drug as an antidote. It is, of course, an utterly silly thing in legislation, and neither necessity nor expediency can be pleaded in its defence.

We have seen that the theory of a sanitary basis for the Sunday laws is historically erroneous, because the very idea of such laws originated with a set of religious enthusiasts, and the spirit of the first laws, which survives in all the later statutes to a greater or less degree, is the assertion of a dogma of the Cromwellian Church Militant. That this ground for sustaining Sunday laws is an *afterthought* of the courts—that is to say, that it is an attempt to find a sanction for these statutes in considerations which have never been the moving causes for their enactment—is also sufficiently proven by the contents of the statutes themselves. Obviously, if they had been designed to afford men the physical benefits of "rest," they would not have gone further and prohibited play as well as work. Rather, in the plenitude of their paternal jurisdiction, they would have provided specially for that relaxation or change of scene and interest without which mere rest may quite as likely prove an injury as a benefit. Thus, they would embrace requirements that theatres should be open at half-price, that railroads and steamboats should "run" extra excursions at reduced rates, that all public institutions, as libraries, museums and the like should be open, &c., &c. But none of these things are provided for; and there is not a Sunday law on the statute books of England or America which does not, by its very contents, refute the judicial assumption that it was passed for the worldly benefit of the citizens.

The fallacy of all attempts to sustain the Sunday laws on physical or social grounds has been pointed out merely in order to cover the subject with some degree of completeness. For the fact is that every position here assailed may be conceded, and still the constitutionality of Sunday laws will remain to be established. Those positions are briefly, but correctly, summarized in the North Carolina decision. With the word "religious" (as has been said) we have nothing to do here. But suppose this weekly rest is "essential to the physical and social elevation of a people," will it follow that an American legislature may, therefore, make such rest compulsory? By no means. This would arrogate to the legislature the authority of Lycurgus. There are many social as well as personal benefits most desirable for us to have, which, yet, no American law-makers can bestow on their constituents. Sunday laws interfere with the citizen's use of his own energies and of his own property. Such interference in a free country requires the most cogent arguments for its justification. The general result of this interference is, as has been well said, to establish a special "peace of Sunday." Now, the establishment and regulation of public peace, whether general or for certain times or occasions, is an exercise of what is known as the "police power" of the state. So, in Louisiana, the court relies on the "police power" for the sanction of Sunday laws, and gives a brief extract from Mr. Tiedemann's late work on "Limitations of the Police Power" as supporting this view.[1] And the "police power" is also relied on in Texas.[2] Now, no thoughtful mind can dispute the correctness of what was once said by Mr. Justice Chase: "By the rules which have been laid down for the construction of statutes and the latitude which has been indulged in their application, the British judges have assumed legislative power, and, under the pretence of judicial exposition, have in fact made a great portion of the statute law of the kingdom. Of these rules of construction, none can be more dangerous than that which, distinguishing between the intent and the words of the legislature, declares that a case not within the meaning of the statute (according to opinion of the judges) shall not be embraced in the operation of the statute, although it be clearly within the words, or *vice*

[1] *Walker's Case*, 39 La. Ann. 132 (1887).

[2] *Lundstrom's Case*, 25 Tex. App. 133 (1888).

versa, that a case within the meaning, though not within the words, shall be embraced."[1] And this observation applies with far greater force to constructions of the fundamental law, as embodied in a constitution, than it does to statutes, as Mr. Tiedemann's quotation from Judge Christiancy (*post*) shows that he appreciates. Bold, indeed, is the step for any court to take to declare that the "self-imposed restrictions on the will of the majority," contained in the very instrument to which the court itself owes its existence, do not mean what they clearly and distinctly assert. And it would seem that the historic importance, which the founders of our republic attached to the total separation of church and state, requires that the courts should jealously guard against their coalition, directly or indirectly, and that the necessity of the utmost individual liberty to the preservation of free institutions ought to be a commanding consideration in favor of making every presumption against the state's right to interfere with the volition of the individual. Yet, so far from finding a conclusive and overwhelming and absolute demand for compelling Sunday idleness, the Louisiana court, in the case just cited, after quoting a portion of Mr. Tiedemann's remarks, which evidently are not satisfactory to himself, can do no more than add, "the foregoing considerations are certainly rational and plausible" —surely hardly sufficient qualities in any argument to justify us in sustaining, on the strength thereof, an exercise of "police power," in spirit contradicting every assertion of individual liberty in our American constitutions.[2] And in connection with this dangerous and critical "police power," the most pregnant source of usurpations in all ages, we should specially bear in mind the wise words of Judge Christiancy: "Powers which can only be justified on this specific ground (that they are police regulations), and which would otherwise be clearly prohibited by the constitution, can be such only as are clearly necessary to the safety, comfort and well-being of society, or so imperatively required by the public necessity as to lead to the rational and satisfactory conclusion that the framers of the constitution could not, as men of ordinary prudence

[1] *Priestmann's Case*, 4 Del. 28 (1800).

[2] The Louisiana court cites a portion of Mr. Tiedemann's apology—it is no more—for Sunday laws, but not the portions which demonstrate that astute writer's perception of their untenable character. A few of these follow: "The most common form of legal interference

and foresight, have intended to prohibit their exercise in the particular case, notwithstanding the wording of the prohibition would otherwise include it."[1] The limits of this power are "difficult to define;" but we cannot go very far wrong in determining the legitimacy of its exercise in a given instance, if we bear in mind that it has no concern whatever with the results of individual conduct to the individual, but is limited exclusively to the consideration of its results to other persons, or the community at large. Thus, under its police power, the state may compel a man to submit to vaccination; this, not because if he remained unvaccinated he would be specially liable to small-pox, and if he were to have that disease he would probably die, but because his special liability in the case supposed is that he will become a source of contagion to others.

[1] *Walker's Case*, 9 Mich. 281 (1878).

in matters of religion is *that which requires the observance of Sunday as a holy day.* In these days the legal requirements do not usually extend beyond the compulsory cessation of labor and the closing of all places of amusement. But the public spirit which calls for the compulsory observance of these regulations is the same which in the colonial days of New England imposed a fine for an unexcused absence from Divine worship. Although other reasons have been assigned for the state regulation of othe bservance of Sunday, in order to escape the constitutional objections that can be raised against it, if it takes the form of a religious institution, those who are most active in securing the enforcement of the Sunday laws do so [*sic*] *because of the religious character of the day, and not for any economical reasons.* * * * The effectiveness of the laws is measured by the influence of the Christian idea of Sunday as a religious institution. But *Sunday as a religious institution can receive no legal recognition.* * * * Notwithstanding the strictly religious aspect the observance of a general day of rest has always assumed among all people and under all systems of religion, although the observance of such a day has always been thought to be a Divine injunction, it is claimed, *with much show of reason,* that this custom *was originally established as a sanitary regulation.* * * * And under our constitutional limitations it is only in its primary character that the observance of the day can be exacted. * * * The failure to observe this *law of nature calling for rest from labor on every seventh day*—for *this has been demonstrated by the experience of ages to be a law of nature*—is, like every other inordinate gratification of one's desires, *a vice not the subject of law.* The possible evil following from this 'vice' will not justify the state authorities in entering the house and premises of the citizen, and there compelling him to lay down his tool or his pen and refrain from labor, on the ground that his unremittent toil will possibly be to do damage to society through his children. How can it be proven *a priori* that that man needs the rest that the law requires him

This is an extreme case; but beyond this the police power certainly cannot go. It cannot, for example, compel a man with *caries* to submit to amputation, a man with a cancer to have it removed, a sufferer from consumption to swallow cod liver oil, a victim of obesity to take exercise, *or an overworked man to rest*, however advantageous these respective proceedings might be for the individuals mentioned. If it may do any one of these things, it may certainly do them all. If it may do any one of them, it may regulate the times and duration of sleep; the hours, quantity and quality of meals; the nature and the doses of medicine; the amount, style and thickness of clothing for all its citizens. And, as the mind is of far more importance than the body, every argument for bringing the control and management of the second within the purview of the police power of the state applies with far more cogency to the subjection of the first to the same supervision and direction. If the

to take? He may be fully able to continue his labor at least during a portion of Sundays without doing any damage to anybody. Furthermore, it may be shown that he has, for special reasons, or because his religion requires it, abstained from labor for the required time on some other day. * * * *The prevention of a trespass is the invariable purpose of a police regulation. It is the right of every one to enjoy, quietly and without disturbance, his religious liberty, and his right is invaded as much by noise and bustle on this day of rest, varying only in degree, as by a prohibition of religious worship according to one's convictions. Noisy trades and amusements, and other like disturbances of the otherwise impressive quiet of a Sunday, may therefore be prohibited on that day in complete conformity with limitations of the police power.* But the prosecution of noiseless occupations and the indulgence in quiet, orderly amusements, since they involve no violations of private right, cannot be prohibited by law without infringing upon the religious liberty of those who are thus prevented, and such regulations would therefore be unconstitutional. It is barely possible, but doubtful, that a law could be sustained under the principles here advanced which required that the front doors of stores and places of amusement should be kept closed on Sunday, but not otherwise interfering with the noiseless occupations and diversions. The total prohibition of such employments and labor on Sunday, except possibly for a reason to be suggested and explained later, could only be justified by the religious character of the day, and we have already seen that that aspect of Sunday cannot be taken into account in framing the Sunday laws. * * * *But there is, perhaps, a constitutional reason why the prohibition of labor on Sunday should be extended to other than noisy trades and employments.* * * * *In the ideal state of nature*, when free agency and independence of the behests of others may be considered factual, the *prosecution of a noiseless trade could not in any sense be considered as constituting a trespass or threatening one.* * * * But we are not living in a state of nature.

state may compel a man to be idle against his will because his digestion and circulation will be thereby improved, it may assuredly compel him to read certain books and refrain from reading certain others, because his mental health will be promoted by such a course; it may prescribe the subjects and the manner of his conversations; the degree and kind of the emotions which he is to manifest and *feel* on stated occasions, as his daughter's marriage, or the funeral of his mother, and so on. Preposterous as all this may sound, the inclusion of every one of these things within the police power of the state follows as a logical necessity from the inclusion therein of the right to compel an adult citizen to be idle at any time against his will, on the ground of advantage resulting to the idler. Is there any sounder reason for the invocation of the police power to establish this special peace of Sunday on the ground of its advantage to the state as a unit, or community? In an industrial civilization, where the "dignity of labor" is the incessant theme of speech and essay, and "labor problems" bid fair to crowd everything else out of newspapers and sermons, it sounds grotesque enough to hear compulsory idleness urged as a measure of public policy. And, indeed, it is sufficiently apparent to any unprejudiced mind, without argument, that, in the industrial stage, a state is directly injured by any obstruction to the activities of its population.

It remains to examine the merits of this "special peace" of Sun-

* * * *Those who most need the cessation from labor are unable to take the necessary rest if the demands of trade should require their uninterrupted attention to business.* And if the law did not interfere, the feverish, intense desire to acquire wealth, so thoroughly characteristic of the American nation, necessitating a reckless rivalry and competition, would ultimately prevent not only the wage-earners, *but likewise the capitalists and employers themselves*, from yielding to the warnings of nature and obeying the instinct of self-preservation by resting periodically from labor, even if the mad pursuit of wealth should not warp their judgment and destroy this instinct. Remove the prohibition of law, and this wholesome sanitary regulation would cease to be observed; no one, if he would, could do so. If the reasoning here presented be correct and the premises in the issues which has been formulated, the following conclusion is inevitable, viz., that no Sunday law is constitutional which does more than prohibit those acts which are noisy and are therefore calculated to disturb the quiet and rest of Sunday worshippers, and which in their prosecution demand, or are likely to demand, the service of others who cannot refuse to serve. * * * It is not maintained that this limitation upon the power of the state to regulate the observance of Sunday is recognized and endorsed by the de-

day with reference to those among whom the unwilling idler dwells. The contention is that if he was permitted to work as usual, he would disturb others. In what? Either in the exercises of public worship, or in private devotion. As to both, this involves an assumption which is as false in fact as it is insulting to the pious. Privately, it is their well-known custom to "seek advice and consolation" without reference to days; and publicly, they engage in worship on many days besides Sunday. To say nothing of Christmas, Good Friday, Ash Wednesday, &c., and the many "saints' days" which are venerated by our Roman Catholic and Episcopalian fellow-citizens, and "observed" by special services in their churches, we find Monday and Wednesday "prayer-meetings" a feature in those communions which are peculiarly interested in Sunday laws. But no one has ever pretended that it would be lawful, or even intimated that it is desirable, for the police power to require those who do not regard the anniversaries named, or attend the weekly prayer-meetings, to cease from their ordinary pursuits while others pray, or preach, or sing. Nor has any one asked that the wheels of commerce shall be stopped during his morning or evening or midday prayer and meditation in the solitude of his chamber, unless they happen on a Sunday. But if the "special peace" be not necessary for the proper and satisfactory performance of religious rites on one day of the

cisions of our courts. * * * The laws which prohibit quiet and orderly amusements cannot be sustained under the rule, and so also those laws which make void commercial paper and deeds which are executed on Sunday. * * * But although not generally supported by the authorities, it is believed to be the correct rule. It has been urged that this law, when founded upon this reason of protection to the individual, may be sustained, if it was confined in its operation to slaves, minors, apprentices and others, and designed to protect them from the cruelty of incessant toil. But the slave and apprentice is no more bound to obey the behests of others, and to work at their command, than a free laborer, and even the employer, under the irresistible force of competition in the struggle for existence and the accumulation of wealth. * * * Although the Jew and the Mohammedan have the same right to the quiet and undisturbed enjoyment of his [*sic*] holy day, the public welfare, which likewise is the mainspring to the Sunday laws, requires that his enjoyment of his religion should sustain the burden and annoyance occasioned by the general prosecution of trades and occupations on their [*sic*] holy days." This long extract is introduced here for the purpose of showing that so keen and competent a logician as Mr. Tiedemann has been able to find no apology for Sunday laws which is satisfactory either to himself or any un-

year, or week, it cannot certainly be necessary for such performance on any other.

But suppose it was. May it, on this ground, be lawfully established? If one man may stop another from working, on the ground that it disturbs him at his devotions on one day in the week, he may do it on all, or at any hour of the day. And if one man, or a set of men, selects one period for sacred service, and another another, and so on, the time for productive labor in the community may be easily frittered away altogether. But the fact is that such matters are, from their very nature, beyond the cognizance of legislatures and courts. Injuries to health or property are things understood of all men, may be estimated in money, and can be punished on an adjusted scale by law; but this is not true of "spiritual wrongs," such as interference with one's prayers by chopping wood or driving a wagon. Many persons would say that the prayers were useless, because the creed of the devotee was heretical; others that the worshipper's moral character was fatal to their efficacy; others, again,

prejudiced reader. As his long and labored argument adds absolutely nothing to the considerations elaborated by the courts, all of its positions will be found examined in the text. By observing particularly the italicized portions, we shall see that Mr. Tiedemann gravely, though perfunctorily, contends, (1) that Sunday laws are statutory embodiments of religious dogma; (2) that as such they can receive no recognition from American courts; (3) that because "it is claimed with much show of reason" that the religious dogma was originally a sanitary regulation, therefore (and therefore *only*) the dogma may be made into an American statute—a position which, if the views of leading investigators be correct, would require him to defend a law (which it is quite thinkable might be passed if "Orthodox Jews" should ever control an American legislature) making compulsory on all the circumcision enjoined by Moses, or a law imposing a fine for neglect of the ablutions favored by Zoroaster, and in fact laws for the enforcement of most, if not all, other ceremonial observances of early religions. But Mr. Tiedemann further maintains, (5) that it "has been demonstrated by the experience of ages" that Sunday or Sabbath idleness is "a law of nature;" but (6) that a violation of this law is a "vice" and not punishable, and that, therefore, though (7) noise disturbs religious devotions to such an extent that to permit A to pursue his noisy vocation when B desires to say his prayers is equivalent to forbidding B to say any prayers, and therefore it is within the "police power" to command A to cease from earning his living whenever the spirit may move B to pray—yet (8) noiseless trades and amusements cannot be forbidden on Sunday, unless "perhaps" on the ground that, if all work were not stopped by law, the community in general would at once proceed to work itself to death in "the feverish, intense

that prayer under any circumstances was a mere waste of time. And to save themselves from unseemly and interminable discussions of this sort, the courts have wisely held that a "spiritual wrong" neither entitles to injunction nor damages, but is *damnum absque injuria*.

So that, by the last ground remaining upon which Sunday laws have been sustained, we are brought face to face with this inconsistency—that A is punished as a criminal for doing that to B which the civil law declares to be a wrong which it can neither prevent nor equalize.

This ends our discussion of the constitutionality of Sunday laws. The aim of these three chapters has been to demonstrate that an established Sunday means an established church, whence it follows that it has no place among American institutions; that Sunday laws are in their essence immoral, demoralizing and un-Christian; and

desire to acquire wealth, so thoroughly characteristic of the American nation," forgetting, for this last point, the non-American origin of Sunday laws, and also omitting to furnish the much-to-be-desired information as to the effect of amusements in hastening that decay of the race which Sunday laws alone can arrest; and, although Mr. Tiedemann has just asserted that a "prohibition" of religious exercises is involved in the permission of "noisy trades" to the non-religious, he, somewhat brusquely, as it seems, announces (9) that "the public welfare, which, likewise, is the mainspring of the Sunday laws," requires that the Jew and the Mohammedan should sustain this "burden" from which "the public welfare" requires that the Christian shall be freed, notwithstanding the fact that "the Jew and the Mohammedan have the same right to the quiet and undisturbed enjoyment of a holy day" as the Christian! Finally, Mr. Tiedemann observes, (10) that his view is "not recognized and endorsed by the courts"—though the courts and he differ often only as to degree and not as to quality in the matter of reasoning—and admits that vital points of Sunday laws—as the prohibition of amusements and business—cannot be sustained. In this connection, the reader should peruse Mr. Tiedemann's conclusive refutation of the practicability, to say nothing of the expediency, of state interference with the contract of hiring, as between adults (section 178), and he will then doubtless consider that the Sabbatarian must be easily satisfied who will accept this writer as an advocate of Sunday laws. It is evident, as above remarked, that Mr. Tiedemann's effort is not wholly satisfactory to himself. The use of "perhaps," "it is claimed," "if the reasoning be correct," &c., sufficiently demonstrates this. For a similar exhibition of a great intellect chafing under galling harness, see *Cooley's "Constitutional Limitations," s. v. "Sunday."*

that every effort to defend them involves the maintenance of palpable absurdities.

With the hope that it may stimulate discussion of the subject, so much is offered as a contribution to the science of jurisprudence, and as essential to the completeness of the work. What follows is a digest, generally without comment, of the decisions on the various Sunday statutes.

CHAPTER IV.

WHAT IS SUNDAY?

We have seen that it is judicially settled that the destruction of Christianity is involved in the act of either working or playing on Sunday. It becomes, therefore, a matter of transcendent importance to know just what Sunday is. Every rightfully-constituted mind must shudder at the possibility that, by failing to observe the precise time of its beginning or ending,[1] some contribution may be unwittingly made to the evil work of disintegrating the religion of the country.

Scientific truth compels the admission that the "sanctity" of this day did not originate with Christianity. Among the Pagans it was known as "*dies solis*," or "the day of the sun," and was consecrated to Apollo.[2] Hence, Constantine, in his "First Sunday Law,"[3] calls it "venerable," a word unquestionably referring to its connection with Pagan rites, and probably introduced to incline the minds of his non-Christian subjects to a favorable view of his new prescriptions for Sunday idleness—which, however, it should be noted, were coupled with no prohibition of Sunday play.

When, then, does this "venerable day of the sun" begin and when does it end? Professor William Smith observes:[4] "The

[1] On this point, see *Shepard's* "*Theses Sabbatical*," Pt. III. The "sacred hours" could not, of course, be the same in different places.

[2] On the origin of the names of the days of the week, see Archbishop Hare's paper in "*Philological Magazine*," Vol. I.: "The earlier laws of Constantine, though in their effects favorable to Christianity, claimed some deference, as it were, to the ancient religion in the ambiguity of their language and the cautious terms in which they interfered with the liberty of Paganism. The rescript commanding the celebration of the Christian Sabbath bears no allusion to its peculiar sanctity as a Christian institution. It is 'the day of the Sun' which is to be observed by the general veneration. The believer in the new Paganism, of which the worship solar worship was the characteristic, might acquiesce without scruple in the sanctity of the first day of the week." *Milman Hist. Christ* (*Harper's Ed.*, 1855), p. 289.

[3] See Corp. Jur. Civ. Cod., L. III., T XII. (Table A.)

[4] Dic. Bible, *s. v.* "*Day*."

commencement of the civil day varies in different nations. The Babylonians reckoned it from sunrise to sunset; the Umbrians from noon to noon; the Romans from midnight to midnight; the Athenians and others from sunset to sunset. The Hebrews naturally adopted the latter reckoning."[1] Now, the first civil or statutory "consecration" of Sunday, as the courts would say, was made by Constantine's edict, already referred to. And this edict consecrated, according to the Roman practice, a period "from midnight to midnight." We may here quote two high English authorities. Coke thus distinguishes between two kinds of days: "*Dierum alii sunt naturales, alii artificiales; dies naturalis constat ex 24 horis, et continet diem solarem, et noctem,*" and, therefore, in indictments for burglary and the like, we say, *in nocte ejusdem diei. Iste dies naturalis est spatium in quo sol progreditur ab oriente in occidentem, et ab occidente, iterum, in orientem. Dies artificialis, sive solaris, incipit in ortu solis et desinit in occasu.* And of this day the law of England takes hold in many cases. Now, divers nations begin the day at divers times. The Jews, the Chaldeans and the Babylonians begin the day at the rising of the sun; the Athenians at the fall; the Umbri, in Italy, begin at midday; the Egyptians and Romans from midnight; and so doth the law of England, in many cases.[2]

Blackstone says: "In the space of a day, all the twenty-four hours are usually reckoned. * * * Therefore, if I am bound to pay money on any certain day, I discharge the obligation if I pay it before twelve o'clock at night; after which the following day commences."[3]

In the United States there is no uniformity on this subject. We are indebted for our compulsory idleness and gloom on Sunday to what has been sometimes eulogized as "the spirit of New England." It would seem, therefore, as if New England authority ought to settle for us the exact time which has been "set apart" from business and pleasure. But, strange to say, the rest of the country, while it has accepted the judgment of New England as to the duty and manner of the "observance" of the day, has refused to adopt her definition of the day itself. And it is further to be observed, that certain New England statesmen, while agreeing that "the

[1] See *Genesis i*, 5; *Exodus xii.*, 18; *Leviticus xxiii.*, 32.

[2] Co. Lit. 135 *a*.

[3] 2 Com. 141.

Sabbath" must be "kept" with great care, yet allowed only eighteen hours to the sacred day—possibly apprehending, for themselves or others, too great a burden in a Sabbath of their devising prolonged to the full twenty-four.

In a Massachusetts case, involving the validity of a writ, which, it was claimed, had been made and delivered to the officer on Sunday, the court called attention to the fact that by their act of 1791, chapter 58, the prohibition of labor, &c., was "limited to the time included between the midnight preceding and the sunsetting of the same day."[1] And the Maine statute names the same period, as was mentioned in a suit on a contract.[2]

On the other hand, some New Englanders have not been satisfied with an ordinary day's "observance." In a suit for damages, on account of the arrest of a delinquent tax-payer, the court of New Hampshire said that the statute of that state, passed in 1700 (12 Wm. III.), prohibited inn-keepers, &c., from allowing others than lodgers to be about their places "drinking, or idly spending their time, on Saturday nights, after the sun is set, or on the Lord's day, or the evening following," and required justices, &c., to prevent people from "opening their shops, or following their secular occasions or recreations in the evening preceding the Lord's day, or any part of the said day, or of the evening following,"[3] and said this law "was explicit as to the time, and evidently extended it beyond twenty-four hours." And the court further observed: "It is a well-known fact that many of the New England Puritans, adhering to the doctrine of the Hebrews, and believing it to be the doctrine of the Bible, held that the Sabbath, or 'holy time,' as they called it, began at sunset on Saturday night, and conscientiously abstained from all labor and recreation after that time, observing the evening preceding Sunday with the same scrupulous strictness as they did the day itself." And, after remarking that a later statute, forbidding labor, &c., gave no other definition of the time than to speak of it as "the first day of the week, commonly called the Lord's day," the court added: "The object of the legislature undoubt-

[1] *Johnson* v. *Day*, 17 Pick. 106 (1835).

[2] *Barker* v. *Fogg*, 34 Me. 391 (1852).

[3] The expression "evening following," after the words "Lord's day," shows that what we call "Sunday evening" was not a part of the "Lord's day" in the minds of those who passed this act.

edly was to prevent unnecessary labor and recreation during one-seventh part of the time. When they used the term 'day,' it is to be presumed that they intended it to be understood in its common acceptation—that is, a civil day, embracing twenty-four hours, and commencing and ending at midnight. Such, it is believed, has been the common understanding and practical exposition of the term in this and all other statutes in which it occurs. Under the statute which requires writs to be served within fifteen days before the sitting of the court to which they are returnable, the uniform practice has been to make service till midnight of the last day, but not afterwards. It has been suggested that the second section of the statute under consideration has qualified the term 'day,' as used in the preceding section, and restricted it to the natural day. The words are, 'that no person shall travel on the Lord's day, between sunrising and sunsetting, unless from necessity,' &c. In reply to this suggestion, it may be observed that the legislature probably considered traveling an offence distinct from those before enumerated. The statutes of Vermont, for some purposes, consider the Sabbath as beginning at sundown on Saturday and terminating at sundown the next day, and, for other purposes, as continued till midnight; and it expressly forbids the service of process between Saturday at sundown and twelve o'clock at night on Sunday, except in cases of treason, felony and breach of the peace, and in favor of bail apprehending their principal."[1]

Where a negotiation for the release of an arrested debtor began on Saturday, and was concluded about two o'clock Saturday night (*i. e.*, Sunday morning), the court in Connecticut allowed recovery on the note which was given "in the night season, preceding the Sabbath, when there is no law which expressly forbids it—and in this particular case it appears to be an interference to prevent the imprisonment of the maker's brother."[2] And, where a note for the same purpose was given between eleven and twelve o'clock on Saturday night, the court said: "All people agree that the artificial or solar day is the Sabbath, and that the Sabbath includes the whole of the natural day of twenty-four hours; but whether it includes the evening and night preceding, or any part of it, or the evening

[1] *Shaw* v. *Dodge*, 5 N. H. 462 (1851).

[2] *Carpenter* v. *Crane*, 1 Root 98 (1785).

and night succeeding, is a matter about which mankind differ." And undoubtedly the law meant to allow them liberty of conscience, in case they do not disturb others, and, accordingly, the note was held valid; "especially, as to hold it void would be to enable the defendant to take advantage of his own wrong act to injure the plaintiff."[1]

In the same state a party sued for assault and battery an officer who had arrested him for debt between twelve o'clock Saturday night and daybreak Sunday morning, and, by five judges against four, it was held that the day on which civil process was prohibited comprised the solar day only.[2] Judge Trumbull, of the majority, differed with the New Hampshire court in *Shaw* v. *Dodge*, in maintaining that the express mention of the time in the prohibition of traveling, as "Saturday night, after the sun has set, or on the Lord's day, or evening following," showed that the "Lord's day" meant only the solar day, and said: "According to the rules of construction, the words 'Lord's day' must be understood in the same manner in every part of the statute."[3] But the four dissenting judges were of opinion that the day was twenty-four hours, from midnight to midnight. (Swift, C. J., Trumbull, Edmond and Brainard, JJ.)

In holding that a verdict rendered at two o'clock Sunday morning was invalid, the Supreme Court of New York, after referring to the Connecticut, Massachusetts and New Hampshire cases, said: "A day consists of twenty-four hours, and commences and ends at midnight. Whenever, therefore, a statute forbids an act to be done on a particular day, it has reference to this mode of computation, unless there is some express declaration to the contrary," and cited instances wherein "our own statutes sometimes adopt the solar day, and sometimes only a part of it," and concluded that "the fact that such statutes have been adopted affords evidence that the acts limited to be done on the solar day might be performed on any portion of the natural day, were it not for legislative interference."[4]

In holding that the forwarding of cattle by a common carrier was

[1] *Mumford* v. *Buel*, 1 Root 145 (1789).

[2] *Fox* v. *Abel*, 2 Conn. 541 (1818).

[3] And the other four of the majority agreed in citing other portions of the statute, as tending to show what was meant by "the Lord's day" in the provision under consideration. See Smith's opinion, 550; Hosmer's opinion, 557; Gould's opinion, 559; Peters' opinion, 561.

[4] *Pulling* v. *People*, 8 Barb. 384 (1850).

a work of necessity, the Maryland court said: "In the regular division of time, Sunday embraces all of the twenty-four hours next ensuing the midnight of Saturday."[1]

Before dismissing the unsettled question, "What is Sunday?" we may note that its identification with "the Sabbath" is judicially established. A contract was made to deliver goods "on the first day of July." In a suit for non-delivery, the defendants pleaded that it would have been against the law for them to deliver, because the day named was "a Sabbath day." It was contended that this plea did not show that it was "Sunday," or "the Lord's day," mentioned in the statute, "which, being a penal act, must be strictly construed." But the court in Maryland, after considering the defects in the declaration, said: "The efforts of the counsel to escape from these obvious difficulties, by taking a distinction between the 'Sabbath' (as the day is described in the plea) and the 'Lord's day,' as mentioned in the act of Assembly, or Sunday, cannot avail. The Sabbath is, emphatically, the day of rest, and the day of rest here is the Lord's day, or Christians' Sunday. Ours is a Christian community, and the day set apart as a day of rest is the day consecrated by the resurrection of our Saviour."[2]

Where a party was indicted for hunting, the court in North Carolina said: "It was suggested in argument that our statute uses the word 'Sabbath,' instead of 'Sunday,' which is the term usually employed in our previous legislation. The words are not strictly synonymous, the word 'Saturday' signifying the seventh day of the week, and the word 'Sunday' signifying the first day of the week, commonly called the Lord's day. But, by common usage, the words are used indiscriminately, to denote the Christian Sabbath, to wit, Sunday. In *State* v. *Williams*, 4 Ired. 100, Ruffin, C. J., uses the words as synonymous."[3]

[1] *P., W. & B.* v. *Lehman*, 56 Md. 209 (1881).

[2] *Kilgour* v. *Miles*, 6 G. & J. 268 (1834).

[3] *Drake's Case*, 64 N. C. 589 (1870).

CHAPTER V.

NATURE OF THE ILLEGALITY OF A SUNDAY CONTRACT.

I. In General—Leaving Parties Where They Stand.

(a) *Between the Parties.*—The exact nature of the illegality of a Sunday contract has been several times considered. Two principles have been stated, in this connection, which appear to lead to opposite results. The first is, that if the contract be executed, it binds the parties.[1] So, in Wisconsin, the court said: "It by no means follows that a sale is void for all purposes. Where there was an actual transfer of property, it is not possible, thereafter, to recover it. Between the parties it was an executed contract, and, unless the defendant (a third person) can show a claim superior to that of the vendor, he cannot disturb that of the vendee."[2]

The nature of the invalidity of a Sunday sale, so far as it affects the vendor's remedy for a subsequent conversion by the vendee, was defined in Massachusetts in 1865, when it was held that such a sale is an illegal and void act, not merely at the election, or for the protection of either party, but upon grounds of public policy, and it would give the vendee no right of action whatever; and if the vendee subsequently converted the animal to his own use, the vendor must adopt the form of action suited to such an injury, and, being entitled to trover, he could not waive the tort, and sue in assumpsit.[3]

It might seem to follow from this, that an executed Sunday contract, since it binds the parties, must be as available, for action or

[1] *Ellis* v. *Higgins*, 32 Me. 34; *Greene* v. *Godfrey*, 44 Id. 25 (1857); *Morton* v. *Gloster*, 46 Id. 520 (1859); *Shuman* v. *Shuman*, 27 Pa. 90 (1856); *Foreman* v. *Ahl*, 53 Id. 325 (1867).

[2] *Moore* v. *Kendall*, 1 Chand. 33.

[3] *Ladd* v. *Rogers*, 10 Allen (Mass.) 209.

defence, between them, as any other contract. But another rule steps in, namely, that the law will leave the parties to an illegal contract where it finds them; and it appears that the execution of a Sunday contract, while it makes it obligatory on the parties, does not so far legalize it that either of them can set it up against the other. So, a vendor cannot recover his property,[1] nor a vendee who has paid, his money,[2] nor a pawnor his pledge (a watch, left to secure the price of a Sunday ride).[3]

In New Hampshire, in 1878, where A had sold B some cows, and had, afterwards, taken them from B, claiming that the title was not to pass until the price was paid, and for this taking B had brought trespass and recovered judgment and damages, on the ground that the cows were B's property, by virtue of the sale, which was absolute, A then sued B for the price of the cows. The court said: "The defendant is not estopped by the judgment in the trespass from setting up the Sunday law as a defence. The maxim *in pari delicto*, &c., was not established for the benefit of one party, or of the other. The law does not leave the weaker at the mercy of the stronger, nor give the vendor a remedy by allowing him to retake the property illegally sold; it leaves the parties where their illegal contract left them; when executed, it will not assist the party who has parted with his money or property to recover it back; when executory, it will not compel performance. It would not leave the parties where their illegal contract left them, if it did not maintain the title acquired by the contract. B was in possession of the cows, as of his own property, by the assent of A. When the latter retook them, B was enabled to maintain trespass, because A could not then be heard to controvert his title."[4]

A and B exchanged horses. A, on Tuesday, took the horse he had given B away. B brought replevin, recovered the horse taken, and kept both. The recovery was sustained; the court said: "The plaintiff was in possession, and the defendant, by force, and without

[1] *Horton* v. *Buffington*, 105 Mass. 399 (1870). See, also, *Clapp* v. *Hale*, 112 Id. 368 (1873); *Chestnut* v. *Harbaugh*, 78 Pa. 473 (1875); *Block* v. *McMurray*, 56 Miss. 217 (1878); *Melchoir* v. *McCarty*, 31 Wis. 252.

[2] *King* v. *Green*, 6 Allen 139 (1863).

[3] *Thompson* v. *Williams*, 58 N. H. 248.

[4] *Kinney* v. *McDermott*, 5 Iowa 674 (1881).

the knowledge of the plaintiff, removed the horse from the plaintiff's stable. The question is, by what right did the defendant possess himself of the horse? The burden was on him to show his right. In doing so, he would necessarily be compelled to introduce the Sunday contract in evidence. There is some conflict upon the question whether a vendee will be allowed to retain the property, without paying the price. In our opinion, he should, on the ground that the law will leave the parties where it finds them."[1]

Whatever the theoretical merits of this rule, it is plain that its unvarying application may result in equity under some circumstances, and, under others, in rank injustice. Thus, it was no more than fair that the person who had pledged his watch to secure the hire of a horse and buggy should be prevented from recovering possession of the pawn, while refusing to pay for the team, as was done by the decision in *King* v. *Green*. But the practical outcome in the New Hampshire case was, that A was compelled to pay $75, and relinquish his cows, without consideration, to B. And in the Iowa case, one party to the exchange was enabled to retain his own horse, and the horse of the other party, also. Such unjust results as these could hardly have been contemplated in the passage of laws ostensibly framed "in the interests of morality and religion."

The unequal working of the rule of leaving the parties where they stand, and its liability to abuse, has been held fatal to its universality in Michigan. There the principle is thus enunciated: "As a general rule, courts of law have left the parties to an executed illegal contract in the position in which they have placed themselves, refusing to aid either of them, when equally in fault. But this is a question purely of public policy, and, consequently, there are exceptions to the rule. Courts should give, or refuse, their aid, as the one or the other course will be most likely to discourage such contracts, and to promote the public welfare. The illegality here in question is of a peculiar kind. The contract is not illegal, in respect to the consideration, or the thing done, or agreed to be done; these are neither immoral, nor forbidden by law. The illegality consists wholly in making the contract on a particular day. And we think it much more in accordance with sound public policy to

[1] *Sergeant* v. *Butts*, 21 Vt. 99 (1849).

treat the contract as utterly void, and to allow the plaintiff, by tendering back what he had received (or doing what is in his power to place the vendee *in statu quo*) to recover back his property, than to refuse him a remedy, and thereby to affirm the contract as valid. To refuse all remedy in such cases, would be to open a wide door to fraud. It would operate not only as a trap to the ignorant and unwary, but as a direct encouragement to swindling. A shrewd and dishonest man, knowing his victim could obtain no legal redress, might, by fraudulent misrepresentations, or by tempting offers, which he could well afford to make, obtain money or property to any extent, without consideration, or liability to pay. One object of the statute was to prevent the making of contracts on Sunday; but to refuse to sustain an action to recover back property sold on Sunday would be offering a premium to the dishonest to make their contracts on that day. The rule we have adopted takes away from all parties this temptation."[1]

The same view of the subject was taken in Massachusetts, where it was said: "It is a question, undoubtedly, to be determined by the court upon considerations of public policy. But those considerations must be general, and not such merely as arise out of the facts of the particular case. Where the payment, or delivery, is made for the furtherance of an immoral or illegal purpose, the court will not help the guilty party to revoke, although another, equally guilty, may thereby make an undeserved gain. But, where the illegality consists in the time or mode in which the transaction takes place, and not in the character of the transaction itself, the court will undoubtedly regard the position of the parties in respect to the subject-matter. Thus, in the case of a horse, delivered in pursuance of an illegal contract on the Lord's day, although the owner cannot recover upon his contract, and can have no remedy for excessive use or injury to his horse, while in the possession of the hirer, yet he is not deprived of his title to the horse, and he may, at any time, retake possession, and thus be restored to all his rights. The fact of an illegal bailment, or delivery, without any purpose to pass the title, will not enable the party receiving the property to convert it to his own use, or withhold it from the

[1] *De Forth* v. *W. & M. Co.*, 52 Wis. 320 (1881).

owner, without any legal liability therefor. In case of a contract of sale, not executed by payment of the consideration, when the contract remains executory on one side, the law which declares the executory part of the contract void might well regard the partial execution ineffectual. It is not necessary, however, to decide the point."[1]

It seems, also, that the parties will not be "left where they are found," if either of them was not mentally competent to contract at the time of their agreement. Thus, in Mississippi, in 1871, the court instructed as follows: "If the jury should decide that the seller was intoxicated to a degree that he was not competent to understand the nature and quality of the business, or to make a contract, then the parties are not *in pari delicto*, and he would not be bound by the sale, although made on Sunday."[2]

II. The Question of Completion.

(a) *When Begun on Sunday.*—The general doctrine that a Sunday contract, to come within the statute, must be complete, was thus laid down in New Hampshire, in 1860: "If anything remain to be done on some other day, the contract will not be void. It is not sufficient to avoid a contract that it grows out of a transaction commenced on Sunday. To render it void, it must be closed or perfected on that day."[3]

Where the vendor called on the vendee and proposed to sell him some land, and the parties agreed to the price, bounds and time of payment, but that no deed should be made out till the vendor's partner should arrive and examine the land, and the vendee subsequently advanced the price, and the vendor's partner refused to give a deed, it was held *assumpsit* would lie for the price paid.[4]

Certain goods were selected and set apart, the prices agreed on and bill made out, and two of the articles delivered; it was agreed that the remainder should be delivered next day; the two delivered were handed to a friend of the defendant, that he might show them to his wife, who wanted such goods. *Held*, that the sale was incomplete.[5]

[1] *Horton* v. *Buffington*, 105 Mass. 399 (1870).

[2] *Scarfe* v. *Morgan*, 4 M. & W. 270.

[3] *Merrill* v. *Downs*, 41 N. H. 72 (1860).

[4] *Ibid.*

[5] *Rosenblatt* v. *Trunsley*, 73 Md. 536.

A's attorney wrote to B, requesting him to say to C that he could purchase certain land of A for a certain sum. B handed C the letter on Saturday, and that night C wrote an answer, addressed to the attorney, and accepting the proposition. On Sunday he carried this letter to B's house, told him of the acceptance, and requested him to read the letter, which he did. At his further request, B next day carried the letter to the post-office. *Held*, that the posting was not the execution of an agency delegated on Sunday, but if it was, the act was capable of ratification.[1]

A sold B, the son of C, his principal, a horse, by a verbal agreement, and the animal was delivered and the price paid on Tuesday. *Held*, that the transaction was not complete till Tuesday, and action would not lie on a warranty.[2]

Where a horse was sold and a check given, and a bill of sale deposited with a third party, who was to hold it for the vendor's security till the check was paid, and it was paid on Monday, and the horse and bill of sale afterwards delivered to the vendee on a secular day, an action on a warranty failed.[3] The court observed: "It is contended that the plaintiff overcomes the obstacles thus presented to his right of recovery, inasmuch as he can trace his claim without a resort to the proof of that part of the transaction which took place on Sunday; that proof of the representations made on Saturday, together with the production of the papers bearing date of Monday, in which the sale and receipt of the purchase-money are acknowledged by the defendant to have been as of that day, are sufficient *prima facie* evidence to establish the right to recover; and that the defendant cannot set up his own illegal act against it. But this is too strict an interpretation of the rule. It is true that a plaintiff can never recover where he has to trace his title through an illegal act. But it does not follow that he can recover where he technically avoids proof of the illegal act. The defendant can show that the plaintiff's evidence is not true. If the whole evidence, properly admissible on both sides, discloses the fact that the plaintiff's claim is founded on an illegal transaction, he cannot recover. A promissory note, dated on a secular day, makes out a *prima facie* case. But that is defeated by proof that such note was, in fact,

[1] *Bryant* v. *Booze*, 55 Ga. 448 (1875).

[2] *Bloxsome* v. *Williams*, 5 D. & R. 84.

[3] *Plaisted* v. *Palmer*, 63 Me. 576 (1874).

made and delivered on Sunday. So, it is admissible to show when the bill of sale in this case was made and delivered, and when the consideration was paid."

It has been intimated that a horse-trade begun within the prohibited time, and completed afterwards, would be void;[1] but, where a horse was "traded" on Saturday, and the vendee then authorized to take possession of him in the vendor's stable, it was held that this amounted to delivery, and the contract was consummated on Saturday, though the horse was not taken from the stable till Sunday.[2]

In Indiana, in 1883, A agreed to trade a colt with B for a mare, if C assented. B was to retain colt and mare till C's assent. Afterwards, though C had assented, A removed his colt from B's custody, and D bought it with notice of the previous transaction. B thereupon sued A for the expense of keeping the colt, but dismissed his action before trial, and sued D in replevin. The court said: "Upon the assent of C, the contract ceased to be executory and be executed, and thenceforth the property and possession were both in B * * * the fact that B brought an action for keeping the colt did not conclude him; it may have been some evidence of assent, to the result of the contract, but it was by no means conclusive. There was no election of inconsistent remedies, creating an estoppel * * * had a judgment been obtained and insisted upon, we should have been faced by a very different question."[3]

A bought fifteen mules from B, and gave his note for them; two of the mules were not delivered till Monday; it was held there could be no recovery on the note.[4]

In the case of a sale of pigs, the court below instructed that, though the pigs were selected and marked, and the price to be paid for them fixed on Sunday, yet, if the pigs were to be weighed and delivered on Monday, and were so weighed and delivered, the contract of sale would not be void. It was held on appeal that this was ambiguous, and that whatever rights the parties had grew out of the acts on Monday, which could not validate the previous void transaction.[5]

[1] *Lyon* v. *Strong*, 6 Vt. 219 (1834).

[2] *Peake* v. *Conlan*, 43 Iowa 297 (1876).

[3] *Kuhns* v. *Gates*, 92 Ind. 66.

[4] *Foreman* v. *Ahl*, 55 Pa. 325 (1867).

[5] *Bradley* v. *Rea*, 14 Allen 20 (1867).

Where nothing passed in reference to the sale of a note, except propositions and negotiations, through a common friend of vendor and vendee, until Sunday, and, on this day, the money was paid, and the note endorsed to the vendee, and delivered to the friend, who, on the same day, delivered it to the vendee, it was held these proceedings constituted the contract itself, and the latter was void.[1]

Where a woman was induced to make a contract of sale of her property by false representation on a previous day, it was held that her right to avoid the contract was independent of the question whether the sale and delivery were made on the Lord's day; that the property remained hers, and a subsequent demand by her of payment, and the vendee's promise to pay, would amount to a sale, and support an action against him not founded on the previous contract, but treating this as never made, by reason of the fraud practiced on the previous day.[2]

A instructed B, a broker, to purchase goods for him, and sell at any profit. On Saturday B made the purchase, and on Sunday called on C and offered to sell the goods; B objected to delivering the contract till Monday, but, on C's importunity, delivered a "contract note," and C paid the brokerage, and on the same night made an entry of his purchase, and filled it up with the name of the party from whom he had made it on Monday. Afterwards, B communicated the contract to A, to whom he delivered the "sold note" some days afterwards. C refused to fulfill his contract, and a suit was brought against him. It was held that the contract was completed on Sunday, and void.[3]

A deed begun on Sunday and executed afterwards is valid,[4] and so, with one signed and acknowledged and afterwards delivered,[5] and a bond subsequently delivered is valid.[6] And so it has been said: "A surety, who authorizes his principal, on Sunday, to deliver an instrument, signed by the surety, on that day, is bound by such delivery. The reason is obvious. The authority to make

[1] *Smith* v. *Foster*, 41 N. H. 215.

[2] *Chiswell* v. *Carey*, 115 Mass. 560 (1874).

[3] *Smith* v. *Sparrow*, 4 Bing. 84.

[4] *Tracy* v. *Jenks*, 15 Pick. 465 (1834).

[5] *Shuman* v. *Shuman*, 27 Pa. 90 (1856); *Love* v. *Wells*, 25 Ind. 503 (1865).

[6] *Pierce* v. *Richardson*, 37 N. H. 306 (1858); *Hall* v. *Parker*, 37 Mich. 594 (1877).

the delivery, but for the statute, is ample and complete. The statute does not affect it, for the reason that it alone prohibits the enforcements of contracts executed on the Sabbath day."[1]

A subsequent delivery also makes a Sunday note valid.[2]

A and B went to C's house on a week-day and arranged for a loan, for which their joint note was to be given. On Sunday, it was drawn and signed. Next day, A went to C with the note and delivered it, and received the money. In a suit on the note, B contended that he was not liable, because the note was executed on Sunday, and it did not appear that he gave authority for its delivery at any other time, and that such authority, given on Sunday, would be equally void with the execution on that day. The court said: "The point is not well taken. C performed no act, in relation to the loan, or the note, on Sunday, and it does not appear that he knew any one else was to do so, or did do so. He made the loan on a week-day, and received the note on another week-day; and he received it from one of the two parties who were to give it, and he had a right to assume that that party had a proper authority from the other to make the delivery. The presumption of such authority is, under the circumstances, conclusive."[3] Where a note was dated Monday, and signed by one maker on Sunday, but not delivered till Monday to the payee, who was ignorant that it was signed on Sunday, and the delivery was by another maker, it was held a ratification, making the note valid; and the case was held not to be affected by the principle that the parol authority to deliver upon another day was void, because the delivery was in pursuance of an arrangement previously made, and because the note was in the control of the makers till the delivery, and the possession of one of the joint makers must be regarded as the possession of both.[4] The question, to whom must the delivery be made, was thus dealt with in Indiana, in 1877: "Signing and delivery of a note to a third person, or co-maker, did not make the contract. It required delivery

[1] *Evansville* v. *Morris*, 87 Ind. 269 (1882). See, also, *Prather* v. *Hanlon*, 6 Bush 185 (1860); *Kendig's Case*, 2 Pa. 448 (1846); *Young's Case*, 23 Minn. 551 (1877).

[2] *Lovejoy* v. *Whipple*, 18 Vt. 379 (1846); *Cass* v. *Whitney*, 27 Id. 272 (1855); *Crosby* v. *Blanchard*, 50 Id. 676 (1878); *Hill* v. *Dunham*, 7 Gray 543 (1856); *Cranson* v. *Goss*, 107 Mass. 439 (1871); *Flanagan* v. *Meyer*, 41 Ala. 132 (1867).

[3] *Beman* v. *Wessels*, 53 Mich. 549.

[4] *King* v. *Fleming*, 72 Ill. 21.

to the payee, to complete the execution. It cannot be said that the delivery to a third person, or co-maker, on Sunday, carried with it implied authority that the latter must deliver it to the payee, as perhaps it would, if so delivered on a business day; for, if the maker so delivered it on Sunday, with the express authority to re-deliver on a business day, the act, having been done on Sunday, would have been void. Where an express authority is insufficient to authorize an act, no implied authority can arise."[1]

A bill of exchange drawn on Sunday is valid, if subsequently presented; and it will not be presumed that a bill was accepted on Sunday, because it was dated on that day.[2]

It was held in Pennsylvania, in 1855, that written guaranty that another will fulfill a contract was not void, because executed on Sunday, unless delivered to the obligee on that day, or he had knowledge of the time of its execution.[3] In Massachusetts, in 1852, where a guaranty was given on Sunday for the payment of rent, reserved in a lease, which latter, though then prepared, was not executed and delivered until a week-day following, in a suit on the guaranty, the court said: "It is urged, on the part of the plaintiff, that this contract of guaranty was executed before the making of the lease, and did not take effect, as a contract, until the execution of the lease. * * * But the difficulty in this case is, that the contract of guaranty was wholly made and executed on the Lord's day. It may have had no legal vitality attached to it until the subsequent execution of the lease, but that does not remove the taint that affects the guaranty, by reason of its being made in violation of the statute."[4]

The rule as to subsequent delivery also applies to a contract of sale,[5] and a receipt for goods.[6]

Arbitrators were chosen and met on Saturday, and remained until after midnight listening to the parties and their counsel. They then retired for consultation, and between one and three o'clock Sunday morning they made their award known, both parties being present, and no objection being made on account of the time when

[1] *David* v. *Barger*, 57 Ind. 54.

[2] *Begbie* v. *Levy*, 1 Tyrw. 130 (1830); *S. C.*, 1 Cromp. & J. 180.

[3] *Sherman* v. *Roberts*, 1 Grant 261.

[4] *Merriam* v. *Stearns*, 10 Cush. 257.

[5] *Lamore* v. *Frisbie*, 42 Mich. 186 (1879).

[6] *Harris* v. *Morse*, 49 Me. 432.

the case was submitted and the award made. The award was sustained.[1]

A board of town supervisors were authorized to issue certain bonds only on petition, signed by a fixed number of tax-payers. A bill for injunction against the issue, on the ground that some of the signatures were procured on Sunday, was sustained.[2]

Where a purchaser on Sunday afterwards resold, it was held the article could not be attached for the original owner's debt.[3]

In England, in 1838, a mare was sent to be served, and the service was performed on Sunday. The owner of the stallion claimed a lien on the mare for his charges and retained possession of her. In replevin for the mare by her owner, the court said: "This lien would be supported, though it were, or might have been, illegal to have performed this operation on a Sunday."[4]

THE QUESTION OF COMPLETION—*Continued.*

(b) *When Finished on Sunday.*—A farmer agreed on Saturday to purchase land, but, as he was unwilling to leave his work to execute the papers, it was agreed they should be signed on Sunday, which was done. In a suit on a note for the purchase-money, the court said: "Inasmuch as the plaintiff was a party to the illegal agreement, that the note should be made on Sunday, the courts will not aid either party to enforce its collection, but leave the parties where it finds them."[5] But where a sale was completed on a previous day, and on Sunday a note was given for a balance of the purchase-money, the court said: "The note, not the consideration, was illegal; but the land having been sold on the week-day, the vendor did not lose the purchase-money by taking an illegal note. He could have brought an action for the balance of the unpaid purchase-money, or filed a bill to enforce a vendor's lien."[6]

An agent of A's bargained with B for a tract of land, and moved A's hands on it. A few days after, on a Sunday, the money was paid, and a deed for the land made. In a suit for the purchase-money, A set up the defence of Sunday contract. The court said: "The parties being *in pari delicto*, the law will leave them where it

[1] *Morgan* v. *Bailey*, 59 Ga. 683.

[2] *Tucker* v. *West*, 29 Ark. 386 (1874).

[3] *Drake* v. *Bush*, 57 Ga. 179.

[4] *Johnson* v. *Wills*, 7 Gray 164.

[5] *Lamore* v. *Frisbie*, 42 Mich. 182.

[6] *Crosby* v. *Blanchard*, 50 Vt. 696 (1878).

found them. The defendant is found in possession of this land, and, though the deed was made and the money paid on Sunday, and the consummation of the contract was thus illegal the law will help neither side." And, referring to 16 Ga. 461, and 44 Ga. 541, 642, it added: "In the case at bar, it seems the verbal trade was really made on another day, and consummated on Sunday. This, therefore, is a stronger case for the defendant than those referred to."[1]

It was laid down in Massachusetts, in 1856, that where money is voluntarily received, in payment of a pre-existing debt, and appropriated by the receiver to his own use, he cannot enforce payment again.[2]

So, in Michigan, in 1879, it seems to have been held immaterial that payments on a contract were made on this day, where the money never was returned, and was allowed on the final accounting.[3]

A and B exchanged horses. It was agreed that, if a swelling on the horse which B got did not subside in a certain time, B should pay damages to be estimated by C. The swelling did not subside. A requested B to go with him to C, to get the damage estimated. B told him he might go alone. This A did, and C, on examining the horse, made an estimate of the damage, but declined to announce his decision, except in the presence of both parties. A requested B to go with him to hear the announcement, but B told him he might as well go alone, and get a memorandum of the sum, signed by C. This A did on Sunday. On B's declining to pay the sum awarded, A brought suit and recovered. The court said that whatever liability the defendant was under to the plaintiff was upon the contract, and the agreement to pay the damages was one wholly dependent upon C's estimating such.[4]

It was said in Indiana: "If it is illegal to make a contract on Sunday, it certainly is illegal to contract to perform one requiring common labor on that day."[5]

[1] *Pate* v. *Wright*, 30 Ind. 476.

[2] *King* v. *Fleming*, 72 Ill. 21 (1874); *Banks* v. *Werts*, 13 Ind. 203 (1857); *Perkins* v. *Jones*, 26 Id. 499 (1866); *Kuhns* v. *Gates*, 92 Id. 66 (1883).

[3] *Adams* v. *Gay*, 19 Vt. 358 (1847). The opinion in this case deserves careful reading.

[4] *Flinn* v. *St. John*, 51 Vt. 334.

[5] *Sayle* v. *Wellman*, 11 R. I. 465 (1873).

III. The Question of Ratification.

It has been held that a Sunday contract may be ratified so as to bind,[1] though, where executory, it can only be affirmed by mutual consent;[2] and that "any act done by the parties on a week-day, which recognizes it as a contract existing between them, is a ratification;"[3] and that "where the defendant retains the property, either on the ground of ratification, or of a new promise, for which the retention of the property would be a sufficient consideration, the plaintiff is entitled to recover."[4]

On the other hand, some authorities declare a Sunday contract incapable of ratification, in the strict sense of the term.[5] It has also been observed that, where a previous contract has been made on Sunday, "a valid contract between the same parties with reference to the same subject-matter may be made upon a week-day."[6] And "when nothing is done towards the execution of the contract, until a subsequent period, the fact that a similar contract had been previously made on Sunday will not bring a subsequent contract within the statute. This is not a ratification of a contract previously made, but a new and substantive contract."[7]

It was said in New Jersey: "Stating, at the time of the bargain, to a scrivener, that he might reduce it to writing, for the purpose of being signed, is not the making of a new bargain;"[8] and it seems to be most generally considered that for such a subsequent contract, a promise on Sunday is a sufficient consideration, "and perhaps the acts and conversations of the parties on Sunday, in reference to a contract, might be shown, as explanatory of their subsequent acts and conversations, tending to show a new contract."[9]

But it is further observed that "there can be no such thing, strictly speaking, as a ratification of a transaction, which, at the

[1] *Pope* v. *Linn*, 50 Me. 83 (1863); *Bradley* v. *Rea*, 103 Mass. 188 (1869); *Shippey* v. *Eastwood*, 10 Ala. 198 (1846).

[2] *Harrison* v. *Colton*, 39 Iowa 16.

[3] *Butler* v. *Lee*, 11 Ala. 885.

[4] *Ryno* v. *Darby*, 5 Gr. (N. J.) 231 (1869).

[5] *Tucker* v. *Mowrey*, 12 Mich. 378 (1864).

[6] *Reeves* v. *Butcher*, 31 N.J. 224 (1865).

[7] *Gwin* v. *Simes*, 61 Mo. 335 (1875). See, also, *Clough* v. *Davis*, 9 N. H. 500; *Allen* v. *Deming*, 14 Id. 133 (1843); *Melchoir* v. *McCarty*, 31 Wis. 252 (1872).

[8] *Tucker* v. *West*, 29 Ark. 386 (1874).

[9] *Smith* v. *Case*, 2 Oreg. 190.

time of its performance, was prohibited by statute. * * * It is going quite far enough to maintain that the consideration emanating from the tainted contract will be sufficient to form the foundation of a new express promise."[1]

So, where money was loaned on Sunday, and a note given therefor, a mortgage, made on a subsequent day, reciting the consideration of the loan, and the giving of the note, which it conceded to be illegal, and stipulating that if the money specified in the note be not paid at the time designated therein, the conveyance shall remain in force, was held valid.[2]

And it was held that where the vendee kept the land, for which a note was given, he could ratify the note by an express promise, on a week-day, to pay it (though the promise would be no ratification as to a party who signed the note as surety); "for the moral obligation was as strong, or stronger, than in the case of a note barred by limitations or discharged by bankruptcy."[3]

A horse which was for sale was left at a tavern. A party came to the tavern on Sunday, said he had bought the horse, and took him away; but, on being sued for the price, alleged that the sale was made on Sunday. The court said: "It was the allegation of the defendant, and he must sustain it by proof. His taking him away on Sunday was no proof that he bought him on that day."[4]

Where a letter was written and received, requesting, and promising to pay for, services, and it did not appear the offer was accepted that day, but the work was performed on next Monday or Tuesday, the court said: "The acceptance on Monday or Tuesday was not, in itself, a violation of the statute. So that the defence must rest solely upon the fact that the defendant himself was guilty of an illegal act, in preparing and sending his offer. By the authority of the cases referred to, this is not sufficient to enable him to avoid his contract; and, independently of any authority, this conclusion is reasonable."[5]

[1] *Catlett* v. *M. E. Church*, 62 Ind. 365 (1878). See, also, *Day* v. *McAllister*, 15 Gray 433 (1860); *Ladd* v. *Rogers*, 11 Allen 209 (1865).

[2] *Bradley* v. *Rea*, 14 Allen 20 (1867).

[3] *Tillock* v. *Webb*, 56 Me. 100 (1868); *Kountz* v. *Price*, 40 Miss. 341 (1866); *Ryno* v. *Darby*, 5 Gr. (N. J.) 231 (1869).

[4] *Hadley* v. *Snevily*, 1 W. & S. (Pa.) 477 (1843).

[5] *Tuckerman* v. *Hinkley*, 9 Allen 452 (1864).

Where the defendant came to the plaintiff's house and said, if the plaintiff would do certain work for him, he would pay when the job was completed; and the plaintiff considered the subject on Monday, and went to work at the job on Tuesday, it was held he could recover.[1]

The court below charged the jury that, though a contract for the plaintiff's labor was made on Sunday, yet, if plaintiff did the work, he was entitled to the reward. On appeal, it was said: "A clear distinction is made by the authorities between a suit to enforce a promise or undertaking entered into on Sunday, and a suit on a contract made on Sunday for work and labor, and for the doing of anything, where the thing to be done is afterwards performed by the party. It would be a fraud in one who has the consideration of a contract on a week day to set up the invalidity of the contract, because made on Sunday. He re-affirms the contract by receiving the consideration. At any rate he is bound for the value of the services."[2]

Where, on Sunday, the defendant requested the plaintiff to give him the service of his horse in a certain contingency, but the plaintiff's reply did not appear, and, the contingency afterwards arising, the service was rendered on another day; and the defendant afterwards asked the plaintiff if the service had been rendered, and, being told it had, said, "It is all right," and admitted to others that it had been, and he owed the plaintiff for it, a suit for the value of the services was sustained.[3]

An agreement that A should superintend putting up of ice by B, but, first, should go South and look over the market, and decide whether it was advisable to put it up, and that B should furnish the money and the profits be shared equally, was held to be an agreement for the formation of a partnership then and there, and was invalid.[4]

It was said in Wisconsin, in 1884, that a subsequent occupation of the premises, and payment of rent, will not render a lease valid, as it is incapable of ratification.[5]

[1] *Stackpole* v. *Symonds*, 3 Fost. 229.

[2] *Meriwether* v. *Smith*, 44 Ga. 541.

[3] *Dickerson* v. *Richmond*, 97 Mass. 45 (1867).

[4] *Durant* v. *Rhener*, 26 Minn. 362 (1880).

[5] *Vinz* v. *Beatty*, 6 Wis. 645.

Of an agreement for renting, it was said in Alabama, in 1853: "Neither party can set it up as an agreement, yet it may be looked to, as a circumstance, with others, to account for their after conduct, in relation to the possession of the premises, after the expiration of the first term of rent;"[1] and it was held that declarations or admissions on Sunday might be used to explain the character of the tenant's possession.

It may also be noted that the retention of money loaned on Sunday is a sufficient consideration for a subsequent promise to repay it.

But, though an executed Sunday contract may form the consideration for a subsequent promise, "while the contract remains unexecuted, when nothing has passed between the parties, and they remain as they were at the time the contract was made, a mere promise to execute it will have no validity;" and, accordingly, where a party made a contract of subscription, and admitted to third persons that he had made it, and would pay it, it was held void, as it would have been, had he made a direct promise to the other party, unless it was founded on some consideration different from the subscription itself.[2] And in all such cases "the rights of the parties depend exclusively upon their agreements on the day when it is lawful for them to perform secular business."[3]

And, finally, it has been held in some states that a Sunday contract is no consideration for a subsequent agreement.[4] Of an agreement for the use and occupation of land, under which it was subsequently occupied, the court said: "It was either a ratification and adoption of a previous imperative contract, or was the foundation of a mere implied provision to pay for the use of the land what the same was reasonably worth."[5]

It was said in Indiana, in 1866: "The question is, will a promise be implied from the mere retention of the money paid on the contract? It is evident that the English authorities have not gone to this extent. The common law binds us, as we have adopted the common law by statute."[6]

But, in an earlier case, in the same state, where the terms of a sale were agreed on, and the property delivered to the vendee on

1 *Rainey* v. *Caffs*, 22 Ala. 288 (1853).

2 *Tucker* v. *Mowrey*, 12 Mich. 378.

3 *Myers* v. *Meinrath*, 101 Mass. 366.

4 *Block* v. *McMurray*, 56 Miss. 217.

5 *Fenneller* v. *Ridler*, 5 B. & C. 406 (1829).

6 *Perkins* v. *Jones*, 26 Ind. 499 (1866).

Sunday, and he retained possession until it was levied on by the sheriff under an execution against the vendor's property, and, in the meantime, with the assent of the vendor, re-sold portions of it, in the ordinary course of business, and, in addition, he, on a day subsequent to the sale, paid, and the vendor received, at least one-half the consideration for which the property was sold, it was held that the contract had been ratified, so as to render it valid.[1]

It was said in Vermont: "A refusal to have the contract rescinded, followed by a retention of the property, cannot be considered a stronger or more unequivocal ratification of such contract than, in this case, are the several payments, which have been made on the note, followed by the same act in retaining the property. If there had been no subsequent payments, and the case had stood upon the mere retention of the property, whether that circumstance alone would ratify the contract we are not called upon to decide. Evidently, it would not have that effect in the English courts."[2]

In Alabama it has been held that the fact that a party retains possession of the property does not imply a promise to pay the consideration; it is necessary that there should have been a demand and refusal of the property, or a promise to pay for it, or something equivalent to a promise.[3]

Where the defendant sold a horse, and the plaintiff gave his check for the price, and, at the same time, a bill of sale was made, and deposited with a third person, who was to hold the same till the check was paid, and the check was paid Monday, and the horse and bill of sale were delivered to the plaintiff on a secular day, it was held that the plaintiff could not rescind the contract, on account of a deceit, practised on him by the defendant, and recover, in an action for money had and received, the price paid.[4]

In an action to enforce a penalty provided for the failure of a telegraph company to transmit and deliver a message, it was held that a retention of the message and the consideration paid for its sending did not constitute a new contract.[5]

[1] *Banks* v. *Werts*, 13 Ind. 203 (1857). See, also, *Lyon* v. *Strong*, 6 Vt. 219 (1834); *Allen* v. *Deming*, 14 N. H. 133 (1843).

[2] *Sumner* v *Jones*, 24 Vt. 317.

[3] *Dodson* v. *Harris*, 10 Ala. —— (1846); *Williams* v. *Paul*, 6 Bing. 653 (1830).

[4] *Plaisted* v. *Palmer*, 63 Me. 576 *et seq.* (1874.)

[5] *Rogers* v. *Telegraph Co.*, 78 Ind. 169 (1881).

Where a loan, for which a note was given, was partly in cash, and partly in a check, it was held that by collecting the latter and retaining the money, and also that advanced on Sunday, the parties reaffirmed the contract; and a surety, who took an active part in getting the money from the principal, informed the lender that he would be mostly paid through himself, and acquiesced in the collection of the check and retention of the money gotten on Sunday, was regarded as having affirmed the contract.[1]

A subsequent payment on account is a sufficient ratification of a Sunday contract;[2] but payment of interest on a note is not sufficient to validate it.[3]

Where A and B met and agreed on a measure of damages for an injury, and A on a week day paid what was agreed on, the court said the settlement was valid.[4]

Where a creditor agreed with his debtor that, if the latter would pay a certain sum by a future date, he would wait a year for the balance, it was held that no action could be maintained on the agreement, nor could it answer as a defence; but, when a sum agreed on was paid, the contract was held perfect, and on valid consideration, and free from objection, arising from the previous conversation.[5]

The mere fact that a person borrowing money on Sunday retains it and converts it to his own use does not raise an implied promise, binding in law, and upon which an action can be maintained.[6] In this case the defendant made default in the service of the writ, which he was bound to serve. On Sunday he agreed with the plaintiff that if the latter would bring another suit, summoning a certain person as trustee, it should not discharge him from liability for the default. After sunset the parties arranged to discontinue that suit, had a new writ made, and, immediately after twelve o'clock at night, gave notice of discontinuance, and served the new writ, the defendant assisting the officer who served it. In case for the default, the court said: "We entertain no doubt that this was a ratification of the contract."

[1] *Campbell* v. *Young*, 9 Bush 240.

[2] *Tucker* v. *West*, 29 Ark. 386 (1874); *Sayle* v. *Wellman*, 10 R. I. 465 (1873).

[3] *Reeves* v. *Butcher*, 31 N. J. 224 (1865).

[4] *Taylor* v. *Young*, 61 Wis. 314.

[5] *Uhler* v. *Applegate*, 26 Pa. 140 (1856).

[6] *Troewert* v. *Decker*, 51 Wis. 46 (1881).

A surety, who signed a note, afterwards told the payee, who called to see him about the payment of it, that the principal had certain property he might sell and apply on the note, and, after the principal had done so, paying part of the note, met the payee on the road, and asked how he and the principal were "getting along" with the note, and the payee answered that he could not wait much longer, whereupon the surety asked him not to sue till he (the surety) could see the principal, as none of the consideration for which the note was given was received by the surety. It was held that there had been no ratification by the latter.[1]

The question has arisen whether a Sunday payment on account of a previous contract will take the debt out of the operation of the statute of limitations. It was held that it will not, because "the payment is a link in the chain of evidence, necessary to sustain the action. When an act essential to complete the right of recovery is in violation of the statute, the plaintiff cannot demand the assistance of the judiciary—the delivery of goods or payment of money may vest the property therein or extinguish an existing obligation so far as the property or money has passed from one party to the other, but cannot be applied to any other purpose."[2]

Where a party bought property, in consideration of antecedent debts, and, during the week subsequent, sent a receipt for the property, as well as the debt, it was held a sufficient ratification of the agreement.[3]

Suit was brought on a promise to indemnify the plaintiff for becoming surety on a promissory note. The whole transaction occurred on Sunday, and, holding both note and agreement of indemnity void, the court said: "The defendant might have made this defence to the suit against him on the note. But, failing to do so, judgment was rendered against him. This has no tendency to give efficacy to the agreement of indemnity, which was void in its inception."[4] A Sunday payment, if retained, discharges a debt.[5]

Payment by one joint contractor ratifies the contract so as to bind the others, being presumed to be with the latter's approbation and operating for his benefit.[6]

[1] *Parker* v. *Pitts*, 73 Ind. 597 (1886).

[2] *Clapp* v. *Hale*, 112 Mass. 368 (1873).

[3] *Wilson* v. *Millegan*, 75 Mo. 41 (1881).

[4] *Hill* v. *Sherwood*, 3 Wis. 343 (1854).

[5] *Shields* v. *Klopf*, 70 Wis. 69.

[6] *Russell* v. *Murdock* (Tex.), 44 N. W. Rep. 237 (1890).

Where a note paid on Sunday is secured by a mortgage also executed on Sunday, "the payment, whether made and applied upon the notes or mortgages, is a ratification of both instruments."[1]

In a suit on a warranty, where the representation which induced the sale was made on Sunday, and the horse sold was delivered on Sunday, it was held in Connecticut that it was "a mere evasion of the statute to regard the sale as made on Monday, because payment was then made."[2]

A Sunday contract in Iowa "will be regarded as valid from the date of its ratification."[3]

IV. The Liability of Common Carriers.

A steamboat company running from Baltimore to Richmond and stopping at "City Point" gave receipts for goods to Petersburg; the goods were delivered at City Point to a railroad company. The latter, receiving a shipment on Sunday, stored it in its warehouse to remain till Monday. Sunday evening, it was destroyed by fire. The steamboat company being compelled to pay for the shipment, sued the railroad company. The Supreme Court of the United States held that the latter's duty to keep the goods safely was not a violation of the Virginia code, and that the plaintiff was entitled to recover.[4]

In a suit for injuries occasioned by the negligence of a passenger-railway corporation, it was said: "It is unnecessary to consider what relation may have existed between other passengers and the defendant. If the plaintiff was lawfully traveling, then the defendant had a right to carry her, and it is enough that between them alone the relation of carrier and passenger existed."[5]

By an act passed in Massachusetts in 1877, it was provided that the prohibition of travel should not constitute a defence to an action against a common carrier of passengers for any tort or injury suf-

[1] *Russell* v. *Murdock* (Tex.), 44 N. W. Rep. 237 (1890).

[2] *Grant* v. *McGratt,* 56 Conn. 333 (1888).

[3] *Russell* v. *Murdock,* 44 N. W. Rep. 237 (1890).

[4] *P. S. Co.* v. *C. R. Co.*, 24 How. 247 (1860). The opinion is long and elaborate, and discusses every aspect of the case with great thoroughness.

[5] *Feital* v. *Middlesex R. R.*, 109 Mass. 398 (1872).

fered by a person or traveler. This statute has been held not retroactive.[1]

Where an accident occurred while a steamer was lying at her "slip," and before she started on a Sunday excursion, an injured party was allowed to recover in New York. The court said: "These are not the cases of travelers on a turnpike, out of condition, by reason of which they meet with an accident upon a Sunday, while upon an errand forbidden by law, for, in that case, the travelers would be trespassers, having no right to enter upon the road. The deceased, however, were not trespassers upon the boat; on the contrary, they were there upon the express solicitation and permission of the defendants. The defendants themselves were, on their own theory, in violation of the law, but the idea is the same. They invited and induced the deceased to come on their boat; they failed to perform their contract to convey them to Staten Island, and to this extent the statute gives them protection. But to hold that they had the right to imperil the lives of passengers by gross negligence, such as was found by the jury to have existed, is a proposition which strikes the mind at once as unreasonable. It would seem useless to look for authorities on this point. It is enough to consider the reason of the case, for nothing is law that is not reason."[2] In this state, it is now established that the liability of a common carrier is not affected by the fact that he is working under a Sunday contract, because it does not grow out of his contract.[3]

But a railroad company is not bound, as a common carrier, to convey passengers on Sunday, and though, where their purpose was to attend the laying of a corner stone of a church, recovery was allowed on a contract to do so, it was held that no damages could be claimed for "annoyance, vexation of mind, mental distress, or sense of wrong."

V. The Question of Warranties.

How does the invalidity of a Sunday contract effect recovery on a warranty contained therein?

[1] *Butcher* v. *Fitchburg R. R.*, 131 Mass. 156.

[2] *Landers* v. *S. I. R. R.*, 15 Abb. Pr. (N. S) 338 (1872).

[3] *Merritt* v. *Earle*, 31 Barb. 38 (1872); *S. C.*, 29 N. Y. 115; *Carroll* v. *Staten Island R. R.*, 58 N. Y. 126 (1874).

[4] *Walsh* v. *Chicago R. W.*, 42 Wis. 23 (1877). See, also, *Apsahl* v. *Yudd*, 30 Minn. 126 (1813).

In England, the doctrine seems to be that the defrauded party may recover. It will be observed that, in the following case, the plaintiff, suing on the warranty, was held not to have violated the law, but the language is general, that the contract being void "would not prevent the plaintiff from recovering." Whether this applies only to contracts which, like that under consideration, are illegal on the part of the warrantor, but lawful as far as the warrantee is concerned, or whether it states a universal rule, as to Sunday contracts, is uncertain. The action was on a warranty in the sale of a horse. The purchase was not within the plaintiff's "ordinary calling," and there was no evidence that he knew the sale was within that of the defendant. The court said: "The contract may have been void, but that does not prevent the plaintiff from recovering back his money paid upon a contract, the consideration for which has failed. If it be not void, then he is clearly entitled to recover for the breach of it, the horse not being sound, according to the warranty."[1]

The North Carolina statute is in very nearly the same words as 29 Car. II., and under it the Supreme Court of that state held that a sale of a horse by a dealer, at private sale, though the vendee knew it was within his ordinary calling, was not such a violation of the statute as to prevent recovery in an action by the vendee for deceit and false warranty. This was decided by two judges against one.[2] Butler, J., holding that the contract was void, as within the "ordinary calling" of the vendor, and that the vendee was "*particeps criminis*, because he knew it to be so."

It is held that there can be no recovery on such a warranty in Massachusetts,[3] and Vermont,[4] and Kentucky,[5] and New York.[6] So, where an operation was performed upon a horse with a warranty of recovery, and the animal died from the effects of it, it was held that no recovery could be had on the warranty.[7]

[1] *Bloxsome* v. *Williams*, 5 Dowl. & Ry. 84 (1824).

[2] *Melvin* v. *Easley*, 7 Jones 356.

[3] *Robeson* v. *French*, 12 Metc. 24 (1846). See *Bradley* v. *Ren*, 103 Mass. 188 (1869).

[4] *Lyon* v. *Strong*, 6 Vt. 219 (1834). Mattocks, J., dissented, holding that, though a contract for "swopping" could not be enforced, action would lie on the warranty where the swopping had been completed. Id. 230.

[5] *Murphy* v. *Thompson*, 14 B. Mon. 419 (1854).

[6] See, also, *Northrop* v. *Fort*, 14 Wend. 248 (1835)—action for deceit.

[7] *Slade* v. *Arnold*, Id. 287.

VI. The Question of Hired Horses.

In Massachusetts, where a horse was hired to be driven to a particular place, and was driven to a different one, beyond the limits specified in the contract, and was driven so immoderately that he died, the court below instructed the jury that if he was injured in consequence of being driven a greater distance than specified, or to a different place from that agreed on, the owner could recover. But this was reversed on appeal; the court holding that, though the action was tort, the verdict was found against the defendants essentially on the ground that they had broken the illegal contract by driving the horse beyond the place specified, and by so doing injured the plaintiff.[1] And this is the Rhode Island doctrine.[2] And in a later Massachusetts case, where the horse had

[1] *Gregg* v. *Wyman*, 4 Cush. 322 (1849).

[2] *Whelden* v. *Choppel*, 8 R. I. 230 (1865); *Smith* v. *Rawlings*, 11 Id. 464 (1875). In this case the plaintiff's counsel sought to avoid the introduction of the illegal contract by limiting his client's testimony to the negative statements that he had not let his property to the defendant or any one to be driven to the place to which it was driven or in the direction to which it was driven, and that the use of his property was without his knowledge or authority. The fact of the illegal contract was brought out on cross-examination. The defendant's counsel ingeniously contended that the want of authority was as effectually proved by the plaintiff's statement to that effect as by proving authority for one thing and leaving it to be inferred there was none for another; that the fact that the illegal contract to which the defendant as well as the plaintiff was a party which was made to appear by the defendant to escape liability for a wrongful use of the property was no more available as a defence than it would have been as a cause of action, but the court said it did not assent to these claims; that the conversion depended on the authority; that the fact that the defendant was not authorized to do as he did was not to be established by the plaintiff's assertion, which might be his inference or opinion, but by putting in evidence all material facts; the plaintiff's statement implied that he had let the property for some purpose, and what it was, was material to a proper understanding of the case. Moreover the contract appeared in legitimate cross-examination upon matters opened in the direct, and was therefore none the less a part of the plaintiff's case than if it had been disclosed in the direct examination. The court added that if the tort had been so distinct from the contract as to be capable of complete proof without affording the defendant the right to show the contract on cross-examination, so that the latter would have been obliged to set it up as a defence, there would have been more force in the plaintiff's claim that it was unavoidable.

been injured by immoderate driving, recovery was denied, and this decision was affirmed, though said to "carry the doctrine to its extreme limit."[1] And later still, it was held that recovery would lie for immoderate driving within the limits specified in the Sunday contract, the *gist* of the wrong being the conversion;[2] and it was said: "The action which the court, in *May* v. *Foster* declined to sustain, was an action for immoderately driving a horse upon the very journey which the plaintiff had knowingly delivered it to the defendant for the purpose of being illegally driven upon. That action, though in form *tort*, was, in substance, founded upon a breach of the contract by which the defendants obtained possession of the horse. To such a case the reasoning in *Gregg* v. *Wyman*, that the question whether the injury sued for was a wrong to the plaintiff depended upon the terms of the contract between the parties might, with more reason, be applied. There is nothing in the decision or opinion, in either of these cases, to support the position that the delivery of possession of a chattel on the Lord's day by way of bailment, will prevent the general owner from maintaining an action against the bailee for using the chattel, not under the possession so acquired, but for an entirely different purpose, not contemplated in the illegal contract, and of itself amounting to a conversion."

So, it was said in Maine, where a party drove a horse six miles further than agreed, and overdrove him, so that he died, "there is a limit to the consequences of such an illegal contract. A party who delivers property to another to be used temporarily under a contract, does not lose his title, and though he has no rights under the contract, for injury to the property unconnected with the contract, he may recover." And the court added that neither the hirer nor any other person became owner of the horse, nor was it forfeited to the state, or derelict, so that whoever found it might slay or appropriate, and if the hirer, after driving beyond the agreed distance, were to sell or leave it with another, the owner might maintain trover;[3] and this is the New Hampshire view,[4] and it being there held that driving the horse beyond the limits for which he was hired

[1] *Way* v. *Foster*, 1 Allen 408 (1861).

[2] *Hall* v. *Corcoran*, 107 Mass. 251 (1871).

[3] *Morton* v. *Gloster*, 46 Me. 520 (1859).

[4] *Woodman* v. *Hubbard*, 5 Fost. (N. H.) 67 (1852).

was as absolute an invasion of the plaintiff's right of property, as if he had been kept for a year, or driven to market, or sold; and that his claim was neither in form nor substance, by, through or under the illegal contract.[1]

But the Massachusetts view is adopted in Connecticut,[2] and the court went further, and held that the defendant would be liable for improper driving within the limits specified in the contract.

Later Maine cases, however, seem to lean against the earlier doctrine in that state. Where a horse hired for an indefinite time and distance, had been injured by careless driving, recovery was refused.[3] And so where the injury was done to a horse during the drive contracted for.[4]

In a case in New York, in the report of which nothing is said about whether the agreed distance was exceeded or not, it was observed: "The action is not for the proceeds of the hiring, but for damages for a wrong done, and for such wrong I suppose the plaintiffs may recover, although they could not recover the price agreed to be paid for hiring." [5]

Where the horses hired had been left standing in the street with-

[1] Of these observations, it was said in Rhode Island: "The court, in *Woodman* v. *Hubbard*, appear to have been influenced in their decision by the apprehension that if the action could not be sustained, a plaintiff who had delivered his property to defendant under an illegal contract between them for its temporary use would be without a remedy, though the defendant should refuse to restore the property, or should sell or destroy it. If this were so, it would indeed be a strong argument for sustaining the action; but such would not be the result, for a retention of the property after a demand, or its sale or destruction, would be a conversion wholly distinct from and independent of the contract, upon proof of which and of his title the plaintiff would be entitled to recover the value of the property. Applied to the former, the language of the court is unobjectionable; in relation of the latter, it seems to us erroneous. If the tort cannot be made to appear without proof of the contract, certainly the contract can hardly be considered immaterial or as not affecting the liability of the defendant, even though it might not be part of the cause of action." Id. 472. And, referring to *Hall* v. *Corcoran*, 107 Mass. 251, it was added: "The court appears to have lost sight of the distinction plainly marked between those cases in which the tort is some breach of duty in violation of the plaintiff's right entirely separable from the contract and those in which the tort and contract are inseparable." *Smith* v. *Rawlings*, 11 R. I. 464 (1875).

[2] *Frost* v. *Plumb*, 40 Conn. 111 (1873).

[3] *Tillock* v. *Webb*, 56 Me. 100 (1868).

[4] *Parker* v. *Latner*, 60 Me. 528 (1872).

[5] *Harrison* v. *Marshall*, 4 E. D. Sm. 271 (1855).

out being tied, and ran away, the Supreme Court of New York said:

"The defendant could not, after obtaining possession of the property, willfully injure it, or suffer it to be injured through his negligence. The owner does not forfeit or become divested of his right to the property by its delivery under it. He has a right to the return of it, and if it is retained after demand, an action could be maintained for the recovery thereof, or its value; and there is no reason or principle why he should not as well be compensated for its deterioration, or any damage to it, by reason of the fault of the party to whom it was hired. Such liability does not arise from the contract, but from a breach of duty, in violation of the plaintiff's rights, wholly irrespective of the contract.[1]

In Arkansas, where a horse hired for riding to a certain point, was afterwards used in a hunt, the court said, "the action is not founded upon the contract, but upon the wrongful conversion," and recovery was allowed.[2]

In a Michigan case the court said it declined to discuss, as not arising, the question whether a party would be liable for injury to a horse from driving, not contemplated by the contract of hiring, if the contract were illegal.[3]

VII. The Question of Third Persons.

The fact that a bill of exchange was signed on Sunday is not available for the acceptor against an innocent endorsee;[4] nor is a Sunday contract of sale a defence against such an endorsee of a note for the purchase money.[5] So, where a note was not dated on Sunday, but an offer was made to show that it was made and delivered on that day, the court said: "The defendant cannot be permitted to set up his own fraudulent misdating of his notes to

[1] *Nodine* v. *Doherty*, 46 Barb. (N. Y.) 59 (1864).

[2] *Steuart* v. *Davis*, 31 Ark. 518 (1876).

[3] *Fisher* v. *Kyle*, 27 Mich. 454 (1873).

[4] *Begbie* v. *Levi*, 1 Cromp. & J. 180; *S. C.*, 1 Tyrw. 130 (1830).

[5] *Ray* v. *Catlett*, 12 B. Mon. 532 (1851). See, also, *Houliston* v. *Parsons*, 9 U. C. Q. B. 681 (1852); *Crombie* v. *Overholtzer*, 11 U. C. 55 (1853); *Pope* v. *Linn*, 50 Me. 83 (1863); *Vinton* v. *Peck*, 14 Mich. 287 (1866); *Cranson* v. *Goss*, 107 Mass. 439 (1871); *Knox* v. *Clifford*, 38 Wis. 651 (1875).

defeat the rights of those who parted with value upon the faith that his notes were dated when by his signature thereto he represented them to be."[1]

But it has been held that the endorsement of a note is secular business, and not of necessity or charity, and is void; and that this defence is open to a maker in a suit by the endorsee, by whose procurement the endorsement was made, as it affected the maker's rights and liberties, and was an element in his contract; and the same privity of contract existed between the parties as if the plaintiff was the payee.[2] After the payee's transfer of a note with endorsement, for value, on Sunday, the maker cannot be held as the trustee for the money for the payee's creditors;[3] and the defence of want of knowledge is not available for an endorsee who became such by violating the positive provision of a statute, as upon a usurious loan;[4] and, under the Massachusetts statute, a note, payable on demand, was open to the same defences, in the hands of the endorsee, as in those of the promisee.[5] A note bore date on Sunday; it was warranted to the endorsee to be "as good as gold." Whether the date brought him within the rule "*caveat emptor*," was held to be a question for the jury under instructions.[6]

A party's creditors cannot take advantage of his illegal contract of sale,[7] but the assignor of such a contract, which was dated on a week day, cannot set up its invalidity against the assignee.[8]

In trover, the defendant alleged that the plaintiff acquired possession on Sunday, but the court said: "The objection cannot prevail, though bills of sale were executed and delivered. One who was not a party to the sale, and has no interest in the property which is the subject of contest, cannot prevent a recovery by showing that the plaintiff violated some statutory provision in acquiring

[1] *Bank of Cumberland* v. *Mayberry*, 48 Me. 198 (1842). The court further observed: "If the note was an accommodation note, it would derive its validity from its endorsement, which was not till Monday. * * * It would seem that it was then first delivered as a binding contract, and the action is maintainable."

[2] *Benson* v. *Drake*, 55 Me. 555 (1867).

[3] *Smith* v. *Foster*, 41 N. H. 215. See, also, *Bank* v. *Thompson*, 42 Id. 369; (1861).

[4] *Saltmarsh* v. *Tuthill*, 13 Ala. 300.

[5] *Stevens* v. *Wood*, 127 Mass. 123 (1879).

[6] *Gilman* v. *Berry*, 59 N. H. 62 (1879).

[7] *Smith* v. *Foster*, 41 N. H. 215 (1860).

[8] *Johns* v. *Baeley*, 45 Ind. 241 (1876).

his title."[1] Where a deed was delivered on this day, it was held that the vendor could not set up its invalidity against subsequent purchasers from his vendee, for valuable consideration, in good faith, and without notice, either actual or constructive, that the deed was executed on Sunday.[2]

[1] *Richardson* v. *Kimball*, 28 Me. 463 (1842).

[2] *Love* v. *Wells*, 25 Ind. 503 (1865). In this case, at the vendor's instance, the deed and certificate of acknowledgement were antedated, so as to make the deed appear valid; and when the vendee resold, the vendor gave the purchasers no notice that the deed was executed on Sunday, and asserted no claim to the land till years after they, in turn, had conveyed it to another; and his conduct, in giving the deed a false date, had enabled his vendee to practice a fraud on innocent purchasers.

CHAPTER VI.

EFFECT OF THE PROHIBITION OF SUNDAY LABOR IN CASES OF TORT.

The extent to which the ordinary relations of the civil law, to one of its citizens, are modified by the fact that, at the time of the event which gave rise to the suit, he was engaged in the commission of an unlawful act, has been considered in two classes of cases in connection with the Sunday statutes.

One class involves the question: How do these statutes affect the liability of others for the results to him of their negligence? This point arose in two early English cases. In a case against a hundred, by a person robbed therein, and who had made "hue and cry;" as required by statute, the court held the hundred was chargeable, although the robbery was made on the Sunday, and in time of divine service—observing that the Sunday law was to be liberally construed; that punishing felons "who attempt to violate the Sabbath" was a work of charity and justice; and that persons, such as physicians, &c., who might be necessarily traveling on Sunday, were entitled to protection. The report proceeds as follows: "Croke, J., put the case, if an insurrection should be upon the Sunday, as it was in London, in the Earl of Essex case, if it be not suppressed immediately, the officers are finable; so, if an affray be made upon a Sunday, in view of the constable, if he doth not suppress it, he is finable; *a multo fortiori*, robbery ought to be suppressed." Montague, C. J., to the contrary: "For the country is not bound to watch upon the Sunday, and therefore resembled it to a case in the year books. The law appoints that men should be at divine service, and therefore they are not bound to pursue robbers, and it is at their peril who travel on Sunday if they be robbed. And this statute is to be taken in equity that robbers should be pursued in convenient times, which is not upon the Sunday, no more than that they should be pursued in the night."[1]

[1] *Waite* v. *Stokes*, Cro. Jac. 496 (1619).

A railroad company having left piles in a river, in such a condition as to injure a vessel, in a suit on account of the injury, the defence was made that the vessel was doing work which was illegal under the Maryland statute. The Supreme Court of the United States said: "If we admit that the master and mariner of a ship or steamboat are liable to the penalty of the act for commencing their voyage from a port in Mayland, it by no means follows that the pilots can protect themselves from responding to the owners of the vessel for the damages suffered in consequence of the nuisance. We do not feel justified, on any principles of justice, equity, or of public policy, in inflicting an additional penalty of $7,000 on the libellants by way of set-off, because their servants may have been subject to a penalty of twenty shillings each, for breach of statute;" and it added that the commencement of a voyage by a vessel, in order to take advantage of the wind and weather, might fairly be considered a work of necessity.[1]

A similar view has been taken in various states. In New Hampshire, where a party sued a town for injuries from a defect in the highway, it was said: "Even if the plaintiff's traveling were to be held a violation of the law, as the illegality of his act could, in no way, have contributed to the accident, it would not protect the town; it is immaterial whether the plaintiff's traveling was illegal or not."[2] So, in Rhode Island, where a party who was driving sued another for colliding with him, the court said the act of traveling was a condition, rather than a cause, of the injury, and it instanced the case of a man walking past a house and struck by something thrown carelessly from a window, or driving, after dark, into a hole, left unlighted on a familiar street, and the case at bar, and said: "We think the act of traveling, though unlawful, could not defeat the action on the ground that it was a contributory cause, unless it was one of the immediate causes of the injury." The defendant who is sued in tort cannot justify the tort, whether willful or negligent, by proving that the plaintiff, when injured, was transgressing the law, so long as the tort and the transgression are independent or disconnected, except in time and place, in their relation to each other.[3]

[1] *P., W. & B. R. R.* v. *P. & H. Co.*, 23 How. 209 (1859).

[2] See, also, *Sewell* v. *Webster*, 58 N. H. 586 (1880); *Wentworth* v. *Jefferson*, 60 Id. 158 (1880).

[3] *Baldwin* v. *Barney*, 12 R. I. 392 (1880).

In a suit for damages, caused by an obstruction erected in a navigable stream, the defence being made that the plaintiff was engaged in worldly employment, the Supreme Court of Pennsylvania said: "A vessel engaged in the slave trade, piracy, or smuggling, and injured by another, or the keeper of a gambling house injured in his business by a neighboring nuisance, could have no remedy. But persons are never outlawed, and their lawful property is under the protection of the state even when used improperly. * * * It is said, however, that had it not been for the plaintiff's transgression of the law, his boat would not have been at the defendant's dam when it was. True enough; and so it might be said of boats arriving at Pittsburg on Monday—they would not have been there on Monday had they not run on Sunday, and would have been saved from a certain accident then happening to them. * * * Time is not one of the circumstances of an event itself, and time cannot be a cause of anything, except figuratively. In cases of this kind the law does not inquire at all into the plaintiff's fault, except on proof that the defendant did the act from which the injury arises. * * * Then to silence his complaint there must be a failure of duty under the circumstances of danger; a failure of duty to the party who caused the danger, so that it may be said he brought the injury on himself." And the court added, that if the defendant's contention were allowed "all freight and wages earned by all on steamboats are tainted with illegality, if partly earned on the Lord's day; no insurance covers the risk of running on that day on inland highways, and all accidents must be absolutely charged to the carriers."[1] So, later, in the same state, in an action against a party who left an obstruction in a road, the defence of the plaintiff's Sunday traveling was disallowed.[2]

The Pennsylvania view is adopted in Wisconsin, the court holding that Sunday traveling was not a contributory cause of an injury caused by a defective bridge, or a matter which in any wise affected the defendant, and adding: "The mere matter of time when an injury like this takes place is not in general an element which does or can enter at all into the consideration of the cause of it."[3] And

[1] *Mohner* v. *Cook*, 26 Pa. 342.

[2] *Piollet* v. *Simmers*, 106 Pa. 95 (1884).

[3] *Sutton* v. *Wauwatosa*, 29 Wis. 21 (1871).

so, in Indiana, where there is a prohibition of labor, it was held that a person riding on a business errand, on the highway, and injured by his horse being frightened by a dog, could recover from the dog's owner.[1]

But a different view of the law has been taken in some states. Thus, it was said in Massachusetts, where a town was sued for injuries from a defective highway: "Evidence that a party is guilty of a violation of law supports the issue of a want of proper care. No specific averment of the particular unlawful act which caused or contributed to produce a result could, in such cases, be deemed necessary. * * * It is true that no direct unlawful act of omission or commission by the plaintiff, done at the moment when the accident happened, and tending immediately to produce it, is offered to be shown in evidence. But it is also true that if the plaintiff had not been engaged in the doing of an unlawful act, the accident would not have happened, and the negligence of the defendants in omitting to keep their road in proper repair would not have contributed to produce an injury to the plaintiff. It is the disregard of the requirements of the statute by the plaintiff which constitutes the fault, or want of due care which is fatal to the action." And the court added that if it was not necessary for the plaintiff to aver he was lawfully on the highway, it was not required by the defendant to deny the fact, or make any averment respecting it in his answer.[2] And so it was held that a party who was injured by a locomotive, while on the highway, could not recover, because "the illegal act of traveling might properly be treated as a cause directly contributing to the injury."[3] And so where a party, who was traveling in violation of the Sunday law, had fastened his horse at the side of the road, where it was injured by another's negligent driving against it, the court said: "If, in the course, and as an incident of the traveling, the traveler sustains an injury, his unlawful act necessarily is a contributing cause of the injury."[4]

A party sailing his yacht, not for necessity or charity, was vio-

[1] *Schmid* v. *Humphry*, 48 Ind. 652.

[2] *Jones* v. *Andover*, 10 Allen (Mass.) 18 (1867).

[3] *Swift* v. *Boston R. R.*, 120 Mass. 490 (1876).

[4] *Lyons* v. *Desotelle*, 124 Mass. 387 (1877).

lating the law, and "no distinction can be made between travelers with their vehicles upon the road, and those who travel for pleasure in their boats upon the river;" but the court added: "The second count of the declaration alleges not a careless and negligent act on the part of the defendant in running down his boat, but a wanton and malicious one. Upon such a state of facts, although the plaintiff was in violation of the law forbidding traveling, his title to an action would be independent of his unlawful act. He would not forfeit the general protection of the law, and the injury would proceed solely from the wrongful act of the defendant."[1] Where a party was injured by another's negligence, while helping the latter to dig sand, it was said: "The rules of law, as applied to actions of tort, for injuries like the case at bar, are that if the illegal act of the plaintiff contributed to his injury, he cannot recover; but, although the plaintiff, at the time of the injury, was acting in violation of law, if his illegal act did not contribute to the injury, but was independent of it, he is not precluded thereby from recovering. The case at bar falls within the first-named class of cases. The illegal act of the plaintiff was inseparably connected with the cause of action, and contributed to his injury. The difference between the two rules may be illustrated by supposing the plaintiff, while engaged in his work, to have been assaulted by a stranger; he could maintain an action therefor, because his violation of law had no connection with the trespass. The two are cotemporary facts, but the one has nothing to do with the other. He could show a complete cause of action independent of his own violation of law. But upon the facts of this case it is different. The plaintiff and defendant were engaged in a mutual illegal work, and the accident which happened was one of the incidents and risks of the employment. The plaintiff was participating in an illegal work which led to the injury he sustained."[2] But where a traveler had stopped at a hotel over night, and left his horse, buffalo robes, &c., in charge of the landlord's servant, and the robe could not be found on Monday morning, the action being trover, the court said: "The claim of the plaintiff to the property did not necessarily require him to show in its support a violation of the Lord's day."[3] So,

[1] *Wallace* v. *Merrimack Nav. Co.*, 134 Mass. 95 (1873).

[2] *McGrath* v. *Merwin*, 112 Mass. 467 (1873).

[3] *Cox* v. *Cook*, 14 Allen 165.

it was said: "If a man, while traveling, is injured by an assault, the act of traveling cannot, in any just sense, be said to be a cause of the injury. It is true that, if he were not traveling, he would not have received the injury, but the fact of traveling is a condition and not a contributory cause of the injury."[1]

The Massachusetts view of responsibility for the result of injuries from a defective highway is also taken in Maine[2] and Vermont,[3] the court observing that the liability of a town for a defective highway was purely statutory, and contending that it could not be designed by the statute that this liability should be imposed on behalf of a party whose traveling on the highway was illegal.

[1] *White* v. *Lang*, 128 Mass. 598 (1880).

[2] *Bryant* v. *Biddeford*, 39 Me. 103 (1855); *Ceralty* v. *Bangor*, 57 Id. 423 (1880). But see *Davidson* v. *Portland*, 69 Id. 116 (1879).

[3] *Johnson* v. *Irnsburg*, 47 Vt. 28 (1874).

CHAPTER VII.

SUNDAY AS A "DIES NON JURIDICUS."

I. Was Sunday a Dies Non Juridicus at Common Law?

The assertion that it was has been frequently made in America.[1] In the *Mirror of Justice*, published in English in 1768, we find enumerated among the "abuses of the common law" the fact "that pleas hold upon Sunday;"[2] and Lord Coke says: "In the common law there be *dies juridici et dies non juridici* the Lord's days throughout the whole year, so called because the Lord and Saviour of the world did arise again on that day;" and that this was the ancient law of England, and extended not only to legal proceedings, but to contracts, &c., and he quotes the words of the statute.[3] And, again, "There be also in the term *dies non juridici;* as in all the four terms the Sabbath day is not *dies juridicus,* for that ought to be consecrated to divine service."[4]

In his "ample and most judicious discourse" on the subject of "the Original of the Terms" (London, 1698, ch. 3, p. 75), Sir Henry Spelman observes: "To beat down the Roman superstition touching observation of days, against which Saint Augustine and others wrote vehemently, the Christians at first used all days alike for hearing of causes, not sparing (as it seemeth) the Sunday itself, thereby falling into another extremity. Yet they had some precedent for it, from Moses and the Jews. For Philo Judæas, in the life of Moses, reporteth that the cause of him that gathered sticks on the Sabbath day was, by a solemn council of the princes,

[1] See *Vechten* v. *Poddock*, 12 Johns. (N. Y.) 177; *Merritt* v. *Earle*, 31 Barb. 38; *Scammon's Case*, 40 Ill. 146 (1866); *Chapman's Case*, 5 Blackf. 111 (1839); *Kiger* v. *Coates*, 18 Ind. 153 (1862); *Nevada* v. *Cal. M. Co.*, 13 Nev. 203 (1878); *White, ex parte*, 15 Id. 146 (1880); *Haynes* v. *Sledge*, 2 Port. 530 (1835).

[2] L. C. 244.

[3] 27 Henry VI., ch. 5; Coke's Inst. 265.

[4] Co. Litt. a [g].

priests, and the whole multitude, examined and consulted of on the Sabbath day. And the Talmudists, who were best acquainted with the Jewish customs, do report that their judges, in the council called Sanhedrim, sate on the week-day from morning to night in the gates of the city; and on the Sabbath day and solemn festivals, in the walls. So the whole year then seemed a continual term, no day exempt. And they that seek the original of our modern laws among them do but spend their time in vain; unless for some things imposed on them by the Roman emperors when they became subjects. How this stood with the Levitical law, or rather the moral, I leave to others." Lord Mansfield said: "When the terms were first framed, and so many return days were made on Sunday, can it be supposed that the court did not then usually sit on Sunday? I myself have sat in Parliament on a Sunday. In Venice they sit on Sunday to administer justice. The Roto sits on Sunday." The distinguished judge also calls attention to the practice of the early Christians to hold their courts on Sunday, and says: "They had two reasons for it; one was in opposition to the heathens, who were superstitious about the observation of days and times, conceiving some to be unlucky and others lucky; and, therefore, Christians laid aside all observations of days. A second reason they had was that by keeping their own courts always open they prevented the Christian suitors from resorting to the heathen courts." He then referred to the canons, &c., mentioned by Spelman, and added: "These and other canons and constitutions were adopted by the Saxon kings of England. They were all confirmed by William the Conqueror and Henry the Second, and thus became part of the common law of England."[1]

Now, several definitions have been given of this phrase, "the common law;" but, by "the common law of England" Lord Mansfield must here intend simply the general law, as distinguished from the local or particular law, for it cannot be supposed that he would so

[1] *Swann* v. *Broome*, 1 W. Black. 496 (1764); *S. C.*, 3 Burrows 1575. In a note on this case, it is stated that on the sudden death of George II. both houses of Parliament met on Sunday, October 26th, 1760, pursuant to the statute of Queen Anne, but, the Lord Stewart not appearing to administer the oath, they departed without proceeding to business or making any formal adjournment.

confuse distinctions as to refer to "the common law" in its strictest sense of "the law for which no enactment can be found," a usage prescribed by express rules, the date and manner of whose establishment are mentioned by himself.

It is not quite clear whether the *Mirror* intends by "abuses of the common law," violations of it, or practices under it, that ought to be prohibited. But it is evident that Sunday was not a *dies non juridicus* by English common law, as adopted in America, because that law is always, in this connection, distinguished from English statutory law; and Sunday has derived its character as a *dies non juridicus* in England from certain easily cited statutes, whose regulations were borrowed from the ecclesiastical or canon law, and whose enactment was one of the many results of that English union of church and state which is nominally repudiated among our people.

Thus, it was well said in New York, that the prohibition of legal proceedings on Sunday "is not strictly on grounds of morality, or of the Christian religion, as recognized by the common law, nor was it the original practice of the Christian Church. It was introduced, like very many other doctrines and practices, some of which are, perhaps, less commendable, into popular Christianity, and thence into common law and usage by the influence of the clergy. It is well known, to lawyers, at least, that until the year 500 the Christian courts were open and legal business transacted in the ordinary way on Sunday as on other days."[1] On the other hand, Judge Hoffman, of New York, referring in 1859 to Spelman's mention of the early custom of keeping open the Christian courts, says that if it ever existed it was checked at a far earlier period than 517, and he refers to the edicts of Constantine and Valentinian, and various canons, acts of Parliament, &c.[2]

It was said in Indiana: "Prior to the establishment of the Christian religion, all acts valid on any day were valid, when performed on the first day of the week. After the establishment of that religion, acts done on the first day of the week were valid, until the rule was changed by law. The Church changed the rule, as matter of discipline, in 517, so far as to prohibit judicial acts on

[1] *Merritt* v. *Earle*, 31 Barb. (N. Y.) 38 (1859).

[2] See Table A; *Campbell* v. *International*, 4 Bos. 298.

that day. This rule subsequently became part of the common law; but this did not apply to ministerial acts; writs still continued to be returnable."[1] So it was said in Pennsylvania: "Decrees of councils of the Church, and of the emperors, and governments, forbade holding courts on Sunday; but they went further, and included many other days—Lent, and other fasts of the Catholic Church, Christmas, Easter, and several days before and after. These were, many of them, established by the civil authority in England, but were never part of the law in this state. Every denomination of Christians in our country has its own regulations for its own members; but we have no general ecclesiastical law, and our courts have no power in such matters, except what is expressly given by legislative enactments.[2]

If the views here maintained be correct, it follows that in one of the United States Sunday is not made a *dies non juridicus* by a declaration in the constitution that "the inhabitants are entitled to the common law of England," or the like. And that with us legal proceedings are valid on Sunday, unless declared otherwise by express terms of constitution or statute.

II. Distinction Between Judicial and Ministerial Acts.

This distinction was taken very early; and it was settled that ministerial acts of a court might be done on Sunday.[3]

In 1835 the question was mooted, but not decided, whether the filling up of a blank writ, and delivering it to an officer, was a judicial or ministerial act.[4]

The distinction has been uniformly observed by our courts. It was held that, under the Nevada provision allowing reception of a verdict, &c., the preparation and execution of an undertaking to perfect an appeal was not prohibited; and, after remarking that it was sometimes difficult to discriminate between judicial and ministerial acts, the court added: "It would hardly be claimed that the preparation of the undertaking by the notary on Sunday, so it

[1] *Kiger* v. *Coates*, 18 Ind. 153.

[2] *Huidekoper* v. *Cotton*, 3 Watts 56 (1834); *Hastings* v. *Columbus*, 42 O. S. 585 (1855). See, also, *Story* v. *Elliott*, 8 Conway 27; *Hastings* v. *Columbus*, 42 O. S. 585.

[3] *Mackally's Case*, 9 Coke R. 61.

[4] *Johnson* v. *Day*, 17 Pick. 106.

could be executed and filed early Monday morning, would be a judicial act, because it was in aid of a court proceeding."[1] The Nevada statute provided that courts should not be open, except, among other things, for the issue of attachments on a certain affidavit. *Held*, that the exception was to be liberally construed, and authorized not merely the issuance of the writ, but also the commencement of the action.[2] Later, considering the provision "for the exercise of the powers of a magistrate in a criminal action," &c., the court said: "A justice of the peace, acting as a magistrate, may prosecute judicial business, issue warrants for the arrest of a party charged with crime, proceed with the preliminary examination, and commit, discharge, or release on bail. In the present case the justice, in receiving the plea of guilty, passing and rendering judgment, acted in the exercise of his powers as a justice of the peace. In this respect he acted without any authority of law. The judgment rendered is void."[3]

The service of a writ of attachment, and the arrest of a defendant is in violation of the North Carolina statute,[4] and in Georgia there can be no attachment, or bail process, unless by authority of special law, and then only under special circumstances.[5] But in Alabama, it is held that the service of the process of attachment is a purely ministerial act; and by common law no valid objection can be urged to its execution, though the issue by the clerk is judicial. And it was held, that while the issue on Sunday was irregular, and if it appeared on the face of the attachment, it would justify the courts in quashing it; the court had no power to order the clerk to change the date, "without intending to decide," said the court, "that the defendant is without remedy."[6]

It was said in Ohio: "Process issued by a ministerial officer in the ordinary course of official duty is not process awarded by a court within the meaning of that phrase in *Swan* v. *Browne*.[7] While at common law a judgment could not be rendered, process

[1] *Cal. M. Co.'s Case*, 13 Nev. 203 (1873).

[2] *Levy* v. *Elliott*, 14 Nev. 435.

[3] *White's Case*, 15 Nev. 146 (1880).

[4] *Devries* v. *Summit*, 86 N. C. 126 (1882).

[5] *Bass* v. *Irvin*, 49 Ga. 436.

[6] *Mathews* v. *Ansley*, 9 Ala. 20 (1857).

[7] Was shown in *Clough* v. *Shepherd*.

awarded by a court on Sunday, an arrest in a civil cause, and service of process of any sort, they being merely ministerial acts, were perfectly valid."[1]

Finally, we may observe that the distinction between ministerial and judicial acts has been repudiated in Iowa.[2]

III. Writs in General.

English Cases.—In 1558 it was assigned for error that the *teste* of a *scire facias* was on Sunday.[3]

In 1628 an information was exhibited in the Court of Exchequer against a party for "forestalling," and it was held good.[4]

In 1641 a process for good behavior was served on Sunday, and the court said "it was not well awarded according to the statute."[5]

It was held in 1798 that a rule *nisi* for an attachment for non-payment of money pursuant to the Master's *allocutur* could not be served. Lord Kenyon said the statute of 29 Car. II. was equally applicable to the service of process as to an actual arrest.[6]

In 1691 a citation on a party "in a case for incontinency" was held valid under 29 Car. II.[7] In the report of this case in Salkeld's reports it is stated that the citation was fixed upon the church door, and that Holt said: "The statute extends not to those processes nor to summons at the church, but only to such processes which may be as well executed at any other time."[8]

In 1701 a motion was made to set aside a judgment in trespass after a judgment by default and a writ of inquiry had been executed, because the declaration was delivered on Sunday. It is reported: "Holt, C. J., seemed to incline that the delivery was ill because 29 Car. II. intended to restrain all sorts of legal proceedings; but Powys and Gould, JJ., *contra*, because such delivery was but *quasi* a notice, and as a letter and not a process. But, it appearing to the court that the defendant had appeared, and that the writ of inquiry had been executed, they would not intermeddle, and said that that had made all good."[9]

[1] *Hastings* v. *Columbus*, 42 O. S. 585 (1885).

[2] *Davis* v. *Fish*, 1 Green 406 (1848).

[3] *Barrett* v. *Cleydon*, 2 Dyer 168.

[4] *Bedoe* v. *Alpe*, Sir W. Jones 156.

[5] *Prisor's Case*, Cro. Car. 602.

[6] *M'Ileham* v. *Smith*, 8 T. R. 86.

[7] *Alanson* v. *Brookbunk*, Corth. 504.

[8] Salk. 625.

[9] *Walgrave* v. *Taylor*, 1 Ray 706.

A declaration was delivered on Trinity Sunday, and it was doubted whether such delivery were not void by 29 Car. II., ch. 7. Holt, C. J., said: "Strongly it is; for, first, it is no act of necessity, as putting of ecclesiastical process upon the church, or making a tender to save a penalty." And he said he would take the word process for "proceeding," and such construction as tends to a better observation is to be made. And this declaration as delivered could not be taken notice of without breaking the Sabbath till Trinity term, for that, by statute 32 Hen. VIII., ch. 21, begins on Monday; but *Quind. Pasch.* is indeed always on the Sunday, but is kept on the Monday. And, *per lui*, if an arrest of the person that skulks all the rest of the week be void on Sunday, *a fortiori* this will be. But Gould *et* Powis, JJ., *dubitabant*."[1]

The question was whether the service of an ejectment were good upon the statute;[2] and *per curiam*, it is not, for "it is a process, though not a judicial one; for it is compulsive on the party to appear, and it may as well be said that the service of a summons in a real action may be good."[3]

The execution of a writ of inquiry is void, and the court is bound to take notice of it, without its being specially assigned for error.[4]

The notice of signing judgment for want of a plea was left with the defendant's attorney upon a Sunday, which the counsel said was irregular, and, therefore, he moved to set aside the judgment. But the court said that this was not within the statute of 29 Car. II., though, if it had been upon the late act of Parliament of vexatious arrests, they admitted it would; for then it would have been in the nature of protest.[5]

The *latitat* was returnable on the Wednesday, and upon debate it was held that the bail bond could not be assigned till after Monday; and where the fourth day was Sunday the party has all the next day to put in bail.[6]

In 1764 a case of common recovery was brought before Lord Mansfield on a writ of error, assigning that the day of the return

[1] *Waldegrave's Case*, 12 Mod. 606 (1702).

[2] 29 Car. II., ch. 3.

[3] *Taylor's Case*, 12 Mod. 667 (1702).

[4] *Holye* v. *Cornwallis*, 1 Stra. 387; *S. C.*, Fort. 373 (1720).

[5] *Anon.*, 1 Bar. 139 (1720).

[6] *Bullock* v. *Lincoln*, 2 Stra. 914 (1732).

of the writ of summons was a Sunday, on which day the vouchee died without issue male. His Lordship discussed the relation of a judgment to the "essoign day of the term," and held that as certain forms were necessary to validate this action, and as the deceased died before the return of the writ, and before he did or could appear, inasmuch as, though the writ was in words returnable on Sunday, the court could not sit, and he could not appear before Monday, and no judgment could be given against him till he had appeared, therefore the action could not be supported; and on appeal to Parliament this judgment was affirmed.

In 1791, under the statute,[1] the court was clearly of opinion that the service of notice of a declaration was bad, and that the defendant could not, by acceptance, waive the irregularity. In 1802 the defendant was served with a copy of a *latitat* on Sunday, and it was held to be an irregularity that could not be waived.[2]

In 1807 service of a notice of a plea filed was held void.[3] The service of a declaration in ejectment was made upon a servant of the tenant in possession, with an affidavit of acknowledgment by the tenant on Sunday that he received the declaration. *Held*, that the service was insufficient.[4]

If the vouchee die on the return day of the writ of summons, being Sunday, shall the common recovery be good? This is the query in the syllabus of the case of *Swann* v. *Broome*, as reported in 1 W. Black. 496.[5]

A party convicted under a Lottery act, and sent to the house of correction, "for want of sufficient distress," asked to be discharged because he was arrested on Sunday. The court said: "There is no case exactly in point. It is most similar to an action for a penalty on the same statute. And it is clear that upon an execution in such an action the defendant could not have been taken; this is to recover a penalty given by the statute, and the effect the same, whether that penalty is to be recovered in a summary proceeding before a justice or in an action."[6] *Capias* was returnable in three weeks, and the

[1] 29 Car. II.

[2] *Taylor* v. *Phillips*, 3 East 155.

[3] *Roberts* v. *Monkhouse*, 8 East 547.

[4] *Mortimer's Case*, 2 D. & R. 232 (1822).

[5] *S. C.*, 3 Burrows 1595. See, also, *Morgan* v. *Johnson*, 1 H. Bl. 628.

[6] *Myers' Case*, 1 T. R. 265 (1786).

last day fell on Sunday. A party arrested on it on a Monday was discharged. A note to this case says: "Writs, therefore, which are returnable on a Sunday, must be executed at the latest on the Saturday before."[1]

American Cases.—In Massachusetts a justice cannot receive a complaint and issue his warrant for a violation of the law by traveling; and an officer cannot serve notices and papers in the progress of a suit, or execute a writ of inquiry of damages.[2]

And in New York it is unlawful to make out a *capias* and deliver it to a coroner for service on a debtor who has escaped from prison.[3]

On the other hand, it has been said in Maine: "There is no prohibition, either at common law or by statute, of the service of process in criminal cases, except in so far as the service of the same might be unnecessary," and where the punishment for a breach of a statutory provision was a fine, in default of payment the prisoner must be committed; and it was held to be immaterial whether the fine was payable for the use of an individual or of the state; the statute was still penal, not remedial, and that the same penalty might be recovered in a civil action could make no difference.[4]

The Illinois statute forbids any to "knowingly disturb the peace by labor," &c. The court said: "To permit officers to intrude upon families for service of civil process would be a violation of the spirit and policy of this law, and unbecoming a Christian community."[5]

A deputy sheriff seized a party's horses on Sunday and put them in a stable. The owner retook them. It was held that, under the circumstances, he could not be convicted of "resisting an officer."[6]

It was held in Michigan that, under the statute forbidding the service of civil process, &c., the service of a writ of *certiorari* on a justice was absolutely void. And the court added: "The payment

[1] *Loveridge* v. *Plaistow*, 2 H. Bl. 29 (1792).

[2] *Pearce* v. *Atwood*, 13 Mass. 324 (1818).

[3] *Ven Vechten* v. *Paddock*, 12 Johns. (N. Y.) 177 (1815). See, also, *Butler* v. *Kelsey*, 15 Johns. (N. Y.) 177; *Field* v. *Park*, 20 Johns. (N. Y.) 146.

[4] *Keith* v. *Tuttle*, 28 Me. 326 (1848).

[5] *Scramnon* v. *Chicago*, 40 Ill. 146 (1866).

[6] *Bryant's Case*, 17 Neb. 651 (1854).

of the justice's fees on a subsequent day does not help the case. That was necessary to make the service effectual, unless waived by the justice, but was not itself service of the writ, and did not constitute any part of the service."[1]

In Alabama, an original writ in trespass on the case cannot be issued,[2] nor can an attachment be levied under the prohibition of process, "except in criminal cases."[3]

It has been said in Maine that an execution cannot be sued out,[4] and a levy under it is void in North Carolina.[5] And the fact that it was returned on Sunday is fatal in Michigan.[6]

Where the return day of a summons is made by mistake to fall on a Sunday, the summons is not void but voidable.[7]

A issued a *fieri facias*, an *alias*, and a *pluries*, on each of which he directed the sheriff "not to do anything till further orders." The *pluries* being in the sheriff's hands without a levy, A, on Sunday, directed the sheriff to proceed; on Monday, when about to levy, an execution by B came into his hands; *held*, B's execution had priority, and the order on Sunday was a nullity.[8] The court, however, observed that if an actual levy had been made on A's writ before B's writ came into the sheriff's hands, intent to proceed on the writ pursuant to the levy might have been supported, as against the idea that it was a colorable proceeding, as well as by declarations to the same effect another day, but the order could not of itself galvanize into life a writ issued for the purpose of security, even if it might have such effect on another day, which the court "did not say it would."

The Kentucky statute provided that certain writs might be executed. It was held, that "the right to have such writs executed gives a right to sue them out, and authorizes the proper officer to perfect this right by issuing them."[9]

And so it was said in Alabama: "Where, from the urgent neces-

[1] *Anderson* v. *Berck*, 3 Mich. 280 (1854).

[2] *Haynes* v. *Sledge*, 2 Port. 530 (1835).

[3] *Cotton* v. *Huey*, 4 Ala. 56 (1842).

[4] *Suhur's Case*, 33 Maine 539 (1832).

[5] *Bland* v. *Whittfield*, 1 Jones (N. C.) L. 122 (1853).

[6] *Peck* v. *Cavell*, 16 Mich. 9 (1866).

[7] *Ostertag* v. *Goldbreitt*, 37 N. W. Rep. 637 (1888).

[8] *Stern's Case*, 54 Pa. 447 (1870).

[9] *Rice's Case*, 3 Bush (Ky.) 14 (1867).

sity of the case, the service of process is authorized, its issuance is a matter of duty;"[1] and "the fact that the statute authorizes the levy of an attachment in case of a debtor's absconding, &c., presupposes the right of the creditor whose demand is thus endangered to receive satisfaction, and it was held that a bill of sale to one who overtook his absconding debtor, if necessary, under the circumstances, would be valid."[2] Later, it was observed that this last case was decided under a statute not incorporated in the Alabama code,[3] but its principle was subsequently approved.[4]

In Kentucky, an order to reinstate an injunction is void; so with the *teste* of a writ; and if any of the proceedings of a suit be entered and record to be done, it is error;[5] but it was held in Illinois that an injunction was valid against a railroad company which seized possession of a street on Sunday, and was insolvent, so that property-holders could obtain no damages for the injury which might incur.[6]

IV. Arrest Without Process—Taking Recognizance, &c.

A party was taken without a warrant on Sunday, and kept locked up till Monday morning and then a writ was got; the court said to the prisoner: "If you were imprisoned without a warrant, you have your remedy by false imprisonment, and then let them show cause why attachment should not go against them." And it was said by Gould, Justice, that attachments have gone frequently in such cases.[7] The syllabus in this case states the law to be that the court will grant an attachment against the officer, but will not discharge the prisoner, "for he may have his action."

In 1705 the court said: "The bail have their principal always upon a string, and may pull the string whenever they please and render him in their own discharge; they may take him up even upon a Sunday and confine him till the next day, and then render him."[8]

[1] *Haynes* v. *Sledge*, 2 Port. 530 (1835).

[2] *Hooper* v. *Edwards*, 18 Ala. 280 (1850).

[3] *Mathews* v. *Ansley*, 31 Ala. 20.

[4] *Reid's Case*, 53 Ala. 402.

[5] *Coleman* v. *Henderson*, 6 Littell's Sel. Cas. 171 (1813).

[6] *Langabier* v. *R. R.*, 64 Ill. 243.

[7] *Lidford* v. *Thomas*, 6 Mod. 96.

[8] *Anon.*, 6 Mod. 231.

A recognizance to prosecute an appeal is void in Maine.[1]

In Massachusetts, persons accused of perjury, forgery, blasphemy, &c., which are neither treason, felony nor breach of the peace, may be arrested.[2]

In New York, arrest without process for liquor-selling is unlawful.[3]

It was held in Indiana that, as by the statute of that state a debtor might be arrested on his creditor's making a proper affidavit, the debtor might procure his discharge by complying with the act subjecting real and personal estate to execution,[4] so the sureties in a recognizance, entered into before a justice for the principal's appearance in court to answer a charge of larceny, were held bound, though the arrest and other proceedings on which the bond was founded, and its execution and approval, took place on Sunday, for it was said that if the arrest was "common labor," it might have been absolutely necessary.[5]

So it was said in Illinois: "We do not consider entering into a recognizance to be such a judicial act as to render it void. It has none of the elements of a judicial proceeding, except that it is taken and acknowledged before a judicial officer, and is not, therefore, void by the common law." And as to its being void "as labor," it observed that any work necessary for "the public safety, by keeping a felon safe, or delivering him to bail, is within the exception (of necessity and charity); and neither the peace nor good order of society is disturbed by such a proceeding, which may be both secretly and silently conducted; and besides, it might be possible a prisoner could not secure the attendance of his surety on the next day, the consequence of which would be that he, though innocent, would have to be committed to jail. It would be a charitable act under such circumstances to take a recognizance."[6]

Where there is an adjournment till Sunday, the court does not lose jurisdiction, but the case is continued till next day.[7]

[1] *Suhur's Case*, 33 Me. 539 (1832).

[2] *Pearce* v. *Atwood*, 13 Mass. 324.

[3] *Wood* v. *Brooklyn*, 14 Barb. 425 (1852).

[4] *White* v. *Wilson*, 6 Blackf. 447.

[5] *Douglas' Case*, 69 Ind. 544.

[6] *Johnston's Case*, 31 Ill. 469 (1863). See, also, *Rice's Case*, 3 Bush 14 (1867); *Watts' Case*, 5 Bush 309 (1869).

[7] *State* v. *King*, 37 N. W. Rep. 410 (1888).

V. Receiving a Verdict, Giving Judgment, &c.

The following general review of this subject is given in North Carolina: "Sunday is frequently called *dies non juridicus;* but this means only that process cannot ordinarily issue, or be executed, or returned, and that courts do not usually sit on that day. It does not mean that *no* judicial action can be had on that day. On the contrary, it is laid down in books of authority that warrants for treason, felony and breach of the peace may be issued and executed on that day. I do not doubt that, if the circumstances made it proper, a coroner and his jury might lawfully hold an inquest of homicide on that day, although I have no authority for the opinion. So I think that a magistrate might, upon that day, hear the case of a prisoner brought before him on a criminal charge, and admit him to bail, or refuse it. The receiving the verdict of a jury, who have, perhaps, been long confined, and may be mentally and physically exhausted, in order that they may be discharged, is a work of necessity within the common and the legal meaning of the word, and may be justified on religious and moral grounds. But whether this be so or not, it is not forbidden by any statute of this state, and is, therefore, a lawful and valid act. I think that, probably, it has repeatedly occurred. We do not say how it would be if a court should undertake to sit on Sunday for the trial of actions, civil or criminal, or for giving judgments when no extreme necessity for it existed. As long as practice makes the law of a court, probably its proceedings in such cases would be deemed irregular, as was held in the case of taking a deposition in *Sloan* v. *Willifred.*"[1]

It was said in New York: "The trial of a cause is a judicial act. No part of it can be had, except what is specifically allowed by the statute, namely the receiving of the verdict." And where a case was submitted to a jury at one o'clock in the morning, and they rendered their verdict at three, it was held the conviction was wrong, "for the error of submitting the cause to the jury on Sunday."[2]

[1] 3 Ired. 307; *Rickett's Case,* 74 N. C. 184. See, also, *Penley's Case,* 12 S. E. Rep. 455.

[2] *Pullings' Case,* 8 Barb. 384.

The court below was actually delivering the charge to the jury Saturday night when twelve o'clock arrived. The appellate court said: "This may have been inadvertence, but, under all the circumstances, it was certainly no grave error. Beyond the conclusion of the charge, and the sending of the jury to their room, nothing was actually *done* in open court on the Sabbath day, and in the course of the Sabbath day, perhaps about three o'clock P. M., the judge received a message from the jury that they had agreed upon their verdict, and the counsel of each party being present, or summoned, consented to its reception. The judge then went into the court-room, and sent for the jury. Upon their entrance, one of the counsel present retracted the consent he had given that the verdict be received, and objected to it. The jury were remanded, and their verdict was not received till Monday. Whatever judicial action was had in the case on the Sabbath day was either inadvertent or inevitable. Of the latter character was the retention of the jury in their room. That being unavoidable, it is inconceivable how they could have been restrained from thinking and speaking of the case. We think what transpired on the Sabbath was not sufficient to vitiate the verdict."[1]

A cause was committed to the jury on Saturday, and they were permitted to seal up their verdict and separate after they had agreed. The evidence tended to show that they were engaged in the consideration of the cause on Sunday, and that they had not agreed upon their verdict until after twelve o'clock at night. The verdict was rendered on Monday. It was impeached under the prohibition of labor, as well as because Sunday is a *dies non*, but declared valid.[2]

It was said in Indiana that the law authorizing the reception of a verdict, "as an incident thereto," authorizes the court to sit to receive it, and to receive any motion or order touching it, and the discharge of the jury rendering it.[3]

A verdict may be received in New Hampshire,[4] and New York,[5]

[1] *Gholsten* v. *Gholsten*, 31 Ga. 625.

[2] *True* v. *Plumley*, 36 Me. 466 (1853).

[3] *McCorkle's Case*, 14 Ind. 39 (1859).

[4] *Webber* v. *Merrill*, 34 N. H. 202 (1853).

[5] *Van Riper* v. *Van Riper*, 1 South. 156.

and in Pennsylvania,[1] and Ohio,[2] and Illinois,[3] and Indiana,[4] and generally in South Carolina,[5] and in Alabama,[6] and in Texas,[7] but not in Georgia.[8]

We have seen that the general rule in South Carolina is that a verdict may be received. But in an early case in that state it was held that the fact that a verdict was delivered Sunday morning, a considerable time after twelve o'clock, the hour limited for a conclusion of the term of the court, was ground for a new trial. And the court said: "It is a well-known rule of the common law that the Lord's day, commonly called Sunday, is not a day in law."[9]

So it was held in Alabama, that where the term of a court was one week, it expired at twelve o'clock on Saturday night, "as the Sabbath then commenced." And a verdict could not be rendered after that hour, and the court added: "It has been a serious question with us how the precise time is to be ascertained, but there can be no other mode than to rest this matter with the presiding judge."[10]

[1] *Huidekoper* v. *Cotton*, 3 Watts 56. In this case it was observed: "The objection goes to a great length; if it is unlawful, or sinful to deliver the verdict to the prothonotary verbally after Sunday has commenced, I must suppose it would be equally unlawful to write and seal it up, to be delivered on Monday; nay, to deliberate upon, and discuss it after Sunday has commenced. Now, whether it would be less sinful in fact, and in its consequences, to keep a jury from Saturday night until Monday morning locked up without food; or to permit them to give a verdict, go home, and attend public worship, I leave to casuists to discuss. In point of fact, I remember cases in the Common Pleas and in Circuit Courts in which the jury charged and sent to deliberate on Saturday did not agree till after twelve that night, and, in some instances, until late in the forenoon of Sunday. In some of these cases writs of error were taken and in some appeals. So far as I know, the present objection has not been taken in our courts before. I have heard of courts sitting, and counsel arguing causes on Sunday. I never saw it and would not do it."

[2] *Hastings* v. *Columbus*, 42 O. S. 585 (1885); *City of Parsons* v. *Lindsay*, 41 Kan. 336 (1889).

[3] 3 Gil. 368 (1846).

[4] *Cory* v. *Silcox*, 5 Ind. 370 (1854).

[5] *Hiller* v. *English*, 4 Strob. 486 (1848).

[6] *Reid's Case*, 53 Ala. 402 (1875).

[7] *Huffman's Case*, 12 S. W. Rep. 588 (1889).

[8] *Bass* v. *Irvin*, 49 Ga. 436 (1878). See, also, *Weldon's Case*, 62 Ga. 449 (1879); and as to "charity and necessity" herein, *Henderson* v. *Reynolds*, 84 Ga. 159 (1889).

[9] *Shaw* v. *McComb*, 2 Bay 232 (1799).

[10] *Nabors' Case*, 6 Ala. 200 (1844).

It has been several times held that a judgment cannot be rendered on Sunday.[1]

So, it was held in New York, that though a justice was required by statute to render a judgment "forthwith" on the announcement of the verdict, where the latter was given on Sunday, the judgment might be pronounced on the Monday following.[2]

But a different view has been taken in Nebraska. The statute in that state provides that no court shall be opened, nor judicial business transacted, except "to give instructions to a jury then deliberating, to receive a verdict and discharge the jury, or to exercise the powers of a single magistrate in a criminal proceeding." Another section of the code provides that a justice must immediately render judgment according to the verdict. The court held that these two provisions were to be construed together, and said: "We have no doubt that where a verdict is received on Sunday it is the duty of the justice immediately to render a judgment thereon."[3] And it was said in Nevada: "The power given to the court to sit on Sunday to receive the verdict necessarily authorizes it to have the verdict then read and recorded, to discharge the jury, and make such other orders as are incident to the power given by the statute."[4]

The arguments were closed, and the jury retired to make up their verdict between twelve and one o'clock Saturday night, and the court adjourned till nine o'clock next morning, when it was ascertained that the jury had not agreed and the court was adjourned till six. At two the jury sent for the judge and requested further instructions, and received them. The judge prepared the order for withdrawing a juror and a mistrial, and at six o'clock, when the jury announced they had not agreed, he signed it and had it spread on the record. The court said there was nothing in the objection that the court was held on Sunday, under the circumstances.[5]

A Dakota statute provides, that while a jury in a criminal case are absent, the court may adjourn from time to time as to other business, but nevertheless shall be deemed open for every purpose con-

[1] *Arthur* v. *Mosby*, 2 Bibb 589 (1812); *York* v. *Ackerman*, Penn. (N. J.) 655 (1818); *Baxter's Case*, 3 Gilm. 368 (1846); *Davis* v. *Fish*, 1 Green 40 (1848); *Hemmens* v. *Bentley*, 32 Mich. 89 (1875).

[2] *Allen* v. *Godfrey*, 44 N. J. 438 (1871). See, also, *Hoghtaling* v. *Osborn*, 15 Johns. 118 (1871).

[3] *Thompson* v. *Church*, 13 Neb 287.

[4] *Rover's Case*, 13 Nev. 17.

[5] *McGimsey's Case*, 80 N. C. 377.

nected with the cause submitted to them till the verdict is rendered or the jury discharged. A jury retired at nine o'clock Saturday night, and at three Sunday afternoon the judge, of his own motion, had them brought in and corrected a supposed error in his former charge. *Held*, that there was no impropriety in his so doing.[1]

An error in giving judgment on Sunday may be proven by an examination of the almanac.[2]

VI. Miscellaneous Instances.

The publication of a legal notice has been held valid in Ohio[3] and South Carolina,[4] and invalid in Illinois,[5] Indiana[6] and Georgia.[7]

Where a judge by mistake appointed Sunday to hear an insolvent debtor's petition for the benefit of the act "for the relief of honest debtors," and the court met and adjourned over until next day, doing no other business, it was held that the hearing would have been necessarily postponed until Monday, "the next working day," without the meeting and adjournment for that purpose, and therefore the meeting and adjournment was a mere nullity, and no injury was done.[8]

In North Carolina it was held that a deposition taken on Sunday in Louisiana was inadmissible, and the court said it was immaterial whether or not Sunday were *dies non juridicus* in Louisiana.[9]

A justice cannot examine and decide a bastardy case on Sunday.[10]

The making or giving a mortgage is not civil process, or the service of civil process;[11] and the proceeding to effect a statute foreclosure of a mortgage is not a judicial proceeding, and is not prohibited by any law.[12]

It has been said in New York, that a settlement between parties to a litigation would be valid,[13] and an award by arbitration is not

[1] *Odell's Case*, 1 Dak. 197.

[2] *Page* v. *Faucet*, Cro. Eliz. 227 (1591).

[3] *Hastings* v. *Columbus*, 42 Ohio 585 (1885).

[4] *Ensor* v. *Witroffsky*, 29 S. C. 239 (1881).

[5] *Seammon* v. *Chicago*, 40 Ill. 146 (1866).

[6] *Shaw* v. *Williams*, 87 Ind. 158 (1882).

[7] *Sawyer* v. *Gargile*, 72 Ga. 290 (1880).

[8] *Cheeseborough* v. *Van Ness*, 12 Ga. 380 (1853).

[9] *Sloan* v. *Willifrod*, 3 Ired. (N. C.) 307 (1843).

[10] *Chapman's Case*, 5 Blackf. 111 (1839).

[11] *Tracy* v. *Jenks*, 15 Pick. 465 (1834).

[12] *Sales* v. *Smith*, 12 Wend. 57 (1834).

[13] *Shank* v. *Shoemaker*, 18 N. Y. 489 (1859).

void in Vermont,[1] though it is so in New York;[2] but even in the latter state, where arbitrators sat, heard the parties and witnesses, and signed the award on Sunday, but it was dated as of the next day, and was delivered to the parties on Monday, the court said the proceedings would not invalidate the award, which purported on its face to have been made, and was actually delivered and published, on Monday.[3] And it was said in Indiana, where an award was made and signed, and copies drawn on Saturday giving notice of the award, that this "not being an act of common labor, not being a judicial act and not being specially prohibited by any statute, but being simply a ministerial act in connection with a judicial proceeding, would seem to be valid, especially as the notice seems to have been received without objection."[4]

Where a jury was discharged on Saturday because they could not agree, and another *venire* was issued, and the court was not actually opened, and did not transact business, but the justices suspended business until the return of the second *venire* on Monday, and considered their court open, in contemplation of law, so far as not to lose jurisdiction of the case, it was held no violation of the New York act.[5]

In Indiana, courts may adjourn "to and on Sunday."[6] It was claimed in Nebraska that, under the statute of that state, an adjournment of court to Thanksgiving day was a nullity, as also the formal opening of the court on that day; but the court said that, although there was no actual adjournment, but practically only a recess, the objection was strictly technical and entirely devoid of merit, and the prisoner could not have been prejudiced by it in the slightest degree. In this case the trial did not proceed until the next day.[7] In North Carolina the statute required an adjournment, where the jury could not agree, "from day to day." An exception was taken to an adjournment from Saturday till Monday "while the jury had a prisoner in charge," and it was overruled.

[1] *Blond* v. *Bates*, 31 Vt. 147.

[2] *Story* v. *Elliott*, 8 Cow. 27 (1827).

[3] *Isacs* v. *B. H. Soc.*, 1 Hilt. 469 (1857).

[4] *Kiger* v. *Coats*, 18 Ind. 153 (1862).

[5] *Vanderwerker's Case*, 5 Wend. 530 1830; *Howard's Case*, 82 N. C. 623.

[6] *Kiger* v. *Coats*, 18 Ind. 153.

[7] *Polin's Case*, 14 Neb. 540 (1883).

CHAPTER VIII.

SUNDAY IN THE COMPUTATION OF TIME

I. In General.

In computing the time mentioned in a contract for the doing of an act, intervening Sundays are to be counted, but when the day of performance falls on Sunday it is not to be taken into the computation.[1] Where a party is to be paid by the day, Sunday is not included, "though parties may agree to pay for seven days a week, or thirty in a month, as well as for six or twenty-six;"[2] and where a statute prescribes that one officer shall fix the compensation for another, if the services to be rendered therefor are necessary on Sunday this day should be included in the estimate of time to be compensated for.[3]

The clause respecting demurrage was a memorandum in the margin of a bill of lading "to be discharged in fourteen days or pay five guineas a day." The ship arrived on December 9th; December 15th was Sunday, and December 21st was a holiday (St. Thomas' day); Christmas day and the three following days were all holidays. The goods were discharged on December 30th. In an action to recover the demurrage, Eldon, J., said: "If no evidence had been offered, but I was to decide on the clause itself, I should have been of opinion that it meant running days; as the law, however, stands, usage may be admitted to establish the meaning of the words. * * * If this was a case of inland trade, the word 'days' must mean working days, as the law of the country prohibits working on such days as those which formed part of the fourteen days."[4]

By a charter party twenty-five "running days" were allowed for lading, &c. The court said: "I think the words 'days' and 'running days' mean the same thing, viz., consecutive days, unless there

[1] *Salter* v. *Burt*, 20 Wend. (N. Y.) 205 (1838).

[2] *Patterson* v. *Patterson*, 2 Phil. 170.

[3] *People* v. *Ulster*, 91 N. Y. 672 (1883).

[4] *Cochran* v. *Retberg*, 3 Esp. N. P. 121 (1800).

be some particular custom. If the parties wish to exclude any days from the computation they must be expressed."[1]

In California, it was said, in the absence of any custom to the contrary, Sundays are computed in the calculation of lay days at the port of discharge; but where the contract specifies working lay days, Sundays and holidays are excluded in the computation.[2]

A statute provided that a railroad company should not allow freight to remain unshipped for more than five days, &c. *Held*, that the act meant running days, and that a final Sunday was one of them.[3] This was afterwards affirmed.[4]

In Connecticut, a party died October 2d, 1841, and devised land on condition that "within one year" after his decease the devisee should give a certain sum of money to A. The court said: "We think that the defendant had, by the terms of the devise, a full year allowed him for paying the money, and, therefore, that he was not bound to pay it on the Saturday preceding the day on which the year expired."[5]

Where it was necessary to prove that a defect in a highway had existed for twenty-four hours, in order to enable one injured in consequence of it to recover against a town, it was held that Sunday was not to be excluded in the computation of time.[6]

"Standard time" cannot be substituted for local, so as to make hours which by latter belong to Sunday a part of Saturday.[7]

Where a statutory holiday falls on Sunday, the following Monday is not a holiday, except as to commercial paper.[8]

II. When Fulfillment of Contract Due when Time for same Expires on Sunday.

There has not been an entire uniformity in the various judicial tribunals, in their decisions as to the time of performance of a contract when the day of maturity, on the face of the contract, falls on a Sunday.[9]

[1] *Brown* v. *Johnson*, 10 M. & W. 331.

[2] *Brooks* v. *Minturn*, 1 Cal. 481 (1851).

[3] *Branch W. & W. Co.*, 77 N. C. 347 (1822).

[4] *Keeter* v. *Same*, 86 N. C. 346.

[5] *Sands* v. *Lyon*, 18 Conn. 18 (1846).

[6] *Flagg* v. *Milbury*, 4 Cush. 243 (1849).

[7] *Henderson* v. *Reynolds*, 84 Ga. 159 (1889).

[8] *King's Case*, 37 N. W. Rep. 310.

[9] *Stebbins* v. *Leowolf*, 3 Cush. 137 (1849).

It was held in Massachusetts, that where a contract was entered into in New York, by parties resident there, and to be performed there, it was governed by the rules of law of that state in reference to the question of the time of performance where, on its face, the day of maturity fell on Sunday.[1]

It was observed in Maryland, that where the day appointed by a contract of sale for delivery falls on Sunday, this does not annul the contract, but the execution is due on another day, and the court said: "We have found much difficulty in determining whether the delivery must be Saturday or Monday. In the commercial community the usage is established in banking transactions, drafts, bills of exchange and negotiable paper. Amongst mercantile men, the pecuniary engagements becoming due on Sunday according to the letter of agreements, are discharged on the previous Saturday, and we think that both analogy and convenience will be consulted by deciding that the same rule shall govern other cases.[2]

But this is contrary to the general view, which distinguishes between negotiable instruments and other contracts in this regard.[3] Thus, in Massachusetts, when the time for paying an insurance premium expired on Sunday, it was held that the tender on Monday was sufficient.[4] And so it was said in New York, that "when, from accident, or mutual error, the day of fulfilling an agreement falls upon Sunday, there is enough of principle and authority to justify the party in deferring his performance till the Monday ensuing."[5]

And in New Jersey, where, by the terms of a contract, a deed was to be delivered and purchase-money paid on May 1st, and this fell on Sunday, it was held that compliance with the contract on Monday was a legal performance.[6]

III. When Demand, &c., to be Made, Where Time for Same Expires on Sunday.

In a case where the time for paying a quarterly premium on an insurance policy expired on Sunday, the Supreme Court of Massachusetts said: "We have, on the one hand, the rule as to

[1] *Stebbins* v. *Leowolf*, 3 Cush. 137 (1849).

[2] *Kilgour* v. *Miles*, 6 G. & J. 268 (1834).

[3] *Hammond* v. *American Co.*, 10 Gray 306.

[4] *Ibid.*

[5] *Campbell* v. *International Soc.*, 4 Bos. 298 (1849).

[6] *Stryker* v. *Vanderbilt*, 3 Dutch. (N. J.) 68. See, also, *Amis* v. *Kile*, 2 Yerg. 31 (1821).

commercial paper or negotiable notes, payable with grace, requiring payments to be made on Saturday, where the third day of grace falls on Sunday, and the other rule, generally adopted as to other contracts to pay money, or perform other specific duties on a certain day named, that if such day falls on Sunday the day of performance is postponed till Monday."[1]

It was observed in New York: "If a note falls due on Sunday in Connecticut it must be paid on Monday; in this state on Saturday."[2]

Among the "points resolved" by Holt, C. J., we find: "If the last of the three days of grace is a Sunday, or great holiday, as Christmas day, upon which no money used to be paid, there the party ought to demand money on a foreign bill of exchange upon the second day, and protest it thereon."[3]

It was said in Massachusetts: "The rule respecting days of grace depends altogether on the custom of merchants, and the established usage, as early as the time of Lord Holt, in the case of foreign bills, has since been extended equally to inland bills and notes of hand,[4] but, if demand is made on Saturday, notice to the indorser on Monday is sufficient."[5]

The rule as to ordinary contracts has been applied to coupon bonds,[6] and to a check "without grace," which, where falling due on Sunday, was held not presentable till Monday;[7] and so where a non-negotiable note was payable sixty days after date, and the sixtieth day was Sunday, it was held that a tender of the amount on Monday following was sufficient; this was settled by a bench of nine judges in Connecticut, of whom three dissented.[8]

IV. Computation of Time in Judicial Proceedings.

Where the writ was returnable on Wednesday, and the bail-bond was assigned on the Monday following, the court held the party was too soon by a day, for that Sunday was not to be reckoned.[9]

[1] *Hammond* v. *American Co.*, 10 Gray 306.

[2] *Strong* v. *Elliott*, 8 Cow. 27 (1827).

[3] *Tassell* v. *Lewis*, 1 Ray. 743 (1699).

[4] *Thayer* v. *Felt*, 4 Pick. 354. See, also, *Jackson* v. *Richards*, 2 Caines 343; *Bussard* v. *Levering*, 6 Wheat. 102 (1821).

[5] *Jackson* v. *Richards*, 2 Caines (N. Y.) 343 (1821); *Cuyler* v. *Stevens*, 4 Wend. 566 (1830).

[6] *Chaffee* v. *Middlesex R. R.*, 146 Mass. 224 (1888).

[7] *Salt* v. *Burt*, 20 Wend. 205 (1838).

[8] *Avery* v. *Steuart*, 2 Conn. 69 (1816).

[9] *Studley* v. *Sturt*, 2 Str. 782 (1727).

A rule of court allowed eight days for pleading. "It seems to have been allowed that two intervening Sundays were not to be counted."[1]

It was determined that Sunday was not to be esteemed one of the four days to be allowed for motions in arrest of judgment, and the practice was said to be the same on the criminal as on the civil side of the court.[2]

Where a defendant has four days to plead, "the Sunday is one."[3]

A defendant had till the fourth day after the return of a *clausum fregit* to appear. The return day was a Sunday. *Held*, he must appear by Wednesday.[4]

Where a declaration was filed on the 17th and the defendant had four days to plead, the 21st coming on Sunday, the plea was filed on Monday. The court held it was too late, "because the four days are reckoned exclusively, and the time expired on the Saturday."[5]

The court was of opinion that if the last of the four days allowed for pleading happen on a Sunday the defendant may plead in abatement the next day; otherwise, as no plea can be filed on a Sunday, the time would be limited to three days in such cases, and Buller, J., added that the note referred to in *Jennings* v. *Webb*, 1 T. R. 278, meant that Sunday should only be considered as one of the days when it was not the last. "For, that in some instances, when any act is to be done by a party in a limited number of days, as in a case of a motion in arrest of judgment, the party has four law days when the court is actually sitting in which to do it, and in those cases Sunday is not one, though it be an intervening day."[6]

In 1792 it was said, if a plea be demanded on Saturday, the defendant has twenty-four hours to plead, exclusively of Sunday.[7]

In 1809, after reference to the master, Lord Ellenborough said that "it appeared to be the settled practice in all rules for pleading against bail in *scire facias* to exclude Sundays and holidays from the computation of time given, though not happening on the last day;"[8] but he is reported as having said in 1811 that "whatever

[1] *Shadwell* v. *Angel*, 1 Burr. 55 (1756).

[2] *Elkin's Case*, 4 Burr. 2129.

[3] *Jennings* v. *Nett*, 1 T. R. 277 (1786).

[4] *Fano* v. *Coken*, 1 H. B. 9 (1788).

[5] *Harbord* v. *Perrigal*, 5 T. R. 210 (1793).

[6] *Lee* v. *Carlton*, 3 T. R. 642.

[7] *Solomans* v. *Freeman*, 4 T. R. 557.

[8] *Walter* v. *Beaumont*, 11 East 271.

the general rule may be, the grammatical construction of the rule of court accords with the practice of reckoning Sunday when intervening as one of the eight days given to the bail to render their principal." And Bailey, J., added that if the proceedings had been by original, the bail would have had till the *quarto die post*, which day would not be altered by the intervention of Sunday.[1]

The following appears among the *Regulae Generales* of 1832: "In all cases in which any particular number of days, not expressed to be clear days, is prescribed by the rules or practice of the courts, the same shall be reckoned exclusively of the first day and inclusively of the second day, unless the last day shall happen to fall on a Sunday, Christmas day, Good Friday, or a day appointed for a public fast or thanksgiving, in which case the time shall be reckoned exclusively of that day also."[2]

In Backus on Sheriffs, &c. (New York, 1812), it is laid down "if the return day of a writ be Sunday, and the return appears to be made on that day, it will be bad, nor can it be made on any day subsequent."[3]

Where the lien of an attachment is limited to thirty days, the last day is not excluded because it is Sunday; and this applies to other statutes, unless a contrary intention is apparent.[4]

Where an officer was allowed to adjourn a sale under execution for three days, it was held Sunday was not included, and the court added: "If it were required that adjournments should only be made from day to day, still no one would doubt that an adjournment from Saturday to Monday would be legal, for every statute must have a reasonable construction."[5]

In Florida, where the time fixed by an order for settling a bill of exceptions expires on Sunday, the settlement may be made on Monday.[6]

It was said in Maine that, even without a statutory exception of Sunday from the time allowed for an appeal, such an exception would be implied.[7] In the same state, where, by statute, a writ of error might defeat an execution, if issued within four days after

[1] *Creswell* v. *Green*, 14 East 536.

[2] 1 Dowl. Pr. C. 200.

[3] 1 Back. Sher. 259.

[4] *Butler* v. *Damon*, 14 Mass. 225 (1818).

[5] *Thayer* v. *Felt*, 4 Pick. 364.

[6] *Bacon's Case*, 22 Fla. 46 (1886).

[7] *Suhur's Case*, 33 Me. 539 (1852).

judgment perfected, it was held this meant four clear judicial days, and where Sunday was the second of the four it was excluded.[1]

But it was held in New York, that Sunday was to be included when the last of the number of days allowed for appealing from a justice's decision had expired, the court saying: "Sunday has, in no case, we believe, been excluded in the computation of statute time,"[2] and the reason of this decision was afterwards said to be that, the day bebeing *dies non juridicus*, the sheriff was not bound to attend to the discharge of the ordinary duties of his office on that day.[3] In this state, where the rule to plead expires on Sunday, the defendant has the next day in which to plead.[4] So, where the last day of a rule to plead in an ejectment happens on Sunday, default is prematurely entered on Monday.[5] And, in the same state, where a claim of property was interposed in an action of replevin on Saturday, and a statute allowed two days to elapse before the claim must be tried, the court said the statute meant law days, and Sunday was properly excluded in the computation.[6] And again, the court said: "We know of no rule or principle by which Sunday is to be excluded from the computation where it is an intermediate day," and, accordingly, where the time for the return of a summons was four days by statute, and it was made returnable in five days, of which Sunday was one, it was held this objection was fatal.[7] And in another New York case, it was said that, "in computing statutory time, when the last day for compliance falls on Sunday, that day is included in the computation, and the act must be done on the preceding day," though it was held that this was not the case where the time was fixed by a rule of court, and, accordingly, that where

[1] *Blunt* v. *Greenwood*, 1 Cow. 15 (1823).

[2] *Dodge's Case*, 7 Cow. 147 (1827).

[3] *Luther's Case*, 1 Wend. 42 (1828).

[4] *Cock* v. *Bunn*, 6 Johns. 325 (1810). The following note is appended: "In *Roberts* v. *Quickenden*, 50 Ga. 111, this case was explained as not meaning to extend the like mode of computation to rules for pleading in actions in general. The practice appears to be this: in rules of pleading in action in general, the Sunday or holiday reckons as a day, except it be the last; but in rules for judgment a Sunday or a holiday does not reckon, though it be not the last day; and in proceedings on *scire facias* against bail, the rules for pleading are assimilated to and operate in this respect as rules for judgment, and are entered as such in a separate book in the office."

[5] *Borst* v. *Griffin*, 5 Wend. 84.

[6] *Anon.*, 2 Hill 375 (1842).

[7] *King* v. *Dowdall*, 2 Sand. (N. Y.) 131 (1848).

the time for putting in special bail expired on Sunday, it could be put in on Monday.[1]

In Pennsylvania, where the last day for an appeal was Sunday, one judge thought it unnecessary to decide the point whether one more day was allowed, but the other expressed the opinion that it should be.[2] A Wisconsin statute allowed twenty-four hours for an appeal from a magistrate's conviction. Where a party was convicted Saturday, and appealed Monday, it was held in time.[3] In the same state, the statute allowed a justice, when taking time to consider a cause, to continue the same for not more than seventy-two hours. The court said: "We are entirely satisfied that it was the intention of the legislature to give the justice seventy-two hours of secular time," and held that the hours of an intervening Sunday were excluded.[4]

It was held in California that, where Sunday was the last day of the period of extension fixed by a court's order for preparing a statement on a motion for a new trial, it should be excluded.[5] The constitution of California provides that the Supreme Court "shall always be open for the transaction of business," and the Superior Court shall be so, "legal holidays and non-judicial days excepted;" and the former provision is inserted among the general exceptions to the rule that no court shall transact judicial business on Sunday. It is also provided, that an order that a judgment of one department of the Supreme Court be heard *in banc*, must be made within thirty days after the judgment of the department. Where the thirtieth day fell on Sunday, an order made on the following Monday was vacated, and the court added: "In point of fact, we believe the universal custom has been to make no distinction where Sunday intervenes, and where it does not. Sunday is always counted as one of the days when the statute has declared that an act shall be performed within a given number of days, whether the number of days specified by the statute is longer or shorter than a week."[6]

[1] *Broome* v. *Wellington*, 1 Sand. (N. Y.) 664 (1847). See, also, *Campbell* v. *International Soc.*, 4 Bos. 298 (1859).

[2] *Sims* v. *Hampton*, 1 S. & R. 411 (1815).

[3] *Ridgeley's Case*, 7 Wis. 661 (1859).

[4] *Meng* v. *Winkleman*, 43 Wis. 41 (1877).

[5] *Muir* v. *Galoway*, 61 Cal. 498 (1882).

[6] *Adams* v. *Dohrmann*, 63 Cal. 417 (1883).

In Connecticut, Sunday is excluded within the computation of time within which motions to set aside a verdict, &c., must be filed.[1]

It was held in Indiana, that the day was not counted where a statute required a replevin bond to be executed within twenty-four hours after the replevy.[2]

The charter of Chicago provides that notice of the filing of a special assessment rule in the clerk's office shall be given by six days' publication in a newspaper, and confirmation be applied for at the next regular meeting of the council after the expiration of the publication, and that objections shall be filed in writing in the city clerk's office at least one day prior to the meeting of the council. The six days of publication ended on Sunday, and a certain assessment was confirmed on Monday. The court said: "It thus appears, Sunday being *dies non juridicus*, and the clerk's office not open for the filing of papers, no opportunity was given parties interested to file objections. As the law requires objections to be filed at least one day prior to the "meetings of the council, it must be construed as intending that a day shall intervene between the last publication and the action of the council."[3] And this case was afterwards affirmed where the last day of publication was Sunday. Whether the publication on Sunday would have been counted if the council had met Tuesday instead of Monday following does not appear.[4]

In Missouri, the time for a prisoner to make his challenges after the list of jurors was furnished him was limited by statute. It was provided that Thanksgiving day, when appointed by the governor, should be a public holiday; and that such holidays should be considered the same as Sunday, as regarded the presenting for payment or acceptance of bills, notes, &c. The court said: "If such holidays are to be considered as Sunday for all general purposes, they would still be counted in computing statute time unless expressly excepted."[5] And in New Hampshire, a person against whom judgment has been rendered for a fine under the militia laws is entitled

[1] *Stone* v. *Stevens*, 12 Conn. 219 (1852).

[2] *Link* v. *Clemens*, 7 Blackf. 479 (1845).

[3] *Burton* v. *Chicago*, 53 Ill. 87.

[4] *Chicago* v. *Vulcan*, 93 Ill. 222 (1869).

[5] *Green's Case*, 66 Mo. 631 (1877).

to two full days, exclusive of Sundays, after the day when judgment was rendered, to pay the fine and costs.[1]

Where the last day of the fifteen months during which a creditor had a statutory right to "redeem" lands sold under an execution happened on Sunday, it was held that tender must be made on Saturday to entitle the creditor to a deed from the sheriff.[2]

But later, where a statute required a judgment to be rendered within four days after the submission of a cause, it was held that Sunday must be included.

Where a party served notice on another that he would move for an order "on the tenth day of the term," the court said the question what day of the month that was depended "on whether Sunday, which intervened between the first and tenth days of the term, ought to be counted as one of the days of the term, and the court is of opinion that it ought not," which opinion the court based on the general understanding and usage in such matters in Virginia, while admitting that a different view might be taken in England.[3]

The law provided that if a judge should not attend on the first day of a term of the court, the same should stand adjourned from day to day till a court should be formed, "if that shall happen before four o'clock of the third day." The first day of the term was Saturday. It was held that the judge's presence at four o'clock on Tuesday was sufficient. In a subsequent Virginia case, where a statute provided that a term should not exceed fifteen days, was construed, the day on which judgment was passed was the sixteenth from the commencement of the term, counting the two Sundays which intervened, and the fourteenth, not counting them. The court said that the fifteen days were judicial days on which the court may lawfully sit, and did not include Sundays.[4] In 1866, in the same state, notice was given that a certain motion would be made on the "tenth day of the term." A Sunday intervened between the first and tenth days of the term. It was held that it ought not to be counted. In a Georgia case, the question whether the service of a writ was sufficient depended on whether or not, when the sheriff had five days to serve writs and the last was Sun-

[1] *Scribner* v. *Whitcher*, 6 N. H. 63 (1832).

[2] *Luther's Case*, 1 Wend. 42 (1828).

[3] *Michie* v. *Michie*, 17 Grat. 109 (1880).

[4] *Read's Case*, 22 Grat. 924 (1872).

day, it should be counted; it was held that it should not be.[1] And it was said in another case: "While we hold that Sunday is not to be disregarded, whether it be the first or the last, or an intervening day, in counting the various times presented by law for the service of writs, notice and all such matters, still we think that a different rule should obtain in relation to appeals; and whether Sunday be the first or last, or an intervening day, it is not to be counted."[2] The Alabama act directing that the court shall be held one week, as distinguished from six judicial days, "does not intend a change with respect to the Sabbath."[3]

When the return day of a summons falls on Sunday, it is not void but voidable, and next day is return day.[4]

Where an adjournment falls on Sunday, the court does not lose jurisdiction, but the case is continued till next day.[5]

A term of court which begins Monday and is to last four weeks, expires at twelve o'clock midnight of the last Saturday.[6]

[1] *Turner* v. *Thompson*, 23 Ga. 49 (1857).

[2] *Neal* v. *Crew*, 12 Ga. 93 (1852).

[3] *Nabor's Case*, 6 Ala. 200 (1844).

[4] *Ostertag* v. *Galbraith*, 37 N. W. Rep. 637 (1888).

[5] *King's Case*, 37 N. W. Rep. 410.

[6] *Juneman's Case* (Tex.), 13 S. W. Rep. 783 (1890).

CHAPTER IX.

SUNDAY LIQUOR-SELLING.

I. As "Business," &c.

Before the passage of laws specially forbidding the sale of liquor on Sunday, attempts were made to punish the act in Delaware and Pennsylvania. The Delaware case was decided in 1844.[1] It was held by a majority of the court that liquor-selling by an inn-keeper was not "worldly business," nor a "sale of goods," within the statute; and that a resident of the town might be served, as a "guest," with a drink. Harrington, J., dissented, distinguishing between an "inn" and a "tavern," and holding that the inn-keeper was bound to entertain "travelers" only, and that a resident calling for a drink at the bar was not a "guest." In 1847 a Delaware statute was passed, declaring Sunday liquor-selling by inn-keepers to be "worldly business." In 1853 it was held in Pennsylvania that liquor-selling by an inn-keeper was "worldly employment and labor," and not excepted under the words "dressing victuals."[2]

II. Clubs—What is "A Tippling-House."

It was laid down in Georgia, in 1882, that "it makes no difference in law whether the place be called a bar-room, or a glee club resort, or a parlor, or a restaurant, if it be a place where liquor is retailed and tippled on the Sabbath day, with a door to get into it, so that anybody can push it open and go in and drink, the proprietor of it is guilty of keeping open a tippling-house on Sunday."[3]

In Indiana, in 1874, where a society, with initiation fees, monthly dues and officers, held regular meetings to which none were admitted but members, and these were furnished with pass-keys, and,

[1] *Hall's Case*, 4 Harr. 132.

[2] *Omit's Case*, 21 Pa. 426.

[3] *Hassey's Case*, 69 Ga. 54.

on each Saturday, the treasurer, by the society's order, purchased a keg of beer with its money, and each member who desired a glass delivered the treasurer five cents, which was placed in the treasury, and of which the treasurer got no part, but which was disbursed by a standing committee for rent, relief of sick members, &c., it was held a "sale" within the statute, made by the society to its members, through the treasurer, as its agent, and it was said to be sufficient that a gain accrued to the principal, the society.[1]

In 1879, in Georgia, the court below was requested to charge that a tippling-house is "a house kept for the purpose of selling liquors by the dram, or small quantities, to the public, and where men are accustomed to tipple," and in lieu thereof, it charged that if liquors were given away by the drink, or other small quantity, every Sunday, and it was a usual thing, it was a tippling-house, whether pay was received for the drink or not; and this was approved on appeal.[2] The articles of association in this case expressed a knowledge that it was against the law for a liquor dealer to sell, and declared that they needed Sunday drinks, and that, in order to comply with the law, the members would pay the sums opposite their names every Saturday night to the treasurer "for the purpose of purchasing the liquor necessary for the use of the club the following Sabbath."[3]

III. What Is "Intoxicating Liquor."

It was said in New York, in 1875, that the courts, "acting upon their own knowledge, derived from observation," would take notice that "whiskey, brandy, gin, ale and strong beer" were intoxicating, but would not do so with reference to lager beer, and that where such notice was not taken the question of the intoxicating character of the liquor was one of fact.[4]

In Indiana, it was held that the courts "could not, from their general knowledge, say that all malt liquors are intoxicating,"[5] and, later, that beer was not, necessarily, a "malt liquor;"[6] that the court would not judicially notice that "common brewer's beer"

[1] *Marmout's Case*, 48 Ind. 21.

[2] *Minor's Case*, 63 Ga. 318.

[3] See, also, *Smith's Case*, 102 Mass. 144 (1869).

[4] *Ran's Case*, 63 N. Y. 277.

[5] *Shaw's Case*, 56 Ind. 188 (1877).

[6] *Weis' Case*, 33 Ind. 204.

was intoxicating, and that "the mere naked opinion of the witness that the liquor sold is intoxicating, founded upon no knowledge of its effects, of what it is composed or how it is made, is not sufficient."[1] But later, in the same state, where a witness said "he bought beer, and beer is an intoxicating liquor," it was held that the fair inference was that the beer, concerning which he was testifying as having been sold him, was an intoxicating liquor.[2] But an instruction that if a witness testified that he bought beer of the defendant, and is asked if beer is intoxicating and says it is, and no different beer is spoken of by the witness or others, it is a legitimate inference for the jury to draw that the witness, in saying beer was intoxicating, had reference to the beer he purchased, was held to be an invasion of the jury's province.[3] Finally, on an indictment for selling intoxicating liquors, it was held that evidence that the liquor sold was beer was sufficient;[4] and that, if other than malted and fermented beer was wanted at a bar, it was to be expected "that the qualifying words would be used, such as spruce beer, root beer, small beer, ginger beer and the like, thus attaching a remote and secondary meaning to the word 'beer,' as descriptive of particular beverages."[5] In 1884, it was said: "Brandy is ranked as an intoxicating liquor by writers upon the general subject, and that it is a liquor of that character is generally and commonly known. The fact is, therefore, one of which the courts will take judicial knowledge. The addition to the term 'brandy' to the word 'blackberry,' does no more than designate it as a particular kind of brandy; it does not indicate that the liquor was not brandy of some kind. The natural and reasonable presumption is that the basis of the liquor was brandy, and, therefore, intoxicating. If it was not, the appellants should have shown it."[6]

IV. "Keeping Open."

A statute which provides that saloons must be "closed," means that the sales shall be stopped, and will be construed in a common

[1] *Klare's Case*, 43 Ind. 483 (1873). See, also, *Lathrope's Case*, 50 Id. 555 (1875); *Plunkett's Case*, 69 Id. 68; *King's Case*, 79 Id. 488 (1881).

[2] *Pancake's Case*, 81 Ind. 93 (1881).

[3] *Ibid.*

[4] *Myer's Case*, 93 Ind. 251 (1883).

[5] *Ibid.*

[6] *Fenton's Case*, 100 Ind. 598.

sense way.[1] A saloon is "open," of which the outer door is closed, but unfastened, and can be opened from the outside;[2] and so where a back door is open;[3] and so where the door was kept open, so that persons had ingress and egress thereto, and persons did go in and out, and the back room was kept for a sleeping-room, and there was a partition between the sleeping-room and grocery, where the liquors were kept, with a door without a shutter, so that persons could pass from one to another.[4]

A saloon is open where a gate is open in a "high paling" around it, as well as door of the saloon itself; and it matters not for what purpose (as to dry fruit, &c.)—"the open door is the crime."[5]

The front room was used as a "card-room;" it opened at the rear into a room where cigars were sold; this communicated by a door with a room where the proprietor of three apartments vended liquor. This door was locked on Sunday; there was evidence that parties were seen coming out of a rear entrance to the third room. *Held*, it was for the jury to say what rooms constituted the "saloon," and whether it was "open."[6]

To keep the door open "but for a moment" is a violation of the statute.[7]

And where the keeper's "living-rooms" were connected with his saloon by "inward" doors, and people passed through the former into the latter, and occasionally drank in the latter, it was held that the "living-rooms" were a part of the saloon, and could not be "opened, except to the family of the saloon-keeper."[8]

[1] *Kuttz's Case*, 37 Mich. 279.

[2] *Lynch's Case*, 8 Gray 384 (1857). See, also, *Hussey's Case*, 69 Ga. 54. The facts of this last case are thus vigorously set forth by the court: "The counter where, on other days, drinking could be done, was covered by a canvass from the ceiling to the floor, so as to be invisible itself and to conceal the bottles on shelves behind it, and on it, in brazen letters, was the announcement, 'bar closed,' and all the drinking was carried on in the rear and restaurant room. This fact that the ostrich thus hid his head in the sand, and thereby imagined that his body was all covered, too, is absolutely assigned as the legal reason why he was not visible to the keen eye of the law, which penetrates and despises all subterfuge and deceit. But one witness, though the canvass tried to hide the bird's head, actually did see poked out through a sort of aperture or window the bill or beak which let out the liquor from the bar to servants in the restaurant. So that the foolish bird did not even keep all his head hid all the time.

[3] *Blahut's Case*, 34 Ark. 447.

[4] *Harvey's Case*, 65 Ga. 568 (1880).

[5] *King's Case*, 77 Ga. 734 (1886).

[6] *Scranton's Case*, 61 Mich. 244 (1886).

[7] *Morse's Case*, 78 Ga. 110 (1886).

[8] *Cox's Case*, 38 N. W. Rep. 235 (1888).

An inn-keeper may keep open a room for supplying meals,[1] but it has been said: "The evidence shows that the plaintiff kept his saloon open in order to supply customers with drinks at his bar. This was not a lawful purpose, and it is no excuse that he may also have furnished meals to boarders at the same place. The lawful business—if it was one—cannot protect the unlawful."[2] In 1882, where the defendant claimed that his saloon was open without the selling of liquor, and with no intention of selling it, and that the persons seen in it were washing and cleaning it, the court said the question of intent was wholly immaterial.[3]

In 1880, in Arkansas, the court said: "The jury hardly believed that the saloon was kept open for the purpose of airing it. Persons were collected there playing billiards, and the defendant stood at the open front door, with his apron on—business fashion—and apparently ready to wait on customers. It is immaterial whether the defendant or his brother was the owner or proprietor of the saloon; the defendant was there, seemingly in charge, with a business appearance, and the front door was open. If he was merely a clerk or servant in the saloon, and was serving in it as such when the door was open on Sunday, he was a participant in the offence."[4]

In the Massachusetts statute, the words "except works of necessity and charity," qualify only the clause "does any manner of labor, business or work," and have no reference to keeping open a shop, or being present at dancing, &c.; and, though it is necessary to allege and prove that a shop was unlawfully kept open, or kept open for unlawful business, the ordinary business of a liquor shop was unlawful, and it is sufficient to prove that the defendant kept open his shop for ordinary traffic with the public indiscriminately.[5]

On an indictment for "keeping open" a shop, evidence is admissible which was previously offered under an indictment for selling liquor.[6]

In Missouri, keeping open and selling are different offences.[7]

Where a witness could not remember what Sunday the place

[1] *Gregory's Case*, 47 Conn. 276 (1879).

[2] *Lynch's Case*, 16 Mich. 472 (1868).

[3] *Weldvogel's Case*, 49 Mich. 337.

[4] *Mane's Case*, 36 Ark. 222.

[5] *Nagle's Case*, 117 Mass. 142.

[6] *Harrison's Case*, 11 Gray 308 (1858). See, also, *Tuckey's Case*, 13 Allen 559 (1866).

[7] *Amb's Case*, 20 Mo. 214 (1854).

was open, but knew it was before a certain trial, tne record of the trial was admitted to prove the date of the opening.[1]

V. The Effect of a License.

A license gives no right to sell liquor on Sunday.[2] Though a party has paid for a license for carrying on his business during a whole year, a city ordinance prohibiting its sale on Sunday is no violation of a contract, and not invalid as divesting vested rights,[3] for "the city council has the same power over the subject within the city limits that the legislature has within the state."[4]

A municipal provision for cancellation of a license for selling liquors by boards of excise, if they find a party holding such to be violating the law relating to their use, &c., is not unconstitutional, as authorizing a conviction without a trial by jury.[5] An injunction will lie against the enforcement of a city ordinance so as to prevent inn-keepers from selling liquor to lodgers, &c., as allowed by statute.[6]

A city ordinance allowing the opening of a saloon from nine to four is void, as conflicting with the state statute requiring them "to be closed during the day."[7]

Where a general statute declares a place where liquor is sold to be a public nuisance in violation of law, a Sunday sale by a licensed saloon-keeper, in the absence of a city ordinance prohibiting the sale of liquor, does not render the place of sale such a nuisance.[8]

Where a state law forbids selling liquor on Sunday, this may not

1 *Quintard* v. *Corcoran*, 50 Conn. 34 (1882).

2 *Omit's Case*, 21 Pa. 426 (1853); *Nesbit's Case*, 34 Id. 36 (1859); *Amb's Case*, 20 Mo. 214 (1854); *Griffin's Case*, 1 Idaho (N. S.) 476.

3 *Bott's Case*, 31 La. Ann. 663 (1879).

4 *Megowan's Case*, 2 Metc. (Ky.) 3. In this case the court said: "The time when the appellant obtained his license as a tavern-keeper is not stated in the record. It does not appear, therefore, that the ordinance was passed after he had been licensed, consequently the questions that might arise on that state of the case are not presented for our decision."

5 *Presmyer's Case*, 59 N. Y. 92 (1874).

6 *Wood* v. *Brooklyn*, 14 Barb. 425 (1852). A case where the law of the state and a village regulation were held not inconsistent arose in New York in 1863. *Cohoes* v. *Moran*, 25 How. Pr. 385.

7 *Sundstrom's Case*, 25 Tex. 133 (1888).

8 *Wacker's Case*, 38 N. W. Rep. 189 (1888).

be done under a municipal ordinance passed by virtue of the city's authority to "regulate," &c., the liquor business.[1]

VI. The Indictment, Evidence, &c.

Where the prohibitions apply only to a class, the indictment must show on its face that the accused belongs thereto (as that he is a "retail liquor dealer").[2]

Indiana has a law providing for permits to sell liquor, but with the reservation that they shall not authorize sales on Sunday, under which it was held, in 1873, not necessary for an indictment to aver that the defendant had a permit,[3] since, if he had one, it would not authorize him to sell on that day.[4]

Under the New York statute, a person not a hotel-keeper cannot, without a license, sell in quantities more than five gallons, or give away liquor in less quantities. The question arose whether a person keeping a hotel without a license was within the prohibition, and the court held that the section was specially designed to prevent hotel-keepers, whether licensed or not, from selling or giving away liquors on Sunday; admitting, however, that the unlicensed keeper would not have been included, if, instead of "hotel-keeper," &c., or "person licensed," &c., the law had read, "hotel-keeper," &c., or "other person licensed," &c.[5]

In an indictment for "keeping open" a saloon it is not necessary to negative the fact that the accused kept it open in order to supply meals to boarders and lodgers;[6] and the court said it was "somewhat doubtful" whether the exceptions "relative to quiet and good order" were applicable to saloon-keepers like the accused.[7]

An indictment need not state the names of the persons to whom the liquor was sold, or that their names were unknown to the grand jurors;[8] but it is sufficient to aver in an indictment that the name of such person is unknown.[9]

[1] *Heinnsen's Case* (Col.), 23 Pac. Rep. 995 (1890).

[2] *Bode's Case*, 7 Gill (Md.) 326 (1848). See, also, *Page's Case*, 3 Park. (N. Y.) Cr. 600 (1857).

[3] *Lehritter's Case*, 42 Ind. 383.

[4] *Id.* 384.

[5] *Murphy's Case*, 5 Park. (N. Y.) Cr. 130 (1861).

[6] *Lynch's Case*, 16 Mich. 472 (1868).

[7] *Id.* 477.

[8] *Parnell's Case*, 16 Ark. 506 (1855).

[9] *Ashley's Case*, 92 Ind. 559 (1883). See, also, *Drake's Case*, 64 N. C. 589 (1870); *Bryson's Case*, 90 Id. 747 (1884).

An indictment under the Massachusetts statute against an inn-keeper for entertaining persons must allege that they were not "travelers, strangers or lodgers," and it must allege how many were entertained, that the court may know how to punish the defendant according to the provisions of the statute.[1]

It has been said that it is not sufficient to state that the selling was "on or about the —— day of ——, which was the first day of the week, commonly called Sunday,"[2] and that a statute which provided that the precise time of the commission of an offence need not be stated in an indictment, but it should be sufficient if shown to have been within the statute of limitations, except where time was an indispensable ingredient of the offence, "did not dispense with the necessity of stating the day on which the offence was committed, but was declaratory of what was the law before, viz., that the state is not bound by the day stated, but may prove any other day within the limitations," &c.[3]

The indictment must aver that the day was Sunday,[4] but it is not necessary to name the day of the month; and if the day of the week is properly set out, the indictment will be good, though the day of the month given in it falls on some other day of the week.[5]

The only case discovered holding a different doctrine from this last arose in Georgia, where an indictment charged the defendant with keeping open a tippling-house on "April 4, 1873, being the Sabbath day," and the 4th of April in that year was Friday. The indictment was held bad, and the court said: "In this case, keeping open a tippling-house is not an offence prohibited by law. It becomes penal only by its being done on the Sabbath day. It is the time when—*the character of the day on which the act is done*—that constitutes the offence."[6]

In an Indiana case the year was laid in the indictment, and the evidence showed that liquor was sold on the 4th day of May, and on Sunday, as charged, but failed to show in what year it was sold. The court held that there was a defect in the indictment, and said:

[1] *Maxwell's Case*, 2 Pick. 138 (1824).

[2] *Clark's Case*, 34 Ind. 436 (1870).

[3] *Ibid.* See, also, *Effinger's Case*, 47 Ind. 235.

[4] *Roy's Case*, 91 Ind. 417 (1883).

[5] *Eskridge's Case*, 1 Swan 413. See, also, *Bull's Case*, 42 Barb. 324 (1862); *Megowan's Case*, 2 Metc. 3 (1859); *Hoover's Case*, 56 Md. 584 (1881).

[6] *Werner's Case*, 51 Ga. 426 (1874).

"We know the 4th of May in this year was Sunday, but this does not show that the year 1873 was intended. It may have been on some Sunday in some other year, which was the 4th of May to which the witness referred."[1] Proof of the precise time at which the liquor was sold is immaterial, provided it was within the time limited for prosecutions, and on some Sunday within the same.[2] The charge was selling without license on July 3d; the proof was of a sale on July 4th, which was Sunday. *Held*, that the variance was immaterial.[3]

Where the prohibition was against keeping open "tippling-houses," it was held in Georgia to be sufficient to charge keeping open "one tippling-house."[4]

The Missouri statute forbids the sale of fermented "or" distilled liquors. An indictment charged the sale of fermented "and" distilled liquors. The court said this did not vitiate the indictment.[5]

It was held in Arkansas that but one offence was charged in an indictment where the first count charged it to have been committe by selling on Sunday a pint of whiskey, and the second by selling on the same day a pint of alcohol; that alcohol is embraced in any one of the terms "goods, wares or merchandise," and that to sell by sample, parcels or quantities, and not in the gross, is to "retail."[6]

Under a Michigan statute against "keeping open," but a single offence is committed where a saloon is opened and closed many times during the day.[7]

The forfeiture of a license is not a "fine" for which an indictment may be sustained under the Missouri statute.[8]

It was held in Missouri that a warrant under a city ordinance need not specify the quantity of whiskey sold, nor the place where it was drank, and the court said: "Selling whiskey on Sunday constituted the offence. The quantity sold, as well as the place where it was drank, were wholly immaterial."[9]

In Pennsylvania, some of the court were of opinion that a con-

[1] *Lehritter's Case*, 42 Ind. 383.

[2] *Pancake's Case*, 81 Ind. 93 (1881); *Marre's Case*, 36 Ark. 222 (1880).

[3] *Krank's Case*, 46 Hun 632.

[4] *Hall's Case*, 3 Kelly 18 (1843).

[5] *Nation's Case*, 75 Mo. 53 (1881).

[6] *Bridge's Case*, 37 Ark. 224 (1881).

[7] *Cox's Case*, 38 N. W. Rep. 235 (1888).

[8] *Burnett's Case*, 77 Mo. 570 (1883).

[9] *Megowan's Case*, 2 Metc. 3 (1859).

viction before a justice for liquor-selling was defective, because it did not set out that the sale was not a work of charity or necessity, while others thought the averment that it was "contrary to the act of assembly" sufficient.[1]

The reputation of a house as one where liquors are sold, and whether it applies to the whole house, or only a part thereof, are for the jury. If the latter, the defendant is entitled to an acquittal; but the reputation of one room may be foundation for ascribing the same to the whole house.[2] The defence that a bar was kept as a part of the business of a hotel cannot be made under a *habeas corpus.*[3]

The principal is guilty, though not present, when a sale is made by his authorized agent,[4] but, in order to convict of the offence of selling liquors on Sunday, proof must be made of the intent on the part of the defendant to violate the statute. Where the sale is not made by the defendant personally, or in his presence, the presumption of his innocence is not overcome by merely showing that the sale was made on his premises, by his bartender, unless the evidence also shows that the defendant in some manner participated in it, connived at it or assented to it. The question whether he assented is one of fact, and not of legal presumption, and belongs to the jury.[5]

In Georgia, it was said: "If the clerk be guilty and keeps the door open, to free himself from crime, the employer of the clerk *must show* not only that he did not consent, but that he did not know. He might consent by private arrangement to do the thing by the clerk, and yet not know it was done at the time it was done; so that, to shield himself, the proprietor must show, at all events, not only no knowledge of the door's being open, but no consent to it, express or implied."[6]

Where the evidence was conflicting, but one witness swore that she purchased intoxicating liquor on Sunday, though her cross-examination threw some doubt on her evidence, and she was contra-

[1] *Omit's Case*, 21 Pa. 426 (1853).

[2] *Ryan's Case*, 5 Conn. 411 (1833).

[3] *Bird's Case*, 19 Cal. 130 (1861).

[4] *Martin's Case* (Neb.), 46 N.W. Rep. 621 (1890).

[5] *Utter's Case*, 44 Barb. (N. Y.) 170 (1865). See, also, *Burke's Case*, 15 R. I. 324.

[6] *King's Case*, 77 Ga. 734 (1886).

dicted by the defendant, yet the court, on appeal, would not say the evidence did not authorize a conviction.[1]

The fact that the words "ale and beer" were used in one section, and omitted in another, of the New York statute "to regulate the sale of intoxicating liquors," &c., has been held immaterial.[2]

In one section of the Tennessee act for licensing the sale of liquor, it was provided that nothing in the act should be so construed as to authorize the sale of liquors on Sunday, and in a subsequent section it was provided that nothing in the act should be so construed as to prevent the sale thereof by the quart or larger quantity, not to be drank on the premises. The court said that the proviso against the "sale" on Sunday applied without regard to the quantity, and the prohibition of the first section applied to the second with as much force as though the proviso of the first had been subsequent to the second.[3]

Where druggists are forbidden to sell except on prescription, the argument of emergency is of no avail.[4]

The question of whether a penalty provided in one section of a statute applies to offences mentioned in others has arisen in Indiana.[5] A different penalty was provided for selling without a license and for selling on Sunday. *Held*, that a party indicted under the first prohibition must be acquitted where the evidence showed that an offence was also committed by him in making the sale on Sunday.[6]

The nature and liability of a liquor dealer's bond has been considered in Connecticut,[7] and the duties and rights of "prosecuting agents" under the laws of that state.[8] What constitutes "delivery" as evidencing a sale was discussed in Massachusetts in 1858.[9]

The defendant made a motion to quash the indictment, which was overruled, and he then pleaded guilty. The court said that the plea cured the defect in the indictment, in not alleging the price at which the liquor was sold, and added: "Perhaps the same

1 *Roy's Case*, 91 Ind. 417 (1885).

2 *Ran's Case*, 63 N. Y. 277 (1875).

3 *Eskridge's Case*, 1 Swan 415 (1882).

4 *Burton's Case*, 99 Ind. 89 (1884).

5 See *Rosenbaum's Case*, 4 Ind. 599 (1853); *Thomasson's Case*, 15 Ind. 449 (1860).

6 *Krank's Case*, 46 Hun (N. Y.), 632 (1887).

7 *Quintard* v. *Corcoran*, 50 Conn. 34.

8 *Wolforth's Case*, 42 Conn. 155.

9 *Harrison's Case*, 11 Gray 308.

doctrine might be beneficially carried still further. It may be doubtful whether, by the plea, the defendant has not shown affirmatively that he is not within any of the provisos or exceptions in the statute."[1]

Where the court below had used language calculated to prejudice the jury against the occupation of a liquor dealer, the Appellate Court said: "This had better have been omitted [*sic*]. The liquor business is as lawful as any other business under the laws of this state, when it is carried on within the restrictions established by the legislature, and rights thereunder should be respected and protected by courts as carefully and to the same extent as those existing."

It was held, in Kentucky, that evidence that the defendant sold liquor on a Sunday subsequent to the date of the warrant was inadmissible.[2]

The state having proven that certain persons were seen in the saloon, may prove in rebuttal that others were seen there.[3]

In Massachusetts, a charge, in general terms, of "unlawful selling" of liquor, is sustained by evidence of a sale on Sunday.[4]

[1] *Rosenbaum's Case*, 4 Ind. 599 (1853).

[2] *Megowan's Case*, 2 Metc. 3 (1859).

[3] *Cox's Case*, 38 N.W. Rep. 235 (1888).

[4] *Harrison's Case*, 11 Gray 310 (1858).

CHAPTER X.

THE PROHIBITION OF SUNDAY LABOR.

I. THE FORBIDDEN ACTS.

The Puritan "Sabbath" is an original institution. All recognition of "Sabbaths" being especially denounced in the New Testament,[1] it can of course find no support in that portion of the Scriptures. But it is equally inconsistent with what we know of the "Sabbath" of the Old Testament. It is of course "kept" on an altogether different day; but, passing by this, in the manner of its observance it differs quite as completely from the Sabbath of the Jews. The latter was a day of feasting and rejoicing, not of gloom and cheerless lounging.[2] It was a day, moreover, on which the labor of all classes of the community was alike prohibited. The priest, as well as the people, "rested." There were no church "services" to overtax clergymen or fret the mothers of large families with morning preparations for the weekly "dress parade."[3] In a word, there were no "exceptions" in the Hebrew statute.

But the Puritan was not prepared to accept the Hebrew Sabbath. There were certain things which he liked to do on Sunday, and as to which he was therefore fully persuaded that it was the will of the Deity they should be done on that day;[4] and accordingly it became necessary for him to make exceptions in his version of the Fourth Commandment.

It is evident that a total prohibition of labor is comparatively easy to understand and enforce. The distinction between the activity of work and other forms of activity is pretty generally recognized and

[1] See texts cited, page 73.

[2] 1 Milman's Hist. Jews 97 (Harper's ed. 1855).

[3] *Ib.*

[4] Such as the cooking of hot dinners—something as far removed as anything could well be from the usual ideas of either "necessity" or "charity." See Table A.

understood. But when we come to make exceptions of any kind to our prohibitions of labor, we at once launch out on a sea of hopeless uncertainty. We may, indeed, name certain specific labors as allowable, and certain other labors as not allowable. But the field of human exertion is so vast that we cannot cover it all explicitly; and hence the effort to classify the exceptions under some general terms.

The terms adopted by the Puritans are "necessity" and "charity." It is safe to say that the vagueness of these words, and the impossibility of applying them with anything like uniformity to every-day life would cause the courts to hold the whole law void for uncertainty if it were anything else but a Sunday law.

Moreover, we shall see presently that the necessity need not be that of the person who does the work, but it is sufficient if his work is necessary for another. This disposes of the claim that Sunday idleness in enforced for the sake of its beneficial effect on the unwilling idler; for it is obvious that his energies are quite as likely to be dissipated in the rendering of services which may chance to be required by another as they would be in work required by or simply advantageous to himself. The same remark applies to the word "charity." If the state's real object in compelling her citizens to be idle on Sunday was their bodily welfare, she certainly would not permit her clergymen, one of the most desirable class among her citizens, to destroy themselves by their reckless defiance of the "law of nature," which demands of all human creatures absolute idleness on one day in every seven.

Again, take the case of the doctor. Plainly his services may be sometimes necessary and sometimes not, on Sunday. Who is to decide this question? If the patient, will his belief in the necessity protect the doctor? If the doctor, then must not every other man be allowed to determine, as well as he, when the service he renders to another is necessary and when it is not?

How these and similar problems are dealt with by the courts, will appear below.

13

I. The Question Whether Sunday Laws are to be Construed Strictly or Otherwise.

The question whether any particular act is within the exception to the statutory prohibitions of Sunday labor depends, to some extent, on whether the statutes are to be construed strictly or otherwise. This point has been considered in three classes of cases: (1) where the illegality of a contract, because made on Sunday, has been set up, in defence; (2) where the service of process on this day has been impeached; and (3) where parties have been indicted for violation of the Sunday law. By observing the nature of the issue involved in each case, we may obtain some clue to the inspiration which has controlled the deliverances now to be quoted, although it still remains impossible wholly to reconcile them with each other. In the case of an indicted baker, Kenyon, C. J., said of 29 Car. II., c. 7: "I think we should construe it equitably, so that it may answer the purpose of public convenience, taking care, at the same time, that Sunday should not be profaned. I agree with Mr. Foster (2 Burr. 780), that I am for an observation of the Sabbath, but not for a Pharasaical observation of it. The most laborious part of the community, who are entitled to some indulgence for the labors of the past week, fare harder on that than on any other day."[1] Where an attempt was made to repudiate a contract, Best, C. J., referred to the opinion of Bayley, J., in Fennell *v.* Ridler,[2] decided one year previously, and said: "In one of the most able judgments ever delivered, he says that the most liberal construction must be put on that statute, because it is in affirmance of the religion which is the basis of the law of this country." And with this Parker, B., agreed.[3] In a suit on a note it was said: "There can be no excuse for any attempt to destroy, by a forced construction of the language, the effect of an enactment so suited to enable man to derive the benefit designated to be bestowed upon him by Providence, in the consecration of the Lord's day to the duty of doing good, and of seeking endless happiness, in accordance with the precepts of the gospel of our Lord Jesus Christ."[4] In an

[1] *Younger's Case*, 5 T. R. 449 (1792).
[2] 5 Barn. & C. 406.
[3] *Smith* v. *Sparrow*, 4 Bing. 84 (1827).
[4] *Towle* v. *Larrobee*, 26 Me. 464 (1847).

action for deceit in the sale of a horse, it was considered that the Sunday law is "a remedial statute, and should be liberally construed."[1] And in a suit for the price of an advertisement, it was said that it is "remedial, and to be construed liberally in respect to the mischiefs to be remedied."[2] And the religious view of the matter has been vigorously sustained as follows, in the case of a party indicted for giving a theatrical exhibition: "The learned counsel for the plaintiffs has entered largely into the question of the origin and sanction of the Christian Sabbath. It may not be essential, but it is far from being irrelevant to sustain the divine authority of its institution. * * * This would throw light upon the nature of legislative provisions, and furnish a guide to a rigorous, or expanded rule of construction."[3] And the court proceeded to give a very broad construction indeed to the law. But later, in the same state, where a Sunday traveler was suing a railroad company for damages on account of an injury, it was observed that "the law subjects the offender to a trivial punishment. The legislature has not seen fit to mark the violation of the statute as a grave offence against the state."[4] Where the offence was the driving of an omnibus on Sunday, the court said: "Our duty requires us to construe the statute so as to accomplish its purpose, which was to enforce the observance of Sunday, instead of obliterating it. We are resolutely opposed to a course of judicial construction which would cheapen its demands and impair its power for good."[5] Where the plaintiff's boat was descending a creek, and was injured by a dam erected by the defendant, the court in the same state said that the Sunday statute "being a law to enforce and protect a general and most valuable custom, it is not to be subjected to a narrower interpretation." Nevertheless, it held the defendant liable, observing that "important as is a day of rest for man; important as are the religious institutions connected with it, and the civilization and moral refinement that grow out of and depend on it and its institutions; important and necessary for all man's highest and noblest

[1] *Northrop* v. *Foot*, 14 Wend. (N. Y.) 248 (1835).

[2] *Smith* v. *Wilcox*, 24 N. Y. 353, 355–6.

[3] *Hoym's Case*, 20 How. (N. Y.) Pr. 76 (1860).

[4] *Carroll* v. *Staten Island R. R.*, 58 N. Y. 126 (1874).

[5] *Johnston's Case*, 22 Pa. 102 (1853).

aims as is the religion which, on that day, sends forth its strongest influence, we cannot protect it by any such latitudinarian interpretation of the law we are appointed to administer as is expected of us here."[1] Where a party was on trial for driving a horse-car, the court said: "While we are ready and willing to sustain the law, whenever it is violated, we will not strain the law, or the facts. * * * A liberal sentiment has prevailed and conservative men have united in sustaining the spirit of the law, while they have accommodated themselves to the wants and necessities of a populous city."[2] But in another case, the same year, it was said: "While this act remains unaltered by the legislature, it is not to be frittered away by judicial construction."[3] The religious aspect of the matter has also strongly influenced the court in Arkansas, where, in a suit on a note, it was said: "One great object of all the American statutes, though varying in their expressions, is to prevent the desecration of the Sabbath by the doing of ordinary work, or secular business." A narrow and literal construction of statute would leave open a wide door for the desecration of the Sabbath. And the court proceeded to give what it called "examples of the numerous instances, in which the Sabbath could be desecrated with impunity, if the words of the statute were narrowly construed."[4] So, in Georgia, the question being whether a bail-bond, executed for the purpose of releasing a prisoner from jail, was valid, the court said: "We think this statute should be rigidly enforced. Independently of the moral obligation resting upon all men to obey the law of the Lord, and to observe by abstention from all secular business the day set apart for His worship, the rest of one day in seven from all physical and mental labor is a great conservative, refreshing, invigorating means, designed by Almighty wisdom for the preservation of health and the recreation of our mental and bodily faculties."[5] The current of decision by this court has been pro-sabbatic in full measure, and with that current runs, we think, the true law, as well as the general moral sentiment of the people.[6] Where an attachment was levied, and the law for-

[1] *Mohney* v. *Cook*, 26 Pa. 342 (1835).

[2] *Jeandelle's Case*, 3 Phil. (Pa.) 509 (1859).

[3] *Johnston's Case*, 22 Pa. 102.

[4] *Tucker* v. *West*, 29 Ark. 386 (1874).

[5] Ga. (1875).

[6] *Weldon's Case*, 62 Ga. 449 (1879).

bade the service of "process," &c., the court said: "The obvious design of the legislature was to prevent the spread of vice and immorality by the desecration of the first day of the week to common secular purposes, unless justified by the necessities of the case"[1]

The Connecticut statute providing that a consideration received must be restored before suit on contract can be defended on the ground that it was made on Sunday, "is broad and remedial and should be liberally construed to prevent fraud or injustice."[2]

In a case involving a sale, the Vermont court repudiated any reference to religious considerations, as affecting the decision of the question whether any particular act was or was not within the purview of the Sunday statute; and said "this is purely a question of law, to be decided by the constitution and statute of this state, and by the application of those principles of law which have been acknowledged and never controverted."[3] Where the validity of an injunction was involved, all reference either to the ecclesiastical or the common law view was repudiated by the Illinois court, which said: "So long as our own statute is not violated—so long as nothing is done which it forbids, there can be no reasonable ground for complaint."[4] It has been said that Sunday laws will be construed on the same principles as those restraining the sales of liquor.[5]

By holding that the statute was intended to apply to private, as well as public conduct,[6] the English courts have given it a liberal construction; but although the use of the words "ordinary calling" would seem to have compelled them to confine its prohibitions to acts fairly to be included under that phrase, the New Hampshire court considered this a narrow view of that statute. In a case where the validity of a will made on Sunday was in issue it said it was apparent from the preamble to 29 Car. II. "that it was the policy of the law to promote the observance of the Lord's day by all classes of persons, without distinction of class or occupation. The construction given by the English courts was probably much influenced by the ancient rule, which was suppose to require a strict

[1] *Cotton* v. *Huey*, 4 Ala. 56 (1842).

[2] *Wentworth* v. *Woodside*, 79 Me. 156 (1887).

[3] *Lyon* v. *Strong*, 6 Vt. 219 (1835).

[4] *Langabier* v. *F. P. & S. W.*, 64 Ill. 243 (1872).

[5] *Bank* v. *Thompsen*, 42 N. H. 369.

[6] *Fennel* v. *Ridler*, 5 Barn. & C. 406.

interpretation of penal statutes. In this state, before the decisions of our courts upon the statute in question, this rule had been materially modified."[1]

It is a point of some interest whether a Sunday law is to be construed with reference to the sentiments prevailing at the time of its passage, or from the standpoint of present society, as manifested by actual practices prevailing at the time when the construction becomes necessary. It has been said: "It is to be remembered that it is the duty of the court merely to give a true interpretation to the language of a human statute, so that it shall speak according to the intention of its framers, and not according to the fluctuating opinions of the schools, leaving it to the legislature, alone, to make such changes in the law, from time to time, as the altered condition of things may demand."[2] This is a deep and far-reaching principle. The inconveniences which might result from its application to many statutes are obvious, but not pertinent to the subject in hand. No case has been found which has considered its effect on the meaning to be given to the word "necessity" in a Sunday law. Yet one can easily imagine the commotion which would be created by an attempt to restrict the Sunday activity of a citizen of one period to such proceedings as would have been deemed necessary by the stern politico-theologians who framed prescriptions for Sunday idleness a century before he was born. The Massachusetts court, however, seems to adhere to this principle. In a suit against a town for injury from a defective highway, received while traveling on Sunday, it said: "Whatever inconveniences might result at the present day from the literal and general enforcement of the act, and whatever hard cases may have arisen under it, it is still the law of the land, to be judicially interpreted, and administered according to its true intent and meaning, and upon the same rules as would govern us in the interpretation of any other statute."[3] So in Pennsylvania: "It is the duty of courts to uphold the institutions and laws, under which our liberties have grown and prospered. Whether these institutions and laws are sufficiently liberal to meet the requirements of modern advancement, it is not for us to determine. Those,

[1] *George* v. *George*, 47 N. H. 27 (1866).

[2] *Ibid.*

[3] *Davis* v. *Somerville*, 128 Mass. 594 (1880).

who consider them insufficient should, instead of disregarding them, endeavor to have them amended, to suit the exigencies of the times."[1] Where a party was indicted for letting a carriage for a purpose not of necessity or charity, and alleged that his information led him to believe the purpose lawful, the court held that proof of information to that effect exonerated him, and that he could not be required to prove its lawfulness in fact; and Gould, J., "applied the general rule in construing penal statutes, that the construction must not be strict, as against the defendant, but liberal in his favor;" and also the maxim "*actus non facit reum, nisi mens sit rea.*"[2] In a case involving the validity of a notice published in a Sunday paper, the court in Illinois said: "If the wise lawgiver, whatever may be his own opinions, or habits, concurs in this setting apart one day in seven, it would ill become the judiciary to give to such enactments a restricted operation. They should be so construed as to accomplish their purpose."[3]

We now pass, *via* cases holding a middle ground in favor of a "reasonable" construction, to those at the opposite extreme from the preceding, which contend for a strict interpretation. In a suit on a warranty given in a horse trade the Kentucky court said: "The statute should not be extended by construction, to embrace cases which are not clearly within its obvious meaning, but, at the same time, it should be fairly construed, with a view to the accomplishment of the objects, contemplated by the legislature, in its enactment."[4] Holding that a verdict might be received, the court in Alabama said: "The Sunday laws must have a reasonable interpretation."[5] Where a party had been indicted for selling cigars, the Indiana court said: "In the United States, where religion can be neither opposed nor supported by law, and where Sunday, under the law, is viewed purely in a secular light, the tendency is naturally to relax the restrictions of the Sunday laws in all things, which do not interfere with the rights of others."[6] It was held in North Carolina: "Considering the act as passed exclusively for promoting public decency, the case of a private sale would not come

[1] *Teaman's Case*, 1 Phil. (Pa.) 460 (1853).

[2] *Myers' Case*, 1 Conn. 502 (1866).

[3] *Seamon* v. *Chicago*, 40 Ill. 146 (1866).

[4] *Murphy* v. *Thompson*, 14 B. Mon. (Ky.) 419 (1854).

[5] *Reid's Case*, 53 Ala. 402 (1875).

[6] *Carver's Case*, 69 Ind. 61 (1879).

within its operation, and it was only by extending its object to the regulation of private conduct and the enforcement of religious duties that such a sale was brought within its operation. This latter purpose is prohibited by our constitution. Cases cited from the New England states have no bearing. Their statutes prohibit all secular labor, and the notions, there entertained, are far more strict and intolerant, than the sentiments that have hitherto prevailed in this state."[1] The New York Court of Common Pleas, in a suit for the price of horse sold, said: "Where parties wish to bring a case within a statutory prohibition, they should produce satisfactory evidence that the facts are such as to make the statute applicable, and not leave to mere inference what should be established by proof, where the intent is to take away a common-law right."[2] The court in Ohio, holding that a contract was good, said: "The law is penal, and is, therefore, to be construed strictly. Such statutes are not to be extended by construction."[3] And the Supreme Court of New York, in a suit by a traveler injured on a steamer, said of the Sunday law: "The fact that a violation has been committed must be established, affirmatively, by him, who claims the protection of the statute."[4] And where suit was brought on a note, the court in Alabama said the provisions of the Sunday law "being penal in their character, must receive strict interpretation."[5] Where a railway company was sued for damages caused by its delay in transporting cattle, the Maryland court spoke as follows: "Of these laws, there has been great diversity of interpretation, some courts holding to them with great strictness, while others have construed them with considerable liberality, and, especially, in cases where, by strict construction, impediments and embarrassments would be raised to the great carrying business of the country."[6] Whether the courts have much regarded the question of convenience in this matter, we shall be better prepared to judge after we see how they have practically

[1] *Melvin* v. *Easley*, 7 Jones (N. C.) 356 (1860).

[2] *Miller* v. *Roessler*, 4 E. D. Smith (N. Y.) 234, 236.

[3] *Bloom* v. *Richards*, 2 Ohio St. 387 (1853). The whole opinion in this case is well worth reading for its clear discrimination between the powers of the English parliament, and those of the American legislature. It was delivered by Judge Thurman.

[4] *Landens* v. *R. R. Co.*, 13 Abb. (N. Y.) Pr. (N. S.) 338 (1872).

[5] *Flanagan* v. *Myer*, 41 Ala. 132 (1867).

[6] *P., W. & B.* v. *Lehman*, 56 Md. 209 (1881).

applied the general principles considered. The following statements are justified by the citations just given: 1. No clear distinction has been made between civil and criminal cases, in regard to the rigidity or liberality of construction; but, 2. The view of this subject has depended largely on whether the court considered the law as designed for the enforcement of a religious tenet, or as a mere civil regulation. 3. The weight of authority is in favor of a liberal construction. 4. There is a conflict of authority in Alabama, and between the higher and lower courts of New York, on the subject. 5. (Already enumerated)—The words used are to be construed as understood when the statute was passed, and it may be added, that the law is to be so construed as to operate equally on all, and, hence, not so as to allow hotels to sell cigars when others cannot do so.[1]

II. Distinction Between Public and Private Labor.

In defining the words "labor," "business," &c., the courts are, of course, much influenced by the view which is taken of the Sunday law's scope and purpose. If it is intended to regulate private conduct, the act of labor, &c., is criminal in itself; but if it is designed merely to prevent one person from disturbing another, the act must be judged with reference to its effect, and labor of one kind may be innocent, while that of another sort is punishable. The English courts have maintained consistency in this matter, and, holding that Sunday laws were passed in order to compel a religious observance, they logically conclude that it is immaterial whether or not the attention of others is drawn to an act forbidden to be done on that day. It is true that in an early case wherein suit was brought on a warranty of soundness in a horse sold on Sunday, Bayley, J., after quoting the provisions of the statute 29 Car. II., c. 7, said: "I apprehend the object of that part of the statute was to prevent handicraftsmen, laborers and others from exercising their ordinary callings in a manner offensive to the eye and with reference to the decent observance of the Sabbath day."[2] And Littledale, J., said: "It is unnecessary to decide

[1] *Ohmer's Case*, 34 Tex. 115.

[2] *Bloxsome* v. *Williams*, 5 Dowl. & Ry. 82, 86.

whether the statute 29 Car. II. extends to contracts entered into by merchants or other persons making no show of business; but it seems to me that the object of the statute was to prevent persons keeping open shop and disregarding the decency of the Lord's day by a public show of their ordinary trades and occupations."[1] But later it was held, that " the spirit of the act is to advance the interests of religion, to turn a man's thoughts from his worldly concerns, and to direct them to the duties of piety and religion; and the act cannot be construed according to its spirit unless it is so construed as to check the career of worldly traffic." And accordingly it was held to apply to a private, as well as a public sale.[2] And some American cases adopt the English doctrine, as thus announced, and repudiate the distinction between public and private labor, &c.[3] On the other hand, in North Carolina, the private sale of a horse was held not within the operation of the statute, though within its words; and the court added: "So the case of a lawyer who sits in his rooms, and reads a law book, or writes a deed, or a merchant who, in his counting-room posts his books, or an old lady who sits by her fireside and knits, if done on Sunday, comes within the words of the statute. But my opinion is that the statute is void, and inoperative, in respect to cases of this kind, and that its operation is confined to manual, visible, or noisy labor, such as is calculated to disturb other people."[4] It was said in Massachusetts that the legislature did not intend to carry the prohibition further than to restrain the exercise of those occupations and employments which make up the common and daily business of mankind—callings carried on for gain and profit, &c.; and this conclusion was based on the subsequent designation in the statute of "keeping open a warehouse," &c., as an employment which would subject the person to the penalty imposed; on the preamble, which spoke of the "damage to members of a Christian society," the "disturbance of well-disposed persons," &c.; and on the consideration that a narrower construction would not promote the

[1] *S. C.*, 5 Dowl. & Ry. 82.

[2] *Fennel* v. *Ridler*, 5 Barn. & C. 406. See, also, *Smith* v. *Sparrow*, 4 Bing. 84 (1827).

[3] *Adams* v. *Hamell*, 2 Doug. (Mich.) 73 (1845); *Lovejoy* v. *Whipple*, 18 Vt. 379 (1848).

[4] *Melvin* v. *Easley*, 7 Jones (N. C.) 356 (1860).

object, "but would produce serious inconvenience, by impeding or preventing the performance of the common and ordinary duties and offices of domestic life."[1] And the idea that "disturbance" of persons was what the legislature meant to prevent was thus assumed in Pennsylvania: "Most of the plaintiffs, if not all, have places of business on streets where passenger cars are passing every few minutes, and no one has complained that they have ever interfered with his addition of items to a bill, &c. * * * The greatest nuisance is the driving up of carriages during the sermon, to take home at the close of the service the rich members of the congregation; * * * as to disturbing persons in private dwellings on Sunday, it is an absurdity which requires no answer."[2] So, the South Carolina court has asked, "Why are we to hold any labor indictable except it might be such as actually to interfere with the rights of conscience, and worship of others, as by disturbing congregations assembled in churches, in their devotions, or the like? If the act of the accused in fact disturbed others in the performing of their duties of piety, that will itself be a specific offence, whether committed on Sunday or any other day. If the particular work or trade be not, in its nature, a nuisance, as prejudicial to the health or comfort of the public, it does not become so by being performed or carried on on one day more than another."[3] The legislature which concocted the Sunday law for New Hampshire seems to have been disposed to concede greater personal liberty than was enjoyed under the laws of the neighboring communities. It permitted work, &c., to be done, provided it was not "to the disturbance of others"—thus using a word which, by construction, the opinions just cited, have imported into the statutes of other states. But in this connection, we encounter a remarkable instance of judicial definition nullifying an intention which the legislature expressed with apparent clearness and distinctness. What is a disturbance? Webster says that, in law, it is the hindering or disquieting of a person in the lawful and peaceable enjoyment of his right, the interruption of a right, as the disturbance of a franchise of com-

[1] *Bennett* v. *Brooks*, 9 Allen (Mass.) 118, 120.

[2] Read's concurring opinion, *Sparhawk's Case*, 54 Pa. 401 (1867).

[3] *Williams' Case*, 4 Ired. (N. C.) L. 400 (1844).

mon, of ways and the like."[1] Blackstone says it is "usually a wrong done to some incorporeal hereditament, by hindering or disquieting the owners in their regular and lawful enjoyment of it."[2] Bouvier repeats this definition.[3] And Abbott, also.[4] Burrill adds: "The hindering of that which, in right, belongeth unto one to do."[5] Thus we see that the idea of a wrong done and a right invaded is involved in the legal definition of a disturbance. Now, it is a fundamental maxim, *volenti non fit injuria*.[6] And it would seem to follow that a man cannot be, in a legal sense, disturbed by the act of another, to which he assents, and in which he participates. But this train of reasoning was explicitly repudiated by the New Hampshire court. In considering what is a "disturbance of others," the court said it was difficult to lay down a general rule; that it might depend on the party's existing pursuit; that the fact that people willingly submitted to and took part in a thing did not make it no disturbance; and that it was safe to give the word a comprehensive meaning; that the object of the statute was to prevent the distracting of people from religious observances, and "nothing should be tolerated that tends to defeat it;" and accordingly, it was held that a proposition to buy a horse was a disturbance of the owner, and that the latter's willingness to be disturbed could not make the contract valid; and the vendee's taking a witness along with him, when he went to make this proposition, was held a further violation of the act in regard to the witness, as was also the additional interruption to the plaintiff's wife (who was in the room at the time *reading a newspaper*). The result that a person present at a transaction might allege that it disturbed him, however quietly conducted, the court said was a necessary hardship, such as must result in some cases from the application of all general rules; that if disturbance to a solitary individual were not enough, it would be impossible to draw the line; and that the question was the application of a principle, and not one of convenience or inconvenience.[7] And later, in the same state, the court defined disturbing acts as "acts calculated to turn the attention of those who are

[1] Webs. Dict., *s. v.*

[2] 3 Com. 16.

[3] Dict., *s. v.*

[4] *Ibid.*

[5] *Ibid.*

[6] Whart. Max. 99; Broom Max. 268.

[7] *Varney* v. *French*, 19 N. H. 233 (1848).

present from their appropriate religious duties to matters of mere worldly concern," and held that the execution of a will in the presence of others was to their disturbance, and added: "It has been urged that the question whether the act under consideration was to the disturbance of others must always be one of fact and should be submitted to the jury; but, if business has been transacted of a secular character and not within the exceptions and in which two or more persons have taken a part, and there be no controversy as to these facts, then upon the interpretation which has been given to these terms, the disturbance is a conclusion of law."[1] And, in a yet later case, this view was sustained.[2]

I. The Words "Ordinary Calling."

The use of the words "ordinary calling" in the English statute 29 Car. II. has given rise to some subtle judicial distinctions.

A was a horse auctioneer. B came to his stable, and, after trying a horse, asked leave to show it to C; A consented, on condition that, if C did not return it by two o'clock, it should be B's horse. As it was not returned till a later hour, A refused to receive it, and sued for the price. The court said "the sale of horses by private contract was not A's ordinary calling nor was it B's, and, therefore, though it is to be lamented, yet the sale must be held good."[3] A very often quoted English case is that of *Bloxsome* v. *Williams*, *supra* (1824). A's son bargained with B for a horse, upon a warranty of soundness, giving nothing in earnest. The horse was delivered on Tuesday, and proved unsound. A sued on the warranty. B was a horse dealer, but there was no evidence that A or his son knew this. "We must assume the plaintiff has not knowingly concurred in enabling the defendant to contravene the law, because there is no evidence of his having been aware that the defendant was a horse dealer at the time of this transaction; and, if the defendant were allowed to insist on this objection, it would be permitting him to take advantage of an illegality for which he alone is culpable."[4] In another report of the same case, Bailey, J.,

[1] *George* v. *George*, 47 N. H. 27 (1866).

[2] *Thompson* v. *Williams*, 58 Id. 248.

[3] *Drury* v. *Defontaine*, 1 Taunt 130.

[4] *Bloxsome* v. *Williams*, 5 Dowl. & Ry. 82, 84.

is represented as saying: "It is not competent to the defendant who alone has been guilty of a breach of the law to set up his own contravention of the law as an answer to this action at the suit of an innocent person."[1] But, if the purchaser was a horse dealer, he cannot sue on such a warranty.[2] An attorney entered into an agreement for the settlement of his client's affairs, thereby rendering himself personally liable. *Held*, that he was not exercising his ordinary calling; and Lyndhurst, B., said: "Has it ever been held that an attorney is within the statute of 29 Car. II.?" * * * and Alderson, B., asked: "Can it be contended that an attorney is a tradesman? * * * The words 'other persons' mean persons *ejusdem generis*."[3] * * * Still later, the question arose whether a pauper had acquired a residence in a certain parish by virtue of a contract of hiring made with a farmer therein whose labor was intended to be prohibited, and it was held that the hiring of a servant was not within the farmer's "ordinary calling,"[4] and still later it was said "the cases show that the act to be illegal within the statute must be done in the exercise of the party's ordinary calling, and that the statute does not apply to all persons, but to persons having such ordinary callings which they exercise on the Sunday. Had the statute intended to prevent the doing of any business on a Sunday, it would have enacted that no one should enter into a contract on that day."[5] A mare was sent to a farm to be served and the service was performed. The farmer claimed a lien on the mare for his charges. *Held,* that the statute did not apply to a case where the defendant, in the ordinary calling of a farmer, happens to be in the possession of a stallion, occasionally covering mares.[6]

It is held in Massachusetts that "upon a contract in the exercise of the ordinary calling of one party, the other may sue, if it was not within his own ordinary calling, and he did not know, when he entered into it, that it was within the ordinary calling of the defendant."[7] But later it was observed that, previous to 1791, all the acts in Massachusetts were framed like the English statute, so as to prohibit only the exercise of a person's ordinary calling, and

[1] *S. C.*, 3 Barn. & C. 232.

[2] *Fennell* v. *Ridley*, 5 Id. 406 (1826).

[3] *Peate* v. *Dicken*, 5 Cromp., M. & R. 422 (1834).

[4] *King* v. *Whitnash*, 7 Barn. & C. 596.

[5] *Begbie* v. *Levy*, 1 Tyrw. 130 (1830).

[6] *Scarfe* v. *Morgan*, 4 Mees. & W. 270.

[7] *Cranson* v. *Goss*, 107 Mass. 439 (1871).

it was said that the existing statute was intended to have a broader application.[1] In a Massachusetts case involving the construction of the Rhode Island statute, which was taken from 29 Car. II., it was observed that to say, as suggested in behalf of the plaintiff, that a contract should not be held void if made through an agent, which would have been valid if made by the owner of the estate in person, would leave professional agents free to pursue their ordinary callings. "A broker or factor is commonly employed to do something which is not within the ordinary calling of his principal, but is within his own ordinary calling. A man who follows his ordinary calling as agent for others is not less within the words of the statute, or the evils which it was intended to prevent, than one who follows his ordinary calling on his own account. The fact that the parties to this action met on the Lord's day at the defendant's request does not estop him to set up this defence. The plaintiffs in meeting the defendant on that day were in equal fault with the defendant, who requested them so to meet him; indeed, more in fault, inasmuch as dealing in real estate was their ordinary calling, and was not his, and the plaintiffs were, therefore, acting in direct violation of the statute."[2] The execution of a release by a creditor to the assignee of a voluntary assignment was held valid in Rhode Island as not within the creditor's "ordinary calling."[3] In 1835, in New York, attention was called to the fact that the qualification "ordinary calling" had influenced the decisions in England, and the court added, "but our statute, in terms, seems confined to servile laboring or working."[4] The English restriction of the prohibition to the "ordinary calling" is adopted in Tennessee.[5] Attention was afterwards called to the fact that a later Tennessee act made "any of the common avocations of life, acts of real necessity or charity excepted," illegal.[6] The word "ordinary" is used in the Indiana statute. The court in that state said the execution of a mortgage does not fall under the prohibition of the South Carolina statute which forbids the exercise of a tradesman's "ordinary call-

[1] *Bennett* v. *Brooks*, 9 Allen (Mass.) 118, 119.

[2] *Hazard* v. *Day*, 14 Allen (Mass.) 487 (1867).

[3] *Allen* v. *Gardner*, 7 R. I. 22.

[4] *Northrup* v. *Foot*, 14 Wend. (N. Y.) 248, 250.

[5] *Amis* v. *Kyle*, 2 Yerg. (Tenn.) 31 (1821).

[6] *Lorry Case*, 7 Baxt. (Tenn.) 95.

ing," &c.[1] The words "ordinary calling" are used in the Georgia statute. But, by construction in one case, they were given a much wider application than they obtained in England. As we have seen, the English courts are strict in confining the prohibition to acts themselves within the ordinary calling; and thus they have held that the hiring of a servant by a farmer is not illegal.[2] But the Puritanism of Georgia has extended the illegality to things which a party does with a view to *afterwards* pursuing his ordinary calling, or, to aid himself therein. In a suit on a farmer's note for the purchase-money of land, it was said "the defendant was a farmer and it was a part of his ordinary business and calling to purchase land and pay for it, in order that he might pursue his ordinary business and calling as a farmer * * * the facts bring this case within the true intent and meaning of the statute, and the note was therefore illegal."[3] In New Hampshire attention was called to the fact that a later statute of that state had substituted the word "secular" for the word "ordinary," and the court said: "We are inclined to think that, if our forefathers had supposed that the word 'ordinary' in the statute of 29 Car. II. had the force and effect which it has been decided in England to have, they would not have copied it into our provisional act."[4] And later, the New Hampshire court has declined to be bound by the English construction.[5] The Pennsylvania act has been spoken of as much more comprehensive than 29 Car. II., and "sufficient to embrace every species of worldly business, not therein specially excepted, whether it appertains to a person's ordinary calling, or not."[6] So it was said of the English decisions in New Jersey: "An individual, so far as the secular magistrate was concerned, could, with entire impunity, desecrate the Sabbath, provided he did so in a business affair, disconnected with his ordinary avocation. A regulation thus mutilated does not appear to have recommended itself to the framers of our statute, and hence the inhibition of all 'worldly employ-

[1] *Hellams* v. *Abercrombie*, 15 S. C. 110 (1880); *Shaw* v. *Williams*, 87 Ind. 158. See, also, *Mills* v. *Williams*, 16 S. C. 593 (1881).

[2] *King* v. *Whitnash*, 7 Barn. & C. 596, 599, see *infra*.

[3] *Morgan* v. *Bailey*, 59 Ga. 683, 685.

[4] *Frost* v. *Hull*, 4 N. H. 153 (1827).

[5] *Smith* v. *Foster*, 41 N. H. 215.

[6] *Kepner* v. *Keefer*, 6 Watts (Pa.) 231 (1837). See, also, *Sparhawk* v. *Union Co.*, 54 Pa. 401 (1867).

ment, or business.'"[1] And the court in Mississippi observed that the statute in that state was broader than 29 Car. II., inasmuch as it forbade "laboring at one's own, or any other calling," &c., and added, "In the absence of all proof, it must be presumed that the transactions thus settled pertain to the ordinary calling of the plaintiff; for a man's business transactions generally arise from the calling in which he is engaged. Hence, when he settles his accounts with a party with whom he has had several dealings, it must be presumed that the transactions were in the course of his ordinary calling, and that the settlement pertained to his usual bnsiness, or employment. Such a settlement necessarily requires 'labor' within the meaning of the statute, and comes fully within its prohibition."[2] But a different view of the burden of proof appears to have been taken in Georgia, where, considering a city ordinance which prohibited the pursuit of a laborer's ordinary business and the selling of merchandise, the court said "the evidence does not show what was the daily avocation of the plaintiff in error, or that he opened any store for the sale of merchandise on Sunday. Indeed, it does not bring him within that portion of the ordinance that the municipal authorities are empowered to enforce; all that it shows is that shoes were sold and exchanged on Sunday; this does not establish any violation of that portion of the ordinance which the authorities of Darien can enforce. It therefore follows that the case should have been sent back to the Police Court for further proceedings."[3]

IV. Contracts as Labor—The General Principle.

One of the most important questions which have arisen in connection with the Sunday law is this: Are contracts void, under a prohibition of "labor," "business," &c.? In this connection, two kinds of contracts are to be considered—those made on Sunday, and those made on a previous day, to be executed on Sunday. With one exception, the following cases belong to the first class. In England, in a case involving the validity of a purchase in *market overt*, the purchaser alleged a prescription to hold the fair

[1] *Reeves* v. *Butcher*, 31 N. J. 224 (1865).

[2] *Miller* v. *Lynch*, 38 Miss. 344 (1860).

[3] *Rothschild's Case*, 69 Ga. 503 (1882).

yearly on August 29th, and the court said "a fair holden upon a Sunday is well enough; although, by the 27 Hen. VI., c. 5, there is a penalty inflicted upon a party who sells upon that day, but it makes it not to be void."[1] But afterwards it was laid down by Holt, J., in a usury case, that "any contract for or about any matter or thing which is prohibited and made unlawful by any statute, is void, though the statute itself doth not mention that it shall be so, but only inflicts a penalty on the offender, because a penalty implies a prohibition, though there are no prohibitory words in the statute."[2] Lord Holt is not reported as giving any authority for this doctrine, and its application to cases under the Sunday law was, as just stated, denied nearly a hundred years previously. But, later (1808), it was re-asserted, in that connection, and, alluding to the ruling in the *Fair Case*, the court said, "The law is since changed, and, if any act is forbidden under a penalty a contract to do it is now held void."[3] But, though this general principle is settled in England, the early statutes there have been so construed as to admit many Sunday contracts. In the case just cited, it was said that a contract, to be void, must be within the contractor's "ordinary calling," and the court added: "Lord Coke, 2 Inst. 22, cites the law of Athelstane, and observes, 'here note, by the way, that no merchandise could be sold on the Lord's day.' But it does not appear that the common law ever considered those contracts as void, which were made on a Sunday." In a later case of horse-selling, this view was endorsed, and Bailey, J., said: "I entertain some doubts whether the statute applies at all to a bargain of this description. I incline to think that it applies to manual labor, and other work, visibly laborious, and the keeping of open shops. But I do not mean to pronounce any decision upon that point."[4] So, it was said, still later, "the act ought to be so construed as to advance the objects contemplated by the legislature, but not so as to make every work or business, done on the Lord's day, illegal."[5] In 1830 an action was brought by the endorsee against

[1] *Comyns* v. *Boyer*, Cro. Eliz. 485 (1596).

[2] *Bartlett* v. *Vinor*, Carth. 251 (1693).

[3] *Drury* v. *Defontaine*, 1 Taunt. 130 (1808).

[4] *Bloxsome* v. *Williams*, 3 Barn. & C. 596 (1824).

[5] *King* v. *Whitnash*, 7 Barn. & C. 596 (1827).

the acceptor of a bill of exchange. Defence that the bill was drawn on Sunday. The court said if any contract had been entered into on the Lord's day, done in the defendant's ordinary calling, and the plaintiff knew it, they would hold the bill void."[1] In the report of this case in another volume, the court is represented as having said, that, had the statute intended to prevent the doing of any business on Sunday, it would have enacted that no one should enter into a contract on that day.[2] Holt's doctrine has been adopted in Vermont,[3] and New Hampshire,[4] and Pennsylvania,[5] and Ohio.[6]

It has been held that Sunday contracts are void in New Jersey,[7] and Kentucky,[8] and Indiana,[9] and Arkansas.[10] But to the contrary are cases in New York,[11] and Nebraska;[12] and in Ohio a Sunday deed has been held valid;[13] but, later, the court had occasion to consider an ordinance of the city of Cincinnati, which provided that no one should engage in any "trading, bartering or selling or buying any goods, wares, or merchandise, or at any common labor," and it was held that buying and selling merchandise were "common labor," though the latter words were also used, and it was observed, as to the general law, that it prohibited "common labor," but not "buying and selling" in terms,[14] and this view was afterwards approved.[15] But, in a later case, Judge Thurman, delivering the opinion that contracts were not "common labor," said:

[1] *Begbie* v. *Levi*, 1 Cromp. & J. 180.

[2] *S. C.*, 1 Tyrw. 130, 131.

[3] *Lyon* v. *Strong*, 6 Vt. 219 (1834); *Lovejoy* v. *Whipple*, 18 Id. 379 (1846).

[4] *Woodman* v. *Hubbard*, 5 Fost. 67 (1852).

[5] *Shuman* v. *Shuman*, 21 Pa. 90; *Mitchell* v. *Smith*, 4 Yeates 84 (1804); *Hagdock* v. *Tracey*, 3 Wils. & S. 507 (1842).

[6] *Bloom* v. *Richards*, 2 Ohio St. 387 (1853).

[7] *Crockett* v. *Vanderveer*, Penn. 626 (1811); *Van Riper* v. *Van Riper*, 1 South. 156 (1819); *Reeves* v. *Butcher*, 31 N. J. 224 (1865).

[8] *Slade* v. *Arnold*, 14 B. Mon. 287 (1853); *Murphy* v. *Thompson*, Id. 419.

[9] *Link* v. *Clemmens*, 7 Blackf. 479 (1845); *Banks* v. *Werts*, 13 Ind. 203 (1857); *Cutlett* v. *M. E. Church*, 62 Id. 365 (1878). It was said by Elliott, C. J., in 1881, that, of the Indiana cases holding contracts incapable of enforcement, "some have carried the doctrine very far, possibly too far." *Rogers* v. *Telegraph Co.*, 78 Ind. 169.

[10] *Tucker* v. *West*, 29 Ark. 386 (1874); *Merritt* v. *Robinson*, 43 Id. 483 (1880).

[11] *Smith* v. *Wilcox*, 24 N. Y. 353 (1862).

[12] *Horacek* v. *Keebler*, 5 Neb. 355.

[13] *Swisher* v. *Williams*, Wright 754 (1834).

[14] *Cincinnati* v. *Rice*, 15 Ohio 225.

[15] *Sellers* v. *Dugan*, 18 Id. 489 (1849).

"It follows that we do not agree with the decision in *Sellers* v. *Dugan*. That judgment was given by a majority only of the court, and is contrary to the former decision, pronounced by two of the judges in *Swisher* v. *Williams*. It thus appears that three judges have been of one, and an equal number of the contrary opinion, upon this question;" the judge added that the popular meaning of toilsome, manual exertion must be given to the word in the statute, unless plainly used in a more enlarged, or restricted sense, that it is obviously not used in its most enlarged sense, for mere thought, writing a letter of friendship, or studying mathematics, or metaphysics, might be laborious, but were still lawful, that a marriage, which, in a legal point of view, is a contract, and nothing more, would be valid on Sunday, and continued: "It is not to be understood, however, that, because a Sunday contract may be valid, therefore business may be transacted upon that, as upon other days; as, for instance, that a merchant may lawfully keep open store, for the disposition of his goods. To wait upon his customers, and receive and sell his wares, is the common labor of a merchant, and there is a broad distinction between pursuing this avocation, and the case of a single sale, out of the ordinary course of business."[1] In Missouri, Judge Thurman's distinction between the prohibitions of "labor" and "business" in this connection has been approved.[2] Under a statute prohibiting "labor" only, whether, if a railway company held itself out as a common carrier of live-stock on Sunday, as on other days of the week, it would be bound to accept for carriage, for an owner, or a connecting road, stock offered on Sunday, the court in Maryland declined to decide in 1881.[3]

It may be observed, here, that there is reason for holding contracts void in states where "business" is forbidden, not because of Holt's doctrine, but simply because it may plausibly be maintained that making a contract is "business," and another well-established principle operates, namely, that the law will not enforce a contract which it forbids to be made.[4] The occasion for the application of

[1] *Bloom* v. *Richards*, 2 Ohio St. 387 (1853).

[2] *More* v. *Clymer*, 12 Mo. App. 11, 15 *et seq.* (1882).

[3] *P., W. & B.* v. *Lehman*, 56 Md. 209, 226.

[4] Chit. Cont., ch. 4, § 1; Pars. Cont. 807 (bottom), ed. 1883.

Holt's doctrine arises where the prohibition is of labor, &c., only, and where it is admitted that making a contract is not labor. Then the question is, is it "for or about" the labor which is forbidden? It must be remembered that this labor is Sunday labor; and, hence, there seems to be some point in the suggestion that the doctrine applies in this connection to contracts made on some other day to do on Sunday an act which is then unlawful, as such a contract would be, to use Holt's expression, "a contract for or about a thing which is prohibited," whereas, a contract made on Sunday, to be executed on another day, can hardly be said to be "for or about" Sunday labor. Moreover, thus construed, the principle has a reasonableness which is lacking in any other acceptation of it. A man, it says in effect, shall not be cast in damages for refusing to do an act which the law forbids, or which it will punish him for doing, even though he has expressly agreed to do it; nor, if he carries out his agreement, will the law allow him to recover the consideration. "Business" is used in the Massachusetts act. In that state, it has been said that "the legislature intended to prohibit secular business and did not confine the prohibition to manual labor, but extended it to the making of bargains, and all kinds of trafficking."[1] The same word is used in the New Hampshire statute. But there it is necessary, for the labor or business to be illegal, that it be to the "disturbance" of others. Yet the court of that state, in 1860, said that it was not a question whether the others were "disturbed," "annoyed," &c.; and it cited the "comprehensive" meaning given to the word "disturbance" in *Varney* v. *French*,[2] and added: "We understand from this decision that a valid contract cannot be made if it relates to the business of one's secular calling, because two or more must necessarily be engaged," and each would disturb the other, or others.[3]

[1] *Pattee* v. *Greely*, 13 Metc. (Mass.) 284 (1847). But see *post*, p. ---, *et seq.*, as to the present Massachusetts doctrine. See, also, *Barker* v. *Fogg*, 34 Me. 391 (1852); *Tucker* v. *Mowrey*, 12 Mich. 378 (1864); *Kepner* v. *Keefer*, 6 Watts (Pa.) 231 (1837); *Kendig's Case*, 2 Pa. 448 (1846); *Foreman* v. *Ahl*, 55 Id. 325 (1867); *Slade* v. *Arnold*, 14 B. Mon. (Ky.) 287 (1850); *Block* v. *McMurry*, 56 Miss. 217 (1878); *Hooper* v. *Edwards*, 18 Ala. 280 (1850); *S. C.*, 25 Id. 528 (1854); *Hill* v. *Sherwood*, 3 Wis. 343 (1854); *Melchoir* v. *McCarty*, 31 Id. 252 (1872); *Knox* v. *Clifford*, 38 Id. 651 (1875).

[2] 19 N. H. 233.

[3] *Smith* v. *Foster*, 41 N. H. 215, 220, 221.

The Vermont statute also has the word "business." But a contract made on Sunday in another state has been held enforceable in Vermont.[1] In this case, the court said the constitutional guaranties of religious liberty "impliedly, at least, forbid the adoption of any law which is not necessary for the quiet enjoyment of religious feeling and worship," and asked, "How can it be said that a contract made out of the state upon Sunday is a violation of the religious feelings or any infringement of the religious devotions of our citizens any more than if made upon any other day?"[2] So, in New York, in holding a private sale of personalty valid, under a provision that "no person shall expose to sale any wares," &c., the court said: "The prohibition of the New York statute is directed against the public exposure of commodities for sale in the streets, or in stores and shops, warehouses, or market places. It has no reference to mere private contracts, which are made without violating, or tending to produce a violation of, the public order, and solemnity of the day. Every man is permitted, in those respects, to regulate his conduct by the dictates of his own conscience."[3] And in the same state, it was held that a Sunday contract is not void, "if it did not contemplate and provide for some prohibited service or act to be done on this day."[4] "Business" is mentioned in the North Carolina statute, and yet it was said in that state that contracts are binding; and the court added: "It has been often so ruled in this state,"[5] though no previous case to that effect has been found. It was observed in Michigan "the rescission of a contract, requiring certain *formulæ*, to be gone through with, by the party making the same, was as much a matter of business as making the contract;" and it was held that where the original contract could not be made, neither could the acts for its undoing be done.[6]

Only one instance has been found of what has been called "the second class of cases," or those in which the contract was made on another day, to be executed on Sunday. This was a case in Penn-

[1] *Adams* v. *Gay*, 19 Vt. 358 (1847).

[2] Id. 366.

[3] *Boynton* v. *Page*, 13 Wend. (N. Y.) 425. See, also, *Miller* v. *Roessler*, 3 E. D. Smith (N. Y.) 234 (1855).

[4] *Eberle* v. *Mehrbach*, 55 N. Y. 682 (1874).

[5] *Williams' Case*, 4 Ired. (N. C.) L. 400, 406.

[6] *Benedict* v. *Bachelder*, 24 Mich. 425 (1872).

sylvania, where a party sued for the hire of horses, which had been let on Saturday to be used on Sunday. The court said the contract for the performance of an illegal act on Sunday, being so founded on an illegal consideration, and standing in the same relation as a contract for gambling, is void.[1]

V. Contracts as Labor—The Question of Sustaining Fraud, &c.

Some cases have been influenced in their view of Sunday contracts by the fact that to hold them void *in toto* would enable a party to take advantage of his own wrong. It was said in England: "The defendant was the only person who had violated the statute, and it would have been against justice to have allowed him to take advantage of his own wrong to defeat the rights of the plaintiff, who was innocent. These cases, therefore tend to support the present objection. * * * The expression that the contract would be void, probably meant only that it would be void so as to prevent a party who was privy to what made it illegal, from suing upon it in a court of law, and not so as to defeat a claim upon it by an innocent party; and so it was considered by this court in *Bloxsome* v. *Williams*. And in Pennsylvania, in a suit for the price of a horse sold, it was observed: "Zeal for religious observance of the Sabbath is commendable, but it may exhibit itself in a very questionable shape. It cannot avail a defendant, who has the possession of property, without paying for it, unless he proves that the plaintiff has violated some law, human or divine."[2] So it was said in Georgia, "it is difficult to suppose that any legislature could intend to aid dishonesty, by allowing parties to repudiate their obligations, merely because incurred on Sunday. Encouraging crime is a poor way to punish crime."[3] The parties to a pending suit before a justice made an agreement on Sunday by which the plaintiff received a certain amount in full and agreed to discontinue the suit. The defendant failed to appear, and the plaintiff prosecuted the suit to judgment, of which proceeding the defendant had no knowledge

[1] *Berrill* v. *Smith*, 2 Miles 402, 403 (1840).

[2] *Hadly* v. *Snevily*, 1 Watts & S. (Pa.) 477 (1841).

[3] *Sanders* v. *Johnson*, 29 Ga. 526.

till the time for appeal had expired. On the defendant's application for an injunction against the judgment, the court said that the plaintiff "having obtained it by making an unjust use of an agreement for a settlement, even though void in law, yet acted on by the other party, who was thereby prevented from appearing, the judgment ought not to stand."[1] So, in North Carolina, an attempt being made to escape liability for a warranty on the sale of a horse by alleging it took place on Sunday, Judge Manley said: "The defence is a novelty in North Carolina, and it has the singular demerit of being unconscientious, and, at the same time, wearing a garb of Christian morality."[2] And it was given as a reason for holding that a subsequent payment would validate a Sunday contract, that otherwise "the payee would receive and hold money paid him without consideration."[3] So, in Ohio, the Supreme Court said to a grantor: "The objection that the deed was executed on Sunday will not avail you. Both parties partook of the sin of violating the Sabbath, and the law does not require of us to enable either party to add to the sin, by breaking the faith pledged on that day, and commit a fraud out of assumed regard for the Sabbath day."[4] And the Indiana court gave, as a reason for holding that a surety, who signed a bond on Sunday, and authorized his principal to deliver it on another day, was bound by such delivery, the fact that, if the law were otherwise, "it would shield the guilty, and punish the innocent."[5] In Michigan, on a trial under an information, alleging that a forged certificate of acknowledgment was made and uttered January 13th, when the prosecution produced the certificate, it appeared that it was dated January 14th, which was Sunday; the defendant objected to its admission on the ground that, purporting to have been made on this day, it was on its face invalid, and hence incapable of being the basis of a prosecution for forgery; but the court held it admissible.[6] On the other hand, some judges, while regretting the result, have felt themselves obliged to disregard this question in applying

[1] *Blakesley* v. *Johnson*, 13 Wis. 530 (1861).

[2] *Melvin* v. *Easley*, 7 Jones (N. C.) 356 (1860). In this case, recovery was allowed on the warranty, because the sale was private.

[3] *Russell* v. *Murdock* (Iowa), 44 N. W. Rep. 237 (1890).

[4] *Swisher, &c.,* v. *Williams, &c.*, Wright (Ohio) 754 (1834).

[5] *Evansville* v. *Morris*, 87 Ind. 269.

[6] *Van Sickle's Case*, 29 Mich. 61 (1874).

the law. In Maine, while holding that money borrowed could not be recovered, the court said: "It is an unfortunate condition of the law when the violator of its commands is rewarded by it for such violation. Juvenal indignantly says: *Multi committunt eadem diverso crimina fato. Ille crucem pretium sceleris tulit, hic diadema.* So now, of two criminals, guilty of the same offence, one is punished and the other rewarded by the law which creates the offence."[1] So, it was said in New Hampshire "with considerations of its policy and expediency, this court has nothing to do. To declare any contract, or any class of contracts, void, may involve consequences which it would be desirable to obviate. The application of a principle often causes individual hardship, but where the law is plain, it must be declared."[2] So, in Vermont, Williams, C. J., delivering the opinion of the majority of the court that an action would not lie on a warranty given in an exchange of horses, said "it becomes our duty to declare the law as we find it, without regard to consequences."[3] So, in New York, in refusing to allow recovery on a contract to publish an advertisement in a Sunday paper, the court said: "It is a strange mode, it will be said, to support religion by sheltering bad faith. Laws involving public policy can seldom be made effectual in any other way."[4]

VI. Contracts as Labor—Contracts Through Agents.

It was said in England, as to the argument that the contract, if effected on a Sunday, was so effected without the plaintiff's knowledge, and that therefore he was not liable to the consequences of his agent's misconduct,—"if we were sitting in another court to decide whether or not under the circumstances the plaintiff should be amenable to ecclesiastical censure, perhaps he might be holden not liable; but here we are deciding on the validity of the contract, and if the contract entered into by the broker be void, there is no

[1] *Meader* v. *White*, 66 Me. 90 (1876).

[2] *Clough* v. *Davis*, 14 N. H. 133. See, also, *Allen* v. *Deming*, Id. (1843).

[3] *Lyon* v. *Strong*, 6 Vt. 219 (1834). In this case, Mattocks, J., in a dissenting opinion, observed, "Eternal justice is a principle older than the Sabbath, and in the New Testament much better defined, and much more frequently enjoined than the observance of that holy day." But see *Grant* v. *McGrath*, 56 Conn. 333 (1888).

[4] *Smith* v. *Wilcox*, 19 Barb. (N. Y.) 581

contract on which the plaintiff can sue, for he stands on a contract which his agent could not make."[1] An agent accepted a guaranty, which was to take effect on delivery and acceptance; it was held that his principals could maintain no action on it, "having, through their agent, participated in the illegal contract," and this, though it was dated on a secular day, and the principals had no knowledge that it was signed on Sunday, till long afterwards.[2] Where a party's agent, to collect the money on a note or get a new one, received a new one, dated on a secular day, and delivered it to his principal, who endorsed it to another, and neither the principal, nor the endorsee was aware that the delivery was on this day; and the maker's purpose, in then taking up his first note, was to defraud, the first note being, as a result of his conduct, barred by limitation, the court held the principal could not sue; that the contract was incapable of ratification; that, as the defence was allowed not for the defendant's benefit but because the court could not aid the plaintiff the defendant's motive in the illegal contract was immaterial.[3]

VII. Contracts as Labor—Bills and Notes.

Under the Massachusetts statute, though "business" is prohibited, yet, in 1813, it was held in a case in which no opinion is reported, that it was no bar to the recovery of a judgment on a note that it was made on this day.[4] Later, it was said that this case was imperfectly reported, and was decided on the insufficiency of the plea.[5] But still later it was formally endorsed.[6] And afterwards, in the same state, it was held to be no ground for arresting a judgment on a note that it was dated on Sunday, and the court said (1) that the fact that the date was Sunday must be proven to the jury; (2) that if it was, it would not be concluded that it was made on the day of its date, and (3) it took effect from delivery, and (4) that if it was made on Sunday, it might have been made after sunset, and so unaffected by the Massachusetts statute.[7] All of which seems to

[1] *Smith* v. *Sparrow*, 4 Bing. 84 (1827).

[2] *Moseley* v. *Hatch*, 108 Mass. 517 (1871).

[3] *Stevens* v. *Wood*, 127 Mass. 123 (1879)

[4] *Geer* v. *Putnam*, 10 Mass. 317.

[5] *Robeson* v. *French*, 12 Metc. (Mass.) 24 (1846).

[6] *Clap* v. *Smith*, 16 Pick. (Mass.) 247 (1854).

[7] *Hill* v. *Dunham*, 7 Gray (Mass.) 543 (1856).

imply that the court did not regard a Sunday note as valid. Yet, that it is so in Massachusetts is generally held elsewhere, on the strength of *Geer* v. *Putnam, supra*. Thus, it was said in Rhode Island, "in Massachusetts it has been held that a promissory note is valid."[1] Under the New York prohibition of labor a note was held not to be void.[2] The Missouri court, in considering the Illinois statute which forbids any one to "disturb the peace and good order of society by labor," said: "It is inconceivable that the making of a loan, or a promissory note, could have disturbed the peace and good order of society."[3] So it was held that under the Missouri prohibition of labor, a note given for an antecedent debt is valid.[4] But it has been held that a note is void under the statutes of Maine,[5] and New Hampshire,[6] and New Jersey,[7] and Michigan,[8] and Wisconsin,[9] and Minnesota,[10] and Georgia,[11] and Oregon,[12] whose statutes forbid "business;" and under the statutes of Vermont,[13] and Connecticut,[14] in which the phrase is "secular business," and in Pennsylvania, under a prohibition of "worldly employment, or business."[15] It has also been held that a note is void under the Indiana prohibition of "common labor," the court saying: "We think the statute intended to prohibit every description of secular business not within the exceptions;"[16] and that the making of a note

[1] *Allen* v. *Gardner*, 7 R. I. 22 (1861).

[2] *Greenbury* v. *Wilkins*, 9 Abb. (N. Y.) Pr. 206, note (1859).

[3] *Moore* v. *Climer*, 12 Mo. App. 11.

[4] *Kauffman* v. *Hamon*, 30 Mo. 387 (1860).

[5] *Towle* v. *Larrabee*, 26 Me. 464 (1847); *Baker* v. *Flagg*, 34 Id. 391 (1852).

[6] *Clough* v. *Davis*, 9 N. H. 500 (1838); *Allen* v. *Deming*, 14 Id. 133 (1843).

[7] *Reeves* v. *Butcher*, 31 N. J. 224 (1865).

[8] *Adams* v. *Hamell*, 2 Doug. 73 (1845).

[9] *Hill* v. *Sherwood*, 3 Wis. 343 (1854).

[10] *Brimhell* v. *Van Campen*, 8 Minn. 13 (1862); *Finneg* v. *Callendar*, Id. 41 (1862).

[11] *Hill* v. *Wilker*, 41 Ga. 449 (1871).

[12] *Smith* v. *Case*, 2 Oreg. 190 (1866). Although this case was decided in September, 1866, and the provision of the Code is quoted, with a reference to the number of the section, the Code of 1874, which alone is accessible to the writer, contains no provision against "business," but only one against keeping open store, &c. And it says that this latter is from an act which took effect March 19th, 1866, so that it would appear to have been the only law on the subject when the case cited was decided. The point was said to be "conceded by counsel" in Mississippi in 1866. *Kountz* v. *Price*, 40 Miss. 341, 345.

[13] *Lovejoy* v. *Whipple*, 18 Vt. 379 (1846).

[14] *Wright* v. *Geer*, 1 Root 474 (1792).

[15] *Kepner* v. *Keefer*, 6 Watts (Pa.) 231 (1837).

[16] *Reynolds* v. *Stevenson*, 4 Ind. 619 (1853).

is "labor" is settled in Iowa,[1] and Arkansas.[2] The Kentucky act of 1801 was curiously phrased. It seemed to prohibit both labor and business. But the court, considering the prohibition of labor only, said: "We are not prepared to decide that the mere execution and delivery of a note or its mere acceptance is laboring in any trade or calling, unless it be a part of some other transaction which may be regarded as labor in some trade or calling. And, if the mere execution and delivery of a note could be deemed such labor, we are satisfied that its mere acceptance could not."[3]

A few more points remain to be noticed in this connection. It was said by Swift, J., in Connecticut: "If a note should be made payable on Sunday, in express terms, it would be void, because it would be a contract to do an unlawful act. But, if it be payable at a future day, which by calculation is found to be Sunday, and the parties did not intend to make it payable on Sunday, then it would not be void."[4] "The buying, and receiving, and selling, endorsing and delivering of a promissory note must be business as much as the executing and delivering of one and the receiving it would be; it is also business of one's secular calling, as much as the other."[5] So, the endorsement of a bill, and delivery of it to the acceptor, to be used for his accommodation, is "worldly business," though the acceptor may not negotiate it until some subsequent day.[6] And the fact that an endorsement of part payment, dated on Sunday, was made in the presence of both parties, with evidence that it was cotemporaneous with the payment, warranted the jury in "inferring that the date of the payment was correct, and known and assented to by both parties to be correct at the time it was written, and that the payment was, therefore, made on the Lord's day."[7] Where a bill did not, in terms, purport to have been given in pursuance of a contract entered into on a previous day, nor to be the consummation of such a contract, giving the bill on Sunday, with a date of the preceding day, was held not to be

[1] *Sayre* v. *Wheeler*, 31 Iowa 112 (1870). The particular business of "buying and selling land" is mentioned.

[2] *Tucker* v. *West*, 29 Ark. 386 (1874); *Stewart* v. *Davis*, 31 Id. 518 (1876); *Edwards* v. *Probst*, 38 Id. (1882).

[3] *Ray* v. *Catlett*, 12 B. Mon. (Ky.) 522 (1851).

[4] *Avery* v. *Stewart*, 2 Conn. 69 (1816).

[5] *Smith* v. *Foster*, 41 N. H. 215.

[6] *Saltmarsh* v. *Tuthill*, 13 Ala.

[7] *Clapp* v. *Hale*, 112 Mass. 368 (1873).

any evidence from which a jury could draw the conclusion that a contract was made between the parties on the latter day; and it was said that, even supposing it to be equivalent to an admission by the party giving it that a parol contract for the payment of the same sum was made on that day, this would not avail the plaintiff in an action on the bill.[1] It may be observed that the English doctrine that, after an enumeration of certain classes, such a phrase as "other persons whatsoever" must be confined to other persons *ejusdem generis* with those mentioned, is disregarded in the Georgia cases, cited above. For, in that state the prohibition of "business," like that of "labor," is put upon "tradesmen," "artificers," &c., and "other persons whatever," but the courts have never thought of holding that the "other persons" must be of the same class with the "artificers," &c. Finally, it is held in Georgia that the fact that the making of a note was not in the "ordinary calling" of the makers, must be proven in defence.[2]

VIII. Contracts as Labor—Marriages.

It has been held in Massachusetts that a Sunday marriage is valid, though "purely a civil contract."[3] And the court in New Hampshire, referring to the above case, said with respect to the marriage contract, "its validity may be put upon the ground that the contract has been executed, and the status of the parties changed by it, and, therefore, as in other cases, where certain acts are forbidden by statute, but not expressly declared void, the law will not interfere, but leave the parties as it finds them." And it gave, as a further reason for sustaining such a marriage, "the idea that the act was not wholly secular, but rather of a solemn nature, ordained of God, and properly to be celebrated with religious rites and ceremonies."[4] The court added: "The conclusion we have reached in respect to marriages will apply with equal, if not greater, force to funerals, which, in all civilized communities, are occasions of great solemnity, and attended with imposing religious exercises; and, in

[1] *Kepner* v. *Keefer*, 6 Watts (Pa.) 231 (1837).

[2] *Sanders* v. *Johnson*, 29 Ga. 526 (1859).

[3] *Bennett* v. *Brooks*, 9 Allen (Mass.) 118 (1864).

[4] *George* v. *George*, 47 N. H. 27 (1866).

our own country, are universally esteemed to be in harmony with the duties of the Christian Sabbath." On the question whether a marriage contract, securing the woman an interest in the man's real estate is valid, the court of Pennsylvania was divided. in 1850.[1]

IX. Miscellaneous Instances of Labor, Business, &c.

In New York, under the statutory prohibitions of labor, and the sale of merchandise, &c., it was held that a contract to publish an advertisement in a Sunday paper was a contract to do a prohibited act, and the price stipulated for could not be recovered; for the court said, that, though work on the paper were not done on Sunday, its sale was a violation of the law.[2] And this view was sustained on appeal, when it was added that the sale "was servile work, in the same sense that the service of the attorney's clerk was, or that of a salesman in a dry goods store would be."[3] On the other hand, considering similar prohibitions, in a suit on contract for publishing an advertisement in a Sunday edition of a newspaper, the Supreme Court of Missouri said that the contract did not require Sunday work, and it would not assume such was intended; and, as to the sale, "it is contended that the evidence shows that copies of this edition of the paper were sold on Sunday, and that such sale was in violation of the statute. I will not stop to inquire whether such sale of newspapers comes within the prohibitions contained in the statute, or not. It is enough for the present purpose to see, that, by the terms of the contract, no such sale is required by the plaintiffs, or even remotely referred to. No one, after looking over this contract, will say that the plaintiffs could not completely perform the contract on their part, without ever selling a single paper, either on Sunday, or any other day. All that is contemplated by the contract is that the advertisement shall be published in the paper, and sent to the subscribers thereto."[4]

It is settled in Arkansas that not every contract for hire by a livery-stable keeper is void; and the court said: "It is necessary that both he and the hotel keeper should, as far as they can, abstain

[1] *In re Gangwere*, 14 Pa. 417.

[2] *Smith* v. *Wilcox*, 19 Barb. (N. Y.) 581 (1855); *S. C.*, 25 Id. 341.

[3] *S. C.*, 24 N. Y. 453 (1862).

[4] *Sheffield* v. *Barmer*, 52 Mo. 474 (1873).

from all employment not strictly necessary," and held that the necessity of any particular service was a question of fact, and should be ascertained by the keeper "upon information and inquiry."[1]

It is not indictable for a carrier, under contract with the post-master-general to carry the mail on each day of the week, to carry the same on Sunday; and it was said in this connection "when the traveling is necessary to execute a lawful contract, it cannot be considered as unnecessary traveling against the prohibition of the statute. But let it be remembered that our opinion does not protect travelers in the stage-coach, or the carrier of the mail in driving about any town to discharge or to receive passengers; and much less in blowing his horn, to the disturbance of serious people, either at public worship, or in their own houses. The carrier may proceed with his mail on the Lord's day to the post-office; he may go to any public house to refresh himself and his horses; and he may take the mail from the post-office, and proceed on his route. Any other liberties on the Lord's day our opinion does not warrant."[2] In New Hampshire, it was said that a man had "an undoubted right to drive his team on the highway, provided that, in so doing, he wrought no disturbance to others."[3] But later a doubt was intimated, as follows: "Whether every ride or drive for mere relaxation and exercise must be regarded as an unlawful recreation it is not necessary to decide."[4] Still later, in the same state, it was said: "Our cases are far from going the length of including a visit which a son makes to his parents under the head of work, labor, or business of his secular calling, and it cannot be held that such a visit is within that provision."[5] And the court expressed the further opinion "that traveling, in an orderly and decent manner, to visit a parent, is not to be regarded as a criminal recreation." Whether traveling was a disturbance of others was considered in New Hampshire in 1866. The court cited the case of *Dutton* v. *Weare*, and said: "It was held that there was no evidence of a disturbance, although the traveler started with a heavy team from his hotel, taking with him two men, and an extra horse and sled, to enable him to get through a snow-drift which he expected to encounter,

[1] *Stewart* v. *Davis*, 31 Ark. 518 (1880).

[2] *Knox's Case*, 6 Mass. 76 (1809).

[3] *Dutton* v. *Weare*, 17 N. H. 34 (1845).

[4] *Woodman* v. *Hubbard*, 5 Fost. (N. H.) 67 (1852).

[5] *Corey* v. *Bath*, 35 N. H. 530 (1857).

and which occupied them all for several hours. In deciding that here was no evidence of disturbance to others, it is clear that the court did not take the view which we have adopted; but it will be perceived that the point was not discussed in the opinion reported."[1] As will be seen elsewhere, the view adopted in this case was, that anything is a "disturbance" which tends to distract one's mind from religious pursuits, and that the fact that the party disturbed made no objection did not affect the question of the disturber's guilt. Authority was given a canal company to make rules, &c., for "orderly navigation and the government of boatmen," &c. In an action by the company against a party who broke a chain across the canal on Sunday, a by-law closing navigation on that day, except in cases of necessity, and forbidding boats to pass under a penalty, &c., was held illegal.[2] An action was brought against a canal company for delay from the stranding of a vessel. The defence was, that the vessel had attempted to pass a lock on Sunday. An effort was made to show the existence of a regulation that no boat should pass a lock on that day, without a written permit from the superintendent, &c., which was not to be granted, except in cases of necessity. The court said it was held that "neither the superintendent nor directors had power to make such a regulation."[3] In New York, a doubt was expressed whether the business of a common carrier, by means of a steamboat, came within the term "servile labor."[4] But it was held in Pennsylvania that the business of running passenger cars was a violation of the act.[5] The New Hampshire court said: "Whether the letting of a horse is necessarily, and in all cases, a work or business to the disturbance of others, it is not necessary to decide."[6]

Indiana has a statute imposing a penalty of $100 for the failure of a telegraph company to transmit and deliver a message; in an action to recover this penalty, it was held a sufficient answer that the contract for the transmission of the message was made on Sunday.[7]

[1] *George* v. *George*, 47 N. H. 27, 35.

[2] *C. N. Co.* v. *Pilling*, 14 M. & W. 76 (1845).

[3] *McArthur* v. *G. B. & M. Co.*, 34 Wis. 139 (1874).

[4] *Merritt* v. *Earle*, 31 Barb. (N. Y.) 38 (1859).

[5] *Sparhawk* v. *Union R. W. Co.*, 54 Pa. 401.

[6] *Woodman* v. *Hubbard*, 6 Fost. (N. H. 67 (1852).

[7] *Rogers* v. *Telegraph Co.*, 78 Ind. 169.

Where a man signed an application for insurance, and executed the premium notes, and the parties knew the day was Sunday, and, to avoid illegality, post-dated the application and the notes, and there was no evidence of subsequent ratification, the contract was held illegal.[1]

A private sale of a horse is not void in New York, and the court added: "The fact of the parties having driven the horse before they made the bargain, but on the same day, does not alter the case. There is no evidence that this was done even for the purpose of trying the horse, preparatory to the bargain, nor that any negotiation was then on foot for the purpose."[2] And, in a later case, where the vendee went in search of some horses to the vendor's place, and the vendor caught a span in a field, and there made them "show off" to the vendee, in the morning, and, in the evening, drove them in a wagon before the vendee, exhibiting them to him, and the latter then purchased, the court observed: "It cannot, I think, be said that the transaction between the parties in the case at bar was necessarily a public exposure of goods and chattels for sale."[3] But, where two horses exchanged were examined by the parties, and were driven up for that purpose, and were tried by them, and the trade was consummated, and a note for the difference agreed upon on the exchange was given, all on Sunday, the note was declared void, and the court said "no case could be more clearly a matter of business within the statute, and no business transaction more evidently demoralizing in its tendency and example."[4]

On petition to supersede a commission in bankruptcy, the Lord Chancellor said: "The act of bankruptcy, on which the petition is grounded, is a denial to a creditor on Sunday. If the petitioner had assigned Sunday for settling the account, it was not an act of bankruptcy by him to say he would not keep that appointment to transact business on that day." And the commission was superseded.[5]

A party is not bound to regard a demand made on this day for

[1] *Heller* v. *Crawford*, 37 Ind. 279 (1871).

[2] *Miller* v. *Roessler*, 4 E. D. Smith (N. Y.) 234 (1855)

[3] *Batsford* v. *Every*, 44 Barb. (N. Y.) 618 (1865).

[4] *Adams* v. *Hamell*, 2 Doug. (Mich.) 73 (1845).

[5] *Preston's Case*, 2 Ves. & B. 311 (1813).

the fulfillment of a contract.[1] So, demand for wheat sold under a contract is a nullity, with which it would be a violation of law to comply; and neither the vendor, nor the warehouseman could validate this (as, by waiver, in putting a refusal to deliver on other grounds), because "the law is not enforced for the benefit of either, but to prevent a desecration of the day; the demand was void, not merely voidable."[2]

An owner of land, calling at another's house, to make a proposition to sell it, was held a disturber within the statute of New Hampshire.[3]

The enlistment of a recruit in the English army is not void, since recruiting is not a part of the "ordinary calling" of the soldiers detailed for that service.[4]

It is, perhaps, safe to say that anything may be done on Sunday which may be done on any other day, unless it is prohibited by some statute.[5] We have seen that it is susceptible of historical demonstration that Sunday was *dies juridicus*, until made otherwise by express enactment. The New Hampshire court has noticed various canons by which judicial proceedings were forbidden, and which were adopted in England, and added, "But the canons extended no further than to prohibit judicial business; for fairs, markets, sports and pastimes might still take place."[6] And, erroneously assuming that judicial proceedings are void at common law, two New York cases affirm that any business, other than judicial, can be done, unless prohibited by statute in that state.[7] So, it was said in England that exercising the trade of a butcher is no offence at common law, and that an indictment for so doing must lay the offence *contra formam statuti*.[8] So, in California, keeping open store, bar, &c., was said to be *malum prohibitum*, and, independent of statute, not an offence.[9]

It was said in New York that the term "working" is used in the statute of that state "as the most comprehensive that the

[1] *Delameter* v. *Miller*, 1 Cow. (N. Y.) 75 (1823).

[2] *Brackett* v. *Edgerton*, 14 Minn. 174, 190.

[3] *Merrill* v. *Downs*, 41 N. H. 72.

[4] *Wilton* v. *Gavin*, 16 Q. B. (71 Eng. Com. L.) 48 (1850).

[5] See *Behan* v. *Ghio*, 12 So. Rep. 996.

[6] *Allen* v. *Deming*, 14 N. H. 133 (1843).

[7] *Sayles* v. *Smith*, 12 Wend. (N. Y.) 57 (1834); *Boynton* v. *Page*, 13 Id. 425 (1835).

[8] *Brotherton's Case*, 1 Str. 702 (1726).

[9] *Koser's Case*, 60 Cal. 177 (1882).

language can supply, to cover the action, and employment of mind or body, in the pursuit of business."[1] But later, in the same state, it was observed that "acts not interfering with the benevolent design of the Sabbath by disturbing and hindering those who, for themselves and families, desire to enjoy and improve it, are not prohibited."[2] In Massachusetts, one clause of the statute forbids keeping open a shop, &c., and another doing business, &c., after which come other prohibitions, and then a section providing that one conscientiously observing the seventh day shall not be liable to penalties for performing secular labor, &c.; *held,* that this exception applies only to the clause against business, &c., and does not authorize an observer of the seventh day to keep open shop, or violate the other express prohibitions.[3] In Rhode Island, a city ordinance which prohibited the opening of places of trade, &c., was held to create two offences—keeping such a place open, and selling in it.[4]

In Maine "walking in the open air, for exercise, is not against the statute."[5] And it was said in Ohio: "It is not unlawful in this state to travel upon public highways for pleasure merely. * * * The only possible doubt is as to the meaning of the word 'sporting;' but, whatever may be included within the meaning of that word, we do not believe that the legislature intended to inhibit the quiet, peaceful, and invigorating exercise of either walking, or riding, although no urgent necessity, or charity may prompt the exercise."[6] In Massachusetts, the courts have a distinction between traveling and ordinary walking in the streets, and it has been said: "We are of opinion that a person walking with a friend on Sunday evening less than half a mile, with no apparent purpose of going to, or stopping at any place but his own house, much less of passing out of the city, and no object of business or pleasure, except open air, and gentle exercise, is not guilty of traveling, or liable to punishment."[7]

It has been held in Massachusetts that signing, declaring, and

[1] *Campbell* v. *International,* 4 Bosw. (N. Y.) 298.

[2] *Smith* v. *Wilcox,* 24 N. Y. 353 (1862).

[3] *Has' Case,* 122 Mass. 40, 41.

[4] *Geary's Case,* 4 R. I. 485 (1857).

[5] *Davidson* v. *Portland,* 69 Me. 116 (1879).

[6] *Nagle* v. *Brown,* 37 Ohio St. 7 (1881).

[7] *Hamilton* v. *Boston,* 14 Allen (Mass.) 475 (1867).

publishing of a will is not business or work within the prohibition, not being *ejusdem generis* with the things enumerated, as keeping open shop, &c., whereby the general prohibition was confined to transactions for profit or dealings connected therewith; whereas making a will, though a secular, is, at the same time, "a solemn act."[1] And the same result is reached in New Hampshire, though there it is considered that the making of a will is not a secular act, but, like marriages, and funerals, "not inconsistent with a due observance of the Lord's day;" and the court mentions as worthy of consideration the point whether the will is not to be regarded as executed at the testator's death; and observes: "If the law has been violated at all it is, or at least may be, by the maker alone, and the devisees and legatees can, in no sense, unless participating in the act, be regarded as *in pari delicto*."[2] A question about the validity of a will arose in Pennsylvania in 1867. The court observed that, though it could hardly be a question whether making a will was worldly business, as to writing them it would not say. But it sustained a will made on Sunday, on the ground that it did not take effect till the testator's death. In this case, the testator was eighty-five years of age, but in his ordinary health.[3] Later this case was cited, and it was expressly said that a will is not void because testator is in good health.[4]

It was recently said in Indiana that a will made on Sunday is valid, though the testator was in good health, as the drafting and execution thereof does not come within Rev. Stat. Ind. 1881, § 2000, making it a penal offence to be found engaged in "common labor," or in one's usual avocation on that day.[5]

It was held in Wisconsin that a loan of money and promise to repay are "business" and presumptively illegal; and it was added "if possible to bring it within an exception, the burden is on the plaintiff, suing for repayment, to do so."[6] The annexation of the schedule of the property, conveyed in an assignment for creditor's benefit, is a void act in Massachusetts.[7] And filling up a writ, and

[1] *Bennett* v. *Brooks*, 9 Allen (Mass.) 118.

[2] *George* v. *George*, 47 N. H. 27 (1866).

[3] *Bateman's Appeal*, 55 Pa. 183.

[4] *Daler* v. *Knepp*, 98 Pa. 389 (1881).

[5] *Rapp* v. *Reehling*, 23 N. E. Rep. 777.

[6] *Troewert* v. *Decker*, 51 Wis. 46 (1881). See, also, *Meader* v. *White*, 66 Me. 90 (1876).

[7] *Clop* v. *Smith*, 16 Pick. (Mass.) 247 (1834).

delivering it to an officer is within the prohibition of labor, &c.[1] In New York, in 1849, the point was suggested, but not solved, whether the duties of a police magistrate are within the prohibition of the statute.[2] It was held in Indiana, that the execution of a replevin bond came within the terms "common labor."[3] It was said in Ohio: "The words 'common labor' cannot extend to the case of a public officer in the performance of official duty."[4] And it was held in Alabama, that a statute against "worldly employment" had no bearing on the question of the validity of the service of a process of attachment.[5] To serve notice on a tenant that he will be charged an increased rent after the expiration of his term is "worldly business" in New Jersey.[6] A Sunday contract to furnish a county court-house or pay a penalty, is valid in Texas.[7]

An order for closing a public library was held a reasonable one for the directors to pass, and in harmony with the Pennsylvania legislation as to service of process, &c.[8] A town board of supervisors was authorized to issue certain bonds only on petition signed by a given number of taxpayers. A taxpayer asked an injunction against the issue of the bonds, on the ground that the required number of signatures was not affixed on a secular day. The court said that going about and procuring the signatures and signing the petition were "business," and the injunction was granted.[9] It seemed doubtful to the Massachusetts court whether it was a violation of the statute to write a letter stating that the writer had that morning been informed his father was dangerously ill, and must go home immediately, and leave for his father's residence early Monday morning, and requesting another to take some goods he had bought, and do the best he could with them, and assuring the latter he should not lose anything.[10] But in Georgia it was said:

[1] *Johnson* v. *Day*, 17 Pick. (Mass.) 106 (1835).

[2] *Palmer* v. *New York*, 2 Sandf. (N.Y.) 318.

[3] *Link* v. *Clemmens*, 7 Blackf. (Ind.) 479 (1845).

[4] *Hastings* v. *Columbus*, 42 Ohio St. 585 (1885).

[5] *Matthews* v. *Ansley*, 31 Ala. 20 (1857). See, also, *Keith* v. *Tuttle*, 28 Me. 326.

[6] *Ryan's Case*, 49 N. J. L. 314 (1887).

[7] *Behan* v. *Ghio*, 12 So. Rep. 996 (1889).

[8] *Granger* v. *Grubb*, 7 Phil. (Pa.) 350 (1870).

[9] *De Forth* v. *W. & M. Co.*, 52 Wis. 320 (1881).

[10] *Tuckerman* v. *Hinkley*, 9 Allen (Mass.) 452.

"We think it is not a breach of law to hand even a business letter to another, and request the conveyance of it to the post-office to take place on the ensuing day, and that a letter thus dealt with may be the medium of closing a lawful contract."[1] A traded a pony with B for a mule, saying he would give a good title. It turned out there was a mortgage on the pony. B offered to return the pony on Sunday. The offer being refused he brought replevin for the mule. The court said an instruction that this offer would bind the defendant was an error.[2] The Maine provision that a valuable consideration received must be restored, before a suit on a contract can be defeated by showing it was made on Sunday, applies to an agreement to pay money on an exchange of horses.[3]

II. THE EXCEPTIONS OF "NECESSITY" AND "CHARITY."

I. "NECESSITY"—THE GENERAL PRINCIPLE.

It has been well said of the exceptions in the English act that they are "vague and indefinite," and "extremely loose."[4] And a New Hampshire judge has remarked: "There are many classes of cases in which the community need a means of knowing what business is lawful on Sunday;" though he may be rather sanguine when he anticipates the "easy" settlement of this difficulty "by legislation specifically declaring what cases shall be exempted."[5] On the other hand, a Vermont judge has said: "I cannot apprehend the least danger on this head. It is a law as easily observed as any in the statute book."[6] But his associate strongly defended the opposite view, and observed: "The statute excepts all acts of necessity and charity. These are lawful, and who is to judge what are such? If the jury, it will depend on the religious opinions of each jury, and of course be pregnant with the utmost uncertainty. If the court, as matter of law, then it will nearly convert a bench

[1] *Bryant* v. *Booze*, 55 Ga. 438 (1875).

[2] *Merritt* v. *Robinson*, 35 Ark. 783 (1880).

[3] *Wentworth* v. *Woodside*, 79 Me. 156.

[4] *Younger's Case*, 5 T. R. 447, 451 (1793).

[5] *Hamilton* v. *Austin*, 62 N. H. 575 (1883).

[6] *Lyon* v. *Strong*, 6 Vt. 219, 228 (1834).

of laymen into an ecclesiastical council, for 'necessity and charity,' in connection with the Sabbath, must very much depend upon the creed or religious belief of the individual to whom the question is submitted. Although the holy observance of the Sabbath is a positive duty, yet, like charity, it is undefined; and different denominations of Christians even, as well as individuals, vary much in the degree of strictness with which it ought to be observed. How ungracious, then, for a court to mark the law upon this duty for all denominations to be governed by, and with judges usually belonging to different religious societies! It would be like a synod composed of the dignitaries of several sects. Unanimity could scarcely be expected. And if it was to be regarded as a mixed question of law and fact, it still would be a vexed one, as the propensities (*query*, prosecutions?) for traveling on Sunday have formerly shown, when scarcely two justices or two juries would agree upon the validity of an excuse or what constituted a necessity for traveling. So much confusion was there upon the subject, that it is believed most pious persons think that such prosecutions do religion more harm than good. And suppose the question of what was necessity or charity was to be decided independent of sectarian views. How extremely embarrassing many cases would be; for instance, a man borrows a considerable sum of money on the Sabbath; it was, perhaps, to pay a debt at a distance on Monday and save a bill of costs; to redeem a mortgage or save an estate, or he so represented, but it was not so. Another sends to a butcher for meat. Are these matters of necessity? Should the meat have been prepared on Saturday, like the manna? Or should the money have been procured before? Or if it was expected and the person disappointed, will that be an excuse? Or if he lied to the lender, will that be as if a necessity existed? And how difficult to arrive at all the facts and motives, and what cases shall *per se* be adjudged necessary or charitable. How with marriage, the greatest of all contracts here among Protestants? It is no sacrament, or other religious rite, but a mere civil contract. Is this void or voidable, or does it come under the saving clause?"[1] And in Ohio it is said: "It is a task of much difficulty, and one that a court ought

[1] *Lyon* v. *Strong*, 6 Vt. 236, 237.

not unnecessarily to attempt, to draw a line that shall clearly distinguish works of necessity from those that are not."[1] It seems, indeed, to be pretty generally conceded that "necessity, like charity, is incapable of definition at once accurate, and sufficiently comprehensive to accomplish the object of this enactment,"[2] for "no one ought to expect sharp definitions of legal duty on such a subject."[3] Nevertheless, from the mass of judicial expositions of the subject, some canons of interpretation may be plausibly framed.

1. The first of these is that, startling as it may appear, the Sunday law is one thing for one man, and another thing for another. It has been considered the great glory of our system of jurisprudence that it is no respecter of persons; but it has been expressly said, in reference to the Sunday law, that necessity may be one thing for the savage, and another for civilized man, and (*sic*) one thing for the rich man, and another thing for the poor one! And again:

"The individual condition and necessities of each man may go far to determine whether it is his duty to labor on Sunday to save property from destruction. The saving of a piece of property to one man might prevent great misery and suffering to himself and family—to another it might be of no consequence."[4]

2. Though the necessity must be "imperious,"[5] yet it is certain that it need not be "absolute."[6] And "it will not do to limit it to dangers to life, health or property, which are beyond human foresight or control."[7] But it is sufficient that the act is one "morally fit and proper to be done on the Sabbath;"[8] though it has been noted that "this phrase may itself require some explanation."[9]

3. It is not enough that the act is merely "convenient;"[10] that it

[1] *McGatrick* v. *Wason*, 4 Ohio 566 (1855).

[2] *Muller's Case*, 76 Ind. 310, 312 (1881); *Dinsmore* v. *Police*, 12 Abb. (N. Y.) N. Cas. 436 (1882); *Johnston's Case*, 22 Pa. 102 (1853).

[3] *Nesbit's Case*, 34 Pa. 398, 408.

[4] *Whitcomb* v. *Gilman*, 35 Vt. 297.

[5] *Ohmer's Case*, 34 Mo. App. 115 (1888).

[6] *Flagg* v. *Milbury*, 4 Cush. (Mass.) 243 (1849).

[7] *Hennersdorf's Case*, 25 Tex. 597 (1888).

[8] *Bennett* v. *Brooks*, 9 Allen (Mass.) 118 (1864); *McClary* v. *Lowell*, 44 Vt. 116 (1881); *Johnston's Case*, 31 Ill. 469 (1863).

[9] *Sampson's Case*, 97 Mass. 407 (1867).

[10] *Phillips* v. *Innes*, 4 Cl. & F. 234 (1837); *Jones* v. *Andover*, 10 Allen (Mass.) 18 (1865); *Johnston's Case*, 22 Pa. 102 (1853); *Allen* v. *Duffie*, 43 Mich. 1 (1880).

is more convenient or profitable if then done, or than it would be to defer, or omit it;[1] or that it is advantageous for business.[2]

4. Yet the necessity may grow out of or be incidental to a particular trade or calling;[3] or, as it is said, may arise from the "exigencies of society or trade," and Judge Thurman, in so holding, observed:

"In using the expression 'exigency of trade,' I have been speaking of trade generally, and not of a necessity created by a particular contract a man may have made. It is true that a man might be ruined by a failure to deliver an article he had contracted to deliver, if he could not ship it upon a Sunday, and this might be without any fault of his; in which case, it would become the duty of the court to consider whether he could save himself only by a violation of the law. And when that question shall arise, it may possibly be found difficult to say that a man may lawfully labor all day to drag a sheep out of a pit, and yet cannot perform one-tenth of that labor to save himself and his family from pecuniary destruction—that he may lawfully work to save one dollar's worth of property, in the shape of an animal, but that he violates the law, if he save all his property by fulfilling his contract."[4] But in Indiana the loading of a vessel was held not a work of necessity, and the court said: "If the vicissitudes of trade and speculation were allowed to fix the rule as to what are works of necessity, there could be no observance of the Sabbath. There are, as a general thing, dangers attending every enterprise, which may be avoided by expedition; but the Sabbath is not the day for common labor, although by such labor dangers may be avoided."[5] Yet it was later observed in the same state that "it is the exigencies of the object to be accomplished that determines to a great extent the means to be resorted to."[6]

[1] *Sampson's Case*, 97 Mass. 407 (1867).

[2] *Davis* v. *Somerville*, 128 Mass. 59 (1880).

[3] *Hennersdorf's Case*, 25 Tex. 597 (1888).

[4] *McGatrick* v. *Wason*, 4 Ohio 566 (1855). In the course of his able and learned discussion of the subject, Judge Thurman incidentally affords strong support to the position of those who regard the "saving of necessity" as one which might well be treated as "void for uncertainty." In this case, the question was whether the danger of a closing of navigation by cold weather justified loading a vessel, and it was held that it did.

[5] *Pate* v. *Wright*, 30 Ind. 476 (1868).

[6] *L. & N. R. R.'s Case*, 89 Ind. 291 (1882).

5. There is no doubt that necessity may be determined by custom. The court in Pennsylvania said: "The law regards that as necessary which the common sense of the country, in its ordinary modes of doing its business, regards as necessary."[1] And work may be a necessity in one state which is not so in another.[2] So, it was said in Indiana: "We are not to seek the physical, metaphysical, philosophical, scientific, moral, or theological meaning of the word 'necessity,' but its legal meaning, as applicable to the rights, duties, and conduct of men."[3] And in Kentucky, "We shall adopt the language in its construction to the manners, habits, wants and customs of the people it is to affect; and, in many cases, the rights and duties of those charged with a public or private duty, and the obligation they are under to others must also be considered."[4] So, among lawful things is "supplying the ordinary demands of our physical natures."[5] But, on the other hand, though "fuel, and food, and clothing are not forbidden, yet the usual means of obtaining them, by merchants, manufacturers, carriers, farmers, gardeners and laborers are forbidden."[6]

6. In Texas, one may engage in "such labor as is a necessary incident to the accomplishment of a lawful purpose;"[7] and it was laid down in Indiana that "the purpose being lawful, the labor was lawful."[8] And again, it was said that lawful labor was "such as may be necessary to the accomplishment of a lawful purpose under the circumstances of any particular case."[9] And this doctrine was afterwards twice endorsed.[10] But it was finally repudiated, as "a rule which cannot be practically applied without nullifying the law."[11]

7. "Generally speaking, it ought to be an unforeseen necessity, or if foreseen, such as could not reasonably have been provided against or foreseen."[12]

[1] *Nesbit's Case*, 34 Pa. 398 (1859).

[2] *Sundstrom's Case*, 25 Tex. 133 (1888).

[3] *Edgerton's Case*, 67 Ind. 588 (1879).

[4] *L & N. R. R.'s Case*, 80 Ky. 291 (1882).

[5] *Johnston's Case*, 22 Pa. 102 (1853).

[6] *Nesbit's Case*, 34 Pa. 398.

[7] *Hennersdorf's Case*, 25 Tex. 597 (1888).

[8] *Crocket's Case*, 33 Ind. 416 (1870).

[9] *Wilkinson's Case*, 59 Ind. 416, 417 (1877).

[10] *Edgerton's Case*, 67 Ind. 588, 590; *Carver's Case*, 69 Id 61, 67.

[11] *Mueller's Case*, 76 Ind. 310 (1881)

[12] *Ohmer's Case*, 34 Mo. App. 115 (1889).

8. It must not be the party's own creating. Thus, where an injured plaintiff had been traveling to meet a letter which would inform him whether or not he would have to go to a certain point to meet an invalid sister, no questions were made as to his errand's being one of charity, but it was held an insufficient defence "that it was more convenient for the plaintiff to postpone his traveling to obtain the letter from his sister, in order that he might perform his private business."[1] The same principle, it would seem, might well apply to the purchase of bread, milk and many other articles, which may be "kept over," with more or less trouble. So a liquor-drinker (and, apparently, a tobacco-smoker—*query*, chewer, also?) must anticipate his wants by previous purchases."[2]

9. And, finally, the act need not be a work of necessity to him who does the labor, for "if so, why protect the apothecary who sells his medicines for the relief of the patient, or the dairyman who furnishes the milk for his customers, or the hotel-keeper who furnishes his guests with food and lodging?"[3] But this would seem not to be the modern English doctrine. Where the question was whether a barber could compel his apprentice to shave customers on Sunday, it was said, "the necessity contemplated was a necessity of the person who worked, and not of him who compelled the work."[4] And yet, in an earlier case, where a baker was charged with baking meats, Lord Mansfield "hinted his opinion that the Sabbath would be much more generally observed by a baker staying at home to bake the dinners of a number of families than by his going to church and those families, or their servants, staying at home to dress dinners for themselves."[5] And afterwards, Ashhurst, J., said: "The case of bakers, though not particularly mentioned in the exception of the act (29 Car. II.), is within the reason of it. Though, by this means, some few journeymen bakers are kept to work on a Sunday, it is for the general convenience of the public, because it enables the rest of the community to attend public worship, which they could not have an opportunity of doing, if they had no means of having their dinners dressed from home."[6]

[1] *Butcher* v. *Fitchburg R. R.*, 131 Mass. 156, 158.

[2] *Mueller's Case*, 76 Ind. 310 (1881).

[3] *L. & N. R. R.'s Case*, 89 Ind. 291 (1882).

[4] *Phillips* v. *Innes*, 4 Cl. & F. 234 (1837).

[5] *Cox's Case*, 2 Burr. 785 (1759).

[6] *Younger's Case*, 5 T. R. 449.

II. Traveling as a Necessity—The Principle.

The necessity here need not be physical.[1] But is, "to a great extent, determined by its moral fitness and propriety."[2] And "riding for exercise" is lawful in Maine; to hold otherwise, it is said would be "contrary to the letter as well as the spirit of a statute which expressly excepts from its prohibition works of necessity or charity."[3] And, in New York, it was said in this connection that "the evident object of the statute was to prevent the day from being employed in servile work, which is exhausting to the body, or in merely idle pastime, subversive of that order, thrift and economy of health and substance, which is necessary to the preservation of society. It was never intended to prohibit such a use of the day as would be conducive to the health and necessary recreation of the citizen."[4] Which would seem to throw either on court or jury the burden of settling just how much and what kind of recreation is necessary for the individual citizen who may chance to be indicted for "desecrating the Sabbath." It seems that the necessity may be one thing at one time and another at another, for "the change in the habits and customs of the people, and the mode and character of transportation and travel, makes that a necessity at this day that half a century since would not have been so regarded."[5] How far is the party's belief in the necessity of the travel a justification of it? It was said in a civil case in Vermont that "the necessity for traveling must be a real, not a fancied, necessity. It is not an honest belief that a necessity for traveling exists, but the actual existence of the necessity, which renders traveling lawful."[6] But in Connecticut, where the owner of a hack was charged with allowing persons to travel in it "not for necessity or charity," it was held that, if he really believed a case of necessity or charity existed, he was not criminal.[7] It should be noted that this was a case under a special

[1] *Knox's Case*, 6 Mass. 76, 77 (1809).

[2] *Feital* v. *Middlesex R. R.*, 109 Mass. 398; *Smith* v. *Boston R. R.*, 120 Id. 490 (1872).

[3] *Sullivan* v. *Maine Cent. R. R.*, 19 Atl. Rep. 169 (1889).

[4] *Landers* v. *R. R. Co.*, 13 Abb. (N. Y.) Pr. (N. S.) 338.

[5] *L. & N. R. R.'s Case*, 80 Ky. 291 (1882).

[6] *Johnson* v. *Irasburg*, 47 Vt. 28 (1874).

[7] *Myer's Case*, 1 Conn. 502 (1816).

statute forbidding proprietors of coaches, &c., to allow travel in them, except for "necessity," &c. Perhaps it is reconciled with the Vermont doctrine, which was applied to the general statute against work, &c., in the proposition that the responsibility of the carriage-owner is primarily determined by his information as to the hirer's purpose; but, having learned this, in letting his carriage, he takes the risk of that purpose being considered a proper one by the law. This case leads us to another branch of our subject. Closely connected with the question of a person's right to travel on Sunday, is that of the right of another to transport him. We have seen already that the necessity need not be on the party doing the labor, but it is sufficient if his labor be necessary for another. Thus, a woman visiting at plaintiff's house on a cold, windy Sunday in December, informed him that she had to go home that night, a distance of two miles. He thereupon took her home with his horse and sleigh. *Held*, that the act was not unlawful, it being justifiable on the ground of necessity or as a deed of charity; and plaintiff was not precluded from recovering for damages caused by his horse slipping on a street.[1] The conclusiveness, if not the application, of this test, in the case of a common carrier, has been disputed in Pennsylvania. A person was tried in that state for running an omnibus, and the court held that he was a common carrier, pursuing his ordinary occupation, and the motives of his customers could not determine the character of his business, which was declared to be a worldly employment, actually contributing to idleness, dissipation and disorder (*sic*). And the defence that the travelers might be riding to church or the cemetery was denounced as "a specious pretext, to make the most of it, to cover up a palpable violation of the law," for, though it was admitted that, "had the persons riding to church, or the cemetery, been prosecuted, they might have alleged a proper and necessary work, or had the defendant been engaged specifically in carrying them and running his omnibus for no other purpose, he would have been blameless; yet, granting that the parties in the omnibus were lawful travelers, the driver was engaged in furnishing them contraband means of conveyance."[2] And this

[1] *Buck* v. *City of Biddeford* (Me.), 19 Atl. Rep. 912.

[2] *Johnston's Case*, 22 Pa. 102 (1853). Black, C. J., and Lewis, J., dissented.

was reiterated later and extended to horse cars.[1] And the court thus dealt with another principle considered above: "It is said judicial construction has established that traveling is not a violation of the act, and then it is argued, with an appearance of logical precision, that if the end be legitimate, all the means which are appropriate, which are adapted to that end, may lawfully be employed to carry it into effect * * * the conclusion, however sound in some cases, is too broad for this occasion."[2] But later, in the same state, it was said that a man might drive his own family to church, or a hired man his employer's family, though they be not "travelers;" this on the ground of uniform custom.[3] And, finally, the necessity of horse cars was recognized, as well as that of steam cars.[4] The New Jersey prohibition of traveling, except for necessity or charity, has a proviso that a railroad may "run one train each day for the accommodation of the citizens of the state." In a suit by a party injured, the court said that to limit the act to the carrying of passengers in such trains traveling from necessity or charity would practically make it a vain one; that the statute was designed to amend the old law in its total prohibition of general traveling, and that it was the evident legislative intention to permit the use in ordinary travel of the specified trains.[5]

III. Traveling as a Necessity—Particular Journeys.

A party who proceeded in a street car from Charlestown entirely across the city of Boston, in which he resided, to Roxbury, on the opposite side, was held to have been traveling, and not from necessity or charity; the facts being that he had left Boston on the morning of the same day, and spent the greater part of the day in Charlestown, for the purpose of collecting a debt.[6] "It would be erroneous to rule, as matter of law, that traveling for the purpose of attending a Spiritualists' camp-meeting is not within the exception."[7] A party going to see his "boss," with the view of induc-

[1] *Jeandell's Case,* 2 Grant (Pa.) 506.

[2] *Id.* 114.

[3] *Nesbit's Case,* 34 Pa. 398.

[4] *Sparhawk's Case,* 54 Pa. 401 (1867); *A. & S. R. R.* v. *Renz,* 55 Ga. 126 (1875). See, also, *L. & N. R. R.'s Case,* 88 Ky. 291 (1882).

[5] *Smith* v. *N. Y., &c.,* 46 N. J. L. 7.

[6] *Staunton* v. *Met. R. Co.,* 14 Allen (Mass.) 485 (1867).

[7] *Feital* v. *Middlesex R. R.,* 109 Mass. 398.

ing the latter to change his hours of labor from night to day-time, is not traveling from necessity.[1] A woman lived at Chelmsford, but was temporarily employed at Lowell. She went on Saturday morning to visit her children in Chelmsford, where she found one of them sick, and she attended it till Sunday evening, when it was better. A doctor lived near her, but she did not call him. Sunday evening she started for Lowell, designing to get a medicine she had previously tried with success for a same complaint in the child, not intending to go back to Chelmsford that night, but to send the physic by another. *Held* to be traveling from necessity.[2] A party who walked from his home in Boston, for the purpose of ascertaining from the person of whom he had hired a house whether it had been cleaned so that he could move into it with his family next day, was held not to have been traveling from necessity, or charity.[3] A maid-servant, without any fault on her part, was prevented from returning from her mother's house to her employer's on Saturday night, and returned early on Sunday morning for the purpose of preparing needful food for her employer's family. This was held a work of necessity, which justified her in traveling, and her employer or his man-servant in driving her over in the former's carriage.[4] A party may travel to go and return from a funeral, and need not return by the same, or the shortest, route, unless the road taken was so unreasonable and inconvenient as to show a purpose outside of the alleged necessity, or charity; but cannot go to another place, not upon the return route, to enable his companion to make a social call, or go to a remote place, occupying a greatly increased time, or make an additional journey for the transaction of business. The court added that if he had taken his companion from her residence, and gone with her to make the visit, without attending the funeral at all, it would have been a clear violation of the statute, and that it made no difference that the determination to make that journey was formed after he had attended the funeral, and was about to return.[5] Where a party, traveling on business, expected that a letter to him would reach Boston in a week, informing him whether he

[1] *Connolly* v. *Boston*, 117 Mass. 64 (1875).

[2] *Gorman* v. *Lowell*, 117 Mass. 65 (1875).

[3] *Smith* v. *Boston*, 120 Mass. 490 (1876).

[4] *Crosman* v. *Lynn*, 121 Mass. 301 (1877).

[5] *Davis* v. *Sumerville*, 128 Mass. 594 (1880).

would have to go to another place to meet his sister, who was ill, for the purpose of taking her home, or whether a friend of hers would escort her thither, and continued his business travels for a fortnight, and, missing a connection of trains, by which he would have reached Boston Saturday night, took passage on a freight train Sunday morning, and was injured; in a suit against the railroad company, it was *held* that his traveling was not an act of necessity.[1] A party (" who had no wife living," says the reporter,) may travel to see his sons.[2] Where a man and his wife were going to Staten Island for the benefit of a sick child, "that he might have the air," it was held to be clearly a work of necessity, and duty, on the part of the parents; and the court added: "Kelly and Maddern, it is contended, were on a pleasure excursion, but it was also for the purpose of recreation and rest, and our courts have not yet decided that such rest is unnecessary to the overworked laborer."[3] But, later, a party who was going from New York to Staten Island for "innocent recreation and the enjoyment of the sea air" was held not to be going in a case of necessity, or charity, or for any purpose within the exceptions of the New York statute.[4] An arrangement between a plaintiff and her brother for traveling on this day, so that the latter might have all the week-days for other work (he being a teamster and jobber at farming, and the like), did not constitute a necessity.[5] Where a party hired a horse to convey an officer, who was taking a prisoner to jail, under legal process, the purpose was held one of necessity. In this case the hirer was not himself an officer.[6]

IV. Agricultural Work, as a Necessity.

Where a party worked as a shoemaker, in co-operation with others, who were obliged to remain idle, unless his work was promptly performed, when ready for him, and expected to go to work at shoemaking on Monday, but worked in his own garden Friday and Saturday, and on Sunday "hoed" a few hills, which

[1] *Butcher* v. *Fitchburg R. R.*, 131 Mass. 156 (1881).

[2] *Johnson* v. *Irasburg*, 47 Vt. 28, 32.

[3] *Landers* v. *R. R. Co.*, 13 Abb. (N. Y.) Pr. (N. S.) 338.

[4] *Carroll* v. *Staten Island R. R.*, 58 N. Y. 126 (1872).

[5] *Holcomb* v. *Danby*, 51 Vt. 428 (1879).

[6] *Fisher* v. *Kyle*, 27 Mich. 454 (1873).

had been left Saturday evening unfinished, in a very bad condition and suffering for want of hoeing, the court said there was nothing to show necessity.[1] In Vermont, it was held necessary to work in making maple sugar "in order to save a great waste of sap.[2] Where a farmer's watermelons were ripening and decaying much faster than, with the facilities and labor at his command, he could get them to market, the court held that he was justified in starting with a wagon-load of melons for his market on Sunday, the market being twenty-six miles away, though he might, by getting up at midnight on Sunday night, and driving all the remainder of the night, have reached the town in time for the Monday market.[3] Feeding hogs is work of necessity, and hauling corn for that purpose, where "according to the practice of good husbandry," &c., is lawful.[4] Where the defendant, having no reaper, joined with a person who had, and they commenced cutting wheat, beginning with the ripest, and the defendant's wheat was prevented from being cut by a rain, and was "dead ripe," so that another rain would have seriously injured it, its cutting was held a work of necessity.[5] On the other hand, in Massachusetts, it was said: "The work was gathering and taking away sea-weed from a beach, on which the tide had deposited it, and from which the next tide might sweep it away. The supposed necessity arises from the fact that the sea-weed was valuable, and that, if not then secured, it might be lost. We think that taking the sea-weed was not a necessity, within the meaning of the law." The court added: "If a vessel had been wrecked upon the beach, it would have been lawful to have worked for the preservation of the property, which might be lost by delay. But if the fish in the bay, or the birds on the shore, happened to be uncommonly abundant, it is equally clear that it would furnish no excuse for fishing or shooting. How it would be if a whale happened to be stranded on the shore, we need not determine. Whether a case wholly exceptional, and involving a large amount of accessible value, would require any modification of the rule is not now in question. The deposit of sea-weed upon the shore by the waves, if not constant,

1 *Josselyn's Case*, 97 Mass. 411 (1867).

2 *Whitcomb* v. *Gilman*, 35 Vt. 297 (1862). See, also, *Morris' Case*, 31 Ind. 189 (1869).

3 *Wilkinson's Case*, 59 Ind. 416 (1887).

4 *Edgerton's Case*, 67 Ind. 588 (1879).

5 *Turner's Case*, 67 Ind. 595 (1879).

16

is frequent. It is not property which has been reduced into possession, and afterwards been exposed to loss or hazard. There was no certainty, or strong probability, that equally good opportunities of gathering it would not often recur on other days. The collecting of it on the beach, as it is found there from time to time, is one of the ordinary branches of agricultural labor."[1] A similar view was taken in Arkansas. In this case, for a week previous to cutting his wheat, the defendant was "swapping work" with his neighbors, who were afterwards to help him. He was poor, had no cradle of his own, and waited to get one from his neighbor, which he did Saturday night. His wheat was very ripe, and waiting, and from appearance, had been ripe enough to cut four or five days before. *Held,* that instructions that "he had a right to preserve his property from waste on the Sabbath, and, if it was likely to be lost from unforseen or unavoidable circumstances, he was justified in laboring to preserve it," and that "if the jury believed he could not have saved it on any other day, and it was necessary either to do so on Sunday or suffer it to be lost, if correct, were abstract, and well calculated to mislead the jury; that there was not a necessity for the work, under the statute, and that the husbandman should look forward to the ripening of his grain as an event which must happen, and make such timely provision for the harvest as not to violate the Sabbath."[2]

V. Manufacturing, &c., as a Necessity.

"Large manufactories, blast-furnaces, salt-works, oil-wells, and other pursuits wherein heavy machinery is used, and where a stoppage is attended with loss or inconvenience, are seldom interfered with in their operations by legal restriction."[3] And it is lawful to replenish the fires of a blast-furnace, which could not otherwise be maintained, for "the use of iron is essential to civilization."[4] And the manufacture of beer is lawful, and working at a malt-house, in turning a heap of barley, for the purpose of malting the same, as a neglect to handle the barley for twenty-four hours would spoil it.[5]

[1] *Sampson's Case,* 97 Mass. 407.

[2] *Goff's Case,* 20 Ark. 289 (1859).

[3] *Carver's Case,* 69 Ind. 61 (1879).

[4] *Manhattan Co.* v. *French,* 12 Abb. (N. Y.) N. Cas. 446.

[5] *Crocket's Case,* 33 Ind. 416 (1870).

Where the work was digging out sand from a wheel-pit, in order to enable a pump to be used to clear it of water, which frequently settled into the pit so as to impede the action of the wheel, and the only reason for doing the work was that it would obviate the necessity of stopping the machinery in future, the court said: "The whole import of this is that it was more convenient and profitable to repair the wheel-pit than it would be to do it on any secular day. This does not make it a work of necessity or charity." And it held that the fact that the plaintiff (who was suing the defendant for injury sustained from his negligence) was doing the work gratuitously, at the defendant's request, "did not take the case out of the letter or spirit of the statute."[1]

VI. Miscellaneous Instances of Necessity, &c.

Baking meats by a baker is lawful.[2] In a case arising in 1880, baking bread was said to be necessary in California, though that was not the principal point involved.[3] In Indiana, it was once held that a hotel might sell cigars, as they were a necessity to those who had acquired a habit of smoking them.[4] Later this decision was expressly repudiated, though the case was one where the sale of cigars, &c., was made in an ordinary store, and not in a hotel. The court said that the monopoly of the tobacco trade on Sundays which would result to hotel-keepers "ought to condemn the interpretation of the law that leads to it. Whether the hotel-keeper may provide and furnish cigars and tobacco on Sunday to his traveling guest, who may reasonably be supposed to have had no opportunity to supply himself for the day, need not be decided, as the question is not before us. But that he may not keep open a stand, bar or other place for the purpose of general sales to resident customers, or boarders, who, like other citizens, ought to anticipate and furnish a supply for their Sunday wants, seems clear. There should be no

[1] *McGrath* v. *Merwin*, 112 Mass. 467 (1873).

[2] *Cox's Case*, 2 Burr. 785 (1759); *Younger's Case*, 5 T. R. 449 (1793).

[3] *Westerfield's Case*, 55 Cal. 550, 551, 552.

[4] *Carver's Case*, 69 Ind. 61 (1879). It does not appear in the report of this case whether the party purchasing the cigars was a guest of the hotel, or not; but from the drift of the decision, and especially the last paragraph, it may be inferred that the court would not regard the question as material.

privilege allowed to the hotel-keeper of selling to his boarders and resident customers which is not allowed to the keeper of a boarding-house or restaurant, or to other classes of dealers." And of the claim that smoking was a necessity to those who had acquired the habit, the court said: "Upon what principle the court can take judicial knowledge of such a fact, if it be a fact, is not plain. It is hardly probably that the law-makers contemplated that the cravings of a morbid and unnatural appetite should be deemed to create such an imperious necessity for appeasement as that the general requirement for Sunday observance should yield to it, while the supplying of the ordinary necessities of life, like food and clothing, by purchase and sale out of the stores, should be forbidden." The court added that a drink was necessary to a drinker in the same sense in which a cigar was so to the smoker, but the sale of liquors was specifically forbidden, and "he who uses them must, therefore, anticipate his necessity, and provide beforehand a supply for Sunday use. If it were conceded that an appetite or craving creates a necessity, it does not appear that Smith was suffering, or bought for the purpose of immediate use. For all that is shown, he may have made the purchase as a matter of convenience only, in anticipation for future wants."[1] It has also been held in New York that "so broad a construction of the word 'necessity' as to include cigars would abrogate the statute."[2] So in Missouri it was said that the use of an article as a "drug or medicine" under such a statute must be "a general or primary one;" and that tobacco is not such because it "may have some medical or curative qualities, and be used occasionally by the medical profession," being, in fact, "sold as a luxury." And the court said of the position that tobacco was a necessity to its habitual users, "Conceding this to be correct, the evidence shows that defendant exposed his cigars to *general* sale, and did sell them to any and every one who applied to purchase, and there is no evidence that defendant only sold to those who had acquired the habit of smoking to such an extent as to make a cigar a 'necessity,' nor is there any proof that the parties to whom the cigars were sold had no opportunity to purchase a supply the day before." The court added: "Tobacco is not 'food.'

[1] *Mueller's Case,* 76 Ind. 310 (1881).

[2] *Anonymous, No.* 3, 12 Abb. (N. Y.) N. Cas. 458 (1882).

Food is a substance which promotes the growth of animal or vegetable life. There is no nutriment in tobacco. It is merely a narcotic. It is not generally regarded as an article of food. It could hardly be said that an indictment for selling unwholesome food could be sustained by proof that defendant sold a bad or unwholesome cigar."[1] It was held in Massachusetts, in 1865, that a temporary inconvenience, through a party's inability to supply meat on Monday to his usual customers, did not justify his servant's making delivery of the same on Sunday.[2] Where a contract of sale required the delivery of flour on board a steamer, it was held in Indiana (1868) that in the absence of a contract to deliver it on Sunday, performance could not be demanded on that day, on the ground that a delay would subject the vendee to a pecuniary loss; there was held to be no "moral fitness" in such a requirement.[3] Forwarding a shipment of cattle by railway has been held a work of necessity.[4] The seizure of swine found at large, by a hogreeve, is work belonging to a secular calling, and not of necessity, or charity, and makes the party seizing a trespasser.[5] "It is the duty of overseers of the poor to make immediate provision for the relief of the sick and suffering paupers under their care, and the performance of that duty is not a violation of the letter or spirit of the statute."[6] An attorney's clerk cannot recover, over and above his weekly salary, for labor in the office on Sunday, for this is no work of necessity, or charity.[7] A barber cannot compel his apprentice to work on Sunday.[8] In this case, the Magistrates of Dundee's Court of Sessions said that a barber's apprentice was bound to work up to ten o'clock only on Sunday and not bound to work at wig-making at all on that day. Lord Brougham said, in the house of lords, on appeal: "This is rather making an act of parliament than construing an act."[9] The Massachusetts court declined "to say, as a matter of law, that it was not morally fit and

[1] *Ohmer's Case*, 34 Mo. App. 115 (1889).

[2] *Jones* v. *Andover*, 10 Allen (Mass.) 18, 19.

[3] *Pate* v. *Wright*, 30 Ind. 476, 481.

[4] *P., W. B.* v. *Lehman*, 56 Md. 209 (1881).

[5] *Frost* v. *Hull*, 4 N. H. 153 (1827).

[6] *Aldrich* v. *Blackstone*, 128 Mass. 148, 151.

[7] *Watts* v. *Van Ness*, 1 Hill (N. Y.) 76 (1841).

[8] *Phillips* v. *Innes*, 4 Cl. & F. 234 (1837).

[9] *Id.* 246.

proper" to shave at his own house an old man "whose shoulder had been injured and who could not well shave himself."[1] It is held in Indiana that the necessity of a Sunday shave is for the jury under instructions,[2] while it was the opinion of an Ohio judge at *nisi prius* that though shaving may be a convenience it is not a necessity.[3] A had worked for B, and there was due him about $50. As A was about to leave, and B had not on hand the means of immediate payment, it was arranged that A should draw an order on B in favor of C, which, being accepted, C was to pay A. This arrangement was carried out, and C brought suit on the order (1880). Recovery was refused, on the ground that the work was one neither of necessity nor charity.[4] A creditor overtaking his absconding debtor in the evening, need not wait till Monday to take a bill of sale; for watching the debtor the whole night might amount to a greater desecration of the day.[5] The execution and delivery of a promissory note is not *prima facie* a work of necessity and charity. If any special facts exist to make it such, they should be introduced in evidence.[6] Where a man about eighty-five years of age signed a will, the court was not prepared to say it was not a work of necessity, as, though he was in ordinary health, "death was certain, at the furthest, by a general law of nature, very soon, and might occur at any moment."[7] It has been held in New York that the publication of an advertisement in a newspaper is not a work of necessity, or charity; and neither is the sale of the "most unexceptional religious newspaper."[8] But the contrary view was taken in Pennsylvania, and it was said: "You must bring the Monday's issue of every daily paper within the exception, for the types are set, and all the work is done, on Sunday, whilst on a Sunday paper all the work is done on Saturday."[9] It was said in Indiana: "Courts cannot declare, as matter of law, that the business of telegraphy is a work

[1] *Stone* v. *Graves*, 145 Mass. 353 (1888).

[2] *Ungericht's Case*, 119 Ind. 379 (1889).

[3] *Schulle's Case*, 23 Week. L. Bul. 450 (1889).

[4] *Mace* v. *Putman*, 71 Me. 238 (1841).

[5] *Hooper* v. *Edwards*, 18 Ala. 280 (1850).

[6] *Sayre* v. *Wheeler*, 32 Iowa 559 (1871).

[7] *Beitenman's Appeal*, 55 Pa. 183 (1867).

[8] *Smith* v. *Wilcox*, 24 N. Y. 353 (1862).

[9] Read's concurring opinion, *Sparhawk's Case*, 54 Pa. 401 (1867).

of necessity. There are doubtless many cases in which the sending and delivery of a message would be a work of necessity within the meaning of our statute. * * * Whether the contract is within the exception must be determined, as a question of fact, from the evidence in each particular case." And it was held that a message reading "Come up in morning; bring all" upon its face implied a friendly invitation to visit the sender, and sending it could not be regarded as a work of necessity.[1]

It has been said in Indiana that among lawful things are the usual avocations of "superintendents, engineers, firemen, conductors and breakmen, while operating railroads, laborers in depots and stock-yards, herdsmen and feeders of cattle."[2] And again, in the same state: "Sailing ships, running steamboats, and railroad trains, carrying the mails, operating telegraph lines, keeping up water-works and gas-works, carrying on distilleries, breweries, and running flouring-mills, are not prohibited, we believe, anywhere in the civilized world, and seldom regulated any differently than on a week-day; and large manufactories, blast-furnaces, salt-works, oil-wells, and other pursuits wherein heavy machinery is used, and where a stoppage is attended with loss or inconvenience, are seldom interfered with in their operations by legal restriction."[3] Operating an ice-factory is a necessity.[4] "The saving of a week-day for employer and employed," does not make the repair of the mill on Sunday a work of necessity in New Hampshire.[5] The ordinary domestic duties may be performed; and persons and brutes rescued from danger,[6] as well as property.[7] Public worship, and traveling to attend it, with all incidental labor connected therewith, as the care of horses, &c., is allowable; and so with funerals and marriages, and all the functions of undertakers, grave-diggers, hearse and carriage-drivers, and others; and the work of a physician, and apothecary, and of a livery-stable keeper "in large towns," and the care of hospitals,[8] and the shoeing of horses.[9]

[1] *Rogers* v. *Telegraph Co.*, 78 Ind. 169 (1881).

[2] *Edgerton's Case*, 67 Ind. 588, 593.

[3] *Carver's Case*, 69 Ind. 61 (1876).

[4] *Hennersdorf's Case*, 25 Tex. 597 (1888).

[5] *Hamilton* v. *Auston*, 62 N. H. 575 (1883).

[6] *McGatrick* v. *Wason*, 4 Ohio 566 (1855).

[7] *Whitcomb* v. *Gilman*, 35 Vt. 297 (1862).

[8] *Nesbit's Case*, 34 Pa. 398.

[9] *Nelson's Case*, 25 Tex. 599 (1888).

VII. Charity.

"Charity is active goodness. The means which long-established and common usage of religious congregations show to be reasonably necessary to advance the cause of religion are not forbidden and may be deemed works of charity, within the meaning of the statute. It is not essential that they be purely charitable; it is sufficient if they so far partake of that character as to be recognized by the congregation as part of its active goodness, and are not expressly forbidden by the statute." So, a contract of subscription to the erection of a church is binding.[1] And a contract with a preacher, singer, sexton, &c., of a church, for "the support of religious societies, is in itself a charity." But "it would be unsafe to take the statute of charitable uses, 43 Eliz., c. 4, as the test of what might be done, for it enumerates many objects which are only charitable in the sense that private provision for them tends to relieve the general public of a burden."[2]

Traveling to church is lawful.[3] But, where a hiring of a horse was not for necessity or charity, the contract, which was indefinite as to time and distance, is not made legal because the hirer did a kind act by conveying a young lady home who had been to meeting during the day.[4] "Charity must include everything which proceeds from a sense of moral duty, or a feeling of kindness and humanity, and is intended wholly for the relief or comfort of another, and not for one's own benefit or pleasure. That a visit to a sick child, or other near relative, is within the exception is well settled. The same reason extends to the case of a sick friend." And where a party was traveling for the purpose of visiting a friend whom he knew to be sick, and thought might need assistance, it was held that evidence of the grounds of his knowledge or belief was immaterial, except as a circumstance to be considered by the jury, in determining whether the real purpose of the journey was as the rest of the evidence tended to show.[5] But, in order to constitute an act of charity,

[1] *Dale* v. *Knepp*, 98 Pa. 389, 392 (1881).

[2] *Ibid.; Allen* v. *Duffie*, 43 Mich. 1 (1881).

[3] *Tashmaker* v. *Edmonton*, 1 Cow. (N. Y.) 354 (1721).

[4] *Tillock* v. *Webb*, 56 Me. 100 (1868).

[5] *Doyle* v. *Lynn*, 108 Mass. 195 (1875).

the act which is done must be itself a charitable act. The act of ascertaining whether a charity is needful is not the charity; and if a party be under an obligation to perform a contract, which it was his duty to complete before going on a charitable journey, and for that reason perform secular labor all day Sunday, such labor would be neither necessary nor charitable.[1] In this case, it was said: "The same duty of ascertaining whether an act of charity towards his sister was to be done had been resting on the plaintiff for two weeks. It would be an extraordinary proposition that he could elect to do an act on Sunday which he could have done equally well on any other secular day within that fortnight, and which he had postponed because he had considered it subordinate to his secular business. Suppose he had traveled the previous Sunday, in order the sooner to finish his business, and reach Boston and obtain this letter, it could not be contended that traveling on the previous Sunday was an act of charity. It is apparent that the plaintiff's duty to his sister was made subservient to his secular business. We are therefore of opinion that the ruling should have been given that there was no evidence which would justify the jury in finding that the plaintiff was traveling from charity."[2] The hiring of a carriage by a son to visit a father created a legal contract, being in discharge of a filial duty.[3] A bail-bond, on which a prisoner was released from jail, is good, as a work not in the ordinary business of the security, and as an act of charity.[4] And the place or mode of the prisoner's confinement, so that he be in actual legal custody, is not essential.[5]

VIII. Are Necessity, Charity, &c., Questions of Law or Fact?

Notwithstanding the elaborate attempts to define "necessity" and "charity," as used in the Sunday laws, it remains an unsettled point whether the determination of the matter in a given case is within the province of the court or the jury.

[1] *Butcher* v. *Fitchburg R. R.*, 131 Mass. 156 (1881).

[2] *Id.* 160.

[3] *Logan* v. *Mathews*, 8 Burr. 421 (1824).

[4] *Salter's Case*, 55 Ga. 244 (1875).

[5] *Weldon's Case*, 62 Ga. 449 (1879).

In Vermont, the validity of an exchange of horses is purely a question of law.[1] And so in Michigan with the validity of a church subscription.[2] And in New Hampshire with the question of "disturbance." After enumerating the English exceptions of "necessity," charity," &c., the court said these expressions are extremely loose and no certain line can be drawn, as a question of law.[3]

It has been said in Massachusetts that "it is not easy to define as a matter of law what state of facts will make traveling an act of necessity or charity, and the question should in most cases be submitted to a jury."[4] "In this case," said the court, "there is no evidence which would justify a verdict for the plaintiff." So later, in the same state, where the question as to the legality of traveling to and from a Spiritualists' camp-meeting, it was held that "it was for the jury to say whether the meeting was of the character claimed by the plaintiff, and whether she attended it for the honest purpose of divine worship, and religious instruction."[5] It is laid down in Indiana that what labor would be work of necessity, is a question of fact for the jury.[6] And so it was said later, in the same state: "Much of the confusion and doubt upon the subject has arisen probably from attempts made to determine and declare, as by a rule of law, that which was properly determinable only as a matter of fact, or at most of combined law and fact."[7]

A purchased some fish for B and left them at C's house. Saturday he sought B to tell him where the fish were. B, being a "Seventh day man,' was at church. Sunday, A undertook to drive to his house, as he claimed, to notify him of the whereabouts of the fish; other witnesses swore that he actually delivered the fish to B. He was injured on the highway, and sued the town which was responsible for the condition of the road. He claimed that the fish were liable to injury unless put in a cooler place, but B testified that the keg kept without taint, and what was not used was sweet a year after. A Vermont jury "under proper instructions" found the traveling was not necessary.[8] But, on the other hand, in

[1] *Lyon* v. *Strong*, 1 Vt. 219 (1834).

[2] *Allen* v. *Duffie*, 43 Mich. 1.

[3] *Younger's Case*, 5 T. R. 447 (1793).

[4] *Smith* v. *Boston R. R.*, 120 Mass. 490.

[5] *Feital* v. *Middlesex R. R.*, 109 Mass. 398 (1872).

[6] *Edgerton's Case*, 68 Ind. 588 (1879).

[7] *Mueller's Case*, 76 Ind. 310.

[8] *Johnson* v. *Irasburg*, 47 Vt. 28.

the same state, where the party suing a town on account of an injury received on a highway had no reason for traveling, except that she and her brother had arranged to travel some weeks before, and Sunday was fixed as the day to do so, in order that her brother might have all the week-days to work in, he being a teamster and jobber at plowing, &c., the court said it should have been ruled as a matter of law that no justifying necessity for the traveling existed.[1]

Of keeping open a shop, &c., it was said in Massachusetts: "It is for the jury to decide, on the whole evidence, whether the acts were of necessity, and charity."[2] In West Virginia, where a railway company was indicted for dispatching trains, it was held to be for the jury under instructions to say whether the dispatch was necessary.[3] So, in Arkansas, it was said to be a question of fact, whether a service, rendered by a hotel livery-stable keeper, was necessary, and proper, or otherwise."[4] And in Connecticut whether the owner of a hack had reasonable ground for believing that the purpose for which it was hired of him was one of necessity, or charity, was held to be for the jury.[5] And it was said in Maine, in a case of traveling, "as a general rule, the jury, under proper instructions from the court, must determine the question from the circumstances presented to them."[6]

It was held in Indiana in 1879 that the question whether gathering corn in the field, hauling it to a feeding-place and there feeding it to hogs was a work of necessity or not was for the jury.[7]

Of the case of manufacturing maple sugar, it was said in the same state, "the necessity of gathering the sugar-water as it runs is manifest, but whether the boiling of it is necessary may depend on the means of storing and saving it which the party has on hand, or under the circumstances ought to have had ready. The necessity in any such case is to be determined evidently as a matter of fact."[8]

Where a party fled from one county into another, and was over-

[1] *Holcomb* v. *Dandy*, 51 Vt. 428 (1879).

[2] *Harrison's Case*, 11 Gray (Mass.) 308 (1868).

[3] *B. & O. Co.'s Case*, 24 W. Va. 783 (1884).

[4] *Steuart* v. *Davis*, 31 Ark. 518 (1870).

[5] *Myer's Case*, 1 Conn. 502 (1816).

[6] *Sullivan* v. *Maine Cent. R. R.*, 19 Atl. Rep. 169 (1889).

[7] *Edgerton's Case*, 67 Ind. 588 (1879).

[8] *Mueller's Case*, 76 Ind. 310 (1881).

taken by an agent of a deputy sheriff, and in consideration of the latter's assuming certain debts, executions for which were in the deputy's hands, &c., gave the agent a bill of sale for certain slaves, with the slaves themselves, it was said in Alabama, "whether it was necessary, under the circumstances, for the party to do what he did was for the jury, under the direction of the court."[1]

[1] *Hooper* v. *Edwards*, 25 Ala. 528, 532 (1850).

ADDENDA.

Constitutional Law.

It is not a "discrimination" to require all places of business to be closed on Sunday, with exceptions, as drug stores, &c.[1]

It is immaterial to the question of constitutionality that persons who "observe other days" are not excepted by a Sunday law.[2]

The Sunday law is not "a local law" under the Texas constitution.[3]

The Massachusetts view, that there can be no recovery for injuries received while traveling on Sunday, binds the Supreme Court of the United States, on writ of error from a court of that state, though not according with the Supreme Court's views.[4]

The constitutional right to a jury trial does not extend to the proceeding before a justice against one who works on Sunday in Virginia.[5]

Contracts—The Question of Completion of a Contract.

Where a tenant was served on Sunday with notice that he would be charged an increased rent after his term expired, and remained in possession after that time, it was held that he was not liable for the increase. The court said: "I do not forget that the contract was not completed on Sunday. It would have arisen only by the fact that retention of possession was an acceptance of the landlord's proposal or demand. But in proving the contract it was essential to prove a business matter occurring upon Sunday. Without proof of the motive the retention of possession had no significance whatever. It

[1] *Scranton's Case*, 61 Mich. 244.

[2] *Scales' Case*, 47 Ark. 476 (1886).

[3] *Sundstrom's Case*, 25 Tex. App. 133 (1888).

[4] *Busher* v. *Cheshire R. R. Co.*, 8 So. Car. 974.

[5] *Marx's Case*, 9 S. E. Rep. 475 (1889).

is unlike those cases in which a preliminary conference held on Sunday has been merged into a contract made upon a secular day. Here the most important circumstance out of which the contract grew was done upon a Sunday by the person who is now seeking to enforce it. In the present case the landlord is the actor, and he has no case against the prosecutor, unless his act of notification is recognized as a legal proceeding."[1]

It was said in New Jersey, in 1887: "The absolute avoidance of all contracts made on Sunday does not arise from any express words in the statute declaring such contracts void. It rests upon the statutory inhibition of all worldly employment or business on Sunday, and comes about from the policy of the courts in refusing to recognize any act or word which, being a part of worldly employment or business, is done on Sunday. I am unable to see how worldly business done upon Sunday can afford any support to a contract. Whether all the negotiations and acts which would make up the completed agreement take place on Sunday, or only a part of them, if such part is essential to the contract, the statutory prohibition is encountered. In the last, as well as the first, condition of affairs, the court, to support the contract, would be compelled to recognize with approval the transaction of worldly business on Sunday."[2]

The execution of a bill of sale on Sunday, where the actual sale was on a preceding day, does not affect the sale; "it is only the manufacture of the evidence" thereof.[3]

In Minnesota a deed is void if delivered on Thursday to a grantee, with the understanding that it was not to go into effect till a certain contingency, which contingency occurred on Sunday. The "contingency" was a conference by the grantee with his partner. It seems he anticipated its occurrence on Sunday, and accepted the deed with that view. *Query.* Would his expectation that the conference would occur on some other day, the degree of its "necessity" on Sunday, or the fact that the contingency was one over which neither party had control, and which happened without (a) the knowledge, or (b) the aid, or (c) the anticipation of either, be material? These points serve to illustrate the beauties of a Sunday law in operation, and the honorable part such statutes play in our jurisprudence.

[1] *Ryan's Case*, 49 N. J. L. 314 (1887).

[2] *Ibid.*

[3] *Foster* v. *Wooten* (Miss.), 7 So. Rep. 501 (1890).

It is irrelevant that negotiations were had on Sunday when the contract was completed on another day;[1] though signed and sealed on Sunday, a deed afterwards delivered is valid.[2]

Contracts—Leaving Parties Where They Stand.

In Mississippi the rule of law as to Sunday contracts is "absolute non-action. It will give neither party to the contract any assistance, nor listen to any complaint. It will leave the parties where it finds them." And an attaching creditor of a party will no more be helped than the party himself.[3]

Though a Sunday loan might be non-recoverable, action will lie for money deposited for safe-keeping on Sunday.[4]

Cases of Tort.

The liability of a railroad company for the killing of cattle on Sunday is the same as if the killing occurred on a secular day.[5]

By usage the receiver of a telegraphic acceptance of his offer was not bound by the acceptance unless delivered to him within twenty-four hours after the receipt of the offer. Such an acceptance was delivered to the company late on Saturday, and to come within the required time it had to be delivered to him on Sunday. The court said: "The contract to transmit the message was wholly made on Saturday, and its validity is not destroyed by a condition that in order to bind it must be delivered within a limited time, though compliance therewith may require a delivery on Sunday. The mere delivery of a telegram on Sunday is not an act prohibited by either statutory or common law; and in the absence of proof we cannot as-

[1] *McKinnes* v. *Estes* (Iowa), 46 N. W. Rep. 987 (1890).

[2] *Schnat* v. *Rigby* (Minn.), 38 N. W. Rep. 101.

[3] *Foster* v. *Wooten*, 7 So. Rep. 501 (1890).

[4] *Zamplin* v. *Still*, 77 Ala. 374.

[5] *Tingle* v. *C., B. &c. R. R. Co.*, 60 Iowa 333.

sume that such delivery is prohibited by the laws of Germany. The defendant cannot set up that the compliance with the condition would necessitate a delivery on Sunday to avoid the consequences of an entire breach of a valid and legal contract."[1]

The family of a brakeman who was fatally injured while on Sunday duty may recover.[2] The court said that the fact that the defective appliances which produced the injury were used on Sunday rather than Monday "neither contributed to nor was the efficient cause of the injury."

"Keeping Open," Etc.

The offence of "keeping open store" is not shown by a single sale because of sickness in vendee's family."[3]

One who has charge and control of a "shop" may be convicted of keeping it "open," though shop and business belong to another, and it may be properly described as the shop of the former.[4]

One who keeps his shop open and makes several sales is guilty of but one offence against the Sunday laws.[5]

A druggist who sells liquor must close on Sunday.[6]

Miscellaneous Cases of Business, Etc.

A "baker" excepted under the Massachusetts statute is "one whose occupation is to bake bread and other articles of food." The word does not include "all who deal in the products of bakeries," and a man who "keeps a shop for the purpose of selling groceries, fancy articles, bread, pastry and milk," is not within the exception, because "he has a small stove in the rear part of his shop, in which his

[1] *W. U. Co.* v. *Way*, 83 Ala. 542 (1887).

[2] 118 Ind. 18; *L., N. O. & C. R. R. Co.* v. *Buck*, 116 Id. 566 (1888).

[3] *Dixon's Case*, 76 Ala. 89.

[4] *Dale's Case*, 144 Mass. 363.

[5] *Friedeborn's Case*, 113 Pa. St. 242.

[6] *Elkins' Case*, 63 Miss. 129.

wife sometimes bakes a few cookies and ginger snaps, which he placed in his show cases and sold with the bread and pastry."[1]

One who believes that the seventh day is the "religious day of rest," but does business on that day, cannot claim the benefit of the Nebraska exception to the obligation of Sunday idleness.[2]

Selling soda water in connection with drugs is "worldly employment."[3]

"Games" prohibited by the Mississippi statute are only "such sports or contests as are exhibited as spectacles to the people, and not such private diversions as card playing, chess playing and the like."[4]

"Common labor," or "usual avocation," within the Indiana Sunday law, is "not an act commonly done, but rather an uncommon act," and "no evil tendencies were growing out of such work on the Sabbath day which required legislation to correct."[5]

In Missouri "the exhibition of athletic games and sports" is not prohibited as "labor," nor are such included among "horse-racing, cock-fighting or playing at cards or games of any kind." It was said: "This court is of opinion that this prohibition is against games of chance, or other games of an immoral tendency, and that it does not involve a prohibition of athletic games or sports which are not of an immoral tendency, but which tend to the physical development of the youth, and are rather to be encouraged than discouraged. Penal statutes are to be construed strictly. It is an established principle of construction, that where general words follow particular ones, they are to be construed as applicable to the things or persons particularly named. * * * The word 'game' is no doubt susceptible of being used in a sense large enough to embrace any contrivance or institution intended to furnish sport, recreation or amusement. But this is not its usually understood meaning when employed in a statute which constitutes it an indictable offence. In such a case it is usually understood to imply some species of gambling."[6]

[1] *Crowley's Case*, 145 Mass. 430 (1888).

[2] *Leiberman's Case*, 42 N. W. Rep. 419 (1889).

[3] *Splain's Case* (Pa.), 12 Atl. Rep. 431.

[4] *Rucker's Case*, 7 So. Rep. 223 (1890).

[5] *Rapp* v. *Reehling*, 23 N. E. Rep. 777 (1890). In this case the court said that a lawyer "engaged in writing a will to be executed on Sunday" (presumably *writing*, as well as contemplating its execution on that day), could no more be indicted than a minister solemnizing a marriage. *Ferris* v. *Schreiner*, 43 Minn. 149 (1890).

[6] *St. Louis Assn.* v. *Delano*, 37 N. E. Rep. 284 (1889).

An agreement that a party shall receive compensation for every day, "Sundays and all," while he is absent, looking after lands in a distant state, is valid.[1]

It is lawful, in Indiana, to carry persons to and from a pleasure party.[2]

While a druggist is allowed to keep his place of business open for "necessary purposes," he would not be allowed to engage in the sale of soaps, canes, combs, toilet-boxes and cigar-holders. "While a drug store may be kept open for necessary purposes, it is not provided that the proprietor may engage in indiscriminate trade on Sunday, but evidently that he may sell such medicines, and only such, as are necessary in any other kind of business."[3]

Miscellaneous Points of Practice, Evidence, Etc.

Each act of selling merchandise on Sunday is a separate offence.[4]

Railroads are included in the West Virginia provision that passengers and baggage may be carried, &c., "by any person having the right to do so under the laws of the United States or of this state."[5]

To shoot at a dog in wantonness and mischief is "Sabbath breaking."[6]

Fifteen mules were bought on Sunday and thirteen delivered; the other two were delivered Monday. In action on money counts it was held error to allow the jury to consider but liability for the two.[7]

The defence that a note was made on Sunday may be raised by demurrer.[8]

In suit on a note it is sufficient to allege in defence the date of its making without alleging that the day was Sunday.[9]

In Missouri the affidavit for a Sunday attachment must state that the debtor "is about fraudulently to secrete or remove his effects."[10]

[1] *Alfree* v. *Gates* (Iowa), 47 N. W. Rep. 993.

[2] *Dongan's Case*, 25 N. E. Rep. 171.

[3] *Scranton's Case*, 61 Mich. 244 (1886).

[4] *Albrecht's Case*, 8 Tex. App. 315.

[5] *Norfolk & W. R. R. Co.'s Case*, 10 S. E. Rep. 813.

[6] *Smith's Case*, 50 Ala. 159.

[7] *Foreman* v. *Ahl*, 55 Pa. St. 355.

[8] *Clough* v. *Goggins*, 40 Iowa 325.

[9] *Finney* v. *Callendar*, 8 Minn. 41.

[10] *Updyke* v. *Wheeler*, 37 Mo. App. 680 (1889).

An indictment charging that a party was found "unlawfully at labor, and engaged in his usual avocation, to wit, selling," &c., sufficiently alleges that the selling was the party's usual avocation.[1]

In an indictment for "keeping open shop, &c.," the added words "and place of business," are surplusage. "At F., in county of B," sufficiently states locality of shop; "not then and there travelers, strangers or lodgers" sufficiently describes persons served in place.[2]

"Unlawfully did labor," &c., "by then and there hunting," &c., was held insufficient in a Missouri indictment.[3]

An indictment for Sunday card-playing need not name the game, but the name, if given, must be proven.[4]

Where exercise of one's "usual avocation" in selling merchandise is charged, it is not necessary to state the kind sold, or to whom it was sold, or the price.[5]

The indictment must not merely mention day of the month, but also allege that it was Sunday.[6]

Exceptions in a subsequent statute need not be negatived.[7]

It is sufficient to charge that defendant was "found laboring" under the Arkansas statute.[8]

That the vendee received a chattel on Sunday does not conclusively imply that the sale was on that day.[9]

Whether the evidence of delivery and acceptance on Monday is sufficient to overcome other evidence that the bargain was made on Sunday is for the jury.[10]

Judicial notice will be taken of the fact that a written notice from a surety to a payee was given on Sunday.[11]

It is presumed that a Sunday law was passed with the requisite formalities.[12]

The acts of labor need not be proven to have been done on the Sunday named in the indictment.[13]

The defence that a note was made and delivered on Sunday, is available against a payee whose agent received it on that day, and

[1] *Foltz's Case*, 33 Ind. 215.

[2] *Crowther's Case*, 117 Mass. 116.

[3] *Carpenter's Case*, 62 Mo. 594.

[4] *Anderson's Case*, 30 Ark. 131.

[5] *Soughrbough's Case*, 122 Ind. 208 (1889).

[6] *Shepler's Case*, 114 Ind. 194 (1887).

[7] *Shanischan's Case*, 145 Mass. 99 (1888).

[8] *Scales' Case*, 47 Ark. 476 (1886).

[9] *Hadley* v. *Sneviley*, 1 Watts & S. (Pa.) 477.

[10] *Bradley* v. *Rea*, 103 Mass. 188.

[11] *Chrisman* v. *Tuttle*, 59 Ind. 155. See, also, *Ryan's Case*, 49 N. J. L. 1887.

[12] *Usener's Case*, 8 Tex. App. 177.

[13] *B. & O. R. R. Co.'s Case*, 15 W. Va. 362.

against the payee's endorsee, though the note was dated on a secular day, and the payee and endorsee were ignorant of the Sunday making and delivery, and these were designed by the maker to defraud the payee.[1]

It is not necessary to prove that cars run over a company's tracks on Sunday were under its control; but mere proof of the transportation of part of a load of coal does not prove its assent without evidence of recurrence of act.[2]

Where charges on plaintiff's day-book, evidence of his claim, show Sunday sales, he must prove the dates wrong to recover.[3]

The burden is on the party who relies on the Sunday law to show that the contract was within the "ordinary calling" of the parties.[4]

The Sunday law of another state must be proven in defence like other facts; production of the statute book is insufficient.[5]

Where one witness swears a deed was delivered on Sunday, and another that it was delivered on Sunday, a verdict in accordance with the latter statement will not be disturbed; the burden of proof is on him who claims a Sunday delivery.[6]

Pleading, Practice, Etc.

A complaint for violation of a Sunday statute need not negative the exceptions of a later statute.[7]

To the plea by a surety that he executed a note on Sunday, the answer by the payee that he received the note on Monday in good faith and on assurance from the other maker that it was all right as to both makers, is insufficient.[8]

In a suit on a foreign note, as it is not invalid at common law, the statute invalidating it must be proved.[9]

The burden is on a party claiming to be within the exception of a Sunday statute to prove that he is so.[10]

[1] *Stevens* v. *Wood*, 127 Mass. 123. *Contra, Harrison* v. *Powers*, 76 Ga. 218.

[2] *B. & O. R. R. Co.'s Case*, 15 W. Va. 362.

[3] *Bustin* v. *Rogers*, 11 Cush. 346.

[4] *Sanders* v. *Johnson*, 29 Ga. 526.

[5] *Adams* v. *Gay*, 19 Vt. 358.

[6] *Phillips* v. *Phillips*, 47 V. W. (Ind.) 110 (1890).

[7] *Shanischan's Case*, 145 Mass. 99.

[8] *Gilbert* v. *Voebon*, 69 Ind. 372.

[9] *O'Rourke* v. *O'Rourke*, 43 Mich. 58.

[10] *Troewert* v. *Decker*, 51 Wis. 46.

Sunday as a Dies Non Juridicus.

A coroner may hold an inquest, and commit an accused murderer to jail on Sunday.[1]

[1] *Blaney's Case*, 21 Atl. Rep. 547.

NOTE TO PAGE 70.—The statement that "Man had not appeared to interfere with the unbroken Sabbath of the lives of the lower animals, when the Creator 'rested,'" applies to the Jahvistic account, as set out in the second chapter of Genesis. The Elohistic version, as contained in the first chapter, states that all the work of creation was completed by the sixth day. But at any rate the curse of labor, for which the Sabbath was designed as a special mitigation in favor of the "chosen people," was not pronounced at the time of the "rest."

APPENDIX.

TABLE A.

Chronological View of the Decrees of Councils, Emperors, Etc., Respecting Sunday Observance.

1. Ecclesiastical provisions for the observance of Sunday are found in what are called the "Apostolic Constitutions." Among these is a provision, that if any clerk fast on the Lord's day or the Sabbath on more than one occasion, he shall be deposed. If a layman do so, he shall be separated from the congregation. 1 Labbe 39. Severinus Binius, in a note on this canon, informs us that the reason why the early Catholic Church does not fast on Sundays is for the discomfiture of the unbelievers, who deny the resurrection, and spend that day in mourning and fasting. Id. 60. We also find an injunction to attend church on Saturday and Sunday, saying prayers standing, in honor of the resurrection, on the latter day (Id. 300); a prohibition of fasting (Id. 426); a warning against neglect of "assembling together" on Sunday (Id. 432, 31); another to remain at church services all of Saturday night (Id. 365), and an exception of one (Easter eve) Saturday night is afterwards made to this last requirement. Id. 371 *ad fin.* The "Constitutions" also contain a canon in the name of Peter and Paul, ordering that servants work five days, but rest on the Sabbath and Lord's day, that they may attend church, because the Sabbath commemorates the creation of the world, Sunday the resurrection (Id. 498); another to keep a Sabbath in honor of Him who ceased from His labor, but not His providence, in meditation on His laws, not idleness of hand, but casting out wicked desires and wrath (Id. 273), and a prayer declaring the Sabbath day is a day of rest, but observing that the Lord's day rises above it. Id. 438. It is further stated that the Deity has dedicated the "Sabbath" to the memory of His work in making the world, because on that day He rested; and that we observe Sunday because (1) on that day He conquered death, and (2) gave us the light of life and immortality. Id. 440, 37. And we are told that we should fast on Saturday, not because God rested on that day, but because the maker of the world lay that day in the grave. Id. 361. On the other hand, "every Saturday but one" is pronounced to be a day of rejoicing, like Sunday; and it is declared to be sinful to fast on Sunday or spend the day in mournfulness—"*moestitia.*" Id. 372. And, again, after fixing the fast days, it is said that Saturday and Sunday

are to be kept as feast days, because the first commemorates the completion of the world and the second the resurrection; but one Saturday, the anniversary of Christ's burial, must be observed as a fast, and not a feast; for then the maker of the world was in the grave, and the grief for His death overcomes the joy at the finishing of the world, as the Creator is greater than the creature. Id. 425, 24. As to the date of the "Apostolic Constitutions," see Smith & Cheatham Dic. Christ. Ant., V. One of the reasons why scholars are generally agreed that these provisions are not of the apostolic time, is the fact that they contain these regulations respecting Sunday. "*Ils ont forgé les Constitutions Apostoliques,*" says Voltaire, flippantly, in his "Essay on Miracles," but of deliberate forgery there is no proof.

2. In a paper (Apologia pro Christianis ad Antoninum Pium, ch. 67) written between A. D. 139 and 150, Justin Martyr says that the assemblings of the Christians for prayer, &c., took place "on the day of the Sun, as it is called;" and he advances as reasons for selecting that day, the facts (1) that upon it God made the world, and (2) Christ rose from the dead, and (3) appeared to His disciples. In another passage, Justin observes that the elements keep no Sabbath, and adds, that there was no need of the observation of the Sabbath before Moses; neither now is there any need of it, after Christ. Id., ch. 23.

3. In a discussion as to the proper time of celebrating Easter, which is reported by Beda (De Ordinatione Feriarum Paschalium) to have taken place at a Council held A. D. 198, it is said that the creation was begun on Sunday, and that it is blessed (1) because the light then appeared; (2) because the Israelites then passed through the Red Sea; (3) because the manna was then given; (4) because Moses commanded the Israelites to observe the first day (Ex. XII., 16; Lev. XXIII., 7, 8), as well as the last; (5) because of certain expressions in the Psalms, and (6) because the Lord then arose. Concerning this canon, in his letter to Clement VIII., Ferd. Mendoza observes that it applies to laymen; that people living in the country were not at first under such an obligation, because of the danger of persecution, &c.; but that afterwards, as Christianity spread, according to a canon he cites from Burchard (Decretorum, Lib. II., cap. 71), it was ordered that the priests should exhort the people to compel or pérmit their shepherds, ploughmen, &c., to come to mass, and that the arrest of Christians going to church to worship, remaining there, or returning, was forbidden in 932. 9 Labbe 593, 3.

4. At a Council held at Illiberis (now Elne), in Gaul, in 305 (1 Labbe 973, 21), it was decreed that any one remaining in a city—("Civitas," see Du Cange, Glos. Med. et Inf. Lat, *s. v.*)—three Sundays without attending church should be arrested. At the same Council, the erroneous supposition that a special fast was to be observed on Saturday was corrected. I Labbe 973, 26. ("Superpositio"—"a special fast." On the distinction between "fasting" and "abstinence," in the Roman Church, see McClintock & Strong's Cyclo. Bib., &c., Lit., *s. v.* "Fasting.") The Bishop of Orleans, in a note on this canon, refers to an early practice in the East, and parts of Spain, to make a feast day of Saturday (with the exception of the day before Easter Sunday). Labbe 995, 26. He also gives a dissertation on the name of the day (*dies dominicus*), and comes to the conclusion that Christians should abstain from work, "as the Apostles wished this day to be no less honored than the Jewish Sabbath." Id. 1162 *seq.* See Ferd. Mendoza's letter on this canon. Id. 1181, 26.

5. There is no evidence of a Sabbatical observance of Sunday in any part of Christendom, prior to the celebrated edict of Constantine (Code Just., III., XII., 3), A. D. 321, "That all judges, people of the cities and artificers rest on the venerable day of the Sun; but husbandmen may labor freely, and at pleasure, at the work of the fields, as it often happens that the sowing of corn and planting of vines cannot be so advantageously performed on another day, lest, by neglect of opportunity, the bounty granted by Divine foresight be lost." (Another version of the text reads, in the first sentence, instead of "judges and people of the cities," "judges of the people of the cities," but the Greek follows the first reading.)

6. Constantine, however, "by a pious provision," expressly appointed markets to be held on Sunday, as we learn from an inscription in a bath rebuilt by him. Gruter's Inscriptions Antiquæ Orbis Romani, CCXIV., 2.

7. Later, in the year 321, Constantine forbade any legal business except the emancipation of slaves, and suits growing out thereof. Code Theo., II., 8, 1, and Code Just., III., 12, 2.

8. In 325, at the Council of Nicæa, it was declared not proper to kneel in prayer on Sunday, but proper to pray standing and bending the head. 2 Labbe 299, 29 and 325, 32. We find an allusion to this practice in a letter written in the same year by Constantine to the church of Nicomedia, the reason given for standing being that it commemorates the Lord's rising. 2 Id. 69. Other edicts of Constantine, not in the codes, are mentioned by Eusebius, in his Vita Const., IV., 18' 19, 20.

9. During Constantine's reign, at the Council of Laodicea, of uncertain date, it was declared that Christians ought not to "Judaize" by resting on the seventh day, but to work on that day, preferring, as Christians, to rest, if they could, on Sunday, and if they did Judaize, they were to be "anathema." 1 Labbe 1501.

10. In about 368, under Valentinian and Volens, it was forbidden for Christians to be visited by the tax collectors on Sunday. Code Theo., VIII., 8, 1.

11. In 386, under Gratian, Valentinian and Theodosius, it was decreed that all litigation and business should cease; that neither regular judges nor arbitrators should try causes, and that a violation of these provisions should be adjudged not only infamous, but sacrilegious. Id. 8, 3.

12. In the same year giving shows was prohibited. Id. XV., 5, 2.

13. It was again made a forensic holiday under Theodosius in 389. Id. II., 8, 2.

14. Among the canons of the African Church, digested about 390, is found one against theatrical and other diversions. 2 Labbe 1085, 61.

15. Fasting was prohibited in 398 at a Council held at Carthage. Id. 1205, 64.

16. In 409, under Honorius and Theodosius, a law was made requiring the judges, on Sunday, to have prisoners brought from jail, and examine them as to their proper treatment in prison, to see that the poor among them are provided with food, and send them to the bath under proper guards, and a fine of twenty pounds of gold was imposed on the judge and his clerk, and three pounds on the provost, for neglect of this duty; and the bishops were enjoined to admonish its performance. Code Just., I., 4, 9.

17. Among the doctrines laid down in a letter of Pope Innocent I., written in the last year of his papacy (416), is that Saturday should be observed as a fast day, as "it shares the sadness and the joy of Sunday, and the Apostles were in great affliction on that day;" and that Sunday ought to be observed as a most fes-

tive day, on account of the joy it brought to the immediate followers of Christ. 2 Labbe 1246, 4.

18. At Gangra, in Asia Minor, in 424, the penalty of "anathema" was denounced against those who fasted on Sunday. Id. 423, 18, and 426, 18.

19. In 425, under Theodosius the younger, abstinence from theatricals and the circus was enjoined, and it was declared that even the honoring of the Emperor should not interfere with this observance. Code Theo., XV., 5, 5.

20. About 432 we find, in a "Collection of Various Canons," a strong protest against the dancing women who shocked the modesty of Christian females on their way to church. 2 Labbe 1649, 27.

21. In 469, under Leo and Anthemius, it was enacted that the feast days of the Most High should not be spent in carnal pleasures, nor collecting of debts, and that the Lord's day be had in honor, and there be no executions of criminals, nor summons, nor holding to bail; that the constable should be still, the lawyer silent, trials be suspended, the crier's voice not heard, litigants should cease from their controversies, and have an interval of agreement, and that enemies should not fear to meet each other, but feelings of regret and sacrifice should pervade their spirits, so that they should talk over their differences and arrange them; and that no one should abuse the leisure of the day and waste his time in obscene delights, nor attend the theatre or the circus, or the wild-beast shows; that if the Emperor's birthday should fall upon Sunday, its celebration should be postponed, and that any one then attending a show, or any constable violating this law under pretext of public or private business, should lose his office and his property. Code Just., III., 12, 11.

22. Burchard gives a canon which he says was passed by a Council presided over by St. Medard (457–545), by which it is forbidden to administer oaths on feast days, except for the preservation of the peace. Burch. Dec., XII., 20. (Notwithstanding, Spelman (Orig. Term 771), says this means "try law causes, or hold pleas," the context, in which it appears here in Gratian, seems to indicate a literal translation. It is given in connection with canons as to the manner of administering oaths, the age at which they may be administered, &c., and appears to have no reference to any other legal proceedings than the actual swearing of witnesses. See Grotian Decret., II., 22, 5, 17. As to what were "feast days" within the meaning of this canon, see Spel. Orig. T. 78.)

23. In 506, at a Council held at Agatha (now Agde), in Gaul, it was ordered that masses should be specially celebrated on Sunday, and the people should not leave the church before the benediction. 4 Labbe 1391, 47.

24. In 511, at a Council held at Orleans, it was decreed that every bishop, unless too infirm, should attend his nearest church. Id. 1409, 31. At a second Council held at Illiberis, in 516, it was decreed that no bishop, priest or clerk should give judgment in any cause; but on other days they might execute judicial functions, except in criminal cases. Id. 1564.

[25. In 529, under Justinian, the bishops were ordered to visit the prisoners on Wednesdays or Fridays. Code Just. 14, 22.]

26. In 538, at a Council at Orleans, "because the people had been persuaded that it was not proper to drive horses or oxen, or travel in vehicles, or prepare anything for eating, or attend to any matter concerning the advancement of their homes or persons (which rules evidently pertain to Jewish rather than to Christian

observance)," it was ordained that everything previously permitted on Sunday should still be lawful; but that work at the plough, or in the vineyard, and cutting, reaping, threshing, tilling and hedging should be abstained from, that people might more conveniently attend church; and the matter was declared to be exclusively one of ecclesiastical jurisdiction. 5 Labbe 302, 28.

27. At the fourth Council of Orleans, held in 541, it was forbidden to any but invalids to break the Lenten fast on Saturday. Id. 381, 2. (See, also, the notes of Binius on this canon (1 Id. 94), and on the Greek in-istance that Saturday was not a fast day. Id. 984.)

[28. In 549, at a Council at Orleans, prisoners were required to be visited by the archdeacon, or præpositus of the church, as formerly by the bishop, on Wednesdays or Fridays. 5 Id. 396, 20. See *ante*, 25.]

29. King Cheldebirt of France, son of Clovis, in 555, forbade dancing girls traveling through the towns "on the approach of the Lord's day." Id. 811.

30. In 578, at the Council of Antissivodurrum (now Auxerre), in Gaul, it was forbidden to yoke cattle, or do other work, except for good reasons (*constitutis causis*). Id. 959, 16. In 585, at the Council of Matisco (now Macon), in Gaul, "because Christians were rashly scorning the day, and pursuing their business as on others," the priests were instructed to admonish them of this matter; and the laity were warned to "watch the day;" the trial of causes was forbidden, and the "making of occasions" to yoke up beasts of burden; the singing of hymns and attendance at the church, if there should be one near, and the uplifting of the hands and eyes to God during the entire day were prescribed; the day was declared to be perpetually one of rest, "as we know from the image or type of the seventh day, in the law and the prophets;" and if a pleader should violate this canon, he was to lose his case; if a peasant or slave, he was to be well lashed; if a priest or monk, to be excluded six months from intercourse with his fellows; and it is enjoined that the preceding night be spent not in sleep but prayer. Id. 980, 1.

31. About 590 Pope Gregory, in a letter to the Roman people, denounced as the prophets of anti-Christ those who maintained that work ought not to be done on the seventh day; declared that this would not Judaize the people; that after Christ's coming the precepts of the law which had been figuratively announced were not to be literally observed; that to hold otherwise would involve the restoration of carnal sacrifices, &c.; that we receive in a spiritual sense what is written of the Sabbath; that the word means "rest;" and that Christ is our Sabbath. The Pope was also particularly severe on those who maintained that a man ought not to wash himself on Sunday, observing that on no day should we wash for mere luxurious enjoyment, but that not only the face but the rest of the body might be carefully cleansed on the first day. But he says we ought to abstain from worldly labor, and be diligent in prayers, that we may expiate the shortcomings of the other six days. Id. 1511, 3.

32. In 650, at the Council of Cabillonum (now Chalon sur Saone), "as in former canons determined," it was forbidden to do farm work, as ploughing, cutting, gathering the harvest, &c., or anything pertaining to the culture of the farm. 6 Labbe 391, 18.

33. In 680, at the third Council of Constantinople, "because (1) on this day manna fell in the desert, (2) He was born, (3) the star shone on the magi, (4) five

thousand were fed on five loaves and two fishes, (5) He was baptized by John in the Jordan, (6) He rose, and (7) the Spirit descended on the Disciples," it was decreed that nothing shall be attended to save prayers and masses, and the matters necessary for eating; that Christians should meet at the Saturday night vigils or the morning office, and should bring their offerings to the mass; and while attending church, there should be no pleading or hearing of causes, or quarrels, but only prayers, and praises, and charities, and praising of God, and spiritual feasting with relations and sojourners. Id. 1206, 8.

34. In 692 it was decreed that hymns should be sung (apparently by priests only and in churches) on Saturday evening, and the festival be prolonged till daylight, that one entire day and night might be given to the celebration of the resurrection. Id. 90.

35. In 721, among the "Capitularies" of Pope Gregory II., we find the prohibition of fasting repeated. Id. 14, 54, 10.

36. In the "Selections from the Canons," made by Egbert, Archbishop of York from 732 to 767, it is said that Saturday was sanctified because of its reference to the suffering of Christ, and His rest in the grave; that the Deity did not rest, like a tired man on the first Saturday (see St. Augustine on this point, *loc. cit.*), but that He is still making men and animals, as Christ says, "My Father worketh hitherto, and I work," and the archbishop adds that we should keep a spiritual Sabbath on Sunday, which has been sanctified by the resurrection. Id. 1589, 36.

37. In 747, at the Council of Cloveslio, in England, it was decreed that the day should be observed with proper respect by all; that abbots and presbyters should remain in their monasteries and refrain from business or traveling, unless necessary; and that the people be summoned to church by their priests, and be present at masses and sermons. Id. 1577.

38. In "Egbert's Pœnitential" (732–736), we find that conjugal pleasures were interdicted on Saturday and on Sunday night. ("*Dominica Nocte et in Sabbato.*" See Haddon & Stubb's Councils, &c., Rel. to Great Britain, &c., III., 423, 7.)

39. At the Council held at Wormatia (now Worms), it was decreed that the day should be had in such honor as already prescribed in the law and canons, and any one offending should be punished as prescribed. 6 Labbe 1794, 1.

40. Among the Capitularies of Pope Hadrian I., published 785, was a prohibition against bishops and their subordinates giving judgments upon Sunday. Id. 1837, 64.

41. In 789, Charlemagne promulgated a law that all should abstain from servile work and farm work—that is, cultivating the vineyard, ploughing, reaping, cutting hay, setting out hedges, digging up roots, cutting down trees, working in store or building houses; also attending court and hunting (but wagons might be used for the army, or for food supplies or funerals); and he decreed that women should not weave, or cut out or sew their garments, or work embroidery, or card wool, or beat flax, or wash their clothing in public, or shear sheap, "in order that the honor and rest of the day might be observed," and he commanded that all should attend mass. The same year the people were admonished by Capitularies of Charlemagne to attend church, and not to invite the priests to their homes to celebrate mass. 8 Labbe 990, 9.

42. At the Council of Friuli, in Italy, in 791, the "Sabbath" was spoken of as a "day observed by the Jews and our rustics." 7 Labbe 1009, 9. At this Council it

was commanded that the observance of Sunday should begin at the hour of the Saturday evening office, not for the honor of the Sabbath, but for that of the Lord's day; that Christians should abstain from sin, from all exercise of the body ("*etiam propriis conjugibus*") and worldly labor, and should be busy about nothing save prayer, going to church, and ceasing from clamor and contentions. The customs of giving charitable gifts is mentioned, and reasons, such as the descending of the Spirit on the Apostles, &c., are enumerated for the sanctity of the day, which is declared to be the "Sabbath of the Lord," to which reference is made by Moses (Ex., XXXV., 1), when he says "whosoever doeth work therein shall be put to death." ("*Servile opus,*" the canon has it, which is interpreted as meaning "a work of sin," and it is added that other feasts are to be honored as well as that of Sunday. Id. 1007, 13.)

43. In 794, at the Council of Francofordia (now Frankfort-on-the-Main), it was ordained that the day should be observed "from evening to evening." Id. 1061, 21.

44. The day was excepted out of the Lenten fast, and declared to be one of obligation, in 797, by a Capitulary of Theodolph, Bishop of Orleans. Id. 1146, 37. He also ordered, because (1) God then gave us light, (2) the manna fell in the desert, (3) the Redeemer arose, and (4) the Spirit descended on the Disciples, that nothing else should be attended to on Sunday save prayers, masses and the matter of eating; but he gave permission to sail and travel, if necessary, provided mass and sermon were not neglected for that purpose; Christians he enjoined to attend the Saturday night vigils, or the matins, and to bring their offerings to the mass; and he directed that while attending church no cause should be pleaded or heard, and no quarrels carried on, but that in the service of God every man should feast spiritually with his friends, relatives and sojourners. Id. 1142, 24.

45. In the same year Charlemagne enjoined on the Saxons of his kingdom that they should not hold meetings, nor attend to matters of public interest on Sunday, unless great necessity, or the hostility of enemies compelled them, but should attend church and be busy with sermons and good works. Id. 1132, 17.

46. During 813 no less than six canons on Sunday observance were adopted. In one, passed at the Council of Arles, it was decreed that there should be no public markets, nor pleadings, nor disputes, and that rural and servile labor should altogether cease, and only things be done which appertained to the service of God. Id. 1237, 16.

47. Again, at the Council of Mentz, it was decreed that the day should be respectfully observed and servile work abstained from, and that there should be no markets, nor courts whereat any one should be sentenced to punishment. Id. 1250, 37.

48. Afterwards, at the Council of Reims, it was decreed, according to the Lord's commandment, that no one should do any servile work, or attend court, or make donations in public, or open markets. Id. 1257, 35.

49. At the Council of Tours, markets, courts and servile labor were prohibited, and Christians were enjoined to spend tho day in giving praise and thanks "till the evening." Id. 1267, 40.

50. Finally, at Chalon sur Saone, "because the observance of the day was greatly neglected," it was declared that it ought to be authoritatively regulated in accordance with the Imperial edict. Id. 1283, 50. (This was possibly intended

as an ecclesiastical sanction of rules prescribed by the reigning Emperor, Charlemagne. It appears from the canons that the early church insisted on exclusive jurisdiction over offences against the Sunday laws.) See *ante*, 26.

51. In 826, at a synod held in Rome, it was decreed that none should engage in business or merchandising, except in preparing food for travelers, so that all might attend church according to their opportunity, and be busy only with prayer to the Deity, and that Christians might conveniently discharge their duty as such; and that persons committing offences might be held to bail, or imprisoned till trial. 8 Id. 111, 30, 31.

52. In 829, at the sixth Council of Paris, it was observed that the Pagans set apart certain days for the honor of their Gods; that the Jews, whose manners were of a worldly sort, kept the Sabbath in a worldly fashion, and that a custom had grown up among Christians as a matter of religious observance, based on an accredited apostolic tradition, and certainly on the authority of the church, to honor Sunday (1) in memory of the Lord's resurrection; (2) as it was in that day God gave light to the world; and (3) the Holy Spirit descended upon the Apostles, and (4), "as some doctors hold," the manna fell from heaven. It was said that these things, and other things of similar character, plainly showed that this day was more to be respected than others, &c. It was further stated that some had fallen away from the Christian religion in this regard, and were in the habit of indulging in worldly pleasures on Sunday, and customs of this sort had grown to be considered as having the force of laws, and respect for Sunday had died out in a considerable portion of Christendom. Then it was told how many of the assembled fathers had seen with their own eyes some people who were engaged in farm work on Sunday struck dead by lightning, others stricken with "constriction of the muscles" (lockjaw), and others again suddenly consumed by fire, so that nothing remained of flesh or bones save the ashes, and how other fathers, though they had not witnessed such occurrences, had heard of them. And it was concluded, not unnaturally, that such miracles showed that the Deity was offended at the desecration of so great a day; wherefore priests, kings and princes we exhorted to see that the day is more devoutly observed, and that there were no markets or courts held, or farm work done. 7 Labbe 1629, 50.

53. By the same Council, the faithful were admonished to pay honor and reverence to the day, since its dishonor is inconsistent with Christianity, and involves danger to the soul of the desecrator. Id. 1660, 5.

54. In 836, at the Council of Aquisgranum, fasting, court sessions and marriages were prohibited and the communion was ordered to be celebrated. Id. 1725, 18, 22.

55. In one of the letters of Pope Nicholas I., who took his seat in 858, it is stated that the Greek Church reproached the Romans because they fasted on Saturday (8 Id. 471 A); and the practice is defended. Id. 472 B.

56. Pope Nicholas declares that the doctrine of Saturday idleness is the doctrine of anti-Christ, and adds that idleness on Sunday and the pretermission of legal proceedings are obligatory; still he seems to think it better for a man to work than dissipate on the holy days of the church. Id. 521, 10; 522, 11, 12.

57. Pope Nicholas answers the question whether it is wrong to engage in battle on any particular day; and he says ordinary business should be let alone on the Christian holy days, except in case of necessity; and then it may be attended to;

and adds that we must trust in God, and not in the observance of days, and that it was for their superstition in this matter that thousands of Jews were slaughtered, when they refused to fight their enemies on Saturday. Id. 529.

58. In 858, among the Capitularies of Herard, Archbishop of Tyre, which are said to be taken from the canons (8 Labbe 627), is one excluding from the Easter communion those who do not fast till the beginning of the Saturday night before that festival. Id. 633, 83.

59. In 853, at the Council of Soissons, the holding of courts by officers of the state was forbidden. Id. 94, 7.

60. Conjugal pleasures during the day and night were interdicted by Pope Nicholas about 858, for, says he, "the day and night are one, and embrace twenty-four hours." Id. 538, 63.

61. Constantine's exception of agricultural labor was expressly annulled by the Eastern Emperor Leo VI. (54 Const.) in 884, and he reflects severely on the motives of his predecessor in making it.

62. In 895, "according to the Statutes of the Fathers," it was ordained that no count or secular person should hold court, or compel the people to attend him, on Sunday, but the day should be spent in vigils and prayers and offerings and given up to God; nor should any count compel one doing penance to come to court, nor come himself while so doing. 9 Id. 458, 35.

63. The selling of merchandise was forbidden in 928, at the Council of Gratelia, England, during the reign of King Athelstane, the penalty being the forfeiture of the goods sold and thirty pieces of gold besides. Id. 584, 6.

64. In 932, by one of the Capitularies of Pope John XI., secular courts were forbidden on this and other feast and fast days. Id. 592, 2. This canon Spelman says he takes "to be one of the foundation stones to our terms." Orig. Terms 77.

65. In 952 secular courts were forbidden. 9 Labbe 592, 2.

66. In 1009, or thereabouts, it was ordained that the feasts of the church should be celebrated on Sunday in the most creditable manner (*cum summo honore magnopere*); that no servile work should be done, and that secular business and public trials should be suspended. 9 Id. 800, 15.

67. In 1050, at the Council of Coyaco, in Spain, it was decreed that Christians should go to church Saturday evening and Sunday morning, and should do no servile labor (at either of those periods, apparently), nor travel, except to church or a funeral, or to visit the sick, or on public business, or in case of an assault by the Saracens. Id. 1065, 6. So that the Spanish Sabbatarians were not willing to go to the extent of inaction preserved by the Jews, who allowed themselves to be slaughtered rather than fight on Saturday.

68. In 1072, at the Council of Rotomagus (now Rouen), among regulations of service, fasting, &c., it is declared that Saturday night belongs to Sunday. Id. 1227, 8.

69. "Because the day ought to be observed with all reverence," it was, in 1255, at the Council of Copriniacum (now Cognac), decreed that the parishioners should be diligently admonished in the churches to abstain from the public meat-houses, and celebrations and feasts, and not to go to the stores and markets to sell or buy; and the penalty for disregarding the injunction should be excommunication; and in order that the people might not be able to plead ignorance of these requirements, the admonition was required to be frequently repeated. 11 Labbe 752, 36.

70. Secular judges were forbidden to try cases on this and other enumerated feast days, under pain of excommunication, in 1299, at another Council of Rouen. Id. 1428, 2.

71. The Holy Saint Gregory, in his response to Marcus of Ephesus, enumerates, among the things abolished as "figures," sacrifices, the Sabbath, &c. 13 Labbe 814 d.

72. In 1368, at the Council of Lavauer, in France, it was decreed that the priests should fast every Saturday except Christmas day, in honor of the Virgin, unless necessity prevented. Id. 2010, 90.

73. In 1473, "following the footsteps of our predecessors," it was decreed by the Council of Toletum (now Toledo) that there should be abstinence from servile labor, and farm and trade work, and cultivation of the fields, unless there was urgent necessity, or an evidently pious purpose, and then only with the priest's license. This applied to the faithful. Unbelievers were prohibited only from publicly attending to their business; punishment to be by the proper officers; and, if violation occurred through negligence, to be severe; if through deliberation, to be no less than excommunication. Id. 1452.

74. It was stated in 1581, at another Council of Rouen, that Sunday was free from the interruptions of business, which frequently interfered with other feasts, but that processions originally religious in character had degenerated into mere revels, and all markets and servile works were prohibited, though sacred processions were still approved; all manual labor, in city and country, was forbidden, and the dedication of churches prescribed. A striking allusion to existing abuses is found in the declaration then made that the house of prayer should not on this day be used as a place of trade, or secular courts; and the complaint concerning the interference with Divine service by the lictors, and the auctioneers of goods. Judges were commanded to hold sessions elsewhere, and the serving of summons on people while going to or from church, or while in the same, or arresting, or otherwise annoying them at such times, was prohibited, and the want of evening masses in some places for servants was lamented. 15 Labbe 825, 5, 6, 8; 848, 20, 21.

75. An interesting dissertation on the "first and second Sabbaths" is found in the address of Archbishop Stephens to the Lateran Council of 1515. 14 Labbe 263, 4, 5.

76. According to the catechism of the Council of Trent (published A. D. 1567), "when the ceremonies of the law were removed, the Sabbath also, as a ceremonial, was removed" (ch. IV., quest. 5), and "the sanctification of the Sabbath is a cessation from bodily labor and business" (Id., quest. 10); and "the Sabbath we observe fully and perfectly when we afford to God the duties of piety and religion" (Id.); and "the proper meaning of the Fourth Commandment tends to this, that a man give himself up at some fixed time, so that, disengaged from bodily labor and business, he may piously worship and adore God." Id., quest. 2. The whole of chapters I. and IV. of the catechism may be profitably read in this connection.

77. The above is believed to be a pretty fair summary of the regulations made by Councils, Popes and Emperors during the first sixteen centuries for the "observance" of Sunday. The only "official statement" of the Continental Protestant doctrine on the subject is, perhaps, that found in the "Confession of Augsburg," drawn up by Melancthon. This, in the edition of 1540, says "the Scripture

allows that the observation of the Sabbath is now a matter of discretion" (*Scriptura concedit ut observatio Sabbati nunc sit libera, Articuli de Abusibus*, &c., VII. "*De potestate Ecclesiastica*"), but the first edition of that work, 1530, declared that the Sabbath was abrogated. "*Scriptura abrogavit Sabbatum, quæ docet omnes cerimonias Mosaicas post revalatum evangelicum omitti posse.*" See Op. Mel. Schwetschke, Brunsvigne, 1858, p. 409. Id., Ed. Lipsiæ Baumgardneii, 1866, p. 183, note. The German of the confession reads: "Denn die Kirche hat den Sabbat nicht verrucht oder aufgehoben, sondern Gott hat selbst gelernt das wir in neuem Testament nicht sollen verbunden sein zum Gesetz Mosi. Darum haben die Gospel den Sabbat fallen lassen, uns damit zu erinnern das wir nicht zum Gesetz Mosi verbunden sind." First E. Cit., p. 661.

78. Luther says: "*Apostolus Galatas arguit quod dies et menses observarent et tempora et annos secundum ritum Judaicum, id est, externe tantum. Ideo istud præceptum cessavit proprie immo quoad perfectos Christianos quin justo non est lex posita.*" Op. Lut. Erlangen, 1844, vol. XII., pp. 70, 71. See, also, Calvin's Just. 8, 32, and Hessey, "Sunday," &c., III.

79. The regulation of Sunday conduct attracted the attention of the English authorities at a very early period. Among the laws of King Ina, the Anglo-Saxon, promulgated about 692, is found a provision that if any slave work on Sunday by his master's order he shall be free, and the master shall be fined thirty pieces of gold; but if he work of his own volition, the slave shall be chastised or fined; if a freeman work without his lord's order, he must either be reduced to slavery or fined sixty gold pieces; and the punishment of a priest shall be twice as great. 6 Labbe 1325.

80. Among the laws of Wihtred, another Anglo-Saxon monarch, enacted in 696, was a provision that if a serf do servile labor, contrary to his lord's commands, from sunset on Sunday eve to sunset on Monday eve, he should pay his lord eighty shillings; if he did so by his own accord, six. Haddon & Stubbs Coll., III., 235, 9, 10.

81. In 885, in a treaty made between Kings Guthrum and Edward the Elder, it was prescribed that if any one presumed to sell merchandise on Sunday he should forfeit it, and be fined twelve "uni," among the Danes, and thirty "solidi" among the Angli; that if a freeman should work at home on a feast day he should lose his liberty, or pay a fine; and a serf so doing should be flogged, with the same alternative; and that if a master compelled his slave to work on such a day, he should suffer the penalty; ordeals and oaths were forbidden, and criminals were not to be executed on the Lord's day, but captured and held. Wilkins Leg. Ang. Sax. 52, 7; 53, 9.

82. In the time of Edgar the Peaceable, about 958, it was enacted that the feast of the Sunday should be kept from the afternoon of Saturday to the dawn of Monday. Id. 77, 5.

83. In 1032, among the laws promulgated by King Canute, we find one declaring that wrong, though always culpable, was especially so on feast days, and days consecrated to the Lord. 9 Labbe 922, 7.

84. Another enacted that no criminal should be put to death, unless in flight or resisting arrest, and that a freeman working on feast days shall be fined enough to exempt him from the pillory. See Toller's Anglo-Sax. Dic., *s. v.* A slave so doing should be thrashed or fined, and if a master compelled his slave so

to do, the latter should be free and his master be punished. This was promulgated in the same year. 9 Labbe 933; 934, 10–13.

85. In 1201, Eustachius, an abbot, preached bitterly in England against the desecration of the day, and he maintained that it ought to be observed from the ninth hour (six o'clock in the evening) of Saturday until sunset on Monday. This clergyman was particularly severe on those who sold goods. 11 Labbe 24, *fin. et seq.*

86. Among the laws of Edward the Confessor, was one prescribing, among other "days of peace," all Saturdays, from the ninth hour, and the whole of the next day till Monday, and putting within the peace people going to or returning from church, going to dedications, synods, &c. William the Conqueror confirmed the laws of Edward the Confessor. Lombard de Pri. Ang. Leg. 172.

87. In the "Customary" of the Normans is found a provision making a forensic holiday the time from nine o'clock Saturday night to sunrise the following Monday. Custom., cap. 80.

88. "Feast days" were so made by Henry I., except as to swearing fidelity to the Lord of the manor, or to keep the peace. Leg. Hen. I., c. 2.

89. A similar exemption to that under Henry I. was made by the laws of Henry II., and Sunday was declared to be no day for the payment of debts or the punishment of criminals. VI., cap. 62.

90. "Ancient laws" were confirmed by Stephen in the charter of Malmsebury. W. Malmes 179.

91. In 1552 it was enacted by the English parliament that Sunday and other days named should be kept "Holy Days" (5 & 6 Edw. VI., c. 3, s. 1); that when the evens of days on which fasting was enjoined (Id. 52) should occur on Sunday, Saturday should be the fast day (Id., s. 5); and that it should be lawful for every husbandman, laborer, fisherman and every other person, on holy days, in harvest, or at any other time in the year when necessity shall require, to labor, ride, fish, or do any kind of work (Id., s. 6).

92. In 1558, all persons "having no lawful or reasonable excuse to be absent," were required to resort to their Parish church, or, "upon reasonable let thereof," to some usual place where common prayer and such service of God shall be used." 1 Eliz., c. 2, s. 14.

93. And increased penalties were provided for those failing to comply with requirement in 1582. 23 Id., c. 1, s. 5.

94. "But it was not," says Hallam, "till about 1595 that the founders of the English Reformation began to place Sunday very nearly on the footing of the Jewish Sabbath, interdicting not only the slightest action of worldly business, but even every sort of pastime." 2 Const. Hist. Eng. 286.

95. James I. published a "Declaration," dated May 24th, 1618, "to be read in churches," permitting all lawful recreations after Divine service, such as dancing, archery, May games and morrice dances, but with a prohibition of bear-baiting. It was addressed to his subjects in Lancashire, whence complaints as to the vigorous enforcement of Sunday observance had come to him. Hallam adds that the provision for reading this in the churches was not carried into effect, and that the declaration was not enforced till the following reign. A bill was, moreover, introduced "for the better observance of the Sabbath, usually called Sunday" (1621), which the king requested parliament not to pass, as being against his

proclamation. Hallam, vol. I., p. 391, note—edition of Crosby & Co., Boston, 1861. As to the application of the name "Sabbath" to Sunday, see Hallam, vol. I., p. 389, note.

96. The catechism of the English Church contains the Decalogue, but, among the things which are enumerated as "chiefly learned" thereby, the observance of Sunday or the Sabbath is not enumerated, nor does it appear in the summary of the "duty towards God." Neither in her canons nor her homilies, does the church make any reference to abstinence from secular pursuits. See the Canon XIII., which puts all holy days on a level, and refers to religious duties, acts of charity, &c., and the "Homily of the Time and Place of Prayer."

97. Nothing can be found in the works of John Knox indicating that he deemed Sunday recreations sinful. He drew the confession which formed the standard of faith in the Scottish Church from 1560 to 1647, when the Augsburg confession was adopted, and it contains no mention of the duty of Sunday observance. See the "Enumeration of Christian Duties Prescribed by the Decalogue," Knox's works, by Laing, II., 107.

98. But the Cromwellian Church Militant went far beyond the ideas of Luther, Calvin and Knox, and it is to them that we are indebted for "our American Sunday," in its full and complete beauty as a day of idleness and gloom, enforced by act of legislature.

99. "Forasmuch as the Holy Keeping of the Lord's day was profaned by a disorderly sort of people in exercising and frequenting bear-baiting, bull-baiting, interludes, common plays, and other unlawful exercises and pastimes, and many quarrels and bloodsheds had grown by the concourse of people going out of their own parishes to such disordered and unlawful exercises and pastimes, neglecting Divine service, both in their own parishes and elsewhere," it was, in 1625, enacted that there should be no meetings, assemblies, or concourse of people out of their own parishes on the Lord's day, nor any bear-baiting, bull-baiting, interludes, common plays, or other unlawful exercises and pastimes used by any within their own parishes; but of meetings or lawful sports by any within their parishes no prohibition was made. 1 Car. I., c. 1, s. 1.

100. This appears to have been designed merely as a temporary concession to the prevailing spirit of Puritanism, as it was provided that the regulations should continue in force "until the end of the first session of the next parliament." But by the succeeding parliament (1627) the act was again continued in force "until the end of the first session of the next parliament." 3 Car. I., c. 4, s. 22 *ad fin.*

101. And "forasmuch as the Lord's day, commonly called Sunday, was much broken and profaned by carriers, wagoners, carters, wain-men, butchers, and drovers of cattle," it was enacted that no carrier with horse, or wagon-man with wagon, or carman with cart, or wain-man with wain, or drover with cattle, should travel on that day; and that no butcher, or any other for him, by his privity or consent, should kill or sell any victual on the same.

102. And a like continuance of the provisions of the act quoted in paragraph 99 was made in 1640. 16 Car. I., c. 4.

103. By ordinance dated April 6th, 1644, parliament required all persons to apply themselves to the sanctification of the Lord's day, by exercising themselves in the duties of piety and true religion, publicly and privately; and that no per-

son should publicly cry, show forth or expose to sale, any wares, merchandise, &c.; or, without reasonable cause, travel, carry burthens, or do any worldly labor or work; or use, exercise, keep, maintain, or be present at any wrestling, shooting, bowling, ringing of bells, for pleasure or pastime, masques, &c., dancing, games, sport or pastime; and it was enacted that all having care, government, tuition or education of children under fourteen, should forfeit twelve pence for every offence against the law committed by such; and because profanation of the day hath been occasioned by May poles, all such were ordered to be taken down, and no more erected, and the "Declaration" already mentioned was commanded to be suppressed and burned, as well as all other books and pamphlets "against the morality of the Fourth Commandment or of the Lord's day;" "provided that nothing in this ordinance shall extend to the prohibiting of dressing of meat in private families, or the dressing and sale of victuals in a moderate way in inns or victualing-houses, for the use of such as cannot otherwise be provided for; or to the crying or selling of milk before nine o'clock in the morning or after four in the evening, from September 10 till March 10, or before eight o'clock or after five, from March 10 to Sept. 10." Scobell's Collection of Acts of Long Parliament, pp. 68, 69.

104. King Charles I. reissued, on October 18th, 1663, the proclamation of James.

105. In the reign of Charles II., in the year 1676, a statute was passed providing that the laws in force concerning the observation of the Lord's day and repairing to church thereon be carefully put in execution; that all persons should apply themselves to the observation of the day by exercising themselves in the duties of piety and true religion, publicly and privately, and that no tradesman, artificer, workman, laborer, or other person should exercise any worldly labor, business or work of their ordinary callings (works of necessity and charity only excepted); that no person should publicly cry, show forth or expose to sell any wares, merchandises, fruit, herbs, goods or chattels; that no drover, horse-owner, wagoner, butcher, higgler, or any of their servants, should travel or come to their inn or lodging; that no person should use, employ, or travel with any boat, wherry, lighter or barge, except upon some extraordinary occasion, to be allowed by some justice of the peace, &c.; but that nothing in the act should extend to the prohibiting of dressing of meat in families, or dressing or selling of meat in inns, cook-shops or victualing-houses for such as otherwise could not be provided, nor to the crying or selling of milk before nine in the morning or after four in the afternoon; that if any person traveling should be robbed, no hundred or its inhabitants should be answerable, if, after notice, pursuit was made; and that no person should serve or execute, or cause to be served or executed, any writ, process, warrant, order, judgment or decree (except in cases of treason, felony or breach of the peace), but such service should be void, and the person serving or executing be liable as if done without any writ, &c. 29 Chas. II., c. 7.

106. An act in reference to the sale of fish was, in 1699, declared not to prohibit the selling of mackerel before or after Divine service on Sunday. 10 & 11 Wm. III., c. 24, s. 14.

NOTE.—For a discussion of the various kinds of Councils, of the authority of their decrees, and of their relations to the Papacy, the reader is referred to the introduction to Hefele's "History of the Christian Councils." The citations of decrees of Councils given above are chiefly taken from the compilation of the Jesuit Labbe, who died in 1667, before completing the work.

The ponderous volumes of Labbe's collection give force to the words of Milman: "Council followed Council. Though we may not concur with the Arian bishops in ascribing to their adversaries the whole blame of this perpetual tumult and confusion in the Christian world caused by these incessant assemblages of the clergy, there must have been much melancholy truth in their statement: 'The East and the West are in a perpetual state of restlessness and disturbance. Deserting our spiritual charges, abandoning the people of God, neglecting the preaching of the Gospel, we are hurried about from place to place, sometimes to great distances, some of us infirm with age, of feeble constitutions or ill-health, and are sometimes obliged to leave our sick brethren on the road. The whole administration of the empire, the Emperor himself, the tribunes and the commanders, at this fearful crisis of the state, are solely occupied with the lives and the conditions of the bishops. The people are by no means unconcerned. The whole brotherhood watches in anxious suspense the event of these troubles; the establishment of post-horses is worn out by our journeyings; and all on account of a few wretches, who, if they had the least remaining sense of religion, would say with the prophet Jonah, "Take us up and cast us into the sea; so shall the sea be calm unto you; for we know that it is on our account that this great tempest is upon us."'" Hist. Christ, pp. 343–4 (Harper's ed. 1856).

The above summary shows: (I.) That the "observance" of Sunday is entirely a matter of ecclesiastical origin, and that it is historically as well as physiologically false to affirm that Sunday idleness and gloom have ever been required on hygienic grounds. (II.) That, in general, the early guardians of the faith did not connect the Fourth Commandment with Sunday, and were not aware of the theological truth judicially established in America, that Sunday idleness was prescribed "from the smoking top of Mount Sinai," but, on the contrary, that among the many reasons adduced for the "observance" of the day, this fact finds no place (see, particularly, paragraphs 1, 2, 3, 17, 33, 44, 52 and 75), with the single exception of the Council of Friuli. (See paragraph 42.) (III.) That Constantine's edict, the first "Sunday law," was among the first fruits of the baneful union of church and state which began for Christianity with the conversion of that Emperor, and to which it owes every blot upon its history, including the plunder of pagans, the slaughter of infidels and the burning of heretics, as well as the Sunday laws. Up to that time it had spread, as it began, by soft persuasion, irresistibly, yet without reproach.

Dr. Kurtz, in his "Church History," thus portrays the evil results which followed the conversion of Constantine: "When Christianity became the religion of the state, a large number of unconverted and worldly persons made a profession of Christianity for the sake of the temporal advantages which it entailed. This influx of the world into the church necessarily exercised a most detrimental influence, and the earnestness, power, devotedness and purity by which the ancient heathen world had been conquered greatly declined in consequence. The world and the church became more assimilated and conformed to one another; discipline became lax and powerless, and the general decline of public morals made rapid progress. The hot discussions, the dissensions and divisions among the bishops and the clergy led to corresponding effects among the people. Party spirit and bitterness characterized the adherents of different views; the demoralization of the court exercised its pernicious influence on the capital and the provinces, while the inroads of the barbarians increased the general decay. Even in the case of those who sought other than merely earthly things, work-righteousness and bigotry too often took the place of genuine piety, while the great mass consoled themselves with the idea that everybody could not be a monk." Lippincott's ed. 1888, p. 239.

No wonder that fifty years after the Emperor Julian was able to defend his "apostasy" by demonstrating the appalling degeneracy of Christian teachers and leaders. It was natural that the Christians should be pleased with the material resources of wealth and power thus placed at their command, and that they should forget the Master's warning that His kingdom and Cæsar's could never be united. It was inevitable that the result of an attempt to join them should be as He foresaw it. If the practical emasculation of the church as a moral agent had been the sole result of this unnatural connection, men's minds might more slowly, or not at all, have been aroused to its evil work. But it has been made fearfully apparent that the state suffers no less than the church, under such conditions, and that, as religion cannot retain its effective influence over the hearts and minds of men, so neither can government rightly discharge its functions in the regulation of their conduct, while a union of church and state subsists. Hence, from sheer necessity, the tendency of modern civilization is towards a complete separation of Church and state. In America, we have set this complete separation before us as a political ideal, and we have practically attained it, with the following exceptions: (1) certain qualifications in the way of belief required in some states of office-holders; (2) the same as to witnesses; (3) the manner of applying the law of "blasphemy;" (4) Sunday laws. With these exceptions, Christianity is no longer permitted to wield "the sword of Peter" in the United States. Those who love and believe in her work may well congratulate themselves that she has proven herself now, as in the past, able to dispense with such assistance.

Just as informations for "heresy" in the olden time were most frequently the outcome of private animosity, so nearly every prosecution under our Sunday laws is the result of petty spite, meanness and malice; and thus, just as of old, we have the secular power invoked in the name of the Master to gratify the vilest and most despicable impulses of the human heart. The advocates for the relegation of the Sunday laws to the limbo of the stake and the thumbscrew, have a right to claim that the accomplishment of their purpose will free the Christian religion from a great reproach, and materially help on the good work of restoring it to those conditions of absolute independence of the state under which for more than three hundred years it lived and grew, and "kept itself unspotted from the world."

TABLE B.

Comparative View of Provisions Regarding Religion, Sunday Observance, &c., in the United States.

I. Constitutional Provisions as to Religious Freedom in the United States.

ALABAMA.

No person within this state shall, upon any pretence whatever, be deprived of the inalienable privilege of worshipping God in the manner most agreeable to his own conscience; nor be hurt, molested or restrained in his religious profession, sentiments or persuasions, provided he does not disturb others in their religious worship. 88, 3.

No religion shall be established by law; no preference shall be given by law to any religious sect, society, denomination, or mode of worship; no one shall be compelled by law to attend any place of worship, nor to pay any tithes, taxes or other rate for building or repairing any place of worship, or for maintaining any minister or ministry; no religious test shall be required as a qualification to any office or public trust under this state, and the civil rights, privileges and capacities of any citizen shall not be in any manner affected by his religious principles. Id. 4.

ARKANSAS.

All men have a natural and indefeasible right to worship Almighty God according to the dictates of their own consciences; no man can of right be compelled to attend, erect or support any place of worship, or to maintain any ministry against his consent. No human authority can, in any case or manner whatsoever, control and interfere with the right of conscience, and no preference shall ever be given by law to any religious establishment or mode of worship above any other. 45, 24.

Religion, morality and knowledge being essential to good government, the general assembly shall enact suitable laws to protect every religious denomination in the peaceable enjoyment of its own worship. Id. 25.

No religious test shall ever be required as a qualification to vote or hold office, nor shall any person be rendered incompetent to be a witness, on account of his religious belief; but nothing herein shall be construed to dispense with oaths or affirmations. 46, 26.

CALIFORNIA.

The free exercise and enjoyment of religious profession and worship, without discrimination or preference, shall be forever allowed, and no person shall be rendered incompetent to be a witness on account of his opinions on matters of religious belief; but the liberty of conscience hereby secured shall not be so construed as to justify practices inconsistent with the peace or safety of this state. 20, 4.

COLORADO.

The free exercise and enjoyment of religious profession and worship, without discrimination, shall forever hereafter be guaranteed, and no person shall be denied any civil or political right, privilege or capacity, on account of his opinions concerning religion; but the liberty of conscience hereby secured shall not be construed to dispense with oaths or affirmations, excuse acts of licentiousness, or justify practices inconsistent with the good order, peace or safety of the state. No person shall be required to attend or support any ministry or place of worship, religious sect or denomination, against his consent. Nor shall any preference be given by law to any religious denomination or mode of worship. 33, 4.

CONNECTICUT.

The exercise and enjoyment of religious profession and worship, without discrimination, shall forever be free to all persons in this state, provided that the right hereby declared and established shall not be so construed as to excuse acts of licentiousness or to justify practices inconsistent with the peace and safety of the state. 45, 3.

No preference shall be given by law to any Christian sect or mode of worship. Id. 4.

DELAWARE.

Although it is the duty of all men to frequently assemble themselves together for the public worship of the Author of the universe, and piety and morality, on which the prosperity of communities depend, are thereby promoted; yet no man shall, or ought to be compelled to attend any religious worship, to contribute to the erection or support of any place of worship, or to the maintenance of any ministry, against his own free will and consent; and no power shall or ought to be vested in or assumed by any magistrate that shall in any case interfere or in any manner control the rights of conscience in the free exercise of religious worship, nor a preference be given by law to any religious societies, denominations or modes of worship. 23, 1.

No religious test shall be required as a qualification for any office or public trust. Id. 2.

FLORIDA.

The free exercise and enjoyment of religious profession and worship shall forever be allowed, and no person shall be rendered incompetent as a witness on account of his religious opinions, but the liberty of conscience hereby secured shall not be so construed as to justify licentiousness or practices subversive of the peace and safety of the state. 21, 4.

GEORGIA.

All men have a natural and inalienable right to worship God, each according to the dictates of his own conscience, and no human authority should in any case control or interfere with such rights of conscience. 100, 483.

No inhabitant of this state shall be molested, in person or property, or prevented from holding any public office or trust, on account of his religious opinions, but the right of liberty of conscience shall not be so construed as to excuse acts of licentiousness or justify practices inconsistent with the peace and safety of the state. Id. 484.

No money shall ever be taken from the public treasury, directly or indirectly, in aid of any church, sect or denomination of religionists, or of any sectarian institution. Id. 485.

IDAHO.

The exercise and enjoyment of religious faith and worship shall forever be guaranteed, and no person shall be denied any civil or political right, privilege or capacity on account of his religious opinions; but the liberty of conscience hereby secured shall not be construed to dispense with oaths or affirmations, or excuse acts of licentiousness, or justify polygamous or other pernicious practices inconsistent with morality or the peace or safety of the state, nor to permit any person, organization or association to directly or indirectly aid or abet, counsel or advise any person to commit the crime of bigamy or polygamy, or any other crime. No person shall be required to attend or support any ministry, or place of worship, religious sect or denomination, or pay tithes against his consent; nor shall any preference be given by law to any religious denomination or mode of worship. Bigamy and polygamy are forever prohibited in the state, and the legislature shall provide by law for the punishment of such crimes.

ILLINOIS.

The free exercise and enjoyment of religious profession and worship, without discrimination, shall be forever guaranteed; and no person shall be denied any civil or political right, privilege or capacity on account of his religious opinions; but the liberty of conscience hereby secured shall not be construed to dispense with oaths or affirmations, excuse acts of licentiousness, or justify practices inconsistent with the peace or safety of the state. No person shall be required to attend or support any ministry or place of worship against his consent, nor shall any preference be given by law to any religious denomination or mode of worship.

INDIANA.

All men shall be secured in their natural right to worship Almighty God according to the dictates of their own consciences. No law shall, in any case whatever, control the free exercise and enjoyment of religious opinions, or interfere with the rights of conscience. No preference shall be given by law to any creed, religious society or mode of worship; and no man shall be compelled to attend, erect or support any place of worship or to maintain any ministry against his consent. No religious tests shall be required as a qualification for any office of trust or profit. No money shall be drawn from the treasury for the benefit of any religious or theological institution. No person shall be rendered incompetent as a witness on account of his opinions on matters of religion. The mode of administering an oath or affirmation shall be such as may be most consistent with and binding upon the conscience of the person to whom such oath or affirmation may be administered. 47, 53.

IOWA.

The general assembly shall make no law respecting an establishment of religion, or prohibiting the free exercise thereof; nor shall any person be compelled to attend any place of worship or pay taxes, &c., for building or repairing such or the maintenance of any minister, &c.; no religious test should be required as a qualification for office, and no person shall be deprived of any of his rights or be disqualified from the performance of any public or private duty or be incompetent to give evidence on account of his religious opinion.

KANSAS.

The right to worship God according to the dictates of conscience shall never be infringed; nor shall any person be compelled to attend or support any form of worship; nor shall any control of or interference with the rights of conscience be permitted, nor any preference be given by law to any religious establishment or mode of worship. No religious test shall be required for any office of public trust, nor for any vote at any election; nor shall any person be incompetent to testify on account of religious belief. 89.

KENTUCKY.

All men have a natural and indefeasible right to worship Almighty God according to the dictates of their own consciences. No man shall be compelled to attend, erect or support any place of worship, or to maintain any ministry, against his consent. No human authority ought, in any case whatever, to control or interfere with the rights of conscience, and no preference shall ever be given by law to any religious societies or modes of worship. The civil rights, privileges or capacities of any citizen shall in no wise be diminished or enlarged on account of his religion. 120, 5, 6.

LOUISIANA.

No law shall be passed respecting an establishment of religion or prohibiting the full exercise thereof.

MAINE.

All men have a natural and inalienable right to worship Almighty God according to the dictates of their own consciences, and no one shall be hurt, molested or restrained in his person, liberty or estate for worshipping God in the manner and season most agreeable to the dictates of his own conscience, nor for his religious professions or sentiments, providing he does not disturb the public peace, nor obstruct others in their religious worship; and all persons demeaning themselves peaceably as good members of the state shall be equally under the protection of the laws, and no subordination or preference of any one sect or denomination to another shall ever be established by law, nor shall any religious test be required as a qualification for any office or trust under this state; and all religious societies in this state, whether incorporated or unincorporated, shall at all times have the exclusive right of electing their public teachers, and contracting with them for their support and maintenance. 33, 3.

MARYLAND.

As it is the duty of every man to worship God in such manner as he thinks most acceptable to him, all persons are equally entitled to protection in their religious liberty; therefore no person ought by any law to be molested in his person or estate on account of his religious principles or profession, or for his religious practice, unless, under a color of religion, he disturb the good order, &c., of the state or infringe the laws of morality, or injure others in their natural civil or religious rights; nor ought any person be compelled to frequent or maintain or contribute, unless on contract, to maintain any place of worship, &c.; nor shall any person otherwise competent be deemed incompetent as a witness or juror on account of his religious belief, provided he believes in the existence of a God, and that under His dispensation such person will be held morally responsible for his acts, and be rewarded or punished therefor either in this world or in that to come.

No religious test ought ever to be required as a qualification for any office of profit or trust other than a declaration of belief in the existence of a God.

MASSACHUSETTS.

It is the right as well as the duty of all men in society, publicly and at stated seasons, to worship the Supreme Being and great Creator and Preserver of the universe. And no subject shall be hurt, molested or restrained in his person, liberty or estate for worshipping God in the manner and season most agreeable to the dictates of his own conscience, or for his religious profession or sentiments, provided he doth not disturb the public peace or obstruct others in their religious worship. 18, 2.

It was formerly commanded that the legislature should require towns to provide for the support of "Protestant teachers of piety and religion," &c., where such arrangement was not made voluntarily; and that it should enjoin upon "all the subjects" attendance on the instruction of those teachers; but that every denomination of Christians who demean themselves peaceably, &c., should be equally under the protection of the law, and no subordination of one to the other should be established by law. 18, 3.

Retaining the latter provision, the former was so amended as simply to authorize religious societies, incorporated or otherwise, to elect and contract with their own teachers, &c. 39, II.

MICHIGAN.

The legislature shall pass no law to prevent any person from worshipping Almighty God according to the dictates of his own conscience, or to compel any person to attend, erect or support any place of religious worship, or pay tithes, taxes or other rates for the support of any minister of the gospel or teacher of religion. 48, 39.

No money shall be appropriated or drawn from the treasury for the benefit of any religious sect or society, theological or religious seminary, nor shall property belonging to the state be appropriated for any such purpose. Id. 40.

The legislature shall not diminish or enlarge the civil or political rights, privileges or capacities of any person on account of his religion or belief concerning matters of religion. Id. 41.

MINNESOTA.

No religious test as a qualification for office shall ever be required, and no preference shall ever be given by law to any religious sect or mode of worship, but the free enjoyment of all religious sentiments and the different modes of worship shall ever be held sacred; provided, the rights hereby secured shall not be construed to justify acts of licentiousness injurious to morals or dangerous to the peace and safety of the state. 20, 23.

The right of every man to worship God according to the dictates of his own conscience shall never be infringed, nor shall any man be compelled to attend, erect or support any place of worship, or to maintain any religious or ecclesiastical ministry against his consent; nor shall any control of or interference with the rights of conscience be permitted or any preference be given by law to any religious establishment, or mode of worship; but the liberty of conscience hereby secured shall not be so construed as to excuse acts of licentiousness, or justify practices inconsistent with the peace or safety of the state; nor shall any money be drawn from the treasury for the benefit of any religious societies or religious or theological seminaries. 18, 16.

No religious test shall be required as a qualification for any office of public trust under the state, or of a voter; nor shall any person be incompetent to give evidence in any court in consequence of his opinion upon the subject of religion. Id. 17.

MISSISSIPPI.

No religious tests shall be required as a qualification for office, and no preference shall be given by law to any religious sect or mode of worship, but the free enjoyment of all religious sentiments and the different modes of worship shall be forever held sacred; provided, that the rights hereby secured shall not be construed to justify acts of licentiousness injurious to the morals or dangerous to the peace and safety of the state.

MISSOURI.

All men have a natural and indefeasible right to worship God according to the dictates of their own consciences; no person shall, on account of his religious opinions, be rendered ineligible to any office of trust or profit, nor be disqualified from testifying, or from serving as a juror; no human authority can control or interfere with the rights of conscience; no person ought by any law to be molested in his person or estate on account of his religious principles or profession; but the liberty of conscience hereby secured shall not be so construed as to excuse acts of licentiousness, nor to justify practices inconsistent with the good order, peace or safety of this state, or with the rights of others. 55, 5.

No person can be compelled to erect, support or attend any place or system of worship, or to maintain or support any priest, minister, preacher or teacher of any sect, church, creed or denomination of religion; but if any person shall voluntarily make a contract for any such object, he shall be held to the performance of the same. Id. 6.

No money shall ever be taken from the public treasury, directly or indirectly, in aid of any church, sect or denomination of religion, or in aid of any priest, preacher, teacher or minister thereof, as such; and no preference shall be given to, nor any discrimination made against, any church, sect or creed of religion, or any form of religious faith or worship. 56, 7.

No religious corporation shall be established, except such as may be created under the general law, for the purpose only of holding title to such real estate as may be prescribed by law for church edifices, parsonages and cemeteries. Id. 8.

NEBRASKA.

All persons have a natural and indefeasible right to worship Almighty God according to the dictates of their own consciences. No person shall be compelled to attend, erect or support any place of worship against his conscience, and no preference shall be given by law to any religious society, nor shall any interference with the rights of conscience be permitted. No religious test shall be required as a qualification for office, nor shall any person be incompetent to be a witness on account of his religious belief; but nothing herein shall be construed to dispense with oaths and affirmations. Religion, morality and knowledge, however, being essential to good government, it shall be the duty of the legislature to pass suitable laws to protect every religious denomination in the peaceable enjoyment of its own mode of public worship, and to encourage schools and the means of instruction. 15, 4.

NEVADA.

The free exercise and enjoyment of religious profession and worship, without discrimination or preference, shall forever be allowed in this state, and no person shall be rendered incompetent to be a witness on account of his opinion on matters of religious belief; but the liberty of conscience hereby secured shall not be so construed as to excuse acts of licentiousness or justify practices inconsistent with the peace or safety of this state. 49, 4.

NEW HAMPSHIRE.

Among the natural rights some are in their very nature inalienable, because no equivalent can be given or conceived for them; of this kind are the rights of conscience. 21, 4.

Every individual has a natural and inalienable right to worship Almighty God according to the dictates of his own conscience and reason; and no subject shall be hurt, molested or restrained in his person, liberty or estate for worshipping God in the manner and season most agreeable to the dictates of his own conscience, or for his religious profession, sentiments or persuasion, provided he doth not disturb the public peace of others in their religious worship. 21, 5.

As morality and piety, grounded on Evangelical principles, give the best security to government, the legislature is empowered to authorize towns, &c., to provide, at their expense, for the support and maintenance of public Protestant teachers of piety, religion and morality, but the towns may elect their own teachers, and no persons of any one particular religious sect or denomination shall be compelled to pay for the support of teachers for another; and every denomination of Christians demeaning themselves quietly and as good subjects of the state shall be equally under the protection of the law; and no subordination of any one sect or denomination to another shall ever be established by law. Id. 6.

NEW JERSEY.

No person shall be deprived of the inestimable privilege of worshipping Almighty God in the manner most agreeable to the dictates of his own conscience; nor, under any pretext whatever, be compelled to attend any place of worship contrary to his faith and judgment; nor shall any person be obliged to pay tithes or taxes, or other rates, for building or repairing any church or churches, place or places of worship, or for the maintenance of any minister or ministry, contrary to what he believes to be right or has deliberately and voluntarily engaged to peform. 33, 3.

There shall be no establishment of one religion in preference to another; no religious test shall be required as a qualification for any office or public trust, and no person shall be denied the enjoyment of any civil right merely on account of his religious principles. Id. 4.

NEW YORK.

The free exercise and enjoyment of religious profession and worship, without discrimination or preference, shall forever be allowed to all mankind, and no person shall be rendered incompetent to be a witness on account of his opinions on matters of religious belief; but the liberty of conscience hereby secured shall not be so construed as to excuse acts of licentiousness, or justify practices inconsistent with the peace or safety of this state. 82, 3.

NORTH CAROLINA.

All men have a natural and unalienable right to worship Almighty God according to the dictates of their own consciences, and no human authority should in any case whatever control or interfere with the rights of conscience. 685, 26.

NORTH DAKOTA.

Perfect toleration of religious sentiment shall be secured, and no inhabitant shall ever be molested in person or property on account of his mode of religious worship.

OHIO.

All men have a natural and indefeasible right to worship Almighty God according to the dictates of their own consciences. No person shall be compelled to attend, erect or support any place of worship, or maintain any form of worship against his consent, and no preference shall be given by law to any religious society. Nor shall any interference with the rights of conscience be permitted. No religious test shall be required as a qualification for office, nor shall any person be incompetent to be a witness on account of his religious belief, but nothing herein shall be construed to dispense with oaths and affirmations. Religion, morality and knowledge, however, being essential to good government, it shall be the duty of the general assembly to pass suitable laws to protect every religious denomination in the peaceable enjoyment of its own mode of public worship, and to encourage schools and the means of instruction. 1725, 7.

PENNSYLVANIA.

All men have a natural and indefeasible right to worship Almighty God according to the dictates of their own consciences; no man can of right be compelled to attend, erect or support any place of worship, or to maintain any minister, against his consent; no human authority can in any case whatever control or interfere with the rights of conscience, and no preference shall ever be given by law to any religious establishments or modes of worship. 23, 3.

No person who acknowledges the being of a God and a future state of rewards and punishments shall, on account of his religious sentiments, be disqualified to hold any office or place of trust or profit. Id. 24, 4.

RHODE ISLAND.

Whereas Almighty God hath created the mind free, and all attempts to influence it by temporal punishments or burdens, or by civil incapacitations, tend to beget habits of hypocrisy and meanness; and, whereas, a principal object of our venerable ancestors in emigrating to this country was, as they expressed it, to hold forth a lively experiment, that a flourishing civil state may stand and be best maintained with full liberty in religious concernments: we, therefore, declare that no man shall be compelled to frequent or to support any religious worship, place or minister whatever, except in fulfillment of his own voluntary contract; nor enforced, restrained, molested or burdened in his own body or goods; nor disqualified from holding any office, nor otherwise suffer on account of his religious belief; and that every man shall be free to worship God according to the dictates of his own conscience, and to profess and by argument to maintain his opinion in matters of religion; and that the same shall in no wise diminish, enlarge or affect his civil capacity. 20, 3.

SOUTH CAROLINA.

No person shall be deprived of the right to worship God according to the dictates of his own conscience, provided that the liberty of conscience hereby declared shall not justify practices inconsistent with the peace and moral safety of society. 26, 9.

No form of religion shall be established by law, but it shall be the duty of the general assembly to pass suitable laws to protect every denomination in the peaceable enjoyment of its own mode of worship. Id. 10.

No person who denies the existence of the Supreme Being shall hold any office. 47, 6.

SOUTH DAKOTA.

The right to worship God according to the dictates of conscience shall never be infringed. No person shall be denied any civil or political right, privilege or possession on account of his religious opinion, but the liberty of conscience hereby secured shall not be so construed as to excuse licentiousness, or the invasion of the rights of others, or to justify practices inconsistent with the peace and safety of the state. No person shall be compelled to attend or support any ministry or place of worship against his consent; nor shall any preference be given to any religious establishment or mode of worship. No money or property of the state shall be appropriated for the benefit of any sectarian or religious society or institution.

TENNESSEE.

All men have a natural and indefeasible right to worship Almighty God according to the dictates of their own consciences; no man can of right be compelled to attend, erect or support any place of worship, or to maintain any ministry, against his consent; no human authority can, in any case whatever, control or interfere with the rights of conscience, and no preference shall ever be given by law to any religious establishment or mode of worship. 66, 3.

No religious test shall be required as a qualification to any office or public trust under this state. Id. 4.

TEXAS.

All men have a natural and indefeasible right to worship Almighty God according to the dictates of their own consciences. No man shall be compelled to attend, erect or support any place of worship, or to maintain any ministry, against his consent. No human authority ought, in any case whatever, to control or interfere with the rights of conscience in matters of religion, and no preference shall ever be given by law to any religious society or mode of worship. But it shall be the duty of the legislature to pass such laws as may be necessary to protect equally every religious denomination in the peaceable enjoyment of its own mode of worship. 1, 6.

No money shall be appropriated or drawn from the treasury for the benefit of any sect or religious society, or theological or religious seminary; nor shall property belonging to the state be appropriated for any such purpose. Id. 7.

VERMONT.

All men have a natural and unalienable right to worship Almighty God according to the dictates of their own consciences and understandings as in their opinion shall be regulated by the word of God; no man ought to, or of right can, be compelled to attend any religious worship, or erect or support any place of worship, or maintain any ministry, contrary to the dictates of his conscience; nor can any man be justly deprived or abridged of any civil right as a citizen on account of his religious sentiments or peculiar mode of religious worship. No power can or ought to be vested in or assumed by any power whatever that shall in any case interfere with or in any manner control the rights of conscience in the free exercise of religious worship; nevertheless, every sect or denomination of Christians ought to observe the Sabbath, or Lord's day, and keep up some sort of religious worship which to them shall seem most agreeable to the revealed will of God.

VIRGINIA.

Religion, or the duty which we owe to our Creator, and the manner of discharging it, can be directed only by reason and conviction, not by force or violence; and therefore all men are equally entitled to the free exercise of religion according to the dictates of conscience; it is the mutual duty of all to practice Christian forbearance, love and charity towards each other. 69, 18.

WEST VIRGINIA.

No religious test-oath shall be required as a prerequisite or qualification to vote, serve as a juror, plead, appeal, or pursue any profession or employment. 8, II.

No man shall be compelled to frequent or support any religious worship, place or ministry whatsoever; nor shall any man be enforced, restrained, molested or burthened in his body or goods, or otherwise suffer on account of his religious opinion or belief; but all men shall be free to profess and by argument maintain their opinions in matters of religion; and the same shall in no wise affect, diminish or enlarge their civil capacities; and the legislature shall not prescribe any religious tests whatever, or confer any peculiar privileges or advantages on any sect or denomination, or pass any law requiring or authorizing any religious society, or the people of any district within this state to levy on themselves or others any tax for the erection or repair of any house for public worship, or for the support of any church or ministry, but it shall be left free for every person to select his religious instructor, and to make for his support such private contract as he shall please. 9, 15.

No religious tests shall ever be required as a qualification for any office of public trust under the state, and no person shall be rendered incompetent to give evidence in any court of law or equity in consequence of his opinions on the subject of religion. 18, 19.

WISCONSIN.

The right of every man to worship Almighty God according to the dictates of his own conscience shall never be infringed; nor shall any man be compelled to attend, erect or support any place of worship, or to maintain any place of worship, against his consent; nor shall any control of or interference with the rights of conscience be permitted, or any preference be given by law to any religious establishments or modes of worship; nor shall any money be drawn from the treasury for the benefit of any religious societies or religious or theological seminaries. 18, 18.

II. What is Sunday.

ILLINOIS.

From midnight to midnight. 424, 260.

MAINE.

From twelve o'clock Saturday night till twelve o'clock Sunday night. 906, 22.

MASSACHUSETTS.

From midnight to midnight. 621, 16.

From Saturday evening to Sunday evening, in provision against being present at game, public diversion, &c. 519, 1.

Begins evening before, in provision against allowing people not travelers to spend time idly at or about inns, &c. (and ends when ?)

MICHIGAN.

From midnight to midnight. 2022.

MINNESOTA.

From midnight to midnight. 922, 21.

NEW YORK.

From midnight to midnight. Penal Code 259.

UTAH.

From midnight to midnight. 1986.

VERMONT.

As to service of process, from sunset on Saturday till twelve o'clock on Sunday night. 870.

As to work, traveling and sports, twelve o'clock Saturday night to sunset Sunday. 4315.

WASHINGTON.

As to work, from midnight till midnight. 4595.

III. Sunday in the Computation of Time, &c.

ALABAMA.

If the last day of time within which an act is provided by law to be done, excluded. II.

ARKANSAS.

Commercial paper falling due payable the day preceding, and may be then noted and contested, but notice need not be given till next day. 465.

CALIFORNIA.

A holiday. 10.

If another holiday fall on it, the Monday following is a holiday. 11.

Same provision repeated. 5007, 5008.

COLORADO.

Commercial paper falling due is payable and may be protested the preceding day. 115.

Holidays to be construed as Sunday in this regard: if one of them falls on Sunday, the next day is a holiday and paper due on either is payable the day previous to the first of the days. 1630.

GEORGIA.

If the last day of a number prescribed for the exercise of a privilege or the discharge of a duty, excluded. 4, par. 8.

ILLINOIS.

Where last day of time within which notice required by law court's order, or contract, excluded. 841, 6.

So where act provided by law to be done. 1166, I., par. 10.

INDIANA.

If the last day of the time within which an act is to be done, "as herein provided," excluded. 1280.

KANSAS.

If the last day "within which an act is to be done," excluded. 4541.

KENTUCKY.

Holidays treated as Sunday as regards presenting, protesting and giving notice in respect to negotiable paper. 513, 1.

If any of these occur on Sunday, next day to be regarded as a holiday; but negotiable paper may be presented and proceeded upon on a Saturday. 514, 2.

If the day on which the proceeding is directed by law to take place, or an act to be done, either shall be on the next day. 245, 9.

If the law authorizes an adjournment of a tribunal or officers' proceedings to be from day to day, an adjournment from Saturday till Monday shall be legal. 245, 10.

MASSACHUSETTS.

Bills, notes, &c., or contracts falling due or to be performed, are payable or performable the business day preceding, and the former may then be noted and protested; but holder need not give notice of dishonor, &c., till the business day following. 427, 8.

Where a convict's term expires, he shall be discharged the Saturday preceding. 1246, 24.

MICHIGAN.

Excepted from days allowed governor for considering bills. 45, 14.

MINNESOTA.

If the last day of the time within which an act is to be done, excluded. 71, 82.

If last day for serving process or notice, excluded; in other cases reckoned. 17.

Excepted from time allowed governor for signing bills. 24, 24.

MISSOURI.

When a holiday falls on a Sunday, next day is a holiday; holidays regarded as Sunday in respect to negotiable paper, which, when falling due on a holiday, is payable the next succeeding day, unless that be a Sunday or holiday, when it is payable the day previous. 551.

NEBRASKA.

If the last day of time within which an act is appointed to be done, "as herein provided," excluded. 730, 895.

NEVADA.

Holidays treated as Sunday, as regards dishonor of commercial paper, if coming within the three days of grace, counted as one. 4879.

If such paper is due on Sunday, it is payable the day previous. 4880.

Excepted from days allowed governor to consider bills. 109, 25.

If the last day of the time within an act is to be done as required by the act regulating civil procedure, excluded. 3528.

NEW HAMPSHIRE.

Excepted from the days allowed the governor for considering bills. 32, 44.

NEW JERSEY.

Excepted from the time allowed the governor to consider bills. 23, 7.

NEW YORK.

Excepted from the time allowed the governor for considering bills. 97, 92.

If the last day of time within which an act in judicial proceedings must be done, excluded; so, where it is to required to be done within two days, and Sunday is an intervening day. Code Crim. Pro., s. 788.

NORTH CAROLINA.

Where a holiday falls on this day, Monday is a holiday; paper due is payable Saturday, and paper due Monday is payable Tuesday. 3784.

When a holiday falls on Saturday, paper due Sunday is payable Monday; when it falls on Monday, paper due on the holiday is payable Tuesday. 3785–6.

OHIO.

If the third day of grace, demand must be made on the preceding business day. 3176.

Holidays are considered as Sunday in regard to demand and notice of dishonor of paper, and if a holiday falls on this day Monday is so considered. 3177.

Unless otherwise specially provided, if the last day of the time within which an act must be done, "by common or statute law," excluded. 4951.

When Sunday is the last day of time within which act is to be done by law or rule of court, it is excluded. 1636.

Where a holiday happens on Sunday, Monday is a holiday. 270, 2–4.

SOUTH CAROLINA.

Excepted from the days allowed the governor to consider bills. 35, 22.

TENNESSEE.

Paper falling due on a holiday is due the day preceding, unless that day is Sunday, when it is due the Saturday preceding. 2723.

Excepted from days allowed governor for considering bills. 80, 18.

Where last day of time within which act provided by law to be done, excluded. 46.

TEXAS.

Excepted from the days allowed governor for considering bills. 10, 14.

VERMONT.

Not excepted from the days allowed the governor to sign bills. 38, 16.

But so by amendments. 44, 11.

Paper without grace falling due, payable the day following. 2011.

If subject to grace, it is payable the preceding business day. 2012.

VIRGINIA.

Not included in the days allowed the governor to consider bills. 73, 8.

Where court directed to be held or other proceeding by law to take place on a day of the month which is Sunday, the same shall take place the next day; and where an adjournment of court or officers' proceedings from day to day is authorized, adjournment from Saturday till Monday is legal. 195, 9.

WASHINGTON.

Not included in days allowed governor to consider bills. 24, 10.

When a holiday falls on this day, Monday is a holiday. 2577.

Paper falling due is payable next preceding secular day. 1684.

WEST VIRGINIA.

Not included in days allowed governor for considering bills. 21, 14.

IV. Sunday as a Dies Non Juridicus.

ALABAMA.

Attachments may issue and be executed when the plaintiff makes oath that the defendant is absconding, or about to abscond or remove his property from the state under color of Sunday, by reason of which the debt will probably be lost, or he will have to sue for it in another state. 3266. See 2578 at bottom of same page.

ARKANSAS.

No court shall be opened or transact business, unless to receive a verdict or discharge a jury, and adjournment on Saturday shall be to some other day, except when a cause has been committed to a jury; this not to prevent the exercise of a magistrate's jurisdiction where necessary to preserve the peace or arrest offenders. 1483.

Summons or order for provisional remedy may issue on affidavit of plaintiff or some other that unless it is issued there is reasonable cause to believe that it cannot be executed. 5310.

Order for attachment or the delivery of property may be executed if an affidavit of the plaintiff or some other, made to the effect that the affiant believes that the property is about to be concealed or removed or that the process cannot be executed afterwards. 5311.

So with a summons, *subpœna*, order of arrest or of injunction, if such belief, &c., that it cannot be executed afterward. 5312.

COLORADO.

A suit shall not abate by reason of the return or adjourned day coming on a holiday, but stand continued to the next day, unless that be Sunday, and then to the next day. 1630.

Attachment may issue on oath of the plaintiff or another that it is necessary. 2018.

CONNECTICUT.

Civil process issued or served is void. 398, 8.

GEORGIA.

Attachment may be issued and be served when the plaintiff, &c., swears he has reason to apprehend the loss of the debt otherwise. 3274.

ILLINOIS.

If it appear by the affidavit in attachment that a debtor is absconding, concealed, or in defiance of the officer authorized to arrest him, or has left the state or intends leaving with the intention of having his personalty removed, the clerk may issue and sheriff serve an attachment. 153, 12.

An attachment may issue if the plaintiff, &c., make affidavit that it would be unsafe to delay proceedings till Monday. 65, 34.

An injunction may issue and be served, &c., if affidavit of complainant, &c., that the benefits of it will be lost or endangered or irremediable damage occasioned unless it immediately issue, giving reasons, and if the officer to issue is satisfied of the facts. 644, 23.

INDIANA.

No person shall be arrested in a place of worship during service or on Sunday, except in cases specified by law. 2659.

Attachment may issue if the plaintiff shows in his affidavit that the defendant is about to abscond to plaintiff's injury. 920.

Execution may be issued where affidavit filed by plaintiff, &c., that he will otherwise lose his judgment, as he fears and believes. 684.

When the return day of an execution falls on Sunday it shall be returned on Monday. 788.

A writ or process authorized by the section on *habeas corpus* may issue and be served in emergency. 1129.

Process may be issued whenever it shall appear by affidavit that its object would probably be defeated by delay to another day. 1454.

No recognizance, undertaking or bond in a criminal proceeding shall be void because taken on Sunday. 1715.

KANSAS.

Any one causing to issue or serving a civil process from a Justices' Court on that day shall be fined $100 or imprisoned thirty days, or both. 5404.

KENTUCKY.

Process or notice on which legal proceedings are to be founded, "except as herein provided," is void; but *habeas corpus*, or process on a charge of treason, felony, riot, breach of the peace, or upon an escape out of custody may be executed. 781, 12.

MAINE.

Service of process void, and party serving liable in damages. 687, 81.

MASSACHUSETTS.

Service of civil process is void, and the person serving it is liable to damages. 520, 6.

A party committing malicious mischief may be arrested by any one and detained without warrant, but not more than twenty-four hours. 1152, 104.

Courts shall not be open on Sunday nor on the following day when a holiday, unless to enter or continue cases, receive a verdict or adjourn; this not to prevent the exercise of a magistrate's jurisdiction to preserve the peace or arrest offenders. 918, 4.

Persons committed to jail on Sunday or the afternoon or evening preceding may be admitted to bail. 1191, 52.

MICHIGAN.

Service of civil process is void, and the party serving liable in damages. 2019.

No court shall be open, unless to instruct or discharge a jury or receive a verdict; but this shall not prevent the exercise of a magistrate's jurisdiction where necessary to preserve the peace or arrest offenders. 702, 50.

MINNESOTA.

Courts shall not be open, except to receive a verdict or discharge a jury; this not to prevent the judges from exercising jurisdiction where necessary for the preservation of the peace or the sanctity of the day, or for the arrest or punishing of an offender. 633, 7.

The service or execution of civil process is void, and the party executing is liable in damages. 922, 22.

Injunctions and all other remedial processes may be granted, issued and executed, if the judge considers it proper. 1904.

Attachment may be issued and executed. 2471.

MISSOURI.

No court shall be open or transact business, except to receive a verdict, or discharge a jury, and adjournments of court shall be to some other day, except after a cause has been committed to a jury (this not to prevent the exercise of a magistrate's jurisdiction to preserve the peace, or arrest an offender, or prevent the issue and service of an attachment, where the debtor is about fraudulently to secrete or remove his effects). 1054.

No service of process, except in criminal cases, or for a breach of the peace, or when a defendant is about leaving the county, or attachments where the debtor is about fraudulently to secrete or remove his effects; and a party serving is liable in damages. 4039.

NEBRASKA.

No court shall be opened, or judicial business transacted, except (1) to give instructions to a deliberating jury; (2) to receive a verdict or discharge a jury; (3) to exercise a magistrate's powers in a criminal proceeding. 274, 38.

NEVADA.

No court shall be open nor judicial business be transacted, except (1) to give, on request, instructions to a deliberating jury; (2) to receive a verdict or discharge a jury; (3) for the exercise of a magistrate's powers in proceedings of a criminal nature; (4) for issue of attachment on oath of plaintiff, &c., that affiant has good reason for his belief that it will be too late to acquire a lien by the writ if he waits till a subsequent day. 2469.

Any process authorized by the act regulating attachments may be issued and served. 3705.

No judicial business shall be transacted, except deliberation of a jury, instructed "on a week-day, so called," but they may receive further instructions at their request, or deliver a verdict; but civil process shall not be served, nor any record made by an officer, but process may issue for the apprehension of a person charged with crime, and criminal examination be proceeded with. 4848.

NEW JERSEY.

Service and execution of process is void, except in criminal cases, or for breach of the peace, and the party serving is liable in damages. 1229, 5.

Every day of the stated terms of the Supreme Court, except Sunday, shall be a return day. 216, 18.

The Orphans' Court shall be open at all other times. 755, 12.

So with courts of law for return of all writs, with certain exceptions. 854, 41.

Party going to or from religious meetings not to pay toll. 833, 28

Election committee not to sit. 355, 95.

Those who religiously observe the seventh day are exempt from answering process as parties, witnesses or jurors, except in criminal cases; executing official duties, except when the interest of the state requires. 1234, 33.

NEW YORK.

Any processes by which the defendant's body is ordered to be taken in an action for forfeiture of a penalty under the acts relating to the salt springs of the state, may be issued and served. 732, 129.

No service of writ, process, warrant, order, judgment, decree or other proceeding of any court or officer of justice, except in cases of breach of the peace, or apprehended breach of the peace, or for the apprehension of persons charged with crimes or misdemeanors, or the violation of provisions against disturbing religious meetings, or of the Sunday law; and the party serving is liable in damages. 1975, 69.

Any one who maliciously causes process to issue from a Justices' Court in a civil suit on Saturday against a person keeping that day, or serves such process, is liable to a penalty of not more than $100, or more than thirty days, or both. Id. 2.

So with one who procures a suit pending against such a person to be adjourned to be tried on such day. Id. 3.

And a party guilty of either of these things commits a misdemeanor. Penal Code 271.

Courts shall not be open, or transact business, except to receive a verdict or discharge a jury; and adjournment on Saturday, unless after a cause has been committed to the jury, must be to some other day; this not to prevent the exercise of the jurisdiction of a magistrate, were necessary to preserve the peace, or, in a criminal case, to arrest, commit or discharge an offender Code Civ. Pro., § 6.

Habeas corpus may be issued and served, but cannot be made returnable. Code Civ. Pro., § 2015.

Sale under foreclosure must be on some other day. Id. 2393.

Arrests may be made for felonies, but not for misdemeanors, unless by the magistrate's direction, endorsed on the warrant. Code Crim. Pro. 170.

No service of process, except where breach of the peace, or when such apprehended, or when sued out for the apprehension of a person charged with a crime, and where specially authorized by statute. Penal Code 268.

OHIO.

No person shall be arrested. 5458.

PENNSYLVANIA.

Service or execution of writs, judgments, &c., except in cases of treason, felony, or breach of the peace, is void, and the party serving, &c., is liable in damages. 1591, 1.

Persons whose religious faith and practice it is to keep Saturday as a day set apart by divine command as the Sabbath of rest from labor and dedicated to the worship of God, shall be then subject to jury duty in a Justices' Court. 1976, 1.

RHODE ISLAND.

Service of civil process is void. 571, 34.

SOUTH CAROLINA.

No civil or criminal process shall be served, except for treason, felony, or breach of the peace. 663.

TENNESSEE.

Civil process may issue on oath that the defendant is removing, or about to remove, himself beyond the jurisdiction of the court or justice. 3529, 3531.

But not otherwise. 3532.

And, if otherwise, the action may be abated by plea. 3612.

TEXAS.

No civil suit shall be issued, nor process served. 1184.

VERMONT.

With the exception of escape warrants and warrants for apprehending a principal in favor of bail, and in cases of treason, felony or breach of the peace, service or execution of process is void. 870.

VIRGINIA.

No civil process shall be served, except in cases of persons escaping out of custody, or where it may be specially provided by law. 474, 25.

Attachments may issue on oath that the defendant is actually removing his effects. 1011, 10.

WASHINGTON.

No court shall be opened or transact any business (this not to prevent the exercise of a magistrate's jurisdiction, when necessary in criminal cases, to preserve the peace, or arrest offenders). 2576.

No civil process shall be served or executed. 4595.

WEST VIRGINIA.

Coroners' proceedings, summoning jurors and witnesses, and holding inquisitions, are legal. 1230, 12.

No civil process or order shall be executed, except in cases of persons escaping from custody, or where it may be specially provided by law. 273, 15.

Attachments may issue on oath that the defendant is actually removing his effects. 650, 9.

Coroners' proceedings, summoning a jury and witnesses, and holding inquisitions, are allowed. 837, 11.

V. Work, Amusements, &c.

ALABAMA.

Forbidden.—Compelling one's child, apprentice or servant to labor, except at the customary domestic duties of daily necessity or comfort, or works of charity; shooting, hunting, gaming, card-playing, racing; keeping open store, except for druggists; first offence not less than $10 nor more than $20; any subsequent offence not less than $20 nor more than $100 and possible imprisonment or sentence to hard labor for not more than three months; exceptions—railroads, stages, vessels, manufacturing establishments requiring to be kept in constant operation. 4443.

Also.—Opening public market-house or shop connected therewith, or bringing for sale thereto or buying therein; same penalties; any place where people assemble for the purchase of goods is a market, within the meaning hereof. 4444.

Contracts, unless for the advancement of religion, or in the execution or for the performance of some work of charity, or in case of necessity, are void. 2138.

ARKANSAS

Forbidden.—Keeping open store, &c., or dram-shop, or retailing liquor; penalty not less than $10 nor more than $20. 1887.

Charity or necessity may be shown in justification of a violation of the preceding section. 1888.

Forbidden.—Running a single horse or cock-fighting for wager or amusement; penalty not less than $20 or more than $100. 1889.

Forbidden.—Playing brag, bluff, poker, seven-up, three-up, twenty-one, vingt-un, thirteen-card, the odd trick, forty-five, whist, or any other game of cards for wager or amusement; penalty not less than $25 nor more than $50. 1890.

Forbidden.—Hunting; penalty not less than $5 nor more than $25 for each offence. 1891.

For last offence committed by a minor with parent or guardian's consent, &c., the latter shall be fined. 1892.

Forbidden.—Running horse-race for wager or amusement (later than preceding provision herein), not less than $25 nor more than $100. 1893.

COLORADO.

Forbidden.—Opening theatres and circuses; not less than $50 nor more than $100. 2113.

Also.—Being present at a concert or other public diversion. 522, 58.

Also.—Keeping open liquor-selling place. Id. 60.

CONNECTICUT.

Forbidden.—Traveling, labor or sporting (from sunrise to sunset). 521, 527.

Forbidden.—Traveling, secular business or labor, except works of necessity or mercy, opening a shop, &c., or manufacturing establishment exposing property for sale, engaging in sport or recreation; penalty not less than $1 nor more than $4. Haywards may perform official duties. Ib.

Forbidden.—Being present at concert or music or other public diversion. 522, 58.

Also.—Keeping open place where it is reputed that intoxicating liquors are kept for sale, or sports or games of chance carried on (from twelve to twelve); penalty $40, or thirty days, or both. Id. 60.

Forbidden.—Allowing persons to travel in vehicles not carrying the United States mail, except from necessity or mercy; penalty $20. Id. 62.

A person who conscientiously believes the seventh day ought to be observed as the Sabbath, and refrains from work thereon, may work, provided he disturbs no other person while attending public worship. Id. 63.

Forbidden.—Being present at concerts, dancing, &c., on Sunday or the evening thereof. Id., 58.

DELAWARE.

Forbidden.—Worldly employment or business, works of necessity and charity excepted; penalty $4 or twenty-four hours' imprisonment. 784, 4.

Forbidden—Traveling by a carrier, peddler, wagoner, driver of public stage, carter, butcher or drover, with his wagon, drove, &c.; exposing for sale by a retailer; penalty $8 or twenty-four hours' imprisonment. Ib.

Forbidden.—Fishing, fowling, horse-racing, cock-fighting, hunting; penalty $4 or twenty-four hours' imprisonment. Ib.

Also.—Assembling to game, play or dance, and assisting in such act; same penalty. Ib.

Also.—Liquor-selling. 262, 114.

FLORIDA.

Forbidden.—Following business or trade by manual labor, or animal or mechanical power, except it be work of necessity or justified by the accident or circumstances of the occasion. 425, 19.

Also.—Keeping open store and selling; but merchants in case of emergency or necessity may dispose of the comforts and necessities of life without keeping open doors. Id. 10.

Penalty under above not less than $20 nor more than $50. Id. 11.

Forbidden.—Shooting, fishing, &c. (from sundown Saturday night till sunrise Monday morning). 433, 40.

Also.—Employing an apprentice or servant in labor or other business, except the ordinary household business of daily necessity or other work of necessity or charity; penalty $10. Id. 12.

Forbidden.—Keeping open goods; penalty $20 (1832, earlier provision than the preceding one on the same subject). Ib. 13.

Also.—Hunting or firing at targets; penalty not less than $5 nor more than $25, or not more than twenty days. Id. 14.

Forbidden.—Fishing for shad. Id. 40.

Penalty for above not less than $25 nor more than $100, and forfeiture of boat and fishing tackle, or not more than thirty nor less than ten days. Id. 41.

GEORGIA.

Forbidden.—Pursuit of ordinary calling by tradesman, artificer, workman, laborer, or other person whatsoever, except works of necessity or charity; penalty as above. 4579.

(Penalty not exceeding $1,000, or not exceeding six months; work in chain-gang not exceeding twelve months; or any one or more of these punishments. 4310.)

Forbidden.—Hunting; penalty same. 4580.

Also.—Keeping open tippling-house. 4535.

Penalty same. Ib.

Forbidden.—Running freight train (superintendents liable to indictment in each county through which it runs, and punishable as above); but trains with live stock may run on to the next stock-pen, &c. 4578.

And freight trains running on Saturday night may run through to destination, provided the time of arrival according to the schedule shall not be later than eight o'clock Sunday morning. Supp. 312.

Forbidden.—Bathing in view of a road leading to a place of worship; penalty not more than $500 or —— months. 4581.

ILLINOIS.

Forbidden.—Disturbing the peace and good order of society by labor (works of necessity and charity excepted), amusement or diversion; penalty not more than $25 (this not to prevent watermen and railroads from landing passengers, loading cars, &c., nor interfere with ferrymen or travelers, or the exercise of the rights of conscience by one thinking it proper to keep any other day as a Sabbath). 424, 261.

Forbidden.—Disturbing the peace of a private family by noise, riot or amusement. Id., 262.

(Facilities for attending religious services shall be afforded convicts, and they shall not be required to labor or do unnecessary work for the state. 886, 31.)

Forbidden.—Keeping open a tippling-house or place where liquors are sold or given away; penalty not more than $200. 424, 259.

INDIANA.

Forbidden.—For one over fourteen to riot, hunt, fish, quarrel, engage at common labor, or in his usual avocation (works of charity and necessity only excepted); penalty not more than $10 or less than $1 (this not to affect those who conscientiously observe the seventh day of the week as the Sabbath, travelers, families removing, keepers of toll-bridges and gates and ferrymen acting as such). 2000.

Forbidden.—Selling or giving away liquor. 2098.

So doing by druggists. 2099.

The day is "a holiday" as to commercial paper. 5517.

KANSAS.

No person whose religious faith and practice is to keep Saturday as a day set apart by divine command as the Sabbath of rest and dedicated to the worship of God shall be subject on that day to jury or military duty, except in time of war, &c. 5403.

KENTUCKY.

Forbidden.—Work or business, except in ordinary household offices, being found at one's own or any other trade or calling, employing an apprentice or other person in labor or other business for profit or amusement, unless such as permitted; penalty not less than $2 or more than $50. (Every person employed is deemed a separate offence; members of a religious society who observe as the Sabbath day any other day not liable to the penalty if they "observe as a Sabbath one day in seven as herein provided.") 344, 10.

Forbidden.—Hunting with gun or dog; penalty not less than $5 nor more than $50 for each offence. 345, 11.

Forbidden.—Ball-playing; $60 and forfeiture of license, and no license to be afterwards granted. 747, 5.

(Provisions of general statutes regarding its observance shall not apply to street railway companies. 917, 1.)

Forbidden.—For licensed tavern-keeper, &c., to keep open a bar-room, &c., or sell, give away, or otherwise dispose of liquor; penalty forfeiture of license for the third offence of keeping open. 18, 1, 2.

MAINE.

Forbidden.—Keeping open shop, or place of business, traveling, doing any work, except works of necessity or charity, using any sport, game, or recreation, being present at any dancing, show, or entertainment, encouraging the same; penalty not more than $10. 906, 20.

Forbidden.—For an inn-keeper to suffer any person but travelers, &c., to abide in his house, yard, or field, drinking or spending time idly at play, or doing any secular business, except works of charity or necessity; penalty not more than $4 for each person; if again guilty, not more than $10 for each offence, and on a third conviction inn-keeper be incapable of holding license; and each person so abiding shall be fined not more than $4. Id., 321.

No contract, &c., is void for being dated on Sunday, without other proof than its date that it was then made and delivered. 710, 115.

No person who receives a valuable consideration for a contract, express or implied, shall defend action thereon on the ground that it was made on Sunday, until he restores such consideration. Ib.

Jailers are to furnish prisoners with such religious instruction as may be obtained without expense. 662, 30.

Whoever, on Sunday or at any other time, disturbs public worship, &c., shall be imprisoned not more than thirty days and fined not more than $10. 905, 17.

Sunday is a "close time," during which hunting is prohibited. 330, 27.

Where Sunday is the third day of grace, only two such days are allowed; where a holiday is Monday and the third day of grace, or a Saturday and the following Sunday is the third day of grace, or a Sunday and the second day of grace, four such days allowed. 334, 9.

No person conscientiously believing that the seventh day of the week ought to be observed as the Sabbath, and actually refraining from secular business and labor on that day, is liable to the penalties for labor on Sunday, if he does not disturb other persons. 906, 23.

MASSACHUSETTS.

Forbidden.—Keeping open shop, doing labor or business, &c., except works of necessity or charity, taking part in any sport, game, or play, being present at any dancing or public diversion, show, or entertainment; penalty not more than $50 for each offence. 519, 2.

Forbidden.—Traveling; penalty not more than $10 for each offence (but this no defence for common carriers for injuries to the person). 520, 3.

Forbidden.—Keeping open house, shop, cellar, or place of public entertainment or refreshment; entertaining any but travelers, or suffering others to abide therein, or in the yards, orchards, or fields appertaining thereto, drinking, or spending time idly at play; penalty not more than $50 for each person, and, on any conviction after the first, not more than $100; an inn-keeper convicted three times to be incapable of holding a license. Id. 4.

The same provision is made with regard to the "evening of the Lord's day," but the word "idly," is omitted, and a fine of not more than $5 provided for each offence. Id. 5.

Forbidden.—For an inn-keeper or person keeping implements used in gaming for hire to suffer them to be used on his premises; first offence, not more than $100 or house of correction for not more than three months; for every subsequent offence, same for not more than one year and bond for good behavior; and against violation of this section, for three months. Id. 14.

Forbidden.—Being present at any game, play, sport, or public diversion, except a concert of sacred music, if licensed; penalty not more than $5 for each offence. 519, 1.

Railroad commissioners may authorize the running of through trains as in their opinion the public necessity and convenience require, having regard to the due observance of the day. Ib.

Behaving rudely, &c., in a place of worship, not more than $10; discharging fire-arms in the pursuit of game, not more than $10. Id. 10.

Attempting to catch fish. Id. 11.

Whoever conscientiously believes the seventh day ought to be observed as a Sabbath and actually refrains from secular business, travel and labor on that day, shall not be liable to the penalty for Sunday labor, &c., if he disturbs no others. Id. 13.

MICHIGAN.

Forbidden.—Keeping open shop, &c., doing work, being present at dancing or public diversion, show or entertainment, taking part in any sport, game, or play; penalty not more than $10 for each offence (this not to apply to works of necessity and charity or mutual promises to marry or solemnizations of marriage). 2015.

Forbidden.—For any tavern-keeper, &c., to entertain others than travelers, or suffer them to abide in his house, or the yards, &c., pertaining thereto, drinking or spending their time idly at play, or doing any secular business. 2016.

For the first offence, under the above section, $5 for each person entertained, &c.; for the second, $10, and after a third the keeper cannot hold a license; and the person abiding, &c, shall be fined not more than $10. 2017.

Forbidden.—Being present at any game, &c., or resorting to any public assembly, except for religious worship, moral instruction, or concerts of sacred music; penalty not more than $10 for each offence. 2018.

Forbidden.—Disturbing an assembly for worship; penalty not less than $2 or more than $50, or not more than thirty days. 2020.

No person conscientiously believing that the seventh day ought to be observed as the Sabbath and refraining from labor thereon, shall be liable to the penalties for work, provided he disturb no other person. 2021.

Forbidden.—Keeping open saloons. 2274.

Holidays are to be considered as Sunday in regard to bills and notes and the holding of courts; and in case any holiday falls on Sunday, Monday is a holiday. See 1591.

For a trespass on other days, the penalty is not more than thirty days or $20; on this day, not less than five days or $5.

Municipal corporations may punish violations and require places of business to be closed. 2555 (p. 660, par. 10).

MINNESOTA.

Forbidden.—Laboring at one's own or other trade, &c., or employing one's apprentice or servant, except in ordinary household offices of daily necessity, or other work of necessity or charity; penalty not more than $20 for each offence, the employment of every apprentice, &c., being deemed a separate offence (not to apply to railroads or steamboats). 2949.

Forbidden.—Keeping open shop, &c., doing work, &c., except works of necessity and charity, being present at any public diversion, dance or entertainment, taking part in any sport, game or play; penalty $2 for each offence (this not to apply to any person who conscientiously observes the seventh day as the Sabbath, so far as relates to work, &c.).

Forbidden.—Keeping open store, &c., by any except druggists, disposing of merchandise, &c.; penalty not more than $20 for each offence. 2950.

Forbidden.—Giving a show, cock-fight, &c.; penalty not more than $50. 2951.

Forbidden.—Keeping open bar, or selling liquors; penalty not less than $50 nor more than $100 for each offence. 2953.

Forbidden.—Liquor-selling; penalty not less than $25 nor more than $500, or imprisonment not less than one week or more than three months, or both. 1113.

Bills, notes, &c., or contracts falling due or to be performed on a holiday, or on the following day when a holiday falls on Sunday, are payable or performable on the business day preceding; and bills and notes shall be noted and protested on such day, but notice of dishonor, &c., need not be given until the next business day. 36, 10.

MISSOURI.

Forbidden.—Labor, compelling or permitting apprentice or servant or other person under one's charge or control to do any work but the household offices of daily necessity, or other works of necessity or charity, hunting, shooting; penalty not more than $50. 1578.

(This not to extend to a member of a religious society by whom another day is observed as the Sabbath, provided he observes it, nor to prevent ferrymen from "crossing passengers." 1579.)

Forbidden.—Exposing goods for sale, keeping open tippling-house, &c., liquor-selling; penalty not more than $50. 1581.

(This not to prevent the selling of drugs, medicines, provisions, or other articles of immediate necessity. 1582.)

Forbidden.—Horse-racing, cock-fighting, playing cards or games of any kind; penalty not more than $50. 1580.

NEBRASKA.

Forbidden.—For any one, sporting, rioting, quarreling, hunting, fishing, shooting; penalty not more than $20 nor twenty days, or both. Labor, except work of charity or necessity; penalty not more than $5 nor less than $1. (This not to extend to those who conscientiously believe the seventh day ought to be kept as a Sabbath, or to prevent emigrating families from traveling, watermen from landing passemgers, tollgate-keepers from attending to tolls, ferrymen from conveying travelers, &c., or railways from running necessary trains.) 803, 241.

Forbidden.—Selling or giving away liquors. 415, 14.

NEVADA.

Forbidden.—Keeping open, &c., of play-house, race-grounds, cock-pit, playing game of chance for gain, engaging in any noisy amusement. 4847.

NEW HAMPSHIRE.

Forbidden.—Work, &c., to the disturbance of others; game, play or recreation. 617, 3.

Also.—Keeping shop (this not to prevent the sale of bread from bakeries, or drugs or medicines). 618, 10.

Penalty for above not exceeding $10 or thirty days or both. Id. 11.

Forbidden.—Behaving rudely, &c., in a house of worship. Id. 4.

Penalty for above not more than $6. Id. 5.

Bills, notes, &c., or contracts due or to be executed on Sunday or a holiday, are payable the preceding day, if that be not a holiday, and bills and notes may then be noted and protested. 509, 9.

And notice may be given the day following, not being a holiday. Id. 10.

NEW JERSEY.

Forbidden.—Traveling, worldly employment, servile labor (works of necessity and charity excepted), shooting, fishing, hunting, racing, frequenting tippling-houses, plays, music for merriment, foot-ball, fives, nine-pins, bowls, long bowls, quoits or other sports; penalty for offenders over fourteen, $1 for the poor. Exposing for sale or selling merchandise; penalty $2 or not more than ten days. Dancing, fiddling, playing with cards, &c. (but one may travel to or from church, if within twenty miles, or, if one be a physician, or carrying the mail, or going express by order of a public officer—this not to prevent dressing meat in private families, or in inns for travelers, &c.), and railroads may run one passenger train each way for the accommodation of citizens of the state. 1227, 1.

Forbidden.—Transportation of freight, except milk (this not to prevent transportation of mail, or regular trips of ferryboats). 1231, 13.

Forbidden.—Stage-driving, except in case of necessity or mercy; penalty $8 for each offence. 1229, 4.

Forbidden.—Disturbing religious meetings; penalty $10, or not more than ten days. 1230, 9.

And any person may apprehend an offender under the above, and he may be detained till next day, if he gives no bail. 1232, 17.

Forbidden.—Casting a seine; penalty $14, or imprisonment till paid. 1128, 2.

Also.—Fishing in the Delaware river. 428, 17.

This extended to portions of the river within the concurrent jurisdiction of the state and Pennsylvania. 431, 31.

Forbidden.—Fishing with hook and line. 459, 15.

Forbidden.—Hunting or trapping (but those who observe the seventh day can hunt on their own grounds); penalty $25. Ib.

Convicts are to be kept at work every other day but Sunday. 1117, 7.

Forbidden.—Liquor-selling. 495, 64.

Or offering it for sale; penalty $20. 238, 61.

There is a general fine at the end of the act. 1223, 29.

Or for not more than ten days' imprisonment. 1234, 30.

Those who religiously observe the seventh day are exempt from working on the highways and doing militia duty except when in actual service. Id., 33.

And proof that the defendant keeps this day is a defence to an indictment for working, provided the work was on his own premises, and has not disturbed others in the observance of the first day (this not to allow him to openly expose goods). Id. 34.

NEW YORK.

Forbidden.—Shooting, hunting, fishing, sporting, playing, horse-racing, gaming, frequenting of tippling-houses, unlawful exercises and pastimes; traveling, unless in necessity or charity, or going to or from church within twenty miles, or for medical aid, or visiting the sick, carrying mail, or going express by order of some public officer, or the removal of the family, &c., commenced on some other day; servile labor, unless of necessity or charity, except by a person uniformly keeping Saturday as holy time, and not then laboring, and whose labor shall not disturb others in their observance of the first day of the week as holy time; penalty for every offender over fourteen $1. 1975, 70.

Forbidden.—All labor, except works of necessity or charity, which includes whatever is needful for the good order, health or comfort of the community. Penal Code 263.

Forbidden.—Trades, manufactures and mechanical employments, except that, when necessary, they may be performed in the usual and orderly manner so as not to interfere with the repose and religious liberty of the community. Id. 266.

It is a defence to a prosecution for labor that the defendant uniformly keeps another day of the week as holy time, and does not then labor, and that his labor did not disturb others in observing the first day as holy time. Id. 264.

Selling, except articles of food before ten o'clock, and meals and prepared tobacco in places where liquor is not sold; and fruit, confectionery, newspapers and drugs and surgical appliances may be sold in a quiet and orderly manner. Id. 267.

Forbidden.—Exposing merchandise, except meats, milk and fish before nine o'clock; penalty forfeiture of the articles. 1975, 71.

Forbidden.—Selling liquors, except to lodgers at a tavern or persons traveling as allowed; penalty $2.50. Id. 72.

Also.—Selling or giving away liquors, with an exception. 1983, 21.

Forbidden.—Parades in cities, except funerals, or to and from a place of worship in connection with a religious service there celebrated; and in the excepted cases there shall not be any music, fireworks, discharge of cannon or firearms, or other disturbing noise; but the Grand Army of the Republic may play at their funerals, except within one block of a place of worship, where worship is being celebrated; penalty not more than $20 or ten days, or both. 2148, 3.

This privilege of music is extended to military funerals, the burial of a National Guardsman, &c., without the saving as to "one block," &c. Penal Code 276.

Forbidden.—Hunting, trapping, &c.; penalty $25. 2106, 32.

Forbidden.—Shooting, hunting, playing, horse-racing, or other public sports, exercises or shows, and noise disturbing the peace of the day. Id. 265.

Forbidden.—Theatrical performances; and persons aiding them, letting buildings for them, &c., are guilty of a misdemeanor, and liable in $500. Penal Code 277.

Penalty for "Sabbath-breaking" not less than $1 nor more than $10, or not more than five days, or both. Id. 269.

Persons whose religious faith and practice is to observe Saturday are not on that day subject to military duty, except in case of invasion. 1976, 1.

Contracts with publishers of Sunday papers are valid. Ib.

NORTH CAROLINA.

Forbidden.—For any tradesman, planter or other person to labor at his ordinary calling (works of necessity and charity excepted), or to hunt, fish or fowl, or use any game, sport or play, if the offender is over fourteen; penalty $1. 3782.

For any person to hunt, or be found off his premises having a shot-gun, rifle or pistol; penalty not more than $50. If failure to pay, hard labor for not more than three months (this not to apply to one defending his own property). 3783.

Forbidden.—Hunting wild fowl. 2837.

OHIO.

Forbidden.—To any person over fourteen, engaging in sporting, rioting, quarreling, hunting, fishing or shooting; penalty not more than $20 or twenty days, or both. 7032.

To any of same age engaging in common labor (works of necessity and charity excepted); penalty not more than $10. (This not to extend to those who conscientiously observe the seventh day as the Sabbath, or prevent families emigrating from traveling, watermen from landing passengers, tollgate-keepers, &c., from attending to their duties, or ferrymen from conveying travelers over water.) 7033.

No unnecessary labor shall be required of convicts. 7427.

Forbidden.—Selling liquor; penalty not more than $5. 6944.

Also.—Selling liquors, except by druggists on physicians' prescriptions, for medical purposes, keeping open place where they are sold, except drug stores; penalty not more than $100, and not more than thirty days. "Place" applies to bar-room in hotel. Municipal corporations may control the sale of beer and native wine. Supp. 688, 9.

Forbidden.—Theatrical performances. Id. 405, 7052 (*a*)

PENNSYLVANIA.

Forbidden.—Worldly employment, &c., except works of necessity or charity, practicing any unlawful game, hunting, shooting or diversion; penalty $4 or six days (this not to prevent dressing of vituals in private houses or in inns for travelers, or interfere with the business of watermen or ferrymen, or the delivery of milk or the necessaries of life before nine o'clock in the forenoon, or after five o'clock in the afternoon). 1572, 3.

Railroad and canal companies need not attend their works. 1592, 2.

Forbidden.—Liquor-selling. 1077, 12.

Also.—Selling liquor, and for a tavern-keeper to allow it to be drank on his premises. 1573, 7.

Penalty for above $50, forfeited to the poor, and a fine in a criminal proceeding, or not less than $10 or more than $100. Id. 39.

Forbidden.—Tippling in taverns, &c.; penalty for the tippler one shilling, for the landlord ten shillings. Id., 5.

(But inns may supply the "necessary occasions" of lodgers with vituals and drink in moderation, and of the necessary occasion for refreshment the magistrate shall be the judge. Id. 6.)

RHODE ISLAND.

Forbidden.—Labor or sport of ordinary calling, game, sport, play or recreation, or suffering the same by children, servants or apprentices (works of necessity and charity excepted); penalty not more than $5 for first offence, or than $10 for each subsequent offence. 686, 15.

Also.—With the servant of another to work, &c. 687, 16.

Forbidden.—For any tradesman, artificer, &c., "or other person whatsoever," to do any worldly business or work of ordinary calling, works of necessity and charity excepted, if party over fifteen; penalty $1. 1632.

Forbidden.—Engaging in public sports, bear-baiting, foot-ball or "interludes or common plays," or other pastimes; same penalty. 1633.

Forbidden.—Permitting games to be played (on gaming-table); penalty $50. 1634.

Forbidden.—Loading or unloading or running of railroad trains, except as hereinafter provided, and when loaded with animals. 1475.

Companies may run regular mail-trains, and construction and other trains rendered necessary by extraordinary emergencies other than those incident to freight or passenger traffic. 1476.

And a train running by schedule, but delayed by accident or other unavoidable circumstance, may run till it reaches the point where it is usual for it to rest on Sunday. 1477.

Penalty under above $500. 1478.

Forbidden.—Liquor-selling. 230, 2.

For selling liquor or suffering it to be sold or offering it for sale, first conviction $10 and ten days; second, $50 and three months, with forfeiture of license and disqualification to hold one for two years. 238, 31.

That a person is seen drinking is evidence that liquor is sold. 242, 57.

Forbidden.—Theatrical performances. 244, 2.

Also.—Pawnbroker's business. 249, 9.

And discharging fire-arms when not on military duty. 252, 3.

Sabbatarians, &c., may labor, but not keep open stores, load vessels, &c., or work at mechanical trades, except in certain villages; nor may they fish or fowl in public places or out of their own possessions. 687, 18.

TENNESSEE.

Forbidden.—For a merchant, artificer, tradesman, farmer, "or other person," to exercise his common avocation of life, or cause or permit the same to be done by his children or servants (acts of real necessity or charity excepted); penalty $3. 2289.

Forbiddon.—Selling within view of a religious assembly so as to disturb the same (this not to extend to one lawfully selling at his usual place of business). 2013.

Forbidden.—Selling liquor. 5671.

Forbidden.—Hunting, fishing, playing or being drunk; same penalty. 2290.

TEXAS.

Forbidden.—For any person to labor or compel his employes to do so; penalty not less than $10 nor more than $50. Penal Code 183.

This not to apply to household duties, works of necessity or charity, necessary work on farms to prevent the loss of a crop, running of vessels or railroads or wagon trains, or to common carriers, or to their delivering, receiving or storing goods, nor to stages, foundries, sugar-mills, herders with stock, travelers, ferry-men, keepers of toll-bridges, hotels, boarding-houses, restaurants and livery stables, nor to one who conscientiously believes any other day of the week ought to be observed as the Sabbath, and refrains from business on that day for religious reasons. Id. 184.

Forbidden.—Dealers selling merchandise; same penalty; this not to apply to markets or dealers in merchandise selling before nine o'clock A. M. Id. 186.

Nor to the selling of drugs or medicines. Id. 187.

Forbidden.—Horse-racing, allowing use of ten-pin alley, match shooting, gaming within the limits of any town; penalty not less than $20 nor more than $50. Id. 185.

The chaplain of the penitentiary shall preach at least once on Sunday to the convicts. 3544.

No labor shall be required of the convicts. 3560, 3591.

Holidays are considered as Sunday in regard to presenting, protesting and giving notice as to paper. 2835.

If a holiday happens on Sunday, Monday is a holiday; and paper may be presented the Saturday preceding, and proceeded on accordingly. 2837.

Municipal corporations may close drinking places and places of amusement. 391.

UTAH.

Forbidden.—Keeping open workshop or place of business for the purpose of transacting business therein; penalty not less than $5 nor more than $100. 1980.

This not to apply to hotels, boarding-houses, baths, restaurants, taverns, livery stables, or retail drug stores, or manufacturing establishments usually kept in continued operation. 1981.

Forbidden.—Unnecessary labor; penalty not more than $25. 1984.

This not to apply to mills or works usually kept in constant operation, or used in irrigating. 1985.

Forbidden.—The exhibition, &c., of bull, bear, cock or prize fighting, horse-racing, circus, or any barbarous or noisy amusement, opening gambling-house or saloon or theatre, where liquors are sold, and purchasing tickets for such show; misdemeanor. 1979.

VERMONT.

Forbidden.—Business or employment, except works of necessity and charity, being present at any public assembly, except for social and religious worship and moral instruction, traveling, except from necessity or charity, visiting from house to house, except from motives of humanity or charity or for moral or religious edification, holding or resorting to a ball or dancing, exercising, game or sport, resorting to inns, &c., for amusement or recreation; penalty not more than $2. 4315.

Forbidden.—Hunting, discharging fire-arms, except in defence of person or property, or performance of military or police duty; penalty $10. 4316.

WASHINGTON.

Forbidden.—Keeping open shop, &c., labor and business, except works of necessity and charity, being present at a dance or public diversion or show, taking part in sport, game or play; penalty not more than $10. 4595.

Forbidden.—For tavern-keepers or other persons to sell or give away intoxicating liquors. 1564.

Any person who conscientiously believes any other day ought to be observed as the Sabbath, and refrains from labor, &c., on that day, may labor, unless he willfully disturbs some other person or some religious assembly. 4596.

WEST VIRGINIA.

Forbidden.—Laboring at any trade or calling, or employing children, apprentices or servants, except in household or other work of necessity or charity; penalty not less than $5 for each offence (each child, &c., employed, &c., a separate offence); hunting, shooting or carrying fire-arms; penalty not less than $5. 809, 16.

This not to prevent transportation of the mails, passengers and their baggage, running trains and steamboats, carrying fire-arms or shooting by a person having the right to do so under the laws of the United States or of the state; and one may labor who conscientiously believes the seventh day ought to be observed as a Sabbath and actually refrains from secular business and work thereon; provided he does not compel an apprentice or servant not of his belief to work, and does not disturb another person in his observance of the day, and no contract shall be deemed void because made on Sunday. Id. 176.

Forbidden.—Laboring at any trade or calling, or employing apprentices or servants, except in household or other work of necessity or charity; penalty $2 (each servant, &c., a distinct offence). 1209, 17.

LATE ENGLISH SUNDAY LEGISLATION.

I. IN GENERAL.

Exclusion in computing time, 45 and 46 Vic. c. 50, § 230.

Prosecutions, restrictions on, 34 and 35 Vic. c. 87.

Remission of penalties, 38 and 39 Vic. c. 80, § 1.

Warrants granted on, 11 and 12 Vic. c. 42, § 4; 12 and 13 Vic. c. 69, § 4; 14 and 15 Vic. c. 93, § 11.

II. PARTICULAR CASES.

Billiards, 35 and 36 Vic. c. 109, § 10, sch. 30.

Bills of exchange, 34 and 35 Vic. c. 17.

Brewing and distilling, 43 and 44 Vic. c. 24, § 24.

Burials, 43 and 44 Vic. c. 41, § 3.

Factories, children and women in, 41 and 42 Vic. c. 16, § 21.

Factories, Jews in, 41 and 42 Vic. c. 16, §§ 50, 51.

Methylated spirits, selling, 52 and 53 Vic. c. 42, § 26.

Pawnbrokers, 35 and 36 Vic. c. 93, § 32.

Public houses, 25 and 26 Vic. c. 35, § 2, sch. A; 39 and 40 Vic. c. 26, § 17; 41 and 42 Vic. c. 72.

Rectifying, 43 and 44 Vic. c. 24, § 43.

Water, supplying, 34 and 35 Vic. c. 84, § 24.

SUBJECT INDEX.

[An *s* following a reference indicates that successive pages should be consulted.]

I.

J.

K.

T.

U.

V.

W.